Irish Men and Women in the Second World War

In memory of

Lieutenant-Colonel Brian D.H. Clark, MC, GM,

The Royal Irish Fusiliers (Princess Victoria's)

1920-1995

Irish Men and Women
in the Second World War

RICHARD DOHERTY

'The minstrel boy to the war has gone,
In the ranks of death you'll find him.'

FOUR COURTS PRESS

Set in 9 on 12.5 point Sabon by Sheila Stephenson for
FOUR COURTS PRESS LTD
Fumbally Lane, Dublin 8, Ireland
e-mail: info@four-courts-press.ie
http:\\www.four-courts-press.ie
and in North America by
FOUR COURTS PRESS
c/o ISBS, 5804 N.E. Hassalo Street, Portland, OR 97213.

A catalogue record for this title
is available from the British Library.

ISBN 1–85182–441–3

Printed in Great Britain
by MPG Books, Bodmin, Cornwall

Contents

TO IRELAND

FEGEN, O'Connor, Doran, O'Moore Creagh,
These names in Ireland's unregenerate day
Would have brought exultation; as we are,
They send back echoes from some mocking star.
What title, what inheritance, what share
Have we in champions of sea, land or air?

Yet hopes have been that Ireland should unite
Through comradeship in some redeeming fight.
Say, for what cause these Irish struck their blow
If not for freedom? Surely we can know
Who are the wrongers, who the wronged today;
If not, let Poland, Holland, Belgium say:
And, should these tortured nations with their cry
Move not our spirit – should the risk too high
Deter us – then at least let there be shewn
Some will to claim our heroes for our own.
They have ensured that on the field of Fame
Ireland shall not be the forgotten name:
Pay them, let not our instincts be denied,
The flowing tribute of a natural pride.

It may be preparation for an hour
When Ireland, trampled by invading power,
Bids North and South in valiant leaguer join
Shoulder to Irish shoulder – on the Boyne.

STEPHEN GWYNN

List of illustrations

26 Soldiers of 2nd London Irish Rifles, supported by a Sherman tank of 16th/5th Lancers and a 17-pounder anti-tank gun, during the battle of Cassino.

27 Officers and men of 56th Reconnaissance Regiment, decorated for gallantry in the Tunisian campaign.

28 Major John Duane, MC, 2nd Royal Inniskilling Fusiliers.

29 Third Officer Elizabeth Beresford-Jones (*née* Chamberlain), Women's Royal Naval Service.

30 Brenda Graham in Red Cross uniform in Italy.

31 Maeve Boyle who served with the WRNS in her native Derry.

32 Wrens based at HMS *Ferret*, the Royal Navy's shore base on the river Foyle.

33 Former adversaries lay wreaths on an Alpine memorial to those who perished on both sides during the Second World War.

34 An anti-submarine training school was established at Derry and Wrens were important members of the staff.

35 Pilot Officer Bertie Truesdale.

36 The grave of P/O Bertie Truesdale

CREDITS

Author's collection 7, 14; Captain Harry Barton 24; Chaz Bowyer 10; Mrs Brenda Clark 30; Squadron Leader Doug Cooper DFC 33; Mrs Elizabeth Dobbs 15, 29; Sean Drumm 11; Major John Duane 12, 28; 56th Reconnaissance Regiment Comrades' Association 27; Mrs Frances Galloway 1, 2, 3, 4; Colin Gunner 26; Mrs Anne Hogan: 8; Imperial War Museum 9, 13, 16, 17, 19, 20, 21, 22, 23, 25; Mrs Maeve Kelly 31, 32, 34; David Truesdale 35, 36; Col. A.D. Woods MC and Bar 5, 6.

Introduction

That Ireland made a contribution to the Second World War is undenied. What has been disputed is the level of that contribution. Ireland had been divided since 1922 when the larger part of the island had seceded from the United Kingdom as 'Saorstat Éireann', the Irish Free State; the six north-eastern counties remained part of the United Kingdom as 'Northern Ireland' with its own regional parliament at Stormont on the outskirts of Belfast. That division of the island, and the antipathy that existed between the two jurisdictions, lies at the root of the dispute over the extent of Ireland's contribution to the war.

The fact that the independent Irish government in Dublin, under Eamon de Valera, chose to remain neutral during the war created considerable resentment in the United Kingdom, but especially in Northern Ireland, the government of which saw the war as an opportunity to demonstrate and underline the loyalty of their people to the Union. When Robert Fisk wrote his seminal work *In Time of War* in 1983 he examined the record of both parts of Ireland in terms of wartime recruitment to the British forces. Although his study was not conclusive, he certainly caused sufficient embarrassment in Northern Ireland to have those files in the Public Record Office in Belfast that dealt with recruitment, and which had been open to researchers, closed for an extended period. However, Fisk's research was not without fault: describing the attitude of the Northern Ireland government to Winston Churchill's suggestion that an Irish Brigade be formed in the British Army, Fisk concludes that the objections raised by Prime Minister John Andrews led to a British stepdown because 'no "Irish Brigade" ever existed to recognize the contribution that men from Éire made to Britain's eventual victory'. The reality is that an Irish Brigade was formed and served with considerable distinction in North Africa, Sicily and Italy, earning the reputation of being one of the finest fighting formations in the British Army.

Fisk does, however, point out that many men from Éire crossed the border, or the Irish sea, to join the British forces. This was recognized in Northern Ireland, but there was, and remains, an inclination to attribute this to financial necessity. Indeed, in September 1944, a Stormont minister, Harry Midgley, who held the public security portfolio, told his cabinet colleagues that a 'considerable number of Éire men enlisted in HM Forces owing to economic pressure and without any sense of loyalty to the Empire'. Midgley was the sole non-unionist member of that cabinet but the argument that he put forth is still used today by many who would call themselves unionists. One recent caller to the BBC Radio Ulster *Talkback* programme echoed Midgley's argument, and there have even been ex-servicemen from the Republic who have claimed that their sole reason for joining one of the British services was financial. However, a British private soldier was paid the princely sum of fourteen shillings (70p) per week, less deductions for 'barrack damages' and charges for such essentials as laundry; and soldiers, married or single, were encouraged to allot part of their pay to their families. When all deductions had been made, the average private soldier was left with about seven shillings (35p) each week and, although there were proficiency and skill increments, the financial lot of a soldier was hardly attractive, even by the standards of the time. It is hard to imagine thousands of men being prepared to risk life and limb solely for financial rewards.

So it can be seen that the question of Ireland's contribution to the war is fraught with many difficulties and raises many questions. To discuss it, even today, can give rise to cries of political bias, of being a supporter of one faction or another; indeed, in some circles, both nationalist and unionist, it would be difficult to have a rational discussion of the matter at all. In many respects, therefore, much less is known about Ireland's contribution to the Second World War than to the Great War. Part of this may well be due to the lingering effects of what John Bowman has described as 'an early form of political correctness which largely obliterated the memory of those who had fought in the Great War'. It may also be attributable to the neutrality policy that has been a hallmark of the Republic of Ireland and which had its first expression during the Second World War.

It would be difficult indeed to mark a country's part in a war in which that country had no *official* part. And yet Irish historians covering Ireland in the period of the Second World War have praised the part she played. John P. Duggan described Ireland's role as 'an extraordinary unsung contribution' in the struggle against the 'great evil' of Nazism and suggested that the country had

> nothing to be ashamed of in its crusading record to combat it. Thousands of Irishmen died at the tip of the spear – that's where they generally were – on the battlefields. Éire got eight Victoria Crosses to prove it. [This statement is not entirely accurate: the Irish Victoria Crosses included five men born in Éire, one of whom was the son of a Welsh soldier; two born in England but who were clearly Irish, and one born in Belfast. Most of their stories are told elsewhere in this book.] Thousands more worked in Britain's munition factories, farms and hospitals.

Paradoxically, the actions of a British government allowed Ireland to be a neutral nation during the war. The division of Ireland had left Britain with naval bases in the Free State – the Treaty Ports of Queenstown (Cobh), Berehaven and Lough Swilly; there were also fuel storage facilities at Haulbowline island, next to Queenstown, and at Rathmullan on Lough Swilly. Under article 7 of the Anglo-Irish Treaty, Ireland was obliged in time of war 'to afford such harbours and other facilities as the British government may require'. Obviously that obligation meant that Ireland, although independent, could not pursue a policy of neutrality in any future European war: no belligerent nation opposed to Britain would have regarded Ireland as neutral when it was providing facilities for the Royal Navy. Since those facilities would have played a pivotal part in the escorting of Atlantic convoys, they would have become prime targets for the Luftwaffe after the summer of 1940.

There is a clear parallel here with Egypt, which had British bases on its soil as a result of the Anglo-Egyptian Treaty of 1936. Although remaining neutral until 1943, when the danger of invasion by the Axis powers had receded, Egypt found itself a battleground. One of the pivotal battles of the war, El Alamein, was fought on its territory, and its cities, particularly Alexandria and Cairo, were subjected to bombing attacks. Those were aimed at British naval and military facilities but the principal sufferers were Egyptian civilians. There can be little doubt that Ireland would have endured similar attacks had the British naval bases still been in existence in the early war years.

However, little actual use had been made of the bases by the Royal Navy's South Irish Flotilla, and the defences for the three anchorages were only lightly manned. When Britain began a programme of defence expansion in the mid-1930s, the question of upgrading the Irish ports' defences was also considered. Since those ports had no adequate up-to-date anti-aircraft artillery protection, and their coastal guns lacked modern hardened protective emplacements, they would have been in grave danger from aerial attack. Moreover, the nearest Royal Air Force fighter aircraft were across the Irish sea; there were no fighters based in Northern Ireland, although an armament training camp was opened there in March 1936 and many fighter squadrons thereafter used that facility.

Making the ports and their defences viable for a future war appeared to be an extremely expensive proposition. A 1936 estimate showed that improvements to the Irish defences would cost £276,000, an enormous sum at the time. In addition, the garrisons manning the defences were isolated, with only the Lough Swilly garrison having any British troops within reach (just over twenty miles away in Londonderry's Ebrington Barracks). The War Office was advised that defending the ports against a possible aggressive move by the Irish army would require a full division of almost 14,000 soldiers at each port. Simply to keep the ports secure against a hostile Irish population would require a brigade group at each port; but if the ports were to be used safely by the Royal Navy, 'then the hinterland of the ports would have to be occupied and that would demand a division plus AA defences for each of them'. Such a commitment of manpower – effectively a full army corps – was unthinkable. Although the British Chiefs of Staff considered the ports to be vital to the security of the United Kingdom in the event of war, they accepted that their defence within a hostile Ireland was impracticable; it was even suggested that their use might require the occupation of all of Ireland. These factors, together with memories of the IRA's guerrilla campaign, conspired to make the British government amenable to any suggestion that the Treaty Ports be handed over to the Irish government. In theory that would also relieve the Royal Navy of the responsibility for defending the Irish coast.

Developments on the political front between Britain and Ireland were also to influence the future of the ports. In 1932 the Fianna Fáil party had obtained sufficient seats in a general election to form a new government in coalition with the Labour party; Fianna Fáil's leader, Eamon de Valera, became President of the Executive Council, or prime minister, of the Irish Free State. A snap general election the following year gave Fianna Fáil an overall majority that allowed de Valera to begin implementing his party's policies. De Valera, who had been sentenced to death by the British in 1916, was keen to distance Ireland as far as possible from Britain – which meant reducing the constitutional ties that bound the Irish Free State to the British crown.

Although de Valera recognized the close natural links between Britain and Ireland, it was not long before the two countries were engaged in an economic war over trade tariffs and the payment of land annuities. Then, in 1937, de Valera's government introduced a new constitution which came into effect on 29 December of that year and which was to have the effect of further weakening the link with Britain.

Under the terms of this new constitution Ireland was to have an elected president as head of state; Gaelic was to be the language of the state; the tricolour officially became the national flag; and the President of the Executive Council was to become prime minister with the Gaelic title of Taoiseach. The name of the country was to be Ireland in English, and Éire in Irish. One article of the new constitution laid claim to all the island of Ireland as the national territory, but the country remained within the British Commonwealth although it was a republic in everything but name. However, the King still had a position in de Valera's dispensation, but one restricted to foreign affairs: he no longer had a role in Irish internal affairs; the introduction of an elected president indicated a clear rejection of that aspect of the British monarch's role. Effectively de Valera had created a new form of Commonwealth membership described as 'external', that is, the form of Commonwealth membership which is the modern norm. De Valera can be said to have pioneered this contemporary concept of the Commonwealth of Nations.

De Valera wanted to see the British naval and military presence removed from Ireland as part of his process of disentanglement from the British state and as further proof of the political sovereignty of Ireland. However, both countries were anxious to resolve as far as possible the differences between them, especially in view of the deteriorating international situation, and talks were held in London in early 1938. These led to an agreement, signed on 25 April, which brought about a resolution of the economic war: Ireland agreed to pay a lump sum of £10,000,000 to settle the land question, while Britain, for her part, agreed to hand over the Treaty Ports to the Irish authorities by 31 December 1938.

The transfer of Berehaven and Lough Swilly took place at the height of the Munich crisis, with the former being handed over two days after the Royal Navy had been placed on war alert. 'Thousands of British merchant seamen and Royal Navy personnel were to die as a result of this monumental blunder,' it has been claimed.

Irish officials were quite surprised that the British had relinquished the ports so easily. In fact, many British politicians were not only amazed but outraged that Neville Chamberlain's government had so readily given away the three anchorages. Winston Churchill, a former First Lord of the Admiralty, regarded it as a 'feckless act' and an 'improvident example of appeasement'. The handover was to rankle with Churchill during the war years. But, even so, he recognized it as what de Valera perceived it to be – an underpinning of Irish neutrality. In Churchill's own words to the house of commons on 5 May 1938:

> It will be no use saying, 'Then we will retake the ports.' You will have no right to do so. To violate Irish neutrality should it be declared at the moment of a Great War may put you out of court in the opinion of the world, and may vitiate the cause by which you may be involved in war ... You are casting away real and important means of security and survival for vain shadows and for ease.

Churchill later wrote that even de Valera had been surprised at how readily the ports had been handed over, as the Taoiseach had included the proposal as a bargaining counter which he was prepared to drop, should other points have been settled to his satisfaction.

It would appear that the Admiralty, at least, believed that the Irish government would restore the Royal Navy's rights to use the ports in the event of war. In September 1939 a Royal Navy Volunteer Reserve officer, Paymaster Lieutenant-Commander O.W. McCutcheon, was appointed to the staff of the Naval Officer-in-Charge, Buncrana, on Lough Swilly. Pending resolution of the Treaty Ports' situation, McCutcheon, a Derryman, was to report to the Flag Officer-in-Charge, Belfast. But there were no concessions on wartime use of the ports, and McCutcheon never saw service in Buncrana.

So it was that the handover of the ports in the autumn of 1938 provided the firm foundation for Irish neutrality. It was, however, a compromise form of neutrality. Professor Joseph Lee has written that

> De Valera was always wise enough to co-operate sufficiently with the Allies to ensure that they did not feel provoked into decisive action against Irish interests, even while his rhetoric satisfied national psychic needs by insisting on Ireland's equal independence from all belligerents.

Lee also noted that de Valera

> could not, and did not keep Ireland strictly neutral during the war. He kept Ireland benevolently neutral for Britain. Out of sheer self-interest, he maintained the supplies of men and food to Britain.

Lee's argument is that Ireland's behaviour was in line with that of other neutrals, including Sweden and Switzerland, both of which, until recently, had generally been lauded for their even-handed behaviour but in reality favoured Germany. One other neutral is mentioned by Lee in this argument – Turkey, which was in the most awkward position of all, being militarily vulnerable from Allies and Axis for much of the war. Turkey, however, did declare war on Germany, and Japan, on 1 March 1945.

Myles Dungan has suggested that Ireland's neutrality

> was both an expression of its sovereignty, a function of its government's republican background and a non-combative status which was of a very partial nature. An independent foreign policy was seen as a vital ingredient of Irish independence. The authorities were predisposed, therefore, towards non-alignment.

This predisposition towards non-alignment would make de Valera's policy a clear matter of principle. However, politics are rarely so simple, and it appears that the Irish leader suffered some of the doubts of Hamlet during the war years. De Valera's director of government information, Frank Gallagher, noted that the Taoiseach ruefully commented to him in late 1941: 'I wish there was some way of knowing who will win this war. It would make decisions much easier.' Ireland's neutrality was, therefore, much more a pragmatic policy than one of pure principle. It was even-handed in theory but not in practice and, although de Valera claimed that he saw the war as an 'imperial adventure', his policy became, effectively, a pro-British neutrality of the type that he had suggested in the 1920 negotiations. It was, therefore, the 'benevolent neutrality' described by Lee. This was demonstrated by the treatment of aircrew who crashed in Éire: although all were interned at first, Allied aircrew were later repatriated and, in many cases, their aircraft were returned. Many of the repatriations were almost immediate, with the explanation that the crew had been on a training flight rather than an operational mission.

As early as 9 September 1939, the first Saturday of war, the London *Times* suggested that:

> From the British point of view it is more than probable that Éire's neutrality is the best possible policy that Mr de Valera's government could have adopted.

Such a benevolent neutrality allowed the Irish government to turn a blind eye to its own citizens leaving the country to join the armed forces of a belligerent nation in what Lee described as 'the supply of men to Britain'. It would have been a simple matter for the Irish government to introduce a ban on enlistment in any forces other than its own. That it did not do so was entirely in keeping with the attitude of an administration that allowed British aircraft to overfly its territory and that permitted the Royal Navy to station an air-sea rescue vessel in Killybegs harbour in County Donegal (the *Robert Hastie*, a trawler, which was supposed to appear as part of the local fishing fleet). It is against such a background that any examination of Irish involvement in the Second World War must take place.

How many Irish served in Britain's forces?

RUMOURS OF WARS

When Adolf Hitler came to power in Germany in 1933, he did so with a sense of destiny and with a mission to redress what he perceived as the wrongs done to Germany in 1919. Hitler had unfinished business to attend to; and his attention to that business would plunge Europe into another round of bloodletting that would be even worse than had occurred between 1914 and 1918. The war that Hitler would precipitate would spread out to touch almost every corner of the globe. By its end between fifty and sixty million people – a total so large that it is almost impossible to conceive – would be dead, and destruction on a scale never seen before on the surface of the earth would have been visited on villages, towns and cities from Britain to Japan.

In its aftermath the historian A.J.P. Taylor described the Second World War as a just war. That was a description also given to the war, whilst it was being waged, by Pope Pius XII. Few wars in history have deserved the term 'just', but there can be no doubt of the evil of Nazism or of the justice of the struggle waged against it; Taylor even went so far as to call it a 'noble crusade', and '[d]espite all the killing and destruction that accompanied it … a good war'.

Against such a threatening evil it is hardly surprising that Irishmen chose to take up arms. For many of them, the fact that their country was neutral was irrelevant: they wanted to fight, and fight they did. A quarter of a century earlier, when all of Ireland was still within the United Kingdom, Irishmen had flocked to join the British forces to fight the Kaiser's Germany. Their numbers filled the ranks of three army divisions, 10th (Irish), 16th (Irish) and 36th (Ulster), as well as numerous battalions of the Army, while many others chose to join the Royal Navy or the fledgling Royal Flying Corps. But for the Irish volunteers of 1939-45 there were no ready-made Irish divisions in which to enlist, and that fact alone makes it more difficult to trace the Irish who fought in the Second World War.

The number of Irish regiments in the Army had also been reduced as a result of the creation of the Irish Free State in 1922. Gone were the Royal Irish Regiment, Connaught Rangers, Leinster Regiment, Royal Munster Fusiliers and Royal Dublin Fusiliers. The Irish cavalry regiments had also suffered reductions: the 4th Royal Irish Dragoon Guards had merged with the 7th Dragoon Guards to become the 4th/7th Royal

Dragoon Guards with little Irish identity remaining; the 6th Inniskilling Dragoons had similarly been amalgamated but, after something of a rethink, had managed to retain more of an Irish identity as the 5th Royal Inniskilling Dragoon Guards;* the 5th Royal Irish Lancers were now to be found within the curiously numbered 16th/5th Lancers;† only the 8th King's Royal Irish Hussars retained its Great War identity. There was another Irish cavalry regiment in the Supplementary Reserve, although, during the inter-war years, this unit, the North Irish Horse, existed only on paper. (The South Irish Horse, another Supplementary Reserve regiment, had also vanished with partition.)

The Irish regiments that survived in the Army included the Irish Guards in the Brigade of Guards and three regiments of Infantry of the Line – the Royal Inniskilling Fusiliers, the Royal Ulster Rifles and the Royal Irish Fusiliers. (From 1922 until 1937 the two fusilier regiments were reduced to single-battalion strength and linked, from 1924, as the Corps of Royal Inniskilling and Royal Irish Fusiliers; second battalions were restored in 1937 and the linkage was broken.) In addition there was a Territorial Army (TA) regiment, the London Irish Rifles, which, since 1937, had been part of the Royal Ulster Rifles.

The Royal Ulster Rifles were unique in being the sole Irish regiment to include a TA battalion. When the Territorial Force was created in 1908, it was not extended to Ireland, where the old Militia, renamed the Special Reserve, continued in existence. After the Great War (in 1919) the Territorial Force was disbanded, but it was reconstituted the following year as the Territorial Army, a title that reflected the War Office's appreciation of the wartime contribution of the Territorials. However, once again, the organization was not extended to Ireland.

It has been suggested that the reason for the non-inclusion of Ireland in the Territorial Army was a result of the Treaty which established the new Irish Free State and in which the United Kingdom government agreed not to raise military forces in Northern Ireland.

> Ulster had always wanted Territorials, but the circumstances were peculiar because the government was in treaty bound with the Irish Free State not to raise an army in Northern Ireland, and was fearful of misunderstandings. These were removed on condition that the parentage of the new force was

---

* The two regiments were amalgamated initially as 5th/6th Dragoons, a choice of title that was unpopular with both sides of the marriage as the 5th had lost their title of Dragoon Guards and the 6th had lost the distinctive Inniskilling. Within the new regiment A Squadron maintained the Inniskilling uniform, badges and other distinctions as Inniskilling Squadron. On 1 January 1927 the regiment was renamed 5th Inniskilling Dragoon Guards and a process of integration began that was eminently successful. In 1935 the regiment became a Royal Regiment as the 5th Royal Inniskilling Dragoon Guards.

† The 5th Lancers were descended from Wynne's Inniskilling Dragoons, raised in 1689 from the Williamite defenders of Enniskillen. As the 5th Royal Irish Dragoons the regiment was stationed in Ireland in 1798 where it was found that a number of United Irishmen had joined its ranks. Although the regiment was not unusual in this, and infiltrators were discovered and executed, King George III ordered its disbandment. In 1858 the regiment was re-raised as 5th Royal Irish Lancers. Disbandment was ordered again in 1921 but a War Office change of mind brought amalgamation with the 16th Lancers. The 5th's break in service from 1799 to 1858 was deemed to make it junior to the 16th and thus the unusual designation of 16th/5th rather than 5th/16th.

accepted entirely by the War Office, and the object of Territorial units in Northern Ireland was for Imperial defence only.

Although the War Office's opinion was that it would have been perfectly legal to raise Territorial units in Northern Ireland, it was reluctant to do so. The Northern Ireland government was keen that such units should be raised; Sir James Craig, the prime minister, thought that there could be an Ulster TA division and pressed the War Office to create one from the Ulster Special Constabulary. In London it was perceived that raising such a division might prejudice relations with the Free State, and there was also a fear that Craig's government might expect to use Territorial soldiers in aid of the civil power should there be an outbreak of civil disturbance. Craig's request was therefore rejected.

When the War Office established a Northern Ireland Defence Committee in 1929, the feasibility of creating a Territorial formation from the Special Constabulary was again explored. By this time, however, enthusiasm for the idea had waned in Northern Ireland. The Inspector-General of the Royal Ulster Constabulary, Sir Charles Wickham, pointed out that many Specials were over military age, the force was all-Protestant, and its members' prime role was to protect their own homes. Wickham further noted that no religious discrimination could be practised with Territorials and that there might therefore be friction between the different religious groupings. More importantly, Territorials would be under War Office control rather than that of the Northern Ireland government.

Lord Craigavon's government* finally agreed that artillery units of the Territorial Army might be raised to man coastal defences in Northern Ireland but had no wish to see an infantry force brought into being. The reason for this reluctance was a fear that subversive elements might use TA infantry units as

> training facilities [for] men – more especially in bomb-throwing and machine-gun practice – who might use the knowledge which they had acquired for subversive purposes. For some years, at any rate, it is thought inadvisable that there should be in Northern Ireland a territorial infantry organization.

As a result no TA infantry units were raised in Northern Ireland before the Second World War. The assigning of the London Irish Rifles to the Royal Ulster Rifles as their TA battalion came about in 1937 when the multi-battalion London Regiment, of which the London Irish constituted a battalion, was broken up, and its various battalions generally joined regiments to which they had previously had an affiliation.† There had long been such an affiliation between the London Irish and the Royal Ulster Rifles, or its predecessors, and thus the Rifles became the only one of the three surviving Irish Line regiments to acquire a TA battalion in the inter-war years.

---

* Craig was ennobled in 1927.
† Some of the London Regiment's battalions, however, became part of the Royal Artillery, the Royal Engineers or the Royal Corps of Signals with one battalion transferring to the Royal Tank Corps (later Regiment).

In the same year that the London Irish became the TA brothers in arms of the Ulster Rifles, Territorial Army units were finally raised in Northern Ireland. The two small units so raised were for coastal defence: a battery of heavy artillery and a supporting fortress company of engineers were both formed to defend Belfast lough. (It could be argued that Article 6 of the Anglo-Irish Treaty allowed such units to be raised as their coastal defence role was one where the Imperial government had undertaken to protect Ireland.) With a fine eye for tradition, 188 (Antrim) Heavy Battery, Royal Artillery (TA) and Antrim Fortress Company, Royal Engineers (TA) were deemed to be the successors to the Antrim Artillery and the Militia Engineers who had in earlier days manned and maintained the same fortifications.

The following year an early form of female emancipation in the services in Northern Ireland was introduced with the formation of a Northern Ireland Group of the Auxiliary Territorial Service (ATS). A plan to recruit 20,000 women for service with the Army throughout the UK was given royal assent on 9 September 1938 and recruiting began before the end of the month with volunteers in Northern Ireland being among the first to sign up. The NI Group was administered by the Territorial Army and Auxiliary Air Force Association of County Antrim, which had been created in 1937. Group Headquarters was based in Belfast together with 10th (Northern Ireland) Motor Driver Section and 8th (NI) Clerical Company; four other companies were based at Belfast, Armagh, Omagh and Greypoint and Kilroot. A further company was later formed as 18th (Ulster) Company, RAF, based at Aldergrove; this company became the nucleus of the Women's Auxiliary Air Force (WAAF) in Northern Ireland when that service was formed by the Air Ministry.

Whatever the niceties about interpretation of the Anglo-Irish Treaty and consideration for the feelings of the Free State's government, these went by the board in 1938 when the announcement of the creation in Northern Ireland of an anti-aircraft (AA) brigade of the Royal Artillery was made. Although it could still be argued that this did not infringe the Treaty, since the role of AA gunners was purely defensive, the opportunity was also taken, less than a year later, to revive the North Irish Horse which had existed only on paper since 1920.

The new AA brigade and the North Irish Horse were to be administered by the Antrim TA and AF Association which also had responsibility for a squadron of the Auxiliary Air Force: this was No. 502 (Ulster) (Bomber) Squadron which had been raised on 15 May 1925 as a Special Reserve squadron, becoming an auxiliary squadron in 1937. In its Special Reserve guise No. 502 Squadron was one of only five, manned by a cadre of regular personnel on permanent service and which could be brought quickly to operational status. The change to the Auxiliary Air Force made it a Territorial-type unit, manned by part-time volunteers with permanent staff administering the squadron and maintaining the aircraft.

Although administered by a Territorial Army and Auxiliary Air Force Association, neither the anti-aircraft brigade's regiments, nor the North Irish Horse were to be TA units. Instead they were part of the Supplementary Reserve, the new name given to the Special Reserve after the Great War. In this the AA brigade, entitled 3rd Anti-Aircraft

Brigade, and the North Irish Horse were unique. The Supplementary Reserve was normally a body of individuals who fulfilled their training requirements with regular units, although there was provision for some small units, sub-units in military parlance, to be formed, for example, railway companies of Royal Engineers and companies of the Royal Corps of Signals. In both cases, however, the personnel were railway and post office telegraphs employees respectively. The anti-aircraft gunners were given an overseas responsibility whereas similar TA units were, at that time, assigned to the gun and searchlight defence of the UK.

While the first public announcement of the creation of the AA brigade was made in July 1938, the brigade, with its constituent regiments, ancillary units and sub units, did not come into being officially until 1 January 1939 when the titles first appeared in the Army List. Officers were being recruited and commissioned and a cadre of regular Royal Artillery personnel arrived to prepare to receive and train the first influx of recruits from December 1938 onwards. Recruiting was opened on 1 April 1939 for 3rd Anti-Aircraft Brigade's two AA regiments, one searchlight regiment and supporting elements of the Royal Corps of Signals and Royal Army Service Corps.* Each of the AA regiments was made up of a headquarters element, three heavy AA batteries and a light AA (LAA) battery. This was also an order of battle almost unique to these regiments as, with one exception, it was not reflected elsewhere in the Royal Artillery's anti-aircraft branch. (The one exception was another Northern Ireland-raised regiment and the first full TA regiment to be raised there, 102nd AA Regiment which came into being in August 1939.)

The creation of this new brigade was part of a continuing development of Britain's air defence assets. Coming into being at much the same time as the cabinet's decision to form a British Expeditionary Force which would be sent to France in the event of war with Germany, it was almost natural that the brigade should be assigned to the BEF. As its formation, and its recruiting programme, also followed the Munich crisis, it gave the first opportunity for men in Northern Ireland to commit themselves to the Army in the event of war.

Recruiting for the brigade was brisk. The bulk of the formation was located in the greater Belfast area, including the regimental headquarters (RHQ) and the three heavy batteries of 8th AA Regiment together with the RHQ and three of the four batteries of the searchlight regiment as well as the Brigade Signal Company, the Royal Army Service Corps Company (RASC) and the Brigade Workshop of the Royal Army Ordnance Corps (RAOC).

The principal element of the brigade to be found outside Belfast was 9th AA Regiment which had its RHQ and two of its three heavy batteries based in Londonderry. The third heavy battery of 9th Regiment was based in Ballymena and the light battery was in Coleraine. Elements of the two Londonderry-based heavy batteries were also to be found as far apart as Enniskillen and Limavady with part of

---

* These were: 8th AA Regiment, RA (SR); 9th AA Regiment, RA (SR); 3rd SL Regiment, RA (SR); 3rd AA Brigade Signal Company, Royal Signals (SR); 3rd AA Brigade Company, Royal Army Service Corps; and 3rd AA Brigade Workshop Company, Royal Army Ordnance Corps (SR).

a battery also in the Strabane area. In fact, 9th AA Regiment had the broadest recruiting base as it included, in addition to the city of Londonderry, counties Fermanagh, Tyrone, Londonderry and Antrim. By contrast only the light battery of 8th AA Regiment was based outside Belfast; this battery was located in the North Down area. Similarly only one battery of the searchlight regiment was to be found outside Belfast – in this case at Lurgan in County Armagh.

With the number of personnel authorized for each unit set at peacetime levels, 3rd AA Brigade had an overall strength of almost 3,000 all ranks. When the TA's 102nd AA Regiment was raised in August 1939 it reached a strength of 1,037 all ranks in less than three months. Some of its officers were transferred in from 9th AA Regiment which had exceeded its officer quota. Thus, by early November 1939, 3rd AA Brigade and 102nd AA Regiment had attracted some 4,000 men to their ranks.

On 9 May 1940 the designations of the brigade and the Supplementary Reserve regiments were amended to reflect their local affiliations, becoming 3rd (Ulster) AA Brigade; 8th (Belfast) AA Regiment; 9th (Londonderry) AA Regiment and 3rd (Ulster) Searchlight Regiment. Less than a month later, on 1 June, 8th, 9th and 102nd Regiments were redesignated Heavy Anti-Aircraft (HAA) Regiments, although 9th continued to include a light AA battery in its order of battle for some time further while 102nd had two light AA batteries.

The ranks of the brigade were added to after the outbreak of war when a further number of volunteers joined up. However, the bulk of the personnel had been peacetime Supplementary Reserve soldiers some of whom had actually crossed the border to enlist. This was obviously easier in 9th Regiment with the proximity of its base to County Donegal. Several natives of that county provided themselves with accommodation addresses in the city in order to become soldiers. Another, however, gave his address as Lifford – just across the border from Strabane – which seemed to pass unnoticed by the recruiting staff.

With few exceptions therefore the volunteer personnel of 3 AA Brigade and 102nd AA Regiment were mainly from Northern Ireland. The regiments of the brigade – 8th and 9th HAA and 3rd Searchlight, which later became 4th LAA Regiment – were to see widespread service but not as constituent elements of the brigade. In most cases they adopted the Red Hand of Ulster as their badge but there was one notable exception to this: 9th (Londonderry) HAA Regiment preferred to adopt symbols relating to Londonderry and Ballymena for its batteries.* By so doing the Londonderry Regiment was following more closely that tradition of the Royal Artillery which holds that a gunner's first loyalty is to his battery.

As volunteers made their way to the recruiting offices of 3 AA Brigade, and subsequently underwent their training programmes, the many Irishmen, from both sides of the border, who were already in the services were also making their preparations for

---

* These included a profile of Roarin' Meg, a famous cannon from the 17th-century siege of Derry, for 24 Bty; a skeleton, from the city's coat-of-arms for 25 Bty; and the seven towers from Ballymena's coat-of-arms for 26 Bty. The Coleraine-based 6 Light AA Bty adopted a shamrock badge.

war. The Irish infantry battalions were widely spread: 1st Royal Inniskilling Fusiliers were in India as were 1st Royal Ulster Rifles, while 1st Royal Irish Fusiliers were in Guernsey; the respective second battalions were in Catterick in Yorkshire, Parkhurst on the Isle of Wight and Malta. Therefore the battalions which would form part of the British Expeditionary Force were to be those stationed 'at home' – 2nd Inniskillings, 2nd Rifles and 1st Irish Fusiliers. The Irish Guards were stationed in London where their 2nd Battalion, in suspended animation since March 1919, was reactivated in July 1939. Both Guards' battalions were to see service in the early campaigns of the war with the 1st Battalion fighting in Norway and the 2nd in the Low Countries and France. Two of the cavalry regiments were at home, 4th/7th Dragoon Guards and 5th Royal Inniskilling Dragoon Guards, with 8th King's Royal Irish Hussars in Egypt and 16th/5th Lancers in India. Thus the former two regiments were to see service with the BEF. The North Irish Horse, reactivated in May 1939, were still in Northern Ireland carrying out training and absorbing volunteers.

As the Army made ready for war, battalions were brought up to full strength by the recall of reservists, men who had left the Army at the end of their period of enlistment but who were obliged, for a time, to return 'to the colours' in the event of an emergency.

In the summer of 1939 there were eight Irish infantry battalions, plus one partially-Irish TA battalion, which, when brought up to strength with reservists, numbered about 7,000 men. Of these the vast majority, some 90%, were Irish. The cavalry regiments were much less Irish: even 8th King's Royal Irish Hussars, the only one not to have undergone amalgamation in 1922, was only about 50% Irish; the other three regular cavalry regiments had even fewer Irish soldiers with 4th/7th Dragoon Guards probably the least Irish of all. In total, the regular Irish cavalry regiments would have mustered no more than 500 Irishmen.

When the strength of the North Irish Horse, 3 AA Brigade, 102nd AA Regiment, 188th (Antrim) Heavy Battery and the Antrim (Fortress) Company were taken into account, there were almost 12,000 Irishmen in units with an immediate Irish identification. There were, of course, many more Irishmen throughout the Army. This was especially so in the infantry battalions of which, including Guards, there were 138. With a nominal strength of 786 officers and men in a battalion, the infantry then totalled, in theory, well over 100,000 men.

At the end of 1937, the year in which both the Inniskilling and Irish Fusiliers were restored to two-battalion status, Army strength was 197,338 men with 45 battalions and a total of 53,951 men in India. It is difficult to calculate the numbers of Irishmen serving at this point from official records. A reasonable assumption might be that about 6-7% of the infantry's strength – other than in the Irish battalions – was Irish. Eight Irish regular battalions would have accounted for 6,288 men, of whom a small proportion would not have been Irish. Allowing a figure of 5,600, therefore, for the Irish battalions and 6% Irishmen in the rest of the infantry would give a total of almost 12,000 Irish infantrymen. Of the other 89,000 regular soldiers in the other regiments and corps, there had traditionally always been a lower proportion of Irish anyway. Allowing an estimate of about 2% for units other than the Irish cavalry regiments – which, as we have seen, probably numbered no more than 500 Irishmen – would account for some 1,770 men, plus those 500 cavalrymen. The Army would probably have had no more than about 14,000 Irish soldiers. There were also reservists who were required to return to their units in the case of a major crisis; this might have increased the Irish total to about 16,000. As the Army had always attracted the largest number of Irishmen who opted for a life in the services, neither the Royal Navy nor the Royal Air Force would have had anywhere near the same numbers of Irishmen. The RAF had a more glamorous appeal in the 1930s, and throughout the war it appears that more Irish served in air force blue than in navy blue. But the total of Irish regulars, plus reservists, in these two services is unlikely to bring the total of Irish in all three services to much more than 20,000. This is still a significant proportion of the British regular forces on the eve of war.

The exact number of Irishmen, and women who served in the British forces during the war has long been a subject of debate. That debate also reflects the political differences between Northern Ireland and the Republic. In the later stages of the war figures as high as 300,000 were being quoted in newspapers, this particular claim appearing in the letters' column of the *Manchester Guardian*. That figure was halved in a *Daily Telegraph* letter which indicated that 150,000 Irishmen had served in the British forces while, in the United States, the *New Yorker* put the figure at 250,000.

Since the number who had joined up in Northern Ireland during the war could be ascertained* and since the Dominions Office supplied Northern Ireland's prime minister, Sir Basil Brooke, with the information that 37,282 men and women from Northern Ireland had served in the forces during the war, even the lowest of the three figures quoted above indicated that a neutral country, perceived to be anti-British, had made a much higher contribution to the war effort than had Northern Ireland, which was so noted for its loyalty to the crown. In early 1945 the Admiralty, War Office and Air Ministry produced figures indicating that 42,665 men and women from Éire were serving in the three forces: 30,900 (that is, 27,840 men and 3,060 women) in the Army; 715 in the Royal Navy; and 11,050 in the RAF. A year later this figure had been reduced to 38,000 with no explanation provided for that reduction. It would seem that some civil servant had decided to make the two figures more balanced but this can only be speculation.

In his book *Ireland in the War Years*, published in 1975, Joseph T. Carroll provides a further figure. After giving a breakdown from Dominion Office files† Carroll quotes a letter from General Sir Hubert Gough – of Curragh incident fame – in *The Times* in August 1944 in which the general stated that there were 165,000 next-of-kin addresses in Ireland for British servicemen and women. Since Gough had been a

---

* By January 1942 the then Northern Irish prime minister, John Andrews, was claiming that 23,000 Ulstermen had joined the forces, a figure that the head of the Northern Ireland civil service thought to be rather an optimistic estimate.

† From DO 35/1228, Carroll lists: Army 28,645; Royal Navy and Royal Marines 483; and Royal Air Force 9,426. This gives the revised total of 38,554.

supporter of the unionist cause, there is no reason to suspect him of bias in favour of nationalists and of de Valera. The fact that he refers to next-of-kin addresses would also cover the many Irish who joined up in Britain, and those from Éire who crossed the border to enlist in Northern Ireland. The figure supplied to Sir Basil Brooke of 38,282 personnel from Northern Ireland serving in the forces during the war must also include a significant proportion of individuals who had crossed the border to enlist. Brian Barton points out that between September 1941 and May 1945, 11,500 individuals volunteered from Northern Ireland while recruiting centres there approved a further 18,600 Éire recruits.

One method of establishing a figure for Irishmen serving in the British forces would be to work from the overall figure of Irish dead. An effort to obtain this figure from the Commonwealth War Graves Commission met with the reply that the Commission's records did not include nationality. By contrast the Army Roll of Honour at the Public Record Office, Kew, does include a code number to indicate the place of birth of each individual on the roll; a further code number indicates the place of domicile at the time the individual joined the Army. For the purpose of this book a sample was taken from the Army Roll of Honour, which includes 171,000 names of men and women. (Royal Navy dead totalled 51,600 with a further 34,902 Merchant Navy dead; Royal Air Force dead numbered 76,300, the majority of whom were Bomber Command personnel.)

From the infantry of the line 34 regiments were selected, from a total of 90 regiments, which included English, Scottish – both highland and lowland – and Welsh, some of which were former TA battalions. No Irish regiments were included in this sample. The dead in the sample numbered over 34,000, of whom 500 were Irish which is slightly under 1.5% of the total. Of the Irish total, 193 had been born in Northern Ireland and the remainder in Éire. The pattern indicated by these figures applied to most regiments in the sample with the exception of the Scottish regiments where those born in Northern Ireland were in the majority.

In the Guards regiments there was a very small proportion of Irish dead in the Grenadier, Coldstream, Scots and Welsh Guards. Of 1,509 dead in the Grenadier Guards, only eight were Irish, of whom five were Éire-born; of 1,468 Coldstream dead there were seven Irish, five of whom were from Éire; the Scots Guards lost 1,107 men, five of whom were Irish, including two from Éire; Welsh Guards' dead totalled 656 including eight Irish, of whom five were Éire-born. The Irish Guards lost 840 killed during the six years of war and of that total 253 were Irish-born with 160 from Éire and 93 from Northern Ireland. A small number of English-born members of the Irish Guards were shown to be domiciled in Éire while many of the names of the non-Irish dead indicate an Irish connection. The regimental entry in the Army Roll of Honour includes many Murphys, Kellys and O'Briens who were born in English towns or cities. As the war progressed regiments were assigned reinforcements who often did not come from the regimental recruiting area and in the latter phase of the war the Irish Guards' roll of honour reflects this change. Of a total of 5,585 dead in the five regiments of foot guards there were 282 Irishmen, representing 5% of the total. About

12% of the wartime strength in battalions of the guards was formed by three battalions of Irish Guards but the fact that the regiment accepted recruits other than Irishmen, especially in the latter part of the war, is clearly shown in the disparity between that 5% of Irish among the dead and the Irish Guards' 12% of the Guards strength.

In the Royal Artillery, the largest regiment in the Army, wartime strength exceeded that of the Royal Navy and there were 30,767 casualties. Of that number 672 were Irish with just over half that figure – 341 – born in Éire. Thus about 2% of gunner fatalities were Irish which is marginally higher than the figure for the sample of infantry regiments quoted earlier. Although there was an anti-aircraft brigade formed in Northern Ireland, as well as two other regiments, the casualties in these units were not excessively high and could not account for the difference between Irish dead in the infantry and the gunners.

Two other corps were studied – the Royal Corps of Signals where the overall death toll was 4,676, and the armoured regiments that formed the Royal Armoured Corps. Royal Signals' casualties included 73 Irishmen, most of whom (45) were from Éire. The armoured regiments included those which had converted from cavalry as well as wartime Royal Armoured Corps regiments and the Reconnaissance Corps. Many cavalry regiments, especially the Territorial Army units, had no Irish dead, although that does not indicate an absence of Irishmen from those regiments. In general, cavalry fatal casualties were low compared to the infantry and do not, therefore, offer the same guide to the possible numbers of Irish on a unit-by-unit basis. For example, the Carabiniers had two Irish dead from a total of 101 dead, thus providing an Irish percentage of two. By contrast, 5th Royal Inniskilling Dragoon Guards, a regiment that was about one third Irish in enlistment in 1939, suffered 98 dead of whom four were Irish, suggesting that less than 4% of the regiment might have been Irish. Another Irish cavalry regiment, 8th King's Royal Irish Hussars, had five Irish dead from a total of 184 while 4th/7th Royal Dragoon Guards, once an Irish regiment, had no Irish dead at all.

In the course of the war a series of numbered armoured regiments were formed within the Royal Armoured Corps and these suffered 1136 dead, of whom 17 were Irish. The Royal Tank Regiment sustained 2,637 fatalities, of whom 1.2%, or 31 men, were Irish. The overall death toll for all the armoured regiments was 9461 and Irishmen accounted for 182, or just under 2%, of those deaths. This figure would more accurately represent the proportion of Irish in the armoured regiments.

The three Irish infantry regiments represent the largest groupings of Irishmen in the Army and their death tolls were: Royal Inniskilling Fusiliers, 1,158; Royal Ulster Rifles (including the London Irish Rifles), 1,238; Royal Irish Fusiliers, 457. From this total of 2,853 dead, Irish-born soldiers accounted for 500 in the Inniskillings, 450 in the Rifles and 156 in the Irish Fusiliers. Thus 39% of the dead in the three regiments were born in Ireland. This represents the changes in composition of the regiments as the war progressed: early in the war most of the men of these regiments, except the London Irish Rifles, would have been Irish-born, but the reinforcement system used during the war did not allow individuals the degree of choice of regiment that existed in peacetime. Infantry regimental depots, on which the regimental system depended, became Infantry Training Centres when war broke out in 1939. They proved too small for the numbers of recruits and were grouped, normally in pairs, in 1941 to provide better facilities for specialized training. Then, in 1942, they became basic training centres for recruits from all arms; these underwent eight weeks' training before moving on to specialist training. Thus as the war went on, and casualties mounted, more and more non-Irish personnel joined the Irish regiments. The same held true for English, Scottish and Welsh regiments as the importance of local identities took second place to the need for speedy reinforcement.

Excluding the Irish infantry regiments, the sample taken from the Army Roll of Honour totals 84,489 dead which represents about half the 171,000 names on the Roll. With such a sample it is safe to project the Irish percentage of the dead to arrive at a figure for the Army. In the sample there were 1,709 Irish dead, a figure that would suggest that the Irish death toll represented about 2% of the total. This would give an overall Irish figure of about 3,418. However, this figure has to be adjusted to take account of the Irish infantry regiments. Once this is done, a figure of 3,362 is obtained to which the 1,106 dead from the three Irish infantry regiments are added to give an overall figure of 4,468. The ratio of dead to serving soldiers in the British Army in the Second World War was 1 in 22 and applying that factor to the Irish dead would indicate that 98,296 Irishmen served in the Army during the war.

The Army Roll of Honour in the Public Record Office at Kew has no parallel for the other two services, the Royal Navy and the Royal Air Force. It has not, therefore, proved possible to carry out the same exercise in those cases. However, it is known that the proportion of Irish in those services was lower than in the Army. Assuming a figure of only 1% Irish naval and air personnel and applying this to the known numbers who served in both services, it is reasonable to estimate that around 9,500 Irishmen served in the Royal Navy and some 12,000 in the Royal Air Force. Thus the total of Irish serving in the British forces during the war would have been about 120,000. It is further possible to estimate the numbers from either side of the border. Excluding the Irish infantry regiments, where those born in Northern Ireland were in the majority, the ratio of Éire-born to Northern Ireland-born in the infantry was about 1.5 to 1; in the Royal Artillery it was almost 1 to 1; in the Royal Signals 1.6 to 1 while in the Guards it was 1.7 to 1. In the Irish infantry regiments it was 1 to 2.9. Overall the figure was about 1.3 to 1 for the Army and the same ratio may be assumed for the other services. On this basis the figures for enlistment would be 78,826 from Éire and 52,174 from Northern Ireland.

On page 22 it was indicated that about 20,000 Irishmen were serving in the British forces on the outbreak of war. The exercise carried out using the Army Roll of Honour would, therefore, suggest that 100,000 Irishmen, from both sides of the border enlisted during the war years. Many of these were already living in England and were conscripted, but it must be remembered that all the conscripts had the option of returning to Ireland. That they chose not to do so must qualify them for the description of volunteers in common with those who enlisted from Northern Ireland, to which conscription was not applied, or from Éire.

The following chapters are, therefore, the story of the many Irish volunteers who served the Allied cause in the Second World War in the British forces. They were joined by further Irish volunteers in the forces of Australia, Canada, Newfoundland, New Zealand, South Africa and Rhodesia (as it then was) as well as both volunteers and conscripts in the forces of the United States of America.

~ 2 ~

Why did the Irish fight?

GONE TO THE WAR

What prompted Irishmen to enlist for service in the Second World War? As with so many questions of motivation, there are many answers. Some joined from a sense of adventure; others believed that they had a duty to do so; there are those who would insist that their motives were purely mercenary; a few would admit that peer pressure led them to the recruiting office; and some claimed that they had joined up to avoid certain problems in their own lives.

Almost sixty years later it is difficult to be certain that the motives individuals would claim retrospectively for their actions in the war years are those which prevailed at the time. In the thirty years since the outbreak of civil strife in Northern Ireland, some ex-servicemen from the Republic, and many Catholic ex-servicemen from Northern Ireland, have felt it politic to attribute motives such as the mercenary one, or the avoidance of personal problems – the Foreign Legion syndrome – to their having been members of the British forces during the war.

In 1939 there were many men living in neutral Ireland who had been British soldiers in the Great War or in the inter-war period. Many had served in the old Irish regiments of the British Army, while others had done their service in an English, Scottish or Welsh regiment. In many of their families there was a respect for the British Army and an inclination to join that body rather than the Irish Defence Forces. One such was Paddy Devlin from Galway who was

> British Army orientated, not intentionally, by my father, who had served in France from 1914 to 1919, as a Blacksmith in the Army Service Corps ... He joined in Glasgow, where he was working on the day war broke out and he was quickly sent to France as they needed blacksmiths and he was in the retreat from Mons in Belgium. I always listened enthralled to his stories about the war in France when he was telling them to grown-ups ...
>
> When the Spanish Civil War broke out, I became anti-Franco and his Fascists and later anti-Hitler and his Nazis. So when war broke out in 1939, I was pleased as I thought at last we will sort out Hitler, it never occurred to me that England could lose the war as they were the British Empire. Even at the

time of Dunkirk I still believed England would win and I never doubted it at any time during the war. I was still at secondary school in 1941 when the opportunity came for me to get into the war. I did not have to join up for economic reasons as my father was foreman of the Galway Foundry where my two elder brothers worked and he also had a lot of influence with business people in the town. So I could have a job despite the hardship of living in neutral Ireland.

At that time Paddy Devlin was too young to join the Irish Army, which had a minimum age for recruits of eighteen. He was soon to discover that the British Army had a similar lower age limit – but there were ways around that for someone determined enough. Along with a friend, Jimmy Jordan, who was two years older, Devlin travelled to Belfast to enlist. In the recruiting office in Clifton Street a warrant officer handed out application forms for completion with the advice that recruits had to be eighteen years old and, furthermore, those between eighteen and twenty needed both a birth certificate and parental permission to join up; those over twenty did not need either.

On his application form Devlin claimed to be twenty and gave his occupation as labourer on Jordan's suggestion.

> I should have put down 'clerk' or 'shop assistant'. When I had the medical examination ... the Doctor looking at my soft schoolboy hands asked me how long I was out of work. I burst out laughing and he laughed as well so he passed me fit and asked no further questions. I was questioned by security people who asked me for identification. I had my birth certificate in my bag but I couldn't produce that. My pal Jimmy had means of identity and he vouched for me and this was accepted, it was obvious that I wasn't 20.

At that time the young would-be serviceman was aged seventeen years and five months.

The two Galwegians then had to decide which service they wanted to join. Since applying for either the Royal Navy or the Royal Air Force would have meant going home for about six weeks to await call-up, the choice was made for them: it was to be the Army. An enthusiastic appeal to become paratroopers was met with the information that they would first have to become trained soldiers before applying for parachute training. A list of some twenty to thirty regiments was presented and Devlin, a cricketing enthusiast, opted for the Royal Sussex Regiment simply because he was an admirer of the county cricket team.

It remained only for the two friends to be sworn in, given the king's shilling, and a travel warrant for the journey to Sussex which was accomplished by steamer to Heysham, train to London, another train to Pulborough and a walk of several miles to the Royal Sussex's holding unit at Beedings Castle. Before long, the pair were immersed in the routine of basic training.

Just as Paddy Devlin had inherited an orientation towards the British Army, so too did many other Irishmen whose families had a tradition of military service. William Gannon, brought up in County Meath, was also the son of a Great War soldier: 'Well, my father was in the First War and I suppose it rubbed off on me. Do you understand me? I wanted to go too ... My father was a sergeant in the Irish Fusiliers.' Gannon was posted to the Hampshire Regiment and found that the training in shooting that he had received from his gamekeeper father had made him an outstanding shot. He became the best shot in the brigade which included 2nd Hampshires and was selected as a sniper.

William Clarke from Dublin also pointed to a military tradition in his family: his father had been a Royal Marine in the Great War and had served in the battle of Jutland and 'I suppose I was pro-British, you know – against the Germans anyway.' In 1941 this pro-British young man boarded a Belfast-bound train in Dublin and enlisted in the Royal Air Force. He was not to take part in flying duties but would become part of an Army-RAF construction group that built airstrips in France in the days following the invasion in 1944.

Paddy Devlin, William Gannon and William Clarke came from a working-class background, but the tradition of service was classless in Ireland. Many families prominent in business or with large landholdings had long and distinguished connections with the Army or the Royal Navy. Among those were the Jamesons, the famous distilling family, and it was no surprise that Patrick Jameson opted to volunteer in 1940, travelling to Enniskillen to join the North Irish Horse, a yeomanry regiment equipped with armoured cars.

Although he enlisted as a trooper in the North Irish Horse, Patrick Jameson went to an Officer Cadet Training Unit after six months and was subsequently commissioned in the 2nd County of London Yeomanry (Westminster Dragoons) which became an armoured regiment of the Royal Armoured Corps in November 1940. Jameson had been educated at Wellington College, a public school in Berkshire founded in 1856 as a national memorial to the then recently-deceased duke of Wellington. The college had provided many cadets to the nearby Royal Military College at Sandhurst, among them the future Field-Marshal Sir Claude Auchinleck. When Jameson was a pupil,

> about a hundred out of six hundred and fifty boys there were the sons of officers who got killed in action.* That was very much orientated towards the Army. But, on my mother's side, her brother was killed at Gallipoli and my father was gassed at the battle of Verdun. So there was a background there of being in the British Army.

Basil Baker's family lived in Fermoy, County Cork, although he and two of his siblings had been born in Rhodesia, where his father had been in the colonial service.

---

* Places were kept at Wellington for the sons of deceased officers. These pupils were known as Foundationers.

When his father retired, the family came to live in Ireland at their mother's family home at Fermoy. A family tradition of service in the forces led Basil Baker to try to join the Royal Air Force before the war, but he failed the medical test for flying duties. When war broke out he travelled to Enniskillen, where he too joined the North Irish Horse. In that regiment he renewed acquaintances with some old schoolmates from Midleton College; three of them were to die in the course of the war.

Born at Mountainstown, County Meath, in 1920, Richard Ker, son of the County Down commandant of the Ulster Special Constabulary – the B Specials – had been sent to England with his elder sister as their lives were believed to be at risk from the IRA, which made two attacks on their parents. On the outbreak of war, Ker volunteered for the Royal Ulster Rifles but later transferred to the Coldstream Guards, with whom he would win the Military Cross at Mareth in 1943. Ker's family had lived in Ulster for three centuries and an ancestor was credited with starting the linen trade in Ulster.

William Brownlow, who was descended from the Lords Lurgan, one of whom owned the famous greyhound Master McGrath which won the Waterloo Cup in 1868, 1869 and 1871, was at school in England when war broke out. An Etonian, as was Richard Ker, Brownlow joined the Army as soon as he was old enough. Commissioned into the Rifle Brigade in 1941, he later served with the 7th Battalion in North Africa and was mentioned in despatches, and seriously wounded, at El Alamein.

Also at school in England when war broke out was John Gorman, whose father, Major J.K. Gorman, MC, was the RUC's county inspector for Londonderry. His reaction to the news that Britain had declared war on Germany was 'rather ungallant'. As a sixteen-year-old he thought

> well, I'll bet that this war's not going to end as soon as people think. With any luck it'll be over before I'm old enough to fight. I really wasn't in the least eager to get into the fighting at all. I think everybody in those days had been brainwashed by Siegfried Sassoon and so on and the First [World] War, and all the terrible things that happened then and also I think we were all very demoralized by what many pacifists in the world had been saying, namely that aerial bombing would completely wipe out whole populations.

The war had a more immediate effect on John Gorman and his brother who were both at Haileybury. Since it was almost impossible to obtain sailing tickets for regular visits home, the two boys were brought back to Northern Ireland and sent to Portora Royal School in Enniskillen. During his eighteen months at Portora, Gorman took a keen interest in the war's progress, from the disasters of 1940 to the successes against the Italians in North Africa in early-1941 and he began to think that he should become involved in the war.

> So when I had finished my Senior Certificate, as it was then, I was just over seventeen and I applied to the RAF to become a pilot and went to Warrington

without my parents knowing it – I was sent a [travel] warrant to go there. But they told me I was too young – you had to be eighteen. So I gave that up.

Soon after this, John Gorman availed of a new scheme for younger would-be servicemen which allowed suitable candidates, after initial training, to attend university for six months. He did some basic training in the Royal Artillery in Exeter and was then sent to Glasgow University where he was paid the princely sum of nineteen and sixpence per week – two-and-a-half new pence short of a pound – which he supplemented by firewatching on some of the city's distilleries or bonded warehouses on a regular basis – one night's firewatching earned him a pound. Invited to go for an interview for the Irish Guards, he was subsequently commissioned into that regiment and posted to its 2nd Battalion which was converting to an armoured battalion as part of the newly-formed Guards Armoured Division. John Gorman would later earn the Military Cross as a tank commander in Normandy on his first day in action in 2nd Irish Guards.

Dalkey man Michael d'Alton was keen to take part in the war but felt that he could put off his enlisting for a time. When war broke out he was training as a chartered surveyor and wanted to complete his course. In those days the course included practical work in a surveyor's office coupled with attendance at night classes and much study. It was a difficult regime but d'Alton wanted his professional qualifications to give him something to return to when the war had ended. He was influenced in this by his contact with a Great War veteran who had been a staff officer in France but was reduced to working as a typist for his father's firm. Although d'Alton's older brother, Robin, joined the Royal Navy and his sister, Jean, the First Aid Nursing Yeomanry, in the early days of the war, Michael waited until he had qualified before enlisting in 1942. However, Michael d'Alton had no doubts about the need to do something to stop Hitler: 'That bloody little German monster had to be stopped. A lot of people down here don't realize that we'd have been the next for slavery if he'd succeeded.' In the meantime he joined the Maritime Inscription, Ireland's second-line naval reserve in which he attained the rank of petty officer.* As a young man who had always had an interest in the sea and in sailing, a naval career was a natural choice for him. Wanting to be 'an ordinary seaman' he did not divulge any information about his professional qualifications as that might have led to a job in charge of stores or buildings in some naval shore establishment. Nonetheless, he was to be commissioned soon after his entry into the Royal Navy.

The Royal Marines was the chosen service for Michael Previty from Moycullen in County Galway. He volunteered to join in the early days of the war because he 'wanted to'.

Most of one's friends had done the same thing. I was a young man, twenty-four; I thought it was the right and proper thing for young people to do that.

---

* Founded in September 1940, the Maritime Inscription was a localized organization, based on ports or coastal areas. Its title was taken from Louis XIV's localized maritime volunteer service, *L'inscription maritime*.

All my contemporaries had already joined the British forces and so I thought I would do the same thing.

Peter Ross, born of Irish parents in north-west India – present-day Pakistan – was a Trinity College graduate home on holidays in Ireland from his teaching job in Dorset when Germany invaded Poland on 1 September 1939. With his brothers Frank and John, Ross had gone to Mulroy bay in Donegal to join an old friend, Reginald Osborne, who had recently been commissioned into the Fleet Air Arm, the flying branch of the Royal Navy. They were dragging a dinghy down to the water when a sailor called to them from the deck of a steamer that was berthed nearby.

> He was very excited.
> 'It's war,' he shouted, 'it's war!'
> 'What do you mean?'
> 'Them Germans has gone into Poland – heard it on the wireless just now!'

Although the four young men rowed out into the bay, they remained silent for some time until Reginald Osborne spoke the words that had been going through all of their minds. 'That means war for us,' he declared, and yet all around them was the calm peace of the Donegal countryside and the tranquil beauty of Mulroy bay. They began conversing, forcing themselves to be cheerful and talking 'a lot of nonsense'. The news meant imminent active service for eighteen-year-old Osborne,* and for Peter Ross there was

> the shock realization of a career interrupted, perhaps finished. An honours degree, a silver medal for composition in the University Philosophical Society, editing *TCD – A College Miscellany*, dreams of pursuing a literary career in the long school holidays – the so-important achievements of university life now rendered trivial and irrelevant.

Ahead of Ross was enlistment in the Army and a commission in a 'famous cavalry regiment' before being posted to North Africa and a battalion of the Royal Tank Regiment with whom he participated in the battle of El Alamein.

Another university student to give up his studies in order to join the Army was Reginald Bryan Woods of Malahide, County Dublin, who was studying at Cambridge when war broke out. His choice of service was probably influenced by his older brother, Desmond, a subaltern in the Royal Ulster Rifles who had earned a Military Cross in Palestine. Their father had also served in the Royal Munster Fusiliers in the Great War. Bryan Woods left Cambridge 'and joined the RUR Depot at Ballymena where he did his recruit training. From there he went to a War Office Selection Board, and was commissioned into the 1st Battalion the Royal Ulster Rifles, an airborne Battalion at that time.' He would never resume his studies: he was fatal-

---

* He would die less than a year later in the wreckage of his Fairey Swordfish.

ly wounded at Arnhem in 1944 when commanding the mortar platoon of 2nd Parachute Battalion.

Gerald Ralph Auchinleck Darling, better known as 'Bunny', was reading Greats at Oxford until war interrupted his studies. A native of County Tyrone, he chose to join the Royal Navy, and in 1941 volunteered for flying duties. Although accident-prone – he survived nine crashes – he saw the war out and attributed his survival to his good-luck charm, a black shamrock painted on his aircraft.

Don Mooney was two years into an engineering course at Trinity College when he decided to join the British Army in 1940. There was no economic motive behind his decision nor was there any

> great moral urge to go because of problems over fascism or anything like that. … We were a bunch of students … we didn't think very much about the depths of what was happening, it was just that it was going on. And I suppose honestly that it was the excitement of it and the only thought we gave it probably was we didn't want to be wasting all this excitement by sitting out at the Curragh or Gormanstown or somewhere like that for the war. So a lot of us just went up to Belfast and signed on the dotted line and went.

Following his enlistment, the Army sent Mooney to Queen's University, Belfast, to complete his engineering studies but he 'didn't work very hard' and was posted to a field company of the Royal Engineers.

Among the best-educated volunteers for military service were doctors and clergymen. Many Irish doctors, from both sides of the border, were quick to offer their skills to one of the three British services, which, in turn, were keen to accept them as the need for skilled medical personnel was great. One early Irish volunteer from the medical profession was to be recommended for the Victoria Cross in Burma in 1944. Desmond Whyte, from County Down, was awarded the Distinguished Service Order instead, but he was always indifferent to the fact that he had been cited for a VC, insisting that he was only doing his duty. It was that same sense of duty that had led him to volunteer in September 1939.

Alfred Denis Parsons, better known as Andy, a native of Athlone, left his job as a medical officer with the Merchant Navy to join the Royal Army Medical Corps whenever war broke out. He was to serve in France, North Africa and Italy before his war came to an end in the Anzio beachhead. During that time Andy Parsons saved many lives in the battle of El Alamein and also saved one of the Army's finest divisional commanders from bleeding to death in January 1943. Parsons was awarded the Military Cross for his work in North Africa.

The expansion of the services brought about by war also demanded an increase in the number of chaplains in each service. Attempts were made even before the outbreak of war to recruit additional chaplains from each of the major denominations. At the Presbyterian Church in Ireland General Assembly in 1939 a representative of the Royal Army Chaplains' Department (RAChD) was invited to speak. Pointing out 'that war was inevitable', he asked 'if there were any young men who would be willing to serve as chaplains to the forces' as he would like to meet them. Samuel Eaton, who had been ordained on 27 July 1939 was one of six who did meet the RAChD representative. However, the Revd Eaton expressed a preference to serve with the RAF and so was not called upon immediately. He was called as an air force chaplain in 1941. Other Irish Presbyterian clergymen were already in the Army. David Henderson, a native of Derry, had enlisted in 1937; in 1941 he would come into contact with many of his fellow citizens in Egypt's Western Desert.

Father Daniel Kelleher, from County Kerry, was a thirty-year-old curate in the archdiocese of Liverpool, for which he had been ordained, when war broke out. He subsequently volunteered to be an Army chaplain and was granted an emergency commission in March 1941. Before the year was out he was serving with 1st Armoured Division in North Africa. From the Irish dioceses a total of over 150 priests volunteered to serve as chaplains. Irish priests, such as Dan Kelleher, serving in English and Scottish dioceses took the total of Catholic Irish chaplains to over 200 while another twenty-two Irish-born priests served as chaplains to the Australian forces.

Both the Church of Ireland and the Methodist Church in Ireland also provided many chaplains with sixty-six members of the former church becoming military padres. Among the best known were Arthur Butler, later to become a bishop, and Cuthbert Peacocke, who also became a bishop. Victor Pike, a well-known figure in rugby, was already serving as a chaplain when war broke out and was later Assistant Chaplain General to Eighth Army in Italy. The Revd Harold Sloan was one of a number of Irish Methodist ministers who became chaplains. Another was Fred Rea who was working in Rhodesia as a missionary in 1939 and became a chaplain to Rhodesian troops who were serving in the South African forces.

Two Derrymen gave identical reasons for becoming soldiers, although their entry into service life was hundreds of miles apart and the pair never met. John Coyle, a Rosemount man, was working for an oil company in London when war broke out while Tommy Tracey, from the Waterside, was working in Glasgow and living with an uncle who had served in the Great War. Both men knew that they were liable to be conscripted before very long.

Coyle had studied for the priesthood in England before deciding that the religious life was not for him after all, and had remained there to find work. He had an older brother who was working at the de Havilland Aircraft Company's factory at Hatfield in Hertfordshire – and who was involved on the design work of the soon-to-be-famous Mosquito aircraft – who telephoned him to suggest that, as conscription was inevitable for those not in 'reserved occupations',* he should return home as soon as possible. The younger Coyle's response was that he would remain in England as 'this country gave me a job and I'll fight for it if it wants me to'.

---

* An occupation regarded as important to the national war effort. John Coyle's older brother was in such an occupation.

In Scotland, Tommy Tracey's attitude was identical. He would serve willingly in the forces of the country that had given him employment. His uncle also provided a role model for Tracey, who cherished that relative's Great War medals more than he did his own from the Second World War. When the call-up papers came, John Coyle was sent to the Royal Artillery and Tommy Tracey to an infantry training centre and eventually to the King's Own Scottish Borderers (KOSB).

A similar reason for being in the British Army was given to a German prisoner in the Anzio beachhead in 1944 by Company Sergeant-Major Pestell of the Irish Guards. When the German asked why he, an Irish neutral, was fighting for the English in filthy ditches, Pestell responded, 'Well, they fed me for seven years, so now I'm earning my keep.'

Some men found their efforts to enlist thwarted. Another Northern Ireland man working in the Glasgow area decided that he would like to join the RAF as an aircrew member. John Doherty, from Drummeny, near Strabane, was rejected for such service on medical grounds. That rejection prevented him from joining the Royal Navy or the Army, although, had the war lasted much longer, he may well have found his services called upon by one of the forces. Hugh Doherty, an older brother of John, was later conscripted into the Army and served as a driver in the Royal Signals before being invalided out as a result of an infection that was probably caused by a contaminated needle when he was receiving inoculations prior to overseas service. He was later awarded a full war disability pension. The Doherty brothers had an older brother, James, serving in the Royal Artillery and a brother-in-law, Alphonso Giblin, who was also a gunner. An uncle, Hugh Sweeney, had served in the Connaught Rangers in the Great War. Such family involvement in the services was a feature of many Irish homes in the course of the war.

Other Irishmen working and living in Britain also chose to remain there and either be conscripted or enlist voluntarily. The latter course had the positive benefit of allowing the prospective serviceman the chance to opt for a particular branch of his chosen service, although, as John Doherty had discovered, this did not always work out as planned. Bill Mannion, from Boyle, volunteered for army service. He considered that he was about to be called up and, not wishing to be an infantryman, opted for the Royal Artillery or the Royal Tank Regiment and was accepted for the Gunners and sent for training to Devonport.

Another Irish gunner was Desmond Fenning, a Dubliner, who became one of the élite of the Royal Artillery, a member of the Royal Horse Artillery. When on parade with their guns the Royal Horse Artillery, the 'Galloping Gunners', take precedence over all other regiments in the Army, including the Household Cavalry and claim the title 'the right of the line and the pride of the British Army'.

Fenning came from a nationalist family and was 'very nationalist' himself but that did not stop him joining the British Army. He was staying in London with his brother when he decided to enlist because 'I didn't like the Germans, the Nazis, and I saw no reason why not to go in and help to get rid of them.' His decision was to lead to active service in North Africa and Italy.

Since the Royal Artillery became the largest element of the British Army during the war – it eventually had more personnel than the Royal Navy – it is hardly surprising that many Irishmen found themselves in its ranks. Matthew Cassidy was yet another Irish gunner who saw service in North Africa and Normandy with the divisional artillery of 7th Armoured Division. Cassidy was

> out of a job and my best friend was already in the Army and was asking me to join him and I just felt that if that was the way life was to be I will accept it and went off. I had nothing to hold me really in Dublin at that time, 1941. [Those] were grim days and there weren't many jobs for people with minimum qualifications which [was what] I had at that time.

Serving in the London Metropolitan Police in 1939, John Duane enlisted in the Army on 3 September 1939, the day on which the United Kingdom declared war on Germany. His decision was prompted by the fact that Hitler had overrun 'much of eastern Europe and a personal contribution towards the defeat of the Germans was demanded'. Joining up did not bring much of a change of scenery for the young Galway man; he found himself in the Irish Guards assigned to regimental headquarters on Birdcage Walk in London. There he was to remain for over a year. Since the police service was a reserved occupation, John Duane could have continued to pound the beat throughout the war, although it should be pointed out that many of his former colleagues in the Metropolitan Police lost their lives in the German air raids and flying-bomb attacks on London.

It was the effects of German bombing that made Dubliner David McCaughey decide to enlist in the British forces. In 1939 he was a nineteen-year-old trainee hotelier in the Welsh capital

> and I was sent home. I went back to finish my training on what they called an Irish work permit ... The short answer is I got involved in bombing. Cardiff was badly bombed [and] I got mixed up obviously in ARP, air raid precautions, in the hotel itself and then I became in charge of an ARP post. And I think that when you are out early morning, trying to dig people out of mud and that kind of thing after a bad bombing, at nineteen years of age, or twenty years of age, you want to hit back some way or other. That is the only reason because there was no history in my family of service in the British forces or anything like that. I think that's the reason.

His experience of the bombing and the toll it took of human life, plus his belief that what was happening in Germany was 'a very evil thing', led McCaughey to the recruiting office. He joined the Royal Navy with the intention of getting into the Fleet Air Arm to fly, but, although he was accepted for aircrew training, he failed in this ambition and returned to being a conventional sailor.

In 1939 flying was still something of a novelty and there was certainly more glamour attached to airmen than to the other services. Thus the Royal Air Force was an attractive choice for would-be volunteers. As we have seen already not all volunteers for the RAF were successful; but many were and included in the latter was another Dubliner, Eric Dunlop. When war broke out he was working for Guinness in Belfast where, during the 'Phoney War' period, the conflict made little impression on his mind, although he was influenced by the British presence in Northern Ireland. That changed in the summer of 1940 in the wake of the evacuation from Dunkirk. It was then that Dunlop realized that

> when France finally collapsed after all the other successes that Hitler had achieved, there was an obligation on people in the British Isles probably to consider what they were going to do because Hitler looked like he was just about to invade England. I felt I had a conscience: if somebody didn't do something, who was going to do it? And I think that was coupled also with the fact that one seeks adventure at the age of twenty, twenty-two. There was excitement and I think that has a big influence on young men taking a step such as I took.

Dunlop chose to join the Royal Air Force for a fairly pragmatic reason. He considered it better to join 'a service where you either survived intact or were written off'. The Army was not his 'cup of tea' as he thought there was too much chance of being terribly injured whereas he believed that in the RAF it was a case of either 'being okay or you were just a cypher and that was the end of it'.

Working in Belfast had brought Eric Dunlop into contact with many unionists and he was not impressed with their attitude to the war:

> It's fair to say that quite a few people up north of the unionist background didn't show great enthusiasm for joining, but a number of people I knew of my own age did join up about the same time.

The RAF was also to provide the wartime home of one young Belfastman who would have preferred to join the Royal Navy but found that the navy did not want him immediately whereas the air force took him as soon as he volunteered. Sam McAughtry was to serve as ground crew before being selected for flying duties as a gunner/observer in Beaufighters. McAughtry was to spend much of his war in the Mediterranean area whereas Dunlop's service was further east, over the jungles of Burma. Another McAughtry brother was to serve in the North Irish Horse; a third would die at sea when his ship, the *Kenbane Head*, was sunk by the German raider, *Admiral Scheer*.

For many Irishman their minds had been made up before the war started. They had chosen to make their careers in the armed forces where, even in peacetime days, there was always an element of risk. Many applied to join the Royal Air Force where the excitement of flying duties, especially in the new monoplane fighters such as the Hurricane and Spitfire, provided a real attraction. One of those was Brendan

Finucane, later to become a legendary figure in the RAF and a household name in wartime Britain. Finucane's family moved from Dublin to live in Surrey in late-1936 and the young Brendan joined the Royal Air Force in the summer of 1938. Another brother, Raymond, was to follow him and his father, Andy, also attempted to join the RAF as a teleprinter operator in 1939 but his efforts were blocked by his English-born wife. Andy Finucane had fought the British two decades earlier when he had served under Eamon de Valera in the IRA. The youngest Finucane brother, Kevin, was commissioned into the Royal Artillery.

There was another de Valera connection in the case of David Power from Clonmel. Power senior had been one of the founding members of Fianna Fáil and was a friend of de Valera. That did not prevent his son from joining the British Army in early 1939. A sixteen-year-old apprentice panel beater in a local coachworks, David Power decided to run away to join the Army after striking his foreman with a wooden mallet. At much the same time two local men were home on leave from Shanghai and 'the beautiful clothes they wore, so different from the shapeless dark sombre of the hungry thirties, was what really changed imaginative longing into realisable adventure'. With his friend Miney Cooney, Power made his way to Dublin before crossing to England where the pair were split up at a recruiting office in Liverpool. Power was accepted for the Royal Signals while Cooney went to an infantry regiment. Both were to survive the war, although Power was to spend most of it as a prisoner.

For those who joined up after the Munich crisis of 1938, it was clear that war with Germany was a distinct possibility: the only question was 'When?' This also applied to those who joined the Supplementary Reserve units in Northern Ireland, or the Territorial Army sub-units there, or, indeed, those working in Britain who joined their local TA unit.

Brian Clark, to whom this book is dedicated, was working in Lloyds when war broke out but he was also a TA soldier in the Artists Rifles, formerly a battalion of the London Regiment but now a Rifle Brigade battalion. Clark, who was actually born and educated in England, was the son of a County Down man, William Clark, who had served in the Royal Irish Fusiliers in the 1914-18 war and who re-enlisted in the fresh conflict, serving in the Royal Indian Army Service Corps. On 3 September 1939, the War Office redesignated the Artists Rifles as 163 Officer Cadet Training Unit (OCTU), one of a number of such organizations established to cope with the wartime demand for large numbers of officers. The transformation of his TA regiment into an OCTU meant that Brian Clark and his fellow Artists Rifles became officer cadets and he was soon commissioned onto the Army's general list. Most of his war was to be spent with his father's old regiment, the Royal Irish Fusiliers.

Among the many volunteers who had joined 9th Anti-Aircraft Regiment in Londonderry in April 1939 was John Ormsby, then employed with the Northern Ireland Road Transport Board in Strabane. A native of Dungannon, he was named for an uncle who had been killed in the Irish Guards at the first battle of Ypres in November 1914. Ormsby, who kept an unofficial – and strictly illegal – journal throughout the war, was quite clear about his motives for joining up:

The six years of my life, the best six years of my life, I gave; but I gave them voluntarily. And, thank God, I was not a conscript. That's what I'm proud of. I was no conscript; I volunteered for whatever was coming – I was going to take it. In a way, I often say to myself, well, you naturally look at the brighter sides, the nicer sides, that's what you do think of, and you'd say, 'well, do you know, I wouldn't have missed that for the world'.

My own father, James Doherty, was another volunteer for the Londonderry regiment. He had been a regular soldier who had served in Egypt, India and Sudan with the Royal Irish Fusiliers and then, as a musician, with the Irish Guards. His reservist's commitment had ended in December 1938 but he was one of the early volunteers for 9th Regiment in April 1939. He and other former regular soldiers were to prove a great boon to the regiment in its varied wartime service.

One of the other former regulars to join 9th Regiment was Matt Mulhern, who had previously served in the Royal Artillery. His reserve commitment had also expired and he was working on the construction of 9th Regiment's new camp at Caw on the outskirts of Derry when he and Sergeant 'Lofty' Muir, one of the permanent cadre of instructors, recognized each other. The pair had served together and Muir soon talked his old friend into enlisting. His previous experience in the Gunners meant that Mulhern was promoted almost immediately to lance-sergeant.

By contrast, Mulhern's younger brother Richard may well have been the youngest soldier in the Army at the outbreak of war. Dickie Mulhern managed to enlist when only fifteen, and his deception was not uncovered until 9th Regiment arrived in Egypt in November 1939 where he celebrated his sixteenth birthday. Instead of a discharge and being sent home, the younger brother was put under his sibling's wing and given the job of being an officer's batman, or personal servant, which excused him from almost all duties. It would be 1943, by which time he was nineteen, before Dickie Mulhern was allowed into an active-service job.

The ranks of 9th AA Regiment were strengthened after the declaration of war by an additional group of volunteers, all determined to make their contribution to the war effort and seeing the local regiment as the most practical way in which to do so. One such was Miles Stott, whose father, a Corkman, had been killed in France serving in 7th Royal Inniskilling Fusiliers in November 1917, some two months after the birth of the young Stott.

Another volunteer who had lost his father as a result of the Great War was George Robinson, another Derryman. His father, Thomas, had died in 1920, at the age of fifty-six, from the effects of poison gas, but neither this nor the fact that he was married with a young child deterred his son from wanting to become a soldier and satisfy an urge for adventure. Unfortunately, a problem with one of his feet, plus his age of thirty-two years, meant that Robinson was not accepted for an infantry regiment as he had wanted. Instead he was sent to the recently-formed Auxiliary Military Pioneer Corps.

Not everyone joined in a burst of enthusiasm such as that shown by George Robinson. There were some suggestions that single unemployed men were subjected

to a form of economic conscription. Tommy McCready, from the Waterside area of
Derry, recalled that enlisting had been suggested to him as a job opportunity at the
local labour exchange. He joined willingly, although, prior to September 1939, this
was only on a part-time basis, because he was convinced that somebody had to stand
up to Hitler. McCready could not abide bullies and, to him, Hitler was the worst of
bullies. However, he remained convinced that some who joined up did so under pressure from the labour exchange rather than from personal conviction. A similar view
was expressed by John Logue, who joined the Royal Inniskilling Fusiliers but felt that
some unemployed single men had been coerced into taking the king's shilling.

The impression gained by both Tommy McCready and John Logue is supported
by entries in Moya Woodside's diary. Mrs Woodside, a surgeon's wife, was involved
in administering social services in Northern Ireland, and in her diary for 7 October
1940 she noted that outdoor relief was 'being refused to single men here ... the
reason, although obvious, is not stated'. Craigavon, the Northern Ireland prime minister, had wanted to introduce a policy of withholding unemployment benefits from men
who, although eligible, had failed to volunteer for military service. He was dissuaded
from such action by warnings from his government colleagues that the Unionist party
would not support him. While no official policy of withholding dole from those who
did not volunteer was ever initiated, it is possible, nonetheless, that individual officials
applied such a policy on their own volition.

Economic reasons for joining up were given by some of the volunteers from southern Ireland. Dubliner Chris Byrne was a thirty-seven-year-old plasterer who had run
out of walls to plaster and had no means of feeding his six sons and four daughters.

> We had no work, everything went wrong. Things went bad, the cement strike
> came off and we'd no other alternative but to join the Army ... I'd a family. I
> had to go.

Byrne had already worked in England but had returned to Dublin before the war.
When war broke out he made the decision to join up and travelled to Belfast to
become a soldier. His age precluded infantry service and he was posted to the Royal
Artillery. In retrospect he saw his war service as defending Ireland: 'We joined the
British Army anyhow and I suppose, more or less the war, we were afraid of the
Jerries coming over, smashing up our little country like they smashed them all over.'

A similar sentiment was expressed by Tony Brehony, from Dunmanway, County
Cork, who joined the Royal Navy as an eighteen-year-old. To him, it was a job 'pure
and simple ... I knew Hitler was a baddie but essentially it was a job. A lot of us had
the mercenary tag and to tell you the truth we were quite proud of it.'

Denis Murnane decided to cross the border from Dublin in 1941 and join the RAF
out of a sense of adventure, a desire to sort out his life and a feeling, confirmed by a
holiday in Germany in 1939, that Hitler had to be stopped. Although he had been
studying law, he had no real desire to follow in his father's footsteps and become a
barrister, which is what his uncle, who was his guardian, wanted him to do.

A sense of duty, born out of a realisation that Hitler was a threat to peace was the impetus that drove Kevin Gibney, from Howth, to join the Royal Navy in 1938. Gibney trained as an observer in the Fleet Air Arm and was posted to a Swordfish squadron. His antipathy towards fascism had been kindled during the Spanish Civil War, even though his mother had been pro-Franco. A similar motivation inspired Michael Morris Lord Killanin, who was a journalist with the *Daily Mail* before the war.

Many from southern Ireland simply boarded a train in Dublin and, on arrival in Belfast, made their way to the recruiting office to sign up. Boarding a Belfast-bound train at Amiens Street, William Shorten, a Dundrum man who was deserting from the Irish Army, found himself in company with many others who shared his reason for that rail journey: 'There were hundreds on the train from Dublin, both deserters* and ordinary civilians joining up. They distributed you amongst the regiments ... two of us went to the West Yorks. A mate of mine who went up to Belfast was sent to the South Staffords.' Shorten had initially joined the Irish Army on a two-year engagement, intending to enlist in the British Army thereafter as a career soldier. However, the outbreak of war meant that he was to be retained indefinitely in the Irish Army and so he decided to discharge himself.

Another deserter from the Irish Army who made the journey north to enlist was George Berrill, a native of Drogheda, whose wartime service was to take him into the jungles of Burma with Orde Wingate's Chindits. Berrill's decision to desert was prompted by the fact that: 'I was on a charge there, [I was a] bad boy. And someone told me I'd get six months, for being absent [without leave], so I skipped.' He went first to Newry when he, and others, were sworn in by Staff Sergeant McEvoy and sent on to the recruiting office in Clifton Street in Belfast. Of the group of thirty who travelled north with George Berrill, all were deserters. When these men reached Aldershot the instructional staff there 'knew right away' that they had been soldiers. As a result their training period was reduced and they were posted to units after eight weeks.

John P. Duggan suggests that desertions from the Irish Army during 1942 totalled 1,062 men, who 'were subsequently apprehended', but offers no overall figure for desertions in the course of the war. Anecdotal evidence suggests that the desertion rate may have been as high as 7,000. Multiplying Duggan's 1942 figure by six would produce a similar figure. Whether all deserters were 'subsequently apprehended' is a moot point; those who died in action could not have been, nor would those who settled in Britain after the war. It may be that Duggan's figure relates only to those who were subsequently apprehended and court-martialled; this would place the overall total of desertions well above the 7,000 mark. Typical of those apprehended and tried were two men who were arraigned before courts martial in Dublin's Collins Barracks in June 1945.

* These were deserters from the Irish Army who had decided that service in the British Army, in spite of all the risks, was a more attractive proposition than service in Ireland where they might never see action. The pay was no better.

Patrick Kehoe, of D Company, 22nd Infantry Battalion, had joined the Irish Army in November 1940 as a fifteen-year-old 'with the intention of getting training before going to join the British forces'. At the age of eighteen, he absented himself and joined the RAF 'to get a crack at the Germans because I am opposed to Nazism on account of what my relations went through'. Kehoe had been born in Rawalpindi, where his Irish father was serving as a soldier. His mother was English, and the family came to live in Ireland when Patrick was a two-year-old. It was the suffering of his English relatives that prompted him 'to get a crack' at Hitler's Germany. He became a flight-sergeant and flew on 22 operational missions with Bomber Command before being shot down on 13 March 1945 between Nuremberg and Leipzig.

Patrick Shannon, 2nd Infantry Battalion, had joined the Defence Forces in January 1940 and absented himself a year later, joining the British Army in July 1941. He was subsequently promoted corporal, serving in North Africa, Sicily and Italy where he was captured near Florence. He said that he joined the British forces 'so that he could support his mother' which he could not do on the fourteen shillings a week paid by the Irish forces.

Both men had been liberated in May 1945 and were given leave. Kehoe's mother had told him during a telephone conversation that there was an amnesty for deserters while Shannon had come home to visit his mother who was dying. Both were arrested in Dundalk. In their defence, Captain Cowan said that desertion was leaving one's post in time of danger, a definition that did not apply in either case as both men had left safety for danger. 'In many countries the accused would ... be considered a hero that deserves honour and deserved reward.' Their reward was to be given 156 days' detention each, which was immediately commuted and both were discharged from the Defence Forces.

Not everyone, deserter or otherwise, travelled north by train. Paddy Lawlor, from County Mayo, walked most of the way from his home to Derry to join 9th AA Regiment. A former soldier, Lawlor had heard that Major Walter Lambert, under whom he had served in India, was the newly-appointed officer commanding a battery of the regiment and he decided to offer his services to Lambert for whom he had great respect.* Others crossed the border in Tyrone to join the Royal Inniskilling Fusiliers at their depot in Omagh, or in Armagh to join the Royal Ulster Rifles whose depot was located in Armagh city at the beginning of the war. Some of these potential recruits were driven by economic necessity in the view of Charles Alexander, then serving in the Rifles at Armagh.

> Each day ... there were three, four, five, six boys from the South of Ireland came over the border, some of them, literally, in their bare feet, because at that

---

* Matt Mulhern, who served with Lawlor under Lambert's command in 24 HAA Battery, was convinced when he spoke to the author that Lawlor had served in the Connaught Rangers. However, the Army List shows that Walter Lambert was a Royal Artillery officer and had never served in an infantry regiment. It is more likely, therefore, that Paddy Lawlor's previous service had also been in the Royal Artillery.

time there was very little work in the South and they came and joined up for two shillings a day.

Many of the would-be riflemen appeared 'small, undernourished, with a hint of desperation – as they came across the border to join the Royal Ulster Rifles'.

By contrast, George Lapsley and Tommy Porter, two close friends from Donegal, appeared fit and healthy specimens as they volunteered to join 9th AA Regiment in Derry. Since they joined prior to the declaration of war they were concerned that they might be rejected if it were known that they came from Éire and so they arranged accommodation addresses. Each man had a brother living in the city and the brothers' addresses were given to the recruiting officer. Porter was to be 25 HAA Battery's first fatal casualty in the Western Desert some two years later. By that time his home address situation had been regularized: his entry in the Royal Artillery Roll of Honour shows his places of birth and domicile as Éire.

Another volunteer for 25 HAA Battery who was to lose his life in action was Neill Murray from Bridge Street in the city. A former Irish soldier – he may even have deserted from the Irish Army to enlist in his home city's regiment – Murray was much admired by his comrades as an outstanding soldier and a good friend. His death occurred in April 1943 during the battle of Wadi Akarit in Tunisia when he was serving with Mac Troop, an *ad hoc* troop formed from volunteers from the Londonderry and 51st HAA Regiments and equipped with captured German 88mm guns, which was supporting 2nd New Zealand Division.

Stuart Lovell, who had been born in Ceylon in 1916 where his Irish father was a tea-planter, had followed in his late father's footsteps when he left Ampleforth College where he had been educated. When war broke out in 1939, Lovell was on his first leave in five years and 'being something of a live wire and a dare-devil' he volunteered for the RAF in which his younger brother, Tony, was already serving. In July 1941 he began flying training at Kidlington in Oxfordshire and was commissioned into the Royal Air Force Volunteer Reserve (RAFVR) on 20 September. Both Lovell brothers were to die flying.

In Northern Ireland an element of peer pressure influenced the decisions of some volunteers. Billy Jarvis saw many of his friends join the services and felt that he should follow in their footsteps. When war broke out he was not yet seventeen. He was underage and had only reached his seventeenth birthday at the height of the Dunkirk crisis in 1940. Many of his friends had joined the Army, but he was turned down as being too young. Told that he had to be seventeen and a half before he would be accepted by the Army, he took himself off to a Royal Naval recruiting office where he was accepted and

> there I was. We did ten weeks' training down in Devonport and then we were sent up to Rosyth, and everyone on that ship was given leave except me. The reason they didn't give me any leave was because I was Irish, they thought I wouldn't come back again. If I had known what I was going into I wouldn't have come back!

Billy Jarvis' experience would indicate that the naval authorities, at least, could not differentiate between Northern Ireland and Éire. In fact, Jarvis was a Protestant from Derry who was unlikely to have fled across the border to escape service.

Most of those who joined the British forces were male but the Second World War saw large numbers of women in uniform in the auxiliary services such as the Women's Royal Naval Service (WRNS), Auxiliary Territorial Service (ATS) and Women's Auxiliary Air Force (WAAF). Women also served in the naval, military and air force nursing services and volunteer organisations including the St John Ambulance Brigade and the British Red Cross, which combined during the war years and contributed members to the Voluntary Aid Detachments (VADs). Irish Red Cross members wore a harp and shamrock badge to indicate their nationality.

On 19 November 1941 Dubliner Romie Lambkin travelled north to Belfast on the 'Smugglers' Express' to join the ATS at the age of twenty-two. Her father had served in the Royal Navy in the Great War and she had enlisted in September, but had to wait until she was called up for her initial training, which took place at Ballymena castle. She travelled with

> my new 7/6d. striped silk pyjamas, dressing gown, underclothes, powder compact, cold cream, lipstick and wash things in my little suitcase, bound for Belfast and the Big World War.

She was clear in her motives for her journey to Belfast and the ATS

> Even if Éire is staying neutral, I am not. I don't want to be left out of world-shaking events – the Battle of Britain decided me on that – and I do want to be in uniform and driving all sorts of exciting people instead of being cooped up in a ghastly boring office behind the Four Courts.

Brenda Graham's father had also served in the Great War, as a medical officer in the Royal Army Medical Corps, where he had won the Military Cross. It was in Flanders that Thomas Graham also met his future wife. Subsequently he had become one of Ireland's most respected doctors and was elected president of the Royal College of Surgeons in Ireland, a position he held in 1942-3. Thus it was that the idea of service was almost second nature to Brenda Graham, a languages' student at Trinity College when war broke out.

Soon after the war started out, Dr Thomas Graham established a St John Ambulance Brigade corps in Dublin to be available to assist the medical services should the need arise. Through this organization his daughter Brenda received first aid training and a knowledge of basic nursing care. But she, in common with many of her friends, found life in wartime Ireland to be boring and restrictive and they 'wanted to get away'. They had a sense of adventure and wanted to do something positive in the war. This seemed impossible at home and so, in 1941, Brenda and three friends made their way to England, in two pairs, to work as nursing aides in Botley Park War Hospital in Chertsey, Surrey. One of her companions was Elizabeth Chamberlain, daughter of a Church of Ireland canon, who longed to wear the uniform of the Women's Royal Naval Service but found that she could not enlist in the Wrens from Ireland. Elizabeth's aim in travelling to England was to join the Wrens.

The Tottenham family, of Tudenham House, Mullingar, decided to join up en masse. Major Harold Tottenham – Harold Walter Loftus Tottenham – had served in the Great War and lied about his age to re-enlist. At fifty-one he was a year too old for the Army, but he shaved that year off his age and persuaded the War Office that he should be accepted. He was commissioned into the Royal Norfolk Regiment. His wife, Veronica, with her two eldest daughters, Joan and Barbara, joined the Women's Auxiliary Air Force in which Veronica became an officer dealing with personnel matters. Joan had been picking potatoes with the Land Army in north Wales before joining the WAAF in which she trained as a radar operator. By contrast Barbara became a radar mechanic.

Two other members of the Loftus Tottenham family were to become combatants. The family's two eldest boys had 'travelled to Australia to learn a bit about farming' and both joined the Australian forces: Nicholas joined the Australian Imperial Force in 1940, while Anthony joined the Royal Australian Air Force in 1942 and was accepted for pilot training.

Following the fall of France in 1940 the German navy – the Kriegsmarine – was able to establish bases for its U-boats on the western Atlantic coast so increasing the danger to UK-bound convoys and forcing them to use the north-western approaches around the north coast of Ireland. This led to the development of a naval base at Londonderry on the Foyle which, with additional facilities in Lough Foyle, became the Royal Navy's most important escort base in the battle of the Atlantic.

The Derry base needed a large administrative element, much of which was provided by Wrens, the popular name given to members of the Women's Royal Naval Service, and at that stage in the war almost 300 Wrens were based in the city. Many of them were local girls who volunteered as they saw their home city move into the front line of the naval war. Among them was Maeve Boyle who enlisted in 1942, inspired by the example of her older sister. Much of the local recruiting had been encouraged by a visiting naval officer, Commander Aherne, an Irishman who, Maeve Boyle recalled, made some calls on a local antique dealer and auctioneer, Florence O'Sullivan. Aherne suggested to O'Sullivan that there were job opportunities for local girls in the Wrens where they might learn office skills that could help them in post-war civilian life. O'Sullivan then encouraged many of his friends' daughters to enlist and word of mouth brought about a sizeable response.

On a subsequent visit to the city Aherne was surprised to learn that none of the girls had been called for service. He visited the Guildhall where their applications were being processed to discover they were lying in a tray. The official story was that they were 'being processed', but Maeve Boyle is convinced that applications from Catholics were being held up. She recalled that as many as 200 local girls, some of them from Donegal, joined the Wrens and most were Catholic. One of Maeve Boyle's closest friends was Molly Mason, who became a nun after the war and was later principal of Thornhill College, the Catholic girls' convent grammar school on the banks of the Foyle north of the city. And there were many strongly nationalist households which saw one or two daughters don the dark blue uniform of Britain's navy.

Not everyone who applied to join the Wrens was successful, and there were some who were not allowed even to apply. The latter included my own aunt and godmother, Barbara Coyle, who, at eighteen, decided that she would like to follow some of her friends into the ranks of the WRNS. Her age meant that she needed her parents' permission to join and that was refused. As far as Barbara Coyle's mother was concerned, no daughter of hers was going to join the British forces. In spite of the war, Mary Ann Coyle, who came from a strongly nationalist family, regarded the British as the enemy. Perhaps the fact that one of her younger sisters had, over twenty years earlier, married an auxiliary policeman – a Black and Tan – may have had something to do with her attitude, although she later accepted another daughter, my mother, marrying a soldier.

Whatever the attitudes that prevailed among some members of Irish society, there were many Irish men and women, from both sides of the border, who believed that there was a moral imperative to become involved in the war. The majority of those who felt this way made their contribution through joining the British forces, and many made the ultimate sacrifice in doing so. Among the many men and women whose experiences are recounted in this chapter, a large majority assert that their participation in the war, as well as being voluntary, was as a result of a conscious decision that the evil that was evident in Nazism had to be fought. There were others who claimed that their decision to enlist was based purely on mercenary motives, but they are in a minority and there is no real evidence to support claims that they were better off, financially, in the British forces than in the Irish forces, or as civilians in employment.

Is it reasonably possible, therefore, to arrive at the conclusion that Irish involvement in the Second World War was born out of the nobler sentiments that mark mankind at its best: the willingness to help others, the desire to fight against injustice and oppression, the craving for a better world for future generations? If so, then it is right that Ireland should remember with honour and pride those who displayed those sentiments in the years between 1939 and 1945.

~ 3 ~

Attitudes to
Irish servicemen and servicewomen

IF YOU'RE IRISH ...

How did those Irish volunteers of the war years adapt to the military life? Those with previous service, either in the British or Irish forces, had little difficulty in adjusting to their new lifestyles; others found it a strange existence at first but soon became used to it; and there were some who could not adapt and who took the first opportunity to desert and return home. Perhaps those who joined an Irish regiment had the least difficulty in coming to terms with military life. They were, after all, in an environment that contained many of the cultural elements to which they were used. The initial training regime varied little but there were distinct differences in the further training that followed, this depending on whether the individual had been selected for the armoured regiments, the artillery, the infantry or one of the other corps.

Those who found themselves in a minority in an English, Scottish or Welsh regiment, or in the Royal Navy or Royal Air Force, would have had more problems in settling in. Billy Jarvis joined the Royal Navy from his native Derry in 1940. He had been thwarted because of his age in his efforts to enlist with some of his friends in the Army and so went to Belfast to become a sailor. As indicated in chapter Two, Jarvis received special treatment because he was Irish: he was not allowed leave prior to his ship's departure from the UK. The naval authorities seemed to believe that he might desert, a possibility that they appear not to have considered with any of other crew members of the cruiser HMS *York*.

As the sole Irishman aboard the vessel, Jarvis felt a loneliness that was exacerbated as *York* sailed from Scapa Flow into the Atlantic and around the north coast of Ireland, en route to the Mediterranean.

> We had all been given injections against typhus and typhoid and our arms had swollen up terribly and were very painful and we were all seasick. These hardened sailors on board used to come down and we'd be lying there really sick, anybody that's been seasick will know what I mean. They had big plates of pork and bacon and it made us worse. Every so often they would announce over the ship's radio, 'We are now in such and such a position.' Coming out of Scapa Flow into the Atlantic it was really rough, and I heard the voice saying,

'We are now three-hundred-odd miles off the north-west coast of Ireland.' and I thought, 'God, if I could swim, I would swim home tonight.' But after a few days we got used to it.

Billy Jarvis was delighted to hear an Irish accent when *York* put in at the west African port of Freetown, its first port of call on its voyage round the Cape to the Suez canal. Crew members were ferried ashore in motorboats to visit a local bar and, at the landing stage

> this big man was standing, dressed in naval whites … and I heard him saying, 'Now, you go that way, and hi, hi, you, get you that way there', and I thought, 'an Irish voice'. I was the only Irishman on this big cruiser, I went up to him and I said, 'Excuse me, are you Irish?' 'Naw,' he said, 'I'm not, I'm from Ballymena.' That finished me altogether.

York was to serve in the Mediterranean where she saw considerable action against the Italian navy until they put her out of service in Suda bay in Crete in March 1941. *York* settled on the bed of the bay and was used to bolster the anti-aircraft defences of the island, which was preparing for a German attack. Many crew members were given jobs on shore, and Billy Jarvis was among those re-assigned. He found himself boiling water for anti-aircraft gunners and it was whilst so engaged that he met another Irishman.

> I was the only Irishman on board the boat and was very homesick. There was no mail getting through and the Germans were bombing the island all the time. Sitting outside this cavalry barracks one day this friend of mine and I, we were responsible for keeping a big boiler going with hot water for soldiers to come down from surrounding gun positions to have a bath. I was sitting outside feeling very sorry for myself when I heard this broad Derry voice saying, 'What about a cuppa tay?' When I heard the voice it was like God talking to me, I was so glad to hear it and I called out, 'Is there anybody there from Derry?' 'Aye, who's that?' And it was a gentleman from the Bogside.* I didn't care what he was, I was so delighted to hear that Derry voice.

Thus ended Jarvis' homesickness. Crete was invaded by the Germans in late May 1941, but Billy Jarvis was one of those fortunate enough to be evacuated from the island. Following his return to Alexandria he was posted to a small gunboat in which the crew felt more like a family. He also discovered that he was near many more friends and acquaintances from Derry as the AA defences of Alexandria at that time

---

* Jarvis used the description Bogside in his interview with the author in 1989 at which time the description encompassed a large part of the area west of the river Foyle. In 1941 the Bogside was a single street. Jarvis' fellow Derryman was a member of 20 HAA Battery from Lecky Road.

included 9th (Londonderry) HAA Regiment. He was never to feel as lonely again as he did during his days on board HMS *York*.

Paddy Devlin, from Galway, underwent basic training with the Queen's Regiment where he found that there were many more Irish volunteers, so he had little difficulty in fitting in. The drill sergeants tended to use the ex-Irish army soldiers to demonstrate drill to those with no military experience whatsoever. The only problem with the Irish drill was that the response to the order 'Slope arms' was to throw the rifle across the body and then onto the shoulder – which differed from the British drill of throwing the rifle up the right side and then onto the shoulder. Devlin's first experience of different treatment for Irishmen came when he was put on a charge at Stoughton Barracks, outside Guildford. His crime was to bring food to a sick comrade in the barrack block, a practice that was forbidden as the presence of food scraps could bring rats into the blocks.

As a result Devlin was placed on a charge and marched in front of the company commander who awarded him three days' CB (confined to barracks). In addition to not being allowed to leave the barracks,

> it meant I would have to report to the Guardroom in the evening and do fatigues, scrubbing and cleaning. But that afternoon I was told to report to the Captain who informed me that my 3 days C.B. were cancelled and a fine of 3 days' pay awarded instead as I was Irish. How's that for discrimination? General MONTGOMERY, being Irish himself, ordered that all Irishmen in his command were to lose pay instead of being confined to barracks as this was the only way they could be punished. C.B. to them was only a way of getting fatigues in the cook-house where they gorged on food and spent their time drinking tea, especially when they had no drink money left. So by taking some of this drink money off them it was a better form of punishment.

The change in punishment meant that Devlin lost seven shillings and sixpence instead of spending three days carrying out fatigues. Taking a meal to a sick friend had proved to be both an expensive act of charity and an expensive breakfast; 'it also taught me to be more careful when I broke the rules to ensure that I did not get caught. There was really only one rule in the army, the 11th Commandment, "Thou shalt not be found out."'

During Paddy Devlin's first winter in the Army there was a heavy fall of snow and someone from his platoon decided to climb on to the roof of the gym to trace out the slogan 'Up the IRA' in very large letters in the snow. As the roof was pitched at about 45 degrees and faced the barrack square across from the main entrance to the barracks, it could be seen by anyone entering. In spite of this the slogan was ignored and was allowed to melt away. No action was taken to discover the perpetrator, although it 'had to be somebody from our platoon'.

Paddy Devlin's experience was that he was welcomed as an Irishman into Britain's Army. Apart from the policy of monetary fines in place of CB instituted by Montgomery in his command, there was no evidence of Irishmen being treated in a different manner than English, Scots or Welsh. While the majority of Irishmen found themselves welcomed in their chosen service, not all Irish servicemen had a similar experience.

Many Irishmen found themselves dubbed 'Paddy' or 'Mick' irrespective of the names with which they had been christened. But that was a slight burden compared with the hostility that was encountered on a few occasions. Denis Murnane, a warrant officer in RAF Bomber Command, met with such an attitude in London while travelling home to Ireland on leave. Since his home was in Éire, Murnane was in civilian clothing because British uniform could not be worn on Irish soil. In a London pub he was approached by two very well-built soldiers who were curious about his accent; both men were in that stage of intoxication when a drinker can become aggressive. When Murnane told the men that he was Irish, one of the pair responded with 'You're one of those bastards who won't give us the ports.' An attempt to explain that he had no personal part in the refusal to give Britain the ports and to emphasize that he was in the RAF and was going home on leave to Ireland proved of little value. The two soldiers remained on the same theme: 'You're still one of those bastards who won't give us the ports.' At this stage the Irishman became convinced that a rapid exit was his best option but, as he looked for a way out, he became aware of another two large individuals, one on either side of him. His initial reaction to the appearance of the newcomers was that he was now in really serious trouble until one of them asked him if he was having any trouble with the pair of soldiers. The man's accent was unmistakably from Belfast. Murnane's would-be oppressors looked at the Ulsterman and said, 'But he's from the South.' The Belfastman's response was, 'It doesn't matter a damn, he's Irish.' The two Englishmen left and Denis Murnane retired to the bar with his relief force; this turned out to consist of two Belfastmen, one of whom was a Catholic from the Falls Road and the other a Protestant from the Shankill Road.

When he joined the RAF in Belfast in 1941, Denis Murnane had discovered that forty-seven of the party of sixty recruits with whom he travelled to England for basic training were from the south, and three of them were men he knew quite well from Dublin. He had, therefore, never felt out of place in the Royal Air Force. His experience in that London pub was unusual for him. By contrast, another Irish airman, Sam McAughtry from Belfast, found himself being welcomed in a pub precisely because he was Irish. This was at Padgate where he was stationed for his first Saint Patrick's Day in uniform. To mark the occasion, McAughtry and a fellow Irishman, Paddy Johnston, decided to go into town with sprigs of shamrock in their caps. Johnston hailed from the Falls Road and was a Catholic, whereas McAughtry came from the strongly-Protestant Tiger's Bay area of Belfast. But both were united as Irishmen on this Saint Patrick's Day. The shamrock in their caps

> was spotted right away by the locals and the people we were serving with. They treated us differently. A light came into their eyes when they saw the shamrock … I wasn't long in picking all this up. I loved it. It's no wonder the Irish won so many Victoria Crosses because the English expected you to be like

this. I was inclined to play up to the Irishness a lot and do daring things and
be cheeky with sergeants. Now your typical archetypal North of Ireland man,
from Ballymena or wherever, was not naturally this way. Yet I saw them come
out of their shells whenever they were referred to as 'Paddy'. I used to sit on
the bed in the barrack room and watch some guy who was Scotch-Irish by
nature, reserved and cautious, and I used to watch them to some degree come
out of their shell and become 'Irish'.

McAughtry's evidence would suggest that the term 'Paddy', and the alternative 'Mick',
was much more a term of endearment and affection than it was a slight or a racial
slur. 'Paddy' was the name by which the Irish fighter ace Brendan Finucane was
known to the British public and there can be little doubt of the respect in which he
was held.

Eric Dunlop found that the attitude to Irishmen in training in the Royal Air Force
was positive. He attributed this to the fact that most flying personnel tended to be
volunteers, whether Irish, English, Scots or Welsh, and came from similar educational and social backgrounds.

There was a bit of surprise [at a neutral Irishman] but there again the chaps
who had volunteered in Britain for aircrew were themselves to an extent
volunteers. The fellow who wanted a less risky war would have had other
branches of the service, or the Army itself, or even the Navy, which he could
have gone into. So I think that all the flying people had some bond together. In
my case ... it included three chaps who joined with me from the North* who
were very much the same type of fellow as I was as far as background and
education was concerned.

Although there were a couple of times when Dunlop was penalized for being negligent
on drill or on guard duty, there were no harsh punishments and 'apart from peeling a
few potatoes and that sort of thing there wasn't much that was severe about it'. There
was certainly no attempt to single him out for being Irish.

That Irishness which Sam McAughtry identified as something expected by the
English of his countrymen, north or south, was sometimes used to good effect by Irish
servicemen. In the summer of 1941 a group of soldiers from 25 Heavy Anti-Aircraft
Battery, detached to the Western Desert from 9th (Londonderry) HAA Regiment, went
on leave to Cairo. Among the group was Gunner Dodger Greene from Kilkenny; the
rest were Derrymen. On arrival in Cairo the first priority was a bath to remove the
sand of several months' service in the desert and then a trip to a bar for a drink.
Leaving the leave hostel to look for a bar the group spotted a barber's shop and decided that haircuts would feature as the next item on their agenda. That done they set off

* These were Ronnie West, from Ballinamallard, County Fermanagh, and two past pupils of Methodist
College, Belfast, Granville Wilson (see page 122) and Arthur Graham-Cooke. All three were killed on operations.

again in search of a bar but, hardly had they left the barber's, than they came upon a tailor's shop with a window display that included items of uniform clothing. Dodger Greene noticed that the display included ties and made the suggestion that they should all buy ties. At that time in the British Army ties were worn only by officers but, undeterred, the gunners entered the shop, invested a few pence each in neckwear, and came out sporting their ties.

Their next port of call was the bar of a hotel. After a few drinks they decided to move on elsewhere for a meal but, before quitting the hotel, they paid a visit to the gents. As Greene and Bertie Cuthbert were drying their hands, a Royal Artillery captain – described by the latter as being similar to Captain Mainwaring of *Dad's Army* – entered. The staff officer, for such he undoubtedly was, did a double take when he saw these Other Ranks wearing ties and Royal Artillery shoulder titles. He began to dress down the pair, pointing out that, as ORs, they had no right to be wearing ties. Greene, who was much taller than the captain, looked down at the officer and said, in an exaggerated version of his own accent, 'But, Captain, we're the Free Irish, don't you see?' The puzzled officer looked up at Greene, then muttered, 'The Free Irish? Oh, that's all right then.' The improperly-dressed pair promptly made their retreat and urged their friends to make haste as well before the bemused captain realized that, while there may have been Free French, Free Poles, Free Czechs and many others, there was no such grouping as the Free Irish. No one ever managed to track down the offenders on this occasion.

A number of Irish veterans have written accounts of their wartime experiences and many others have been interviewed about those experiences. In his memoir of his service in the Royal Armoured Corps, Peter Ross recounts one incident that annoyed him. It occurred when he was a staff officer in a brigade headquarters after the battle of El Alamein. The officers in the headquarters had the habit of playing cards, usually pontoon, for money each evening after supper. On the first occasion that Ross took part in this recreation he was sitting feeling lonely and listening 'to the flat aristocratic tones' around him when he 'was suddenly startled and delighted to hear someone speaking with a strong West of Ireland accent'.* The Irishman was the brigade's Catholic padre, whom Ross refers to as Father Joyce, who loved cards but hated losing and, therefore, used to cheat. This disappointed Ross who felt that it was contrary to the padre's Christian calling that he should stoop to cheating. But what angered him was the amused tolerance of the other officers. ' "Well," they'd drawl, "it's not really important. He gets a great kick out of thinking he's fooling us." And then, what really infuriated me, they'd add with a knowing smile, "You see, he's Irish!" '

Soon after this incident the headquarters was attacked by German divebombers, the screeching Ju87s, or Stukas, and a number of men were seriously injured when an ammunition lorry exploded and an anti-aircraft gun was hit. In the midst of chaos and devastation Father Joyce went to the help of the injured and dying, in spite of the

---

* Ross was born in India, educated in England, at Repton, and at Trinity and would not have had an Irish accent.

explosions and the bullets striking the ground near him. He bound wounds, gave spiritual comfort and 'never even ducked when the bombs landed near him'. Later he was seen digging graves for the dead. Ross was prompted to ponder:

> Which was the real Father Joyce – the man who cheated at cards to win a few pence, or the man who risked his life to help those soldiers? It is an imponderable question, since it suggests that the complexity of human motives and feelings can be expressed in black and white. I know that Father Joyce didn't cheat for the money, which could mean nothing to him. It may have been an act, a 'playing Irish' to amuse his fellow officers, or even a fling of contempt and defiance at their assumption of authority. I have come to believe that his heroism was always there, always a part of him. In war it was evinced in spectacular manner, in peace it would have served in hidden ways to give sufferers his strength and faith.

In her account of her wartime service in the Auxiliary Territorial Service, Dubliner Romie Lambkin refers only to one example of prejudice and that was the racism in the US forces which extended to at least one centre of entertainment in Northern Ireland.

> En masse, at dances and such, none of us care for the Yanks too much, certainly not their attitude to their own coloured troops. I've liked the Negroes I've talked to when waiting about for my passengers in their camps, but I was really taken aback when one told me he had never spoken to any white girl before me. To our utter disgust, the Ulster Hall has now put up a 'No Coloured Troops' notice. We won't go there again, I can tell you.

David Power wrote an account of his wartime experiences, most of which were as a prisoner of war of the Germans. He joined the Royal Corps of Signals in early 1939 and went through basic training at Catterick before moving to the Signals' Depot at Canterbury for technical training. At neither establishment was he singled out for being Irish, although, as with all recruits, he took a considerable amount of abuse as the instructors tried, in age-old fashion, to toughen the recruits and turn them into soldiers. He was also the butt of a practical joke when an instructor sent him to the Quartermaster's Stores to fetch ten rolls of Army Form Blank. Having been sent for glass hammers and round squares in his panel-beating days, Power was wise to this trick. Another recruit had been sent out with a paint brush and tin to whitewash 'the Last Post'.

It was only when he became a PoW that Power found that a distinction was made between the Irish and the other members of the British forces. And that distinction was made by their German captors who made a point of putting large numbers of Irish together and who seemed to believe that they could form an Irish contingent in the German forces to fight the British.

Most of the Irish who served in the Royal Navy, Army, Royal Air Force or Merchant Navy during the war years were welcomed as comrades in arms, and the only requirement for full assimilation into any unit was the ability effectively to perform whatever duties were demanded. Some Irishmen – a very small number – failed to live up to that requirement and there were those who deserted. But, in general, whether on the ocean waves, the sands of North Africa, the jungles of Burma, the skies over the battlefield, or in the hospitals of war-torn Britain, Irishmen and women gained respect from all around them. Irish sailors sometimes felt some resentment over the ports. David McCaughey recalled 'that meant lives, these ports would have been very useful to the Navy. But other than that there really was no antagonism.'

Perhaps attitudes to the Irish were best summed up by Winston Churchill in 1948 when he said in the house of commons:

> I well know the grievous injury which Southern Irish neutrality and the denial of the Southern Irish ports inflicted upon us in the recent war but I always adhered to the policy that nothing, save British existence and survival, should lead us to regain those ports by force of arms because we had already given them up. I rejoice that no new blood was shed between the British and Irish peoples. I shall never forget – none of us can ever forget – the superb gallantry of the scores of thousands of Southern Irishmen who fought as volunteers in the British Army and of the famous Victoria Crosses which eight of them gained by their outstanding valour.* If ever I feel a bitter feeling rising in me in my heart about the Irish the hands of heroes like Finucane seem to stretch out to soothe it away.

---

* Of the eight VCs generally accepted as Irish during the war, seven were awarded to men from Éire, either by birth or strong family connection, and one to a seaman from Belfast (see pp 227-9).

~4~

Narvik to Tobruk:
Irish infantrymen at war, part I

TRAMP, TRAMP, TRAMP

Throughout history the main burden of the battlefield has been borne by the foot soldier. Whether he has been supported by cavalry or, in the Second World War, by tanks, it has been the infantryman who has had to take ground and hold it. The advent of air power has not reduced the responsibility of the PBI, the poor bloody infantry. Even in the Gulf War of 1991 the power of the air forces, artillery and armour still lacked the final, vital ingredient for success; that had to be provided by infantrymen. As a result of his role the infantry soldier has suffered a higher casualty rate than any other fighting arm. This was certainly the case in the Second World War and Irish infantrymen were no exception.

Although there were several Irish infantry units with the BEF in France in 1940, none was first to see action in Europe: that distinction fell to 1st Irish Guards, the Micks, who were sent to Norway in April 1940 as part of 24 Guards Brigade with 1st Scots Guards and 1st South Wales Borderers.* Norway's neutrality had been brutally ended on 9 April when German forces invaded. British and French forces were moved to Norway following the German invasion which had been undertaken to ensure the safe passage of high-grade iron ore for its armaments industry from Sweden. Most of that ore passed through Norway, either by rail or via the port of Narvik.

Norway was unable to oppose the Germans since the country's forces were pitifully small. The Royal Norwegian Navy's ships were outdated – even though Norway had the world's fourth largest merchant navy – and its conscript sailors received only thirteen weeks' training per year. There was no independent air force; the country possessed only five airfields, eighteen scout aircraft, thirty seaplanes for naval co-operation and six fighters. (Nineteen newly-arrived Curtis fighters from the United States were destroyed in their shipping crates by the Germans at Oslo airport on the first day of the invasion.) The army numbered only 13,000 men, many of whom had not been mobilized before the invasion.

---

* This battalion had been based in Ebrington Barracks in Derry and many of its soldiers married local girls and settled in the city after the war.

The invaders quickly seized the airfields and other key points. For Norwegians it had every appearance of being *Ragnarokk*, the last day, foretold in the *Edda*, those ancient Norse poems known to every Norwegian child. *Ragnarokk* is the time when the very principles of brotherhood will be forgotten and it will be 'axe-time, sword-time, wind-time, wolf-time [when] flames will leap down from the sky' and, as German Fallschirmjäger, or paratroopers, jumped from their aircraft onto their land-ing zones, and German aircraft struck at their targets, it certainly must have seemed as if flames were leaping from the sky.

The British contingent sent to Norway was commanded by Admiral of the Fleet the earl of Cork and Orrery, GCB, GCVO, who became Supreme Commander on 20 April. However, the overall situation was confused, the Allied command was not well co-ordi-nated and objectives were not clear. As the Irish Guards sailed on the *Monarch of Bermuda* from Glasgow for Norway on 11 April, that morning's papers were proclaim-ing the recapture of Bergen and Trondheim; Swedish sources claimed that British troops had taken the former and Norwegians the latter. Such inaccurate reports were excellent examples of the 'confusion and wild rumours which existed after the German landing'.

While the Irish Guards were at sea the Germans took Narvik and so, on 15 April, the battalion landed at Harstad, north-west of Narvik. As the Micks went ashore

> all they knew was that they were the men who would do the first fighting of the war, who would engage the German Army on the ground the German generals had chosen. Except for their families and friends, no one knew that they were there. The only British troops ever named as fighting in Northern Norway were 'two companies of Scots Guards'. The German wireless announced that the landing had been made by 'hired volunteers and unemployed'.

Perhaps that reference to 'hired volunteers' was a back-handed compliment to the Irish Guards.

Norway was to be a tragedy for 1st Irish Guards. The absence of a well-defined plan meant that their brigade remained around Ofoten Fjord, moving gradually closer to Narvik and waiting for the order to attack the port. (An opportunity had been lost when a Royal Navy flotilla sailed into Narvik harbour on 13 April and bombarded the German ships, putting them all out of action.) After several days of waiting and harassing by German aircraft the battalion moved by sea to Liland in Bogen bay. Once more they waited to take part in an attack on Narvik which came under naval bombardment again on 24 April. Although a heavy blizzard put paid to those plans, an Allied ring was closing around Narvik and the Micks deployed on the northern shore of the Westfjord to guard roads leading from Narvik, a duty they carried out through the first two weeks of May.

German air supremacy led to the evacuation of Allied forces from southern Norway on 2/3 May. This allowed the Luftwaffe to concentrate its attentions around Narvik; the Micks suffered considerable harassment from aircraft that were operating freely since there were no airfields from which the Allies could deploy fighters. One soldier, Lance-Corporal Ludlow, opened fire with his Bren gun on a plane only to be placed on orders for firing at Lord Cork's aircraft. Ludlow later told his comrades that he had been reprimanded 'for missing a low-flying admiral'.

With southern Norway abandoned only token opposition faced a German advance northward; 24 Guards Brigade was ordered to Mö, the narrowest part of Norway where a fjord ran inland almost to the Swedish frontier, to delay the Germans while French and Polish troops advanced on Narvik.

On the morning of 13 May the Brigade's battalions converged on Skaanland to board ships for Mö; 1st Irish Guards were to travel on the former Polish liner, MV *Chobry*. Not until 6 p.m. on the 14th was the vessel ready for sailing, and the guardsmen were angry that the wait had exposed them to the risk of bombing. Worse was to follow. At 6.30 the ship sailed down the fjord shadowed by a German reconnaissance plane. When one officer commented that sailing on a ship such as the *Chobry* was the way to go to war, the commanding officer's response was: 'It's all very well, but it only needs one bomb. It would go through this ship like a hot knife through butter.'[14]

At midnight the ship was attacked.* Bombs landed near the cabins occupied by the senior officers, and the commanding officer, Colonel Faulkner, was among the dead. HMS *Wolverine* came alongside to effect a rescue, and its captain subsequently praised the discipline of the Micks which resulted in 694 members of the battalion being saved. Guardsman 'Mushy' Callahan threw a rope over the side and swung from porthole to porthole until he located four men who had been trapped by fire below decks; he then brought all four to safety.[16]

There was little time to ruminate on the tragedy of the bombing as the battalion, now commanded by Captain D.M.L. Gordon-Watson, MC, was in demand from the moment of landing at Harstad. Although a week's rest had been decreed, soldiers had to carry out fatigues, guards and other duties. Then it was another sea trip to disembark near Bodö to delay the Germans in the Saltaden valley. With the Scots Guards being forced back, the Micks took up positions at Pothus where a river, road, two bridges and wooded hillsides combined to form a bottleneck that could be used to impede the enemy advance. In turn this would allow the troops at Bodö to create a strong defence.

Throughout the bitterly-cold night of 24/25 May, 1st Irish Guards waited for the enemy. At about 8 a.m. on the 25th the first Germans appeared on the road; they were cut down by Norwegian machine-gun fire after which their comrades took to the cover of the surrounding countryside as they advanced, supported by machine-guns, mortars and aircraft. Guardsman Tierney was killed, and Captain Basil Eugster was wounded in the shoulder but continued to lead his company; it was later withdrawn with some difficulty. Eugster was subsequently awarded the Military Cross for directing the withdrawal.

The defence of the valley continued until a withdrawal order was issued at noon on the 26th, as British positions were being infiltrated from both flanks. Such was the

---

* The regimental history states that three German aircraft carried out the attack but German records show only one machine and the pilot told the Narvik War Museum that his plane was the sole attacker.

pressure of German ground and air attacks that it was 7 p.m. before the withdrawal could begin. As the Micks pulled back, a single Gloster Gladiator fighter appeared and gave the guardsmen considerable cheer by shooting down three Heinkel bombers before strafing the German troops. In the course of the withdrawal two men earned Distinguished Conduct Medals. Guardsman Wylie of 17 Platoon went back under heavy fire to recover a Bren and tripod which had been left behind; Guardsman O'Shea gathered a group of stragglers and guided them safely through rough country to the battalion concentration area at Fauske.*

Operations had been overtaken by the German attack on France and the Low Countries on 10 May and Norway was to be evacuated. The Irish Guards concentrated with Stockforce in the Valnes peninsula where they could block the approaches to Bodö, which was to be abandoned. Ironically, Narvik was captured on 28 May, after the decision to quit Norway had been taken. After a further move back to Harstad, 1st Irish Guards boarded the liner *Lancastria* on 8 June to sail for England.

By then the regiment's 2nd Battalion, under Lieutenant-Colonel J.C. Haydon, OBE, had gone to war as part of 20 Guards Brigade; 2nd Welsh Guards and 5th Loyals completed the brigade. Many soldiers had left on Whitsun leave when the news of the German invasion of the Low Countries was received and telegrams were sent to speed their return.

Late on 11 May Colonel Haydon was told that he was to command a composite battalion – Harpoon Force – which was to cross to Holland and assist in the defence of The Hague and the Dutch government. Since many officers and guardsmen were en route to Ireland on leave, the Micks borrowed a company of Welsh Guards. Some of those on leave were recalled, having been stopped at Holyhead, but, as they had been travelling to Ireland, they were not in uniform and had to borrow battledress when they rejoined the battalion. Since their own kit had been left at Old Dean Camp,

> most of them, including CSM O'Connor, could not get boots and marched to battle in highly-polished pointed shoes. By a tremendous effort, the Quartermaster, Lieutenant Keating, got back from leave in Ireland. The first thing he thought of was pay for the men; he extracted £2,000 from the local bank and wrapped the notes carefully in a belt under his shirt.

Thus, with funds to pay them and a variety of footwear, the Micks arrived at the Hook of Holland early on 13 May and were asked by the British ambassador to remain there and keep open the road to The Hague.

The reason for this request, which contradicted the original instruction to move to The Hague, became apparent around midday when 'a fleet of long black cars, with motor-cyclist outriders, suddenly swept down the road and drew up sharply by the quay'. At first the cars and their occupants were thought to be Germans as the guards

---

* The citations for both men included their behaviour at the time of the sinking of *Chobry*.

who dismounted from each car were so smartly dressed, but they turned out to be the entourage of Queen Wilhelmina of The Netherlands who was escorted to the destroyer HMS *Malcolm*. Although the queen was hoping to sail to one of the Dutch islands, Captain Halsey persuaded her to sail for England. The Irish Guards remained at the Hook to await the arrival of her government.

At about six o'clock that evening, sentries stopped a convoy of civilian cars on the approach to the village: the Dutch government had arrived. Behind them came the diplomatic corps, in whose wake the Germans launched their first heavy air raid on the battalion area; this killed seven guardsmen and wounded twenty-three. The battalion's anti-aircraft gunners responded furiously:

> They were necessarily in very exposed positions, but they fired continuously throughout the raid. L/Sergeant J. O'Donnell's A/A post was particularly exposed, but he stood to his gun, firing a steady stream of tracer, till he collapsed badly wounded by machine-gun bullets. L/Corporal J. Flynn on another post had a personal feud with one aeroplane which singled him out for special attention. His tripod was hit six times, but he kept on firing till the gun itself was hit twice and destroyed.

Next morning came the news that the Micks were to be evacuated, followed by another German air raid in which four more men were killed and Battalion HQ was given special treatment. But the worst devastation was visited upon civilian refugees; and Father Stoner, the battalion's Benedictine chaplain, and Pipe-Major Cosgrove performed sterling service in organizing stretcher-bearing parties and bringing relief to stricken refugees.

By early afternoon the Irish Guards had embarked on three destroyers – *Whitshed*, *Malcolm* and *Vesper* – to return to Dover some forty-eight hours after leaving that port. If they thought the nightmare was over they were mistaken: six days later they were ordered to France. On 22 May, with 2nd Welsh Guards, they landed at Boulogne to assist the evacuation of elements of the BEF from France. It was a poorly equipped force: 2nd Irish Guards had only 500 men, no signalling equipment, mines, mortars or grenades. Nor was there any transport other than the carriers, a few motor-cycles and the hope that some lorries might be obtained locally.

That latter was not to be realized and the defence of Boulogne was virtually a forlorn hope. The town's perimeter was divided between 2nd Irish Guards and 2nd Welsh Guards who soon came under attack from German troops with armour support. Persistent enemy pressure meant that the perimeter became more and more compressed, and it became clear that the Micks would, once again, be evacuating. Nonetheless, morale remained high as Father Julian Stoner noted: 'I, too, lost all sense of fear; all the more exposed a man was, the more exhilaration I got out of going to see him.'

Orders were received to evacuate Boulogne and, as the Micks pulled back to the harbour area, their Bren gunners and anti-tank riflemen stayed behind to protect the retreating column. Sergeant Gilchrist, L/Sergeant Carragher and L/Corporal Burke performed heroically in this task: Gilchrist was subsequently awarded the DCM, while Carragher and Burke each received the MM, which decoration was also awarded to L/Corporal Mawhinney.

Once again ships of the Dover flotilla took 2nd Irish Guards from a continental port to re-cross the channel. They did so under attack from German aircraft and with German forces pressing in on the embarkation area and the Micks expressed tremendous admiration for the Royal Navy's efforts. In return a naval officer described how

> the courage and bearing of the Guardsmen were magnificent, even under a tornado of fire with casualties occurring every second. They were as steady as on parade and stood there like rocks, without giving a damn for anything.

Subsequently Colonel Haydon wrote a report in which he likened his battalion's efforts at the Hook of Holland and at Boulogne to an orchestra trying to play when only half its members were present:

> [H]ad artillery support, mortar support, air support, grenades, tanks, mines, wire and good communication been available the result in both cases would have been very different. Even as things were, it took a fully equipped, fully supported and highly mobile force a full day to drive the Battalion back a distance of one and a half miles.

Such comments might also have been made about the other Irish battalions involved in the brief campaign in France and Belgium in 1940. Although Britain had given birth to armoured warfare, and to much of the philosophy of such warfare, the British force sent to support the French army in 1939 was unprepared to deal with the strategy and tactics used by the German army in its offensive in May 1940.

Troops of the BEF prepared new defensive positions, known as the Gort Line, but these were abandoned with the German invasion of Belgium, and British troops advanced into that country to meet the German onslaught. Floods of refugees were flowing through the divisional area, and Belgian soldiers were included in those refugees, some in panic and believing that German parachutists were about to descend on them. There seemed to be little spirit left in the Belgians, who had been taken totally by surprise by the German attack, and by its ferocity.

> We were rushed straight up to Louvain in Belgium. Our battalion headquarters was in the cathedral* and our front line was in the railway station. The Germans were on one platform and the Rifles on the other – as close as that.

Within 9 Brigade's front the Ulster Rifles covered some 2,000 yards into which two companies were deployed. The battalion front included a cemetery and a stretch of railway line that passed through the station referred to; this was held by Lieutenant

---

* It was actually in the town hall.

Patrick Garstin's platoon. This caused some problems later, as did another portion of the line on the extreme left flank where a platoon was positioned along the railway with the near line acting as a rifle rest and where sole access was a twenty-four-rung ladder. Worse still was the fact that a tall building only twenty yards away on the other side of the line overlooked this position which became known as the Bala-Tiger post, after the two subalterns who commanded there in turn: Lieutenants Bala Bredin and W.D. Tighe-Wood.

The Rifles had arrived in Louvain wearing respirators, to the surprise of the few remaining residents, as a result of a report that the Germans were using chlorine gas. This was but one of a number of false alarms that were typical of the period. Further reports were investigated rather than being passed on to the troops on the ground. Almost all, such as the parachuting nuns' story, were without foundation; others had been exaggerated in the course of repetition.

During 12 and 13 May defences were improved, mines laid and patrols carried out. Elements of the Belgian army, in good order, retreated into Louvain, and a cyclist unit moved into posts along the battalion front. By the evening of 14 May it was clear that all retreating Allied troops had passed through Louvain. A quiet period was broken by two explosions that marked the destruction of Louvain's bridges. Soon afterwards, as dusk began to fall, German troops began probing the Rifles' defences.

During the night the two remaining companies were deployed, with one available for counter-attack and the other held in reserve. The Belgian cyclist unit was withdrawn under cover of darkness, having suffered some twenty dead from enemy shell-fire. At dawn on 15 May German artillery was pounding the Rifles' positions and an attack penetrated the position at the station, but a speedy counter-attack restored the situation in the Rifles' favour. The Bala-Tiger post also came under attack at intervals during the day. Corporal Gibbens twice broke up German attacks with bren-gunfire and also rescued, under fire, one of his comrades who had been wounded on the railway line. Later in the day Gibbens was killed.

For most of the day there was intermittent shelling and mortar fire with the attacks on the station and on the Bala-Tiger post the only variations. That night the Germans tried to penetrate between 1st Grenadier Guards, on the left, and the Rifles but were repulsed and the two sides faced each other across the railway station where 'Every now and then Lieutenant Garstin would dart up from a subway, fire a burst from his Bren and dash away again, only to reappear somewhere else and repeat the same manoeuvre.'

Fighting intensified next day and, at one stage, both Garstin's platoon in the station and Bala Bredin's on the left flank were cut off.

> The Germans went on attacking and it's very difficult to remember how long this lasted but they finally got into this building in front of us, although we shot quite a few Germans in the building. But one or more snipers got in the top part and began to knock off rather a lot of our own platoon, including my batman, which was pretty sad. He was only about a foot away [from me] and he got a

bullet clean through his tin hat which went clean through his head. We had about twenty-five to twenty-eight men in our platoon and we had about ten casualties during that time, including one unfortunate chap, although he was lucky; his name was Logue and he lost an ear – it just got shot completely off.

Bala Bredin's platoon was cut off when some Germans penetrated between his position and the Grenadiers' platoon to his left. However, the situation was restored after a time. It had placed the platoon in a serious predicament with Germans able to shoot at them from the flank and, especially, at anyone trying to use the ladder to reach the railway line. Artillery support was important in forcing the German withdrawal.

Although the Rifles were holding out well at Louvain, the line was coming under even more severe pressure elsewhere, and a withdrawal was ordered. The Rifles were able to leave Louvain with no interference from the Germans.The BEF was now in retreat as the Belgian army and large elements of the French army collapsed. That retreat would take the army to Dunkirk through a series of rearguard actions that involved the Irish battalions in various locations. The next weeks were a haze of action and confusion, more action and more confusion until, finally, the soldiers boarded ships and boats to take them back to Britain.

For 2nd Royal Inniskilling Fusiliers their first contact with the enemy came on 17 May, three days after the Rifles had met the Germans at Louvain, when a patrol led by Major Butler killed three Germans and took two prisoners. The Inniskillings, in 13 Brigade of 5th Division, had deployed on the river Dendre but had been moved forward to Hals to cover the withdrawal of I Corps from the Dyle.

No sooner was the battalion at Hals than 5th Division was ordered to withdraw to the line of the Escaut, but the order did not reach the Inniskillings until it was too late for them to adhere to the timetable laid down. Small wonder that there was confusion as one newly-arrived subaltern, Billy Megaw from Belfast, recounted:

> As they said in those days, the balloon went up in Belgium. On 10 May the Germans attacked Holland and Belgium. We were turned about … we had no transport so we marched from the Somme to Lille. The transport had gone ahead of us into Belgium and we stayed at night at farms and places like that. The weather was beautiful so it was quite pleasant. We got transport from around Lille and went up south of Brussels and met the Germans at a place called Hals, and eventually after a bit of skirmishing and shooting we had to withdraw because by that time it was evident that things weren't quite right.

By 20 May the Inniskillings were at Avion, enduring almost constant harassment by German aircraft as the latter 'by this time had complete superiority in the air and they were bombing and machine-gunning everybody, including us'. Civilians were strafed and bombed by the Germans and the sight of dead and dying civilians, of all ages, was the cause of much anger and frustration among the soldiers.

We marched past one little baby sitting in the middle of the road and the mother dead beside it and, really, I can see her yet. And there was nothing we could do but march on. It was happening all round us.

To some it seemed as if the entire Belgian population was on the move, and with good reason.

They had been occupied in the First War by the Germans and hated them and had no wish to be occupied again. So they put their bundles under their arms and they said they getting out because the Germans had already gone in by that time, although we didn't know it, to Brussels. And there was a strange procession of the well-off first, in their big cars, and then the not-so-well-off, in carts, and then the poor people on their feet carrying their possessions. It was a pathetic business.

The battalion then became part of Frankforce, under Cork-born Major-General Franklyn, commander of 5th Division, which was to take part in an offensive from the line of the river Scarpe. Following an advance by 1 Army Tank Brigade to clear villages of enemy troops, infantry brigades would follow through and occupy the cleared area. But, although the tanks had some initial success against German armour, defective equipment, in the form of worn tracks, stopped the advance and the infantry were not called forward. In the confusion it was hardly surprising that some infantrymen were unaware that there were British tanks in the vicinity. That was the case with Second-Lieutenant Billy Megaw.

We thought we were every bit as good as they were but we didn't realize how many tanks and how many aeroplanes they would produce and how few we had. We never saw our own tanks. We came through up to the Scarpe ... and there were enormous French tanks ... and the Frenchmen were sitting smoking round behind us, and we marched through the village and someone said, 'We're okay, we've got those boys behind us'. We never saw them again.

On 23 May the battalion came under 'resolute attack' by the Germans, having first suffered bombardment by artillery and dive-bombers, the cranked-wing Junkers Ju87s, or Stukas, which Billy Megaw recalled as 'always petrifyingly frightening'. There followed a period of confused fighting with an enemy attempt to penetrate between the Inniskillings and the Wiltshires foiled. As if the battalion's situation was not bad enough news was received that the BEF was to be put on half rations. With the further news that the Germans had broken through north of Arras came the order to withdraw yet again. Then came reports of disasters to the Belgian army at Menin and the French on the Somme. The BEF was threatened with encirclement and confusion seemed to be the order of the day:

There was total confusion. There was one crossroads where a battalion, no, four battalions, were going four different directions! It wasn't very heartening. You just marched on, that was all there was to it, and when you were told to stop and dig – by that time we didn't even have shovels.

By 26 May 5th Division had deployed along the Canal line, based on the linked canals from the Escaut through La Bassée and St Omer to the coast. It was hoped to make a stand on this line if possible; otherwise the BEF would establish a defensive perimeter to cover a retreat to the channel coast.

The Inniskillings were posted along the Ypres-Comines canal at Hollebeke and had created defensive positions along a railway. On 27 May, as they waited under shell- and mortarfire for the advancing German infantry, the Skins were amazed to see a train, full of women and children, chug along the line from Ypres. Then the full fury of the German attack fell upon them.

The Cameronians were on the right. We were on the railway embankment and it was very difficult. You had to put your head and shoulders up over the rails to fire, and the Germans were infiltrating and evidently some of them had got through a culvert underneath the railway embankment and they ran away back of us ... We had only just one single line of one company, three platoons up, and company headquarters was further back in a little village.

That infiltration between the two battalions was to have serious consequences. Three Inniskilling companies had to withdraw to a position behind battalion HQ. Further German pressure caused two companies to fall back still further, leaving battalion HQ even more insecure. In spite of the efforts of the commanding officer, Lieutenant-Colonel Lefroy, to organize a defence of his HQ the Germans overran his position and all the HQ party were captured.

Enemy pressure continued and increased the following day during which B Company tried, without success, to make contact with battalion HQ. B Company then withdrew

through the wood in single file, and by bounds from cover to cover, platoons covering platoons, crossing the last 300 to 400 yards over open country, fired at by Germans from the left and by a British Regiment, which must have been amazed to see British troops coming at them from where Germans were supposed to be.

Following this the battalion re-organized into three companies and was ordered back to hold a crossroads at Oostaverne where they played a valuable part in the actions that allowed II Corps to be withdrawn successfully to the coast, thus saving the whole BEF from potential annihilation. Finally, the Inniskillings held a bridge position at Loo until the bridge could be demolished to deny its use to the advancing Germans.

On 31 May 2nd Inniskillings reached the sea, the battalion strength reduced to 215 all ranks from its original strength of over 700 officers and men. The Skins had played a vital part in the retreat of the BEF to the coast from where it could be embarked for England.

For 2nd Royal Ulster Rifles the retreat which began at Louvain on 19 May ended at Dunkirk twelve days later. In common with the Inniskillings the Rifles lived through confusion and frustration and were engaged against several enemy attacks, particularly in the last few days of the retreat. The overall memory for the riflemen was of lack of sleep and uncertainty about food. While little could be done about the former problem, soldierly ingenuity helped to ensure that the hunger pangs were not too great. A typical example was when:

> C Company came to a farm ... where they had their company headquarters. There was no food about, but there was a big fat pig and one of my riflemen [was] a fella called Waddell from Limavady who was a butcher. We got this pig and Waddell sorted the pig out and made it into a kind of Irish stew. And there was enough to feed, well we had about one hundred and forty [men]. Everybody got a good meal out of that.

It proved possible to live off the countryside in many cases. On other occasions there were opportunities to obtain supplies intended for someone else that had been abandoned and would otherwise have fallen into German hands. Some soldiers found an abandoned NAAFI* train and helped themselves to some of its contents, packing pockets, ammunition pouches and packs with cigarettes, chocolate bars and other goodies. But it was a pointless exercise as the plundered goods had to be carried and, without transport, the weary infantrymen soon threw away most of their liberated gains, in much the same way as they had already thrown away any items of kit that were considered superfluous. (It was a considerable shock, therefore, to find, soon after their return to England, that their pay was docked to cover the costs of items removed from the NAAFI train: the incident had been witnessed and the 'culprits' identified as the Ulster Rifles.)

The Rifles arrived at the sea in a formed body with all their personal arms and, in spite of fatigue, with good morale since they considered that they had given the enemy a bloody nose on each occasion they had fought him. La Panne, a small coastal town, was the battalion's first planned embarkation point but, arriving there in the middle of the night, the Rifles found a scene of considerable confusion. 'Everybody was shouting and Redcaps [military policemen] saying "Go there" and "Go there" and go everywhere. There was nobody really in charge.' Colour-Sergeant Dick Connell led his company down a defile on to the beach and along a pier that had been improvised by driving lorries into the sea and placing planks along the tops of the vehicles. 'But we

---

* NAAFI, or Navy, Army and Air Forces' Institution, provided a service to the forces at home and abroad through which normal rations could be supplemented at reasonable costs. The NAAFI element with an overseas' force such as the BEF was known as the Expeditionary Forces' Institute (EFI).

stood on that gangway for hours until it was nearly the middle of the next day and couldn't get anything at all. And the tide came in. Of course we were up to our waists in water.' By this stage the Rifles' commanding officer, Lieutenant-Colonel Fergus ('Gandhi') Knox, had decided that it was pointless remaining in La Panne. With the call 'all Riflemen this way' he told his battalion that they were going to march the nine or ten miles to Dunkirk where he believed that there was more likelihood of being evacuated.

The march to Dunkirk took until the early evening and such was the congestion on the roads that the battalion moved on to the beach where

> three or four Messerschmitts came zooming along [over] the beach and just rattling away at everybody and Frank Byrne and I dived into a shell hole, or just a hole in the ground, and a minute or two later I said, 'They're away now – come on, we'll go', and there was no answer. So I gave Frank a dig and said, 'Come on', and he rolled over, and he was dead.*

Similar incidents were occurring on the beaches from which the Royal Navy, assisted by a flotilla of civilian vessels, including countless small boats, was plucking the soldiers of the BEF to safety. In the midst of all this the Rifles' commanding officer proved an inspiring leader.

> The fireworks were everywhere – bombs and bullets, aircraft bullets, flying in all directions. And old Gandhi Knox was really good. He said, 'Follow me, boys', and we headed down towards the harbour, [where] there was a plea-sure-boat pulled alongside, so we all dived onto it. And Gandhi said, 'Every-body who's got a bren gun, get up on top,' because the Stukas were coming down and the Stuka was diving straight at the boat but not hitting anything. It hit the sea several times and the ship bounced up and down. And it hit the land and everybody on the top deck [was] blazing away with their bren guns.

Lieutenant Bala Bredin, by now commanding D Company, found an Isle of Man steamer, *Ben-My-Chree*, whose captain was not prepared to take all D Company on board. However, he was persuaded otherwise and the riflemen boarded although there was a corpse on the gangplank and the vessel was rocking from bombs exploding in the harbour. As the ship made its way out of harbour for the open sea, Bredin went into the saloon to rest, but when he spotted a man in a white jacket he asked if he could have a beer:

> 'Of course, sir, but you know the rules, you can't have a glass of beer until we're three miles out,' and I thought to myself we can't lose the war with people like this around. He brought me a glass of beer when we were outside the harbour.

---

* Frank Byrne, a Dubliner, was a member of the MT (transport) Platoon of 2 RUR. He was not a rifleman and was probably a member of the Royal Army Ordnance Corps.

While the Inniskillings and Rifles had been fighting their way back to Dunkirk, so too had the third Irish infantry battalion in the BEF, 1st Royal Irish Fusiliers, the Faughs. When the bulk of the BEF moved forward into Belgium, the Faughs remained in reserve with 25 Brigade of 50th Division but, on 17 May, the brigade moved to the river Dendre to cover the general withdrawal; the Irish Fusiliers deployed at Meerbeke. After a minor contact with the Germans, the battalion was ordered to pull back to Ninove and then to Oudenarde, where German artillery caused sixty casualties. At Oultre on 20 May, Captain John Horsfall's D Company had a sharp, close-quarter engagement with enemy troops over some two hours. It was there also that the battalion almost lost its commanding officer, Lieutenant-Colonel Guy Gough, DSO, MC.

Gough was out of his staff car studying maps when two German motorcyclists opened fire on his staff car. His driver accelerated rapidly away, swerving the staff car from side to side as the Germans continued their fire. Although Guy Gough's orderly was wounded and the car had been riddled with bullets, the situation could have been much worse. It was an example of the speed with which the German army moved.

> Ours wasn't such a big force altogether against the might of the German army. I saw the German army going down one road and them waving to us on another road. They were that sure they had us. They had a terrific army coming right in. There were hundreds of tanks, there were motorcycles and side-cars with a machine-gun mounted on the sidecar. That was how they came in for a quick run, and they had all the armour and everything that you could name.

In spite of the Germans' superiority, the Faughs were not intimidated as they proved when the battalion deployed along the Bethune-La Bassée canal on 21 May. In this position, holding an extended front of 11,000 yards, the Irish Fusiliers held the Germans for the best part of three days. This feat is all the more remarkable when it is considered that the troops opposed to them were from 7th Panzer Division commanded by Erwin Rommel, later to become famous for his part in the North African campaign where he gained the soubriquet the *Desert Fox*.

The Faughs also faced the problem of thousands of refugees. Before they could take up their positions along the canal they had to move against the flow of refugees.

> By no matter what route one tried to get forward one could make progress only by walking ahead of one's vehicle to force a passage, and then only at an exasperating pace. Although it would be possible to meet few more heart-rending sights than the state of these poor people there was nothing for it but to force them and their lumbering farm wagons off the road as we made an urgent passage for ourselves.

The Faughs had some welcome support from French tanks, a pair of which deployed to cover the weakest sector of D Company and an open flank. Barges in the canal had to be destroyed and the firing of these drew the attention of the Luftwaffe. One Faugh came close to cremating himself in the course of this operation.

> Quentin [Findlater] had got hold of a truckload of French aviation fuel from a nearby dump and sent his Fusilier Crocker ... to supervise. Crocker apparently without considering secondary implications went into the cabin of his first target and emptied a jerrycan of the stuff all over it, himself in the middle – all done 'with typical Faugh thoroughness' as Quentin observed – before striking the first match. Quentin then said that the next time he saw his devoted servant he looked like an Egyptian mummy, swathed in bandages and alive by a miracle.

The battalion showed a great deal more competence and skill in fighting off 7th Panzer Division over the next few days. Several attacks were fought off and the two French tanks made a sally against the Germans which resulted in their destruction; they were the sole survivors of a regiment that had been mauled in an earlier action with German armour. The Faughs had little support: the battalion's own weaponry included nothing heavier than a single 3-inch mortar while anti-tank weapons were limited to Boyes .55-inch armour-piercing rifles. And direct artillery support seemed to be completely absent for some days, as if the battalion had been asked to do a job and had then been forgotten about. The fact that the battalion had been transferred to 2nd Division may have had something to do with this.

On the morning of 25 May an artillery officer arrived to set up an observation post (OP) and the resultant artillery support was most welcome as was a fresh supply of ammunition. The battle continued with the Faughs taking a heavy toll of the opposition. The battalion had also been able to shorten its front a little with the arrival of French troops who took over part of the front. In this sector the Irish Fusiliers found that the French infantry and armour was not demoralized and fought with courage and determination.

The end of the Faughs' battle came on 25 May when the battalion was told to withdraw into reserve; its place was taken by 8th Lancashire Fusiliers. A platoon of 1st Faughs – 13 Platoon – was left behind at the canal, together with a scratch group of troops from 4th/7th Dragoon Guards and other units, and was overrun by the Germans when they launched their next major attack on the morning of 26 May. By this stage 7th Panzer Division had been reinforced by 3rd and 4th Panzer and the Totenkopf SS Divisions.

> Thus was the battle finally and irrevocably lost, and the Faughs owed their escape in part to their own merit and part to the army's need for an intact rearguard, while the rest of the southern front dissolved about us.

Far from being kept in reserve the Faughs were deployed quickly to another sector but the overall picture was becoming ever more gloomy and it was clear to the BEF's commander-in-chief, Lord Gort, VC, that his army's only hope of survival lay in withdrawal to the sea and so orders were issued to that effect. When the battalion reached Roux Croix, Guy Gough received an order to send a number of officers and warrant officers back to England immediately.

> Guy had just been informed by the brigade major that disaster was absolute and that the prospects of saving any of the British Army were slender in the extreme. With this small cadre, if it could be got away, it was hoped to rebuild the regiment. Someone was taking a long view, but the Faughs could hardly have had the military situation spelled out to them in plainer terms, had they bothered to think about it.

The retreat continued with the battalion fighting its way back to the coast where it finally arrived on 29 May, having had several engagements with the enemy. It was an exhausted body of men that reached the Dunkirk area and, in the last phase of the march, the adjutant, Captain Murphy Palmer,* found a bicycle and rode back along the line of retreat to search for stragglers. Those he found were totally exhausted but were encouraged to resume the march by the sight of Murphy's pistol.

In the bridgehead at Bergues a column of buses picked everyone up before driving 'flat out eastwards round the perimeter road of a shattered and burning Dunkirk'. The battalion debussed to prepare to embark under enemy shellfire and bombing from the Luftwaffe. Destroyers, 'small craft, trawlers and others' picked up the survivors to take them across the channel to England and safety where 19 officers and 576 other ranks of the Faughs re-assembled.

There were other survivors of the three Irish battalions who made their way back to Dunkirk by various means. Billy Megaw, wounded at the Ypres-Comines canal, had been fortunate to reach the coast. Shot in the leg, he was taken to a dressing station for treatment where he heard a sergeant comment to a doctor, 'That's the last one, sir,' as an ambulance pulled away carrying his friend Geoff Cocksedge, the carrier platoon commander, who had also been wounded. As he was resigning himself to becoming a prisoner of war, another ambulance arrived and he was stretchered into it to begin a three-day odyssey across France. At Dunkirk he was ordered from the ambulance by military policemen and had to be 'oxter-cogged along' until he got to the pier.

> And don't ask me how I got up it, but I got up it, and one of our British destroyers was there, and again I was helped on by a great big seaman and put in a lovely bed and I never knew another thing until we got to Dover.† That was the end of that and we'll never, of course, forget the Royal Navy, the way they came right in. They lost [a lot of ships]. The destroyer I got out on, they say, bought it the next trip.

---

* Malcolm J.F. Palmer was known to everyone, including his wife, as Murphy. This soubriquet began when he was commissioned into the South Lancashire Regiment and was the sole Irishman in the officers' mess. When the Inniskilling and Irish Fusiliers had their second battalions restored in 1937 he was able to transfer to the Faughs, which had always been his first-choice regiment.
† Billy Megaw was of diminutive stature, not more than 5'6" in height.

The successful evacuation of Dunkirk was made possible by the efforts of many, not least the troops who held the perimeter as the BEF embarked. Among the soldiers carrying out that rearguard action were men of 1st East Lancashire Regiment. One of their company commanders was an Irishman, Captain Harold Marcus Ervine-Andrews, born in Keadue, County Cavan, who was to win the Victoria Cross for his gallantry in the defence of the Dunkirk perimeter.

Ervine-Andrews' VC was the only one awarded for an action within the Dunkirk salient.

> It is printed indelibly on my own mind because the 1st East Lancashires were in 126 Infantry Brigade, the sister brigade to 127 which I was commanding in the 42nd Lancashire Division at Dunkirk.* I had been ordered to move 127 Brigade down to the beaches on May 31st and 126 Brigade were to go on the next day. As we moved off all hell seemed to be let loose in the rearguard position behind held by 126 Brigade – and this, as I afterwards discovered, was when Captain Ervine-Andrews won his VC. Had he and his company not been so steadfast in repelling the fierce German attacks at this critical time it might have been even more difficult than it was to embark the last divisions of the BEF.

The actions of Ervine-Andrews and his company of 1st East Lancashires were remarkable and there can be no quibbling with the award of the Victoria Cross to the Stonyhurst-educated Cavan man. With his soldiers he was in action against a much stronger German force for over ten hours, during which they endured intense artillery and mortar fire, as well as heavy machine-gun fire. Another company of East Lancashires, sent to cover his flank, was unable to reach him to perform that task and, as a result, one platoon was in real danger of being overrun. By this time the company's strength had been reduced to forty men.

The building that the company had been holding was set alight but, instead of ordering a withdrawal, the Irishman told his soldiers that they were going to charge the Germans – less than forty men against some 500. As the enemy soldiers crossed the canal de Bergues at dawn on 1 June, Ervine-Andrews led his depleted company on what should have been a suicide mission. However, the Germans were so shocked by the sight of this charge that they fell back. Ervine-Andrews then dashed to a barn with his men, climbed on to the straw roof himself and opened fire on the foe with rifle and Bren gun. He shot at least seventeen with his rifle and many more with the Bren gun, and all the while German mortars and armour-piercing bullets were punching through the frail roof. When ammunition ran low, he and his men laid into the Germans with bayonets, fists, feet and even teeth, as one survivor subsequently told the *Daily Telegraph*.

Faced with such ferocity the Germans withdrew completely, giving Ervine-Andrews the opportunity to send his wounded back to safety on the company's sole

---

* Brigadier John Smyth, quoted here, was himself the holder of the Victoria Cross, which he had won in France on 18 May 1915.

remaining carrier. By this stage only eight men were left and, determined to lead them to safety, the big Irishman collected them

> from this forward position and when almost surrounded, led them back to the cover afforded by the company to the rear, swimming or wading up to the chin in water for over a mile.

Although it was the last Victoria Cross of the campaign, Ervine-Andrews' award was the first Army VC to be approved in the Second World War. It was Ireland's second VC, the first having been awarded posthumously to the RAF's Donald Garland.

The evacuation of the bulk of the British Expeditionary Force, together with elements of the French and Belgian armies, was dubbed Operation DYNAMO. Ships of the Royal Navy, commandeered merchant vessels and small boats, the owners of which had volunteered to cross to France, all managed to achieve a successful extrication of Allied troops from the beaches of France. A decision by Hitler to halt his advancing divisions some ten miles short of Dunkirk undoubtedly played a part in what Winston Churchill later described as a 'miracle of deliverance'. In the house of commons on 4 June, Churchill stressed that 'wars are not won by evacuation' and that 'we must be careful not to assign to this deliverance the attribute of a victory'.

In the days following the evacuation, much was made of the snatching of a British army from the jaws of a superior foe. The *Daily Mirror* newspaper even marked up a milestone in British journalism by printing a swear word for the first time in its headline BLOODY MARVELLOUS. Defeat was, in effect, turned into victory in the eyes of the British public. There was certainly much to be proud of in the achievements of Operation DYNAMO; but it was no victory in the traditional, and normal, sense of that word. Two Irish generals expressed horror at the popular belief that Dunkirk had been a victory. In his *Memoirs* General Montgomery, who had played a significant part in the successful withdrawal to the French coast, wrote that many soldiers 'thought they were heroes and the civilian public thought so too. It was not understood that the British Army had suffered a crushing defeat at Dunkirk and that our island home was in great danger.'

Montgomery was appalled to see soldiers walking about 'London and elsewhere' with an embroidered flash on their sleeves reading 'Dunkirk' in obvious imitation of the German battle-honours' system. General Sir Claude Auchinleck was amazed to hear talk of a 'Dunkirk Medal' and suggested in a letter to the Vice-Chief of the Imperial General Staff that no one wanted to perpetuate 'the memory of that episode'.

Not all soldiers believed that Dunkirk had been a victory. Some were level-headed enough to appreciate the enormity of what had happened. John Donovan, a bandsman in 2nd Royal Ulster Rifles, commented that 'I'd been a professional soldier and I'd been trained to fight wars, and the British Army fought wars, and here we were, running away. I couldn't understand that ...'

Perhaps the most telling comment from an Irish veteran of Dunkirk came from Lieutenant Billy Megaw of the Inniskillings.

> Oh, it most obviously was a defeat. We were sent packing. But the discipline and spirit of the Army – they got us out, plus the Royal Navy and the wee boats that came in. But there's no talking around it – it was a tremendous defeat.

Following the evacuation from France, which was completed in mid-June, the only British soldiers facing the enemy were in North Africa. Italy declared war on Britain and France on 10 June and attacked Egypt, which, although neutral, was defended by British troops defending the Suez canal zone and Alexandria. It was a half-hearted attack which stopped after a short advance into Egypt in September 1940. Three months later the British Western Desert Force, under the Irishman General Richard O'Connor, swept the Italians out of Egypt and Cyrenaica. Just as it looked as though O'Connor's men were poised to strike to Tripoli and end the Italian empire in Africa, formations were withdrawn for an expeditionary force to Greece. The advance ended at El Agheila.

Then the Germans came to Italy's aid by sending a German force – the Deutsches Afrika Korps – to Libya. The Afrika Korps' commander, Major-General Erwin Rommel, was a man who believed in the value of surprise and he quickly launched an attack on the weakened British forces that regained all that the Italians had lost. And General O'Connor was taken prisoner. However, the port of Tobruk held out and became a thorn in Rommel's side. Efforts to seize it failed, and the garrison endured months of bombing and shelling while being maintained by the Royal Navy.

In late-1941 the newly-created Eighth Army launched its first operation, code-named CRUSADER, in Libya. One of the aims of the operation was to relieve Tobruk, the garrison of which was to strike out through the perimeter to join up with Eighth Army. It was during this operation that another Irish Victoria Cross was won by Captain James Joseph Bernard Jackman.

Jackman was born in Dun Laoghaire, County Dublin, on 19 March 1916, the only son of Dr J.J. Jackman, a Waterford man, and Mrs Jackman of Glenageary. The young Jackman's early education was received at St Gerard's School, Bray, after which he went to Stonyhurst College. He then entered the Royal Military College, Sandhurst, from where he was commissioned into the Royal Northumberland Fusiliers, one of the Army's oldest regiments, and one that had an Irish origin.* Jackman was a popular officer whose life, it seemed, was devoted to one purpose: 'the welfare and efficiency of those under him, he took infinite pains to achieve this, and no man who served in his Company can but have known he served with a friend'.

---

* The Northumberlands were descended from an Irish regiment of British auxiliaries in Dutch pay in 1674 that was commanded by Daniel O'Brien, Viscount Clare. In 1675 this regiment was given to Sir John Fenwick and became an English unit. It remained in the Netherlands until James II recalled it to England at the time of Monmouth's rebellion after which it went back to Holland to return with William of Orange to become a permanent part of the English army. It served at the Boyne as Monk's Regiment and became the 5th Foot when numbers were assigned to regiments in 1751.

In November 1941 Jackman was serving with 1st Royal Northumberland Fusiliers in 70th Division which had relieved Australian troops in besieged Tobruk. The Northumberlands were acting as a machine-gun battalion rather than a conventional infantry battalion, and their role was to provide support for the infantry brigades of the division. A typical machine-gun battalion had three machine-gun companies, each with three platoons of four Vickers .303-inch medium machine-guns and an anti-tank company of four platoons, each of which had four 2-pounder weapons. Captain Jackman was the officer commanding Z Company, one of the machine-gun companies.

Plans were being finalized for the major offensive against the Italo-German forces in Libya with the objectives of destroying a large part of Rommel's command, occupying much of Libya and raising the siege of Tobruk. The main body of Eighth Army was to advance from the Egyptian frontier while the Tobruk garrison was to punch its way out and link up.

Eighth Army's attack began in the early morning of 18 November after a night of rain and sleet. Over the next three days the British armour engaged the German and Italian forces in one of the most confused battles of the Second World War. Inside Tobruk, 70th Division waited for the order to break out. The division, commanded by Major-General Scobie, had been training for its breakout role for the past month. Captain Jackman had carried out an intensive training programme with his company to create an excellent mobile force that was to achieve all that was expected of it. On the night of 20/21 November there was great activity in the southeast corner of the Tobruk perimeter from which 70th Division was to push its way out to link up with 7th Armoured Division. Already known as the 'Desert Rats', the latter formation was at Sidi Rezegh; less than a dozen miles separated the two British divisions.

As day broke on 21 November, Scobie's men opened their assault, accompanied by diversionary attacks from Tobruk by Polish troops and the British 23 Infantry Brigade. Opposition proved much tougher than expected and the attacking troops found themselves pitched against strong defensive positions manned by German and Italian soldiers who were not prepared lightly to give up ground. Although a two-mile wide breach was created in the enemy front line, and broadening attacks were launched, there would be no speedy link up with the tanks of 7th Armoured.

The enemy strongpoints brought the Northumberlands' machine-gun companies into action. There were four such strongpoints, codenamed 'Lion', 'Tiger', 'Jack' and 'Jill'. 'Tiger' proved the toughest of the four; in taking it 2nd Black Watch suffered 75% casualties. Jackman's Z Company was called upon to assist the Black Watch at 'Tiger', lest the depleted highlanders be ejected from their gain by an Axis counterattack. With 'Tiger' consolidated a platoon of Z Company was sent to help capture another enemy position. Z Company had originally been placed under command of 32 Army Tank Brigade,* together with a squadron of King's Dragoon Guards, an anti-

---

* An army tank brigade differed from an armoured brigade in that its primary role was close support for infantry. At the time of CRUSADER a tank brigade deployed 178 infantry tanks which were slower vehicles than the Cruiser tanks of the armoured brigades. The latter also included a motor battalion of infantry, a Royal

tank battery and 1st Essex Regiment. The brigade's objective was the El Duda feature on the El Adem escarpment south of Tobruk.

On the second morning, two platoons of Z Company were detached to defend positions captured the previous day, leaving Jackman with his company headquarters and 14 Platoon. This much-reduced company was deployed to assist 1st York and Lancaster Regiment and a tank squadron in an attack on an enemy position that flanked the approach to El Duda. The position was held by about a battalion of infantry with anti-tank and machine-guns in support. Such was the strength of the defence that the York and Lancasters' attack was brought to a standstill.

> Captain J.J.B. Jackman, on seeing this, made a quick and bold decision. He led No.14 Platoon, under 2/Lieut F. Ward, off to the south and then swung away in a wide circle and came in on the enemy's right flank. Although they had to go through some heavy shell-fire, they got on to the objective and took some prisoners. The drill for getting into action off vehicles had been perfected and No. 14 Platoon were very soon firing hard from the captured positions while their vehicles were being driven away to safety.

German military tactical doctrine dictated that a swift counter-attack be launched on any position that had just been lost in the hope of taking the captors off balance before they had consolidated their gains. This is what happened on this occasion. Under cover of heavy shellfire, and with light tanks in support, German infantry drove up in lorries and forced the British infantry off the positions into which they had not had time to dig. However, one of Jackman's machine-gun sections was ideally located to meet the attack and began pouring sustained fire into the enemy troops. The machine-guns fired off almost all their ammunition and took considerable punishment from both shell- and small-arms-fire but their determined opposition drove off the attackers. The section's commander, Sergeant D. McKay, was later awarded the Distinguished Conduct Medal.

With this phase of the operation over, Z Company returned to 32 Tank Brigade's fold. A narrow wedge had been created in the Axis position and X and Y Companies were ordered forward to provide the base for the defence of this lancepoint while Z Company would go forward to take part in the assault on El Duda. But the stubborn resistance put up by the Axis troops had knocked 70th Division's schedule out of kilter. The attack on El Duda was delayed until 26 November, by which time the timetable for the entire CRUSADER operation was forty-eight hours in arrears.

Two tank regiments led the assault on El Duda by 1st Essex with Jackman's Z Company following in open formation. The tanks' advance was held up by heavy shelling and mortaring. Once again James Jackman put his well-rehearsed tactics into operation and led Z Company forward 'at a terrific speed, under heavy shell and mortar fire – taking no notice of anything but [the] objective'. When the platoons reached a pre-

---

Horse Artillery regiment (plus an anti-tank battery) a light AA battery and other support elements which were not included in the tank brigade.

arranged line they deployed into position ready for action and the vehicles withdrew into cover. As there were no radios with the platoons, Jackman and his company sergeant-major, CSM Hughes, oversaw the deployment. The latter followed Jackman's vehicle and, on the Irishman's signal, drove to a high point on the El Duda feature, debussed from his own vehicle and waved a flag to instruct the platoons to break formation and drive to their positions; each of these was indicated by Hughes with his flag.

Once in position the platoons had an excellent field of fire on to the Trigh Capuzzo, the main Axis supply route. Their Vickers guns wrought havoc among the enemy troops and played a vital part in the capture of El Duda, which was taken for the loss of two I-tanks; the Essex Regiment lost forty men to bombing by British aircraft whose pilots did not realize that the feature was in friendly hands.

James Jackman distinguished himself during this phase of the operation. Calm and cheerful, he drove around the various positions to encourage his men and to co-ordinate their fire. It seemed as if he enjoyed a charmed life. But then his luck ran out. Fusilier R.J. Dishman was an eyewitness to the last moments of the gallant Irish officer.

> Captain Jackman came and lay down on the gun line, and began to observe through his binoculars. He then gave us the order to fire at [a] truck and [motor] cyclist. 'Give them a burst', he said, and just as these words were said a mortar bomb dropped just in front of our left-hand gun, wounding three and killing Captain Jackman and Corporal Gare instantly.

A splinter from the sole mortar to strike that platoon's position passed through James Jackman's neck, severing his jugular vein and causing him to bleed to death. Fusilier Dishman later wrote that 'Captain Jackman was a fine leader and an inspiration to us all, and in losing him we lost a very young, and capable commander.' Of his leadership qualities there can be little doubt: the awards subsequently made to Z Company are positive proof of that. James Jackman was posthumously awarded the Victoria Cross; his second-in-command, Captain Derek Lloyd, and 14 Platoon's commander, Lieutenant Ward, were awarded the Military Cross; both CSM Hughes and Sergeant McKay received the Distinguished Conduct Medal and another DCM and six Military Medals were awarded to Jackman's company. There are few instances of a single company, especially one operating as a machine-gun company, receiving so many gallantry awards for one action. Those awards speak volumes for the training that James Jackman had carried out and for his personal leadership. His own VC was, according to some accounts, awarded for his actions during the action of 19/20 November although the citation specifies 25 November.

> On 25 November 1941, at Ed Duda,* South East of Tobruk, Captain Jackman showed outstanding gallantry and devotion to duty above all praise ... His

* The misspelling *Ed* Duda was used in the original citation and the Northumberlands' regimental history and is repeated in more recent publications, including John Laffin's *British VCs of World War 2 – a study in heroism* (Stroud, 1997).

magnificent bearing was contributory in a large measure to the success of a most difficult and hard fought action. As the tanks reached the crest of the rise they were met by extremely intense fire from a larger number of guns of all descriptions: the fire was so heavy that it was doubtful for a moment whether the Brigade could maintain its hold on the position.

The tanks having slowed to 'hull-down' positions, settled to beat down the enemy fire, during which time Captain Jackman rapidly pushed up the ridge leading his Machine Gun trucks and saw at once that Anti-Tank guns were firing at the flank of the tanks, as well as the rows of batteries which the tanks were engaging on their front.

He immediately started to get his guns into action as calmly as though he were on manoeuvres, and so secured the right flank. Then standing up in front of his truck, with calm determination he led his trucks across the front between the tanks and the guns – there was no other road – to get them into action on the left flank.

Most of the tank commanders saw him, and his exemplary devotion to duty regardless of danger not only inspired his own men, but clinched the determination of the tank crews never to relinquish the position which they had gained.

The regimental historian of the Northumberlands can scarcely be accused of exaggeration for suggesting that there 'can be no instance of a more merited award of the Victoria Cross than that to this courageous officer of the Fighting Fifth'. James Jackman was the fourth Irishman to win the VC in the war; of the four only one had so far survived to receive his award.

The war in North Africa was to continue until May 1943 when the Axis forces surrendered in Tunisia. Although there were many individual Irishmen in infantry units in the campaign it was not until the landings in French North-West Africa in November 1942 – Operation TORCH – that Irish infantry units would be involved. These were the battalions of the Irish Brigade and 1st Irish Guards which played an important part in the Tunisian campaign as part of First Army. Although another Victoria Cross was won by a soldier of the Irish Guards in Tunisia the laureate was not an Irishman even though he had an Irish name and identity. Lance-Corporal John Patrick Kenneally was actually an Englishman, Leslie Robinson, who had deserted from the Royal Artillery and later enlisted in the Irish Guards using the identity of an Irishman with whom he had worked on building sites. The real John Patrick Kenneally had returned to Ireland to avoid being called up. There is a certain irony in the fact that the name of an Irishman who did not want to fight should become forever associated with Britain's greatest gallantry award.

After the CRUSADER battles there was still much fighting to be done in Africa, following which the Allies would cross to Sicily and then to Italy as they strove to destroy the Axis alliance. As ever, Irish soldiers would be present.

~ 5 ~

Battleships and commerce raiders: the naval war, part I

IN PERIL ON THE SEA

The earliest months of the Second World War were dubbed the 'Phoney War' by the British and American press since little appeared to be happening in France to where the British Expeditionary Force (BEF) had been despatched in late 1939. The French themselves had inspired the Anglo-American media with their phrase '*la drôle de guerre*' which seems to have been used first in late-September and which encapsulated French doubts about the war. British troops in France were engaged in exercises and in digging defensive positions in their sector on the left, or northern flank, of the French army where they formed part of the French 1st Army Group. This line of defensive positions being prepared by the British was known as the Gort Line, after Lord Gort of Limerick, VC, commander-in-chief of the BEF.

In the air the Royal Air Force may have been busier but there were no offensive operations against Germany itself. Those British bombers that did fly over Germany (including the first to fly to Berlin on the night of 1/2 October 1939) dropped copious quantities of leaflets, rather than bombs, in Operation NICKEL, an effort to persuade the German people that the war was pointless. In the view of the Air Officer Commanding No. 5 Group, Arthur Harris, later to take control of Bomber Command, all the leaflet raids did was to provide the 'Continent's requirements of toilet paper for the five long years of war'. However, there were offensive operations against the German fleet and naval installations in which Bomber Command suffered its first casualties. But still the press persisted with the 'Phoney War' soubriquet.

There was certainly no phoney war at sea, where ships of the Royal Navy had been on active operations from the very outbreak of war. Harry Barton, son of Archbishop Arthur W. Barton of Dublin, had joined the Royal Navy in 1933 and was an officer serving aboard the R-Class battleship HMS *Ramillies* which was steaming southwards from Stornoway through the Irish sea when the crew learned of the declaration of war. Just a few months earlier, in June 1939, the ship had been in Gibraltar at the same time as one of Germany's pocket battleships. At that time Harry Barton had met some of the German officers and was surprised to find that they all regarded war as inevitable whereas, in the British services, there was still hope that a major conflict would be averted. Now, on this September morning, that hope came to an end.

One always remembers where one was when things like this happen. By then war seemed to us to be inevitable and so one didn't have great bothers about it except that it was astonishing to think that from such and such a time this massive stupidity had begun.

Before hostilities had begun the Admiralty had re-introduced a tactic from the Great War that was designed to protect merchant shipping against submarine attacks – the convoy. Intended principally for merchant vessels travelling at between 9 and 14.9 knots the convoy system was not applied to the fast liners, although all British merchant shipping was brought under Admiralty control on 26 August 1939. Thus it was that *Athenia* was sailing alone off the north coast of Ireland when the German submarine U-30, commanded by Leutnant Fritz Julius Lemp, torpedoed and sank her at 9 p.m. on Sunday, 3 September, less than twelve hours after the British declaration of war on Germany.

The convoy system was quickly expanded after the loss of *Athenia* which went down with 112 souls, a quarter of them American, thus evoking memories of *Lusitania* in the Great War.* But ships travelling in convoy needed escorts to protect them against not only submarines – or U-boats – but also German surface vessels and aircraft. Pitifully short of the vessels needed for escort duty, the Royal Navy deployed a variety of ships on such duties. These ranged from battleships to converted merchantmen.

Merchant ships were not the only targets for the U-boats; two weeks after the sinking of *Athenia*, U-29, which had already sent three British tankers to the bottom, put two torpedoes into the aircraft-carrier HMS *Courageous* which sank with the loss of almost half its crew of 1,000 men. The carrier had been engaged on an anti-submarine sweep when it was struck; U-29 evaded its escorting destroyers. Then, on 14 October, Gunther Prien's U-47 slipped into the Home Fleet's base at Scapa Flow in the Orkneys and sank HMS *Royal Oak* at the second attempt. The battleship, one of only eleven operational capital ships in the Royal Navy, capsized less than fifteen minutes after being struck by the second salvo of three torpedoes launched at her; the death toll was 833 men. Prien made good his escape.

Thus it was that the small U-boat fleet of the Kriegsmarine was perceived as a very real threat. So also were the German surface vessels, including a number of pocket battleships,† two of which, *Admiral Graf Spee* and *Deutschland*, had sailed from

---

* The sinking of *Lusitania*, off the south coast of Ireland, was one of the factors that eventually brought the United States into the First World War.

† Pocket battleships were a German naval innovation: the vessels outgunned the Royal Navy's heavy cruisers, having six 11-inch guns in two turrets with a secondary armament of eight 5.9-inch guns against the 8-inch gun main armament of British heavy cruisers. In addition, the German ships were more heavily armoured than the bigger cruisers and were fitted with 54,000 b.h.p. diesel engines which allowed them to work up to full power almost immediately, thus providing a distinct advantage over steam-turbine-powered ships which took hours to raise steam from cold and could not even accelerate quickly from cruising speed to maximum speed. Although the pocket battleships could make only 26 knots, which was slower than the British cruisers, their ability quickly to work up to higher speeds, and their 10,000 miles unrefuelled range, as well as their mighty armament, made them more than a match for all but the Royal Navy's most modern battlecruisers, of which only two, *Renown* and *Repulse*, were in service. The battlecruiser *Hood* , a Great War veteran, was in need of refurbishment.

Germany on 21 and 23 August respectively. Neither vessel was permitted to engage in hostile acts until 26 September when Hitler, irked at the failure of his peace initiative after the occupation of Poland, gave permission for them to attack Allied shipping. *Graf Spee* was in the South Atlantic by that time while *Deutschland* remained in North Atlantic waters. Their principal targets were vessels sailing alone and unescorted but either raider could destroy a convoy as readily as it could a single ship. *Graf Spee* was hunted down in the South Atlantic and cornered in Montevideo harbour where its captain, Hans Langsdorff, chose to scuttle his damaged ship and commit suicide, rather than either have *Graf Spee* interned by the neutral Uruguayan government or leave the harbour and engage his British pursuers. Among the ships that pursued *Graf Spee* was the cruiser HMS *Exeter*, part of Force G – the other ships in this force were *Ajax* and *Achilles* – which intercepted the German ship on 13 December and began a brutal gun and torpedo engagement. *Exeter* was the most powerful of the three British* ships and Langsdorff concentrated his attention on her to such an extent that the cruiser was badly damaged; the extremely accurate German gunnery eventually forced *Exeter* out of the action with all her turrets either knocked out by shellfire or otherwise disabled. With his ship taking water and listing heavily, *Exeter*'s captain was forced to turn south for the Falklands in an effort to save his vessel from destruction. During this action there were many casualties aboard the cruiser and a number of crew members did sterling work in keeping the ship's systems operating for as long as possible. One of these was Stoker O'Brien from Dublin, who was subsequently awarded the Conspicuous Gallantry Medal.

    Deutschland, renamed *Lützow* in November 1939, was damaged so severely in a torpedo attack by HM Submarine *Spearfish* in April 1940 that it would be 1941 before the pocket battleship was recommissioned.

    The Kriegsmarine had other vessels available that, although less potent than the battleships and pocket battleships, were still a grave threat to merchant shipping. These were the armed merchant raiders; these were better built and more heavily armed than the Royal Navy's answer to them. Six of these long-range vessels were despatched to roam the oceans in the spring of 1940;† by the end of the year they had destroyed 54 ships. Against these, and other German surface vessels, the Royal Navy deployed armed merchant cruisers which were simply ex-liners impressed into naval service in an effort to make good the shortage of ships that resulted from the disarmament policies of the inter-war years. One of those armed merchant cruisers was HMS *Jervis Bay*, a 14,000 tons, eighteen-year-old former liner now fitted with seven 6-inch guns but lacking the armoured skin of a true warship.

    In March 1940 Captain Edward Stephen Fogarty Fegen was appointed to the command of *Jervis Bay*. Although born in England, Fegen was an Irishman, the younger son of a serving naval officer, Vice-Admiral F.F. Fegen of Borrisoleigh, Ballinlanty, County Tipperary, whose father had also been an officer in the Royal

* *Achilles* was manned by New Zealanders and flew the New Zealand flag as well as the White Ensign.
* The German raiders were: *Atlantis, Komet, Orion, Pinguin, Thor* and *Widder*.

Navy. The young Fegen's naval career can be dated to his entry into the naval college at Osborne as a cadet at the age of thirteen in September 1904. Serving as a sub-lieutenant aboard HMS *Amphion* when war broke out in August 1914, he survived the sinking of that ship when it struck a mine some twenty-four hours after the declaration of war. His active Great War career included service on several ships before he obtained his first command, that of HM Torpedo Boat No. 26 from which he progressed to command the destroyers *Moy* and *Paladin*. He continued to command in destroyers in the immediate post-war years during which he also displayed extremely cool courage when he took his ship alongside a blazing oil tanker to rescue the crew; for that deed he was awarded Lloyd's Medal for lifesaving. Following staff appointments in Britain he was promoted to the rank of Commander in 1926 and was posted to Australia to command the Australian Naval College at Jervis Bay.

Following his two-year spell in Australia, a posting to the cruiser HMS *Suffolk* on the China station followed. During his time on *Suffolk* he earned another lifesaving medal, this time from the Dutch government, for rescuing the crew of the merchant ship *Hedwig* which had gone aground on a reef in heavy seas, an action for which he was also commended by the Admiralty. By the time war returned to Europe in 1939, Fegen had vast experience and was a highly-regarded officer. He was also a man with

> an unerring instinct to do the right thing. His command was no more than a projection of his own character. Moreover, he was always on the spot when decisions were due. Whether ships' boats were stove in or washed overboard in those months from September to March, he arrived on the scene first – somehow. In mid-Atlantic Fegen stood on the heaving deck of the *Emerald*, his breath caught at his throat, with scant regard for his own safety but much more for his men's.

This was the man who took command of HMS *Jervis Bay* in March 1940; he was then forty-eight years old.

In November of that year HMS *Jervis Bay* was assigned as sole escort to convoy HX84, eastbound from Halifax to Britain. The thirty-eight merchant ships of the convoy were laden with supplies, including fuel and food, vital to Britain's war effort. Before long the convoy was reduced in size when a Polish ship dropped behind with engine trouble. Once in the ocean the ships formed nine columns with HMS *Jervis Bay* ahead of the main formation, flanked by *Empire Penguin* and *Cornish City*, the latter being the commodore's ship. (The commodore was the civilian officer in charge of the convoy; this post was normally filled by a retired senior naval officer. In the case of HX84, Admiral Maltby fulfilled the role of convoy commodore. Maltby's ship was commanded by a forty-eight-year-old Irishman, John O'Neill of Wexford, a highly experienced seaman who had first sailed as a deckboy at the age of fourteen.)

As the morning of 5 November dawned – fair and calm for a November day in the North Atlantic – Fegen went about his business of shepherding his charges, slowly but surely, eastwards for Britain. Late that morning the British merchant ship *Mopan*, sailing alone, overtook the convoy and steamed ahead to an unexpected rendezvous with one of the Kriegsmarine's pocket battleships, *Admiral Scheer*, commanded by Kapitan Theodor Krancke. The German was already aware of the presence of the convoy, which had been spotted by the battleship's Arado Ar196 floatplane. In mid-afternoon, as *Scheer* came suddenly on the unsuspecting *Mopan*, Captain Fegen was totally unaware of the danger that lay just over the horizon.

Scheer had sailed from Gdynia – now Gdansk – on 23 October to prowl the Atlantic in search of targets of opportunity. *Mopan* was such a target although Krancke at first believed it might be an armed merchant cruiser. The little banana boat was ordered to stop by a morse lamp signal from Krancke's ship; the captain was ordered not to transmit any radio signals and to put his crew into the lifeboats and make for *Scheer*. Then the battleship's anti-aircraft guns blasted the merchantman's hull below the waterline. Thus, as *Mopan* slid below the waves, HX84, and Captain Edward Stephen Fogarty Fegen, continued on their way, still not knowing of the danger waiting for them.

Midshipman Ronnie Butler was on watch on *Jervis Bay* in the afternoon of 5 November. As he scanned the ocean for anything untoward the ship's crew were having their tea; some were settling down to the meal while others had just finished. The sun was setting on the North Atlantic and the ocean's surface had become totally calm. It was a perfect evening. Then, at 4.50 p.m., Butler spotted a ship on the horizon, to the port side of *Jervis Bay*. He immediately notified the captain and gave him a bearing on which to look. Fegen trained his binoculars on the distant vessel and identified it as a German warship. He ordered 'Action stations' to be sounded immediately and for an order to be sent to the convoy instructing it to scatter and make smoke.

The raider's presence and position were notified to the Admiralty and to *Cornish City*; the enemy vessel was twelve miles away, on a bearing of 328° from *Jervis Bay*, steering a course on bearing 208°; its position was 53°N and 32°W. When that message reached the Admiralty in London, it was the first inkling in that establishment that *Admiral Scheer* had slipped through the Denmark Straits into the north Atlantic. The German vessel, assisted by adverse weather conditions, had escaped detection by naval surface vessels and by aircraft of Coastal Command.

With the protection of the convoy foremost in his mind, Fogarty Fegen did not hesitate to order his ship to engage *Scheer*, which was now changing course for an attack. *Scheer*'s first salvo of shells, fired from 17,000 yards range, fell around *Cornish City* but there were no hits. By now HX84 was scattering in three dozen different directions, thus denying the German the opportunity to destroy all of the vessels. But *Scheer* was not even given the chance to concentrate on the fleeing merchantmen. Before the German captain could issue the order to fire a second salvo, Fegen had changed course towards *Scheer* and the puny *Jervis Bay* prepared to match its seven 6-inch guns and thin plating against the pocket battleship's six 11-inch main guns and thick armour plate. It was no contest, but *Jervis Bay*'s attack meant that *Scheer* had to eliminate the escort ship before it could turn its attention to the convoy. Fogarty

Fegen was buying precious time for the convoy; and buying it with his own life, his crew and his ship. For there could be only one outcome to this clash. HMS *Jervis Bay* was doomed.

As Fegen manoeuvred his ship between the convoy and *Scheer*, an enemy shell burst in the water near *Jervis Bay*. The *Scheer*'s captain was now positioning his ship so that he was just outside the effective range of the merchant cruiser's guns. The German could pound the old liner to scrap while taking no damage in return. The second salvo fired at *Jervis Bay* claimed at least one hit: a shell struck the ship, damaging the bridge and hitting the range-finder. The bridge area was on fire and the forward steering gear was disabled. Fogarty Fegen had also been hit but, in spite of terrible injury, continued to direct operations; one arm had been all but severed and hung useless by his side.

Able Seaman Lane, at one of the gun positions, saw a blood-soaked Fegen stagger his way to the second bridge. One of *Jervis Bay*'s rounds had actually struck *Scheer* but, as if in retaliation, the German's next salvo claimed a direct hit on Lane's gun position; he was the only survivor as gun and crew were blown into the sea. Another round had holed *Jervis Bay* below the waterline while the ship was now blazing almost from bow to stern. And yet it continued to fight back, its crew manning its remaining guns, the damage-control parties doing their utmost to cope with the effects of the onslaught. Then the engine room was hit and the power for the pumps was knocked out; no water could now be pumped up with which to fight the fires. *Jervis Bay* began to list.

Fegen was still in command, now on the after-bridge, which was then shot away. By this stage the ship could steam only in a straight line and was an easy target for the German gun crews. As Fegen made his way to the remains of the main bridge *Jervis Bay* was steaming straight for *Scheer*. In a show of defiance one crew member climbed the rigging to nail a fresh white ensign to the mast, the ship's ensign having been shot away. But another hit in the engine room stopped *Jervis Bay* in the water. Her forward guns had been knocked out of action while her aft guns could not be trained to bear on *Scheer*. The ship was blazing and there was the danger of her own ammunition exploding. Crew members threw burning debris overboard and even tried to put out fires by stamping on them. But their efforts were to no avail: *Jervis Bay* was now a dead ship, awaiting only burial by the sea that was washing over her decks as the list grew greater.

Fegen, dying from his injuries and the consequent loss of blood, retained command to the last. On what was left of the main bridge he gave the order 'Abandon ship!' Only one lifeboat was left as *Jervis Bay* settled by the stern. The crew took to the boat and the liferafts, but the boat was holed before it could be lowered and most of the seventy survivors of the crew leapt on to the rafts, although some remained with the lifeboat. Even as *Jervis Bay* slid into the waves, German shells continued to pound the ship, until only the ribs of the hull were visible; shrapnel shells were fired at the men on the liferafts.*

---

* After the war the Admiralty received a letter from a Dutchman who enclosed a scrap of what appeared to be water-damaged paper which had apparently been washed up in a bottle on the Dutch island of Terschelling.

Edward Fogarty Fegen went down with his ship. One of the vessels in HX84 was a Swedish ship, *Stureholm*, whose captain, Sven Olander, had stayed behind and was a witness to *Jervis Bay*'s gallant fight. Watching the *Jervis Bay* through his binoculars, Olander later told of how he watched the British ship slowly sink below the waves with Fogarty Fegen standing on its remains, both arms hanging limp by his side. *Stureholm* picked up sixty-five survivors from Fegen's crew.*

John O'Neill, on the bridge of *Cornish City*, had also witnessed the initial stages of the action between *Jervis Bay* and *Scheer*. He described the uneven struggle to the *Wexford People* shortly after the war ended.

> Within 15 minutes of the epic encounter beginning, *Jervis Bay* was a raging inferno from stem to stern. Billows of smoke soared skywards from the slowly sinking cruiser, from which now and then a solitary salvo was returned in answer to the fire of the raider. As dusk was falling and the smoke ... exceedingly dense, it was difficult for the attacker to see the prey.

The action between *Jervis Bay* and *Scheer* had lasted almost an hour before the weaker vessel succumbed to the greater power of the pocket battleship. That hour was invaluable time for the ships of HX84 which were able to scatter and deny the German captain a juicy and concentrated target. Having sunk *Jervis Bay*, *Admiral Scheer* turned the full weight of its armament to the merchant ships, some of which it had already engaged with its secondary weapons. But, as it grew darker, it could engage only a handful of the convoy's vessels, of which five were lost: *Beaverford*, *Fresno City*, *Kenbane Head*,† *Maidan* and *Trewellard*. A sixth ship, the tanker *San Demetrio* with over 11,000 tons of petrol on board, was set on fire and abandoned by her crew. However, that night one of her lifeboats' crew rowed back to the blazing tanker, boarded her and extinguished the flames in spite of the proximity of the ship's lethal cargo. *San Demetrio* made landfall off the north coast of Ireland some six days later from where she was escorted into the Clyde by a destroyer.

Edward Stephen Fogarty Fegen's actions had saved the convoy from almost certain destruction. The official historian wrote that 'The result was a foregone conclusion but Captain Fegan's action gained enough time to save all the convoy except five ships.' His gallantry seemed to defy belief but it was entirely in character for a man who had so often shown that he was prepared to risk his own life to save others. One of his two brothers – both of whom also served in the Royal Navy and commanded warships – encapsulated his spirit when he said of that last battle: 'It was the end he would have wished.'

The paper had a scribbled message from three survivors of *Jervis Bay* who claimed to have spent three weeks on 'this small craft'. Allegedly, there had been ten on the craft and the message finished with a plea to anyone who found the bottle to 'pray for us'. The Admiralty did not believe that the note was genuine.
* Of the ship's complement on board *Jervis Bay* some two-thirds had been merchant sailors in peacetime yet they had all behaved with the discipline of regular servicemen.
† One of those who died on board *Kenbane Head* was the brother of Senator Sam McAughtry who served in the RAF (see p. 37 above). Another McAughtry brother served in the North Irish Horse.

Admiral Scheer succeeded in disorganizing the convoy system for almost two weeks as major surface vessels were sent to hunt her.* Regular convoys resumed with HX89 which did not depart from Halifax until 17 November. The following day the *London Gazette* carried the news of the posthumous award of the Victoria Cross to Captain Edward Stephen Fogarty Fegen. He had become the third Irishman to be awarded Britain's highest decoration for gallantry in the war. All three services were now represented on the Irish VC roll.

At this time HMS *Ramillies*, with Harry Barton still on board, was finishing its time in the Mediterranean. On its return to the UK the venerable battleship was assigned to convoy escort duties, a task which it carried out over the first six months of 1941. On one such journey from Halifax to Britain, with Convoy HX106, the battleship's presence was enough to save the convoy it was escorting from the attentions of a German warship. As *Ramillies* steamed on her eastward journey Lieutenant John Dreyer, on look-out, spotted the upperworks of a large ship on the horizon. The alarm was raised, but the other ship altered course and moved away from the convoy. Dreyer believed that he had spotted the German battleship *Scharnhorst*, one of the major units of the Kriegsmarine's surface fleet but he could not be certain.† However, a post-war examination of *Scharnhorst*'s surviving log books showed that it had indeed been the German vessel which Dreyer had spotted. Not only that, but *Scharnhorst* had been accompanied by her sister ship *Gneisenau*. Obviously, the German commander, Vice-Admiral Günther Lutjens, did not want to have to engage a British capital ship, even the ancient *Ramillies*, when he could steam off in search of softer targets.

HMS *Ramillies* was also on Atlantic convoy escort duty in May 1941, with Convoy HX 127, when the German battleship *Bismarck* with the heavy cruiser *Prinz Eugen* broke out into the Atlantic on Operation RHEINÜBUNG (Rhine Exercise). On 24 May *Bismarck*, flying the flag of the same Lutjens who had avoided a confrontation with *Ramillies* in January, sank the British battlecruiser HMS *Hood*, once the largest ship in the world and the pride of the Royal Navy; only three of *Hood*'s crew of 1,419 survived. Harry Barton deciphered the coded signal informing *Ramillies* of the loss of *Hood* and sent it to the ship's captain on the bridge. The latter refused to believe what he read and suggested that a mistake had been made in the deciphering. Barton checked his work and came up with exactly the same wording, which he passed back to the captain who once again refused to believe the signal and demanded a further check which a by-now quite angry Harry Barton made. Only on the third reading did the captain accept that *Hood* had gone.

The old battleship, although 900 miles south of *Bismarck*'s position, was ordered to leave the convoy and join in the hunt for the German ship as the Admiralty tried its utmost to trap the enemy capital ship. But *Ramillies* did not play an active part in the

---

* *Scheer* eluded her hunters and sailed into the South Atlantic where she continued to harass shipping and jangle the nerves of their Lordships of the Admiralty.
† *Scharnhorst* and her sister ship *Gneisenau* displaced 31,800 tons, carried a main armament of nine 11-inch guns and could steam at 32 knots.

hunt for *Bismarck* and *Prinz Eugen*. The two German ships were striving to elude their Royal Navy pursuers. *Bismarck* had been hit three times by shells from HMS *Prince of Wales*, one of which had passed through the bow section on the waterline, rupturing two fuel tanks and isolating 1,000 tons of oil. With water coming in, the bow down by several degrees and a marked list to port, speed was restricted to a maximum of 28 knots. Lutjens decided to head south for St Nazaire for repairs; *Bismarck* and *Prinz Eugen* now parted company.

That change of heading, unknown to Lutjens, put *Bismarck* on a course that would bring her closer to Admiral Sir John Tovey's force which was led by HM Ships *King George V* – in which Tovey was flying his flag – and *Victorious*, a battleship and an aircraft-carrier respectively.* Embarked on *Victorious* was the Fleet Air Arm's (FAA) No. 825 Squadron, commanded by Lieutenant-Commander Eugene Esmonde, with Fairey Swordfish biplane torpedo-bombers. Esmonde was an Irishman, although he was born in Yorkshire in 1909 where his father was practising as a doctor; the family returned to his father's home in County Tipperary later that year when his grandfather died and Dr John Joseph Esmonde inherited the family home at Drominagh. Esmonde's great-uncle, Captain Thomas Esmonde of the 18th (Royal Irish) Regiment, had won the Victoria Cross in 1855 at Sevastopol during the Crimean War. Another ancestor, John Esmonde, was executed for his part in the 1798 rebellion.

As a teenage boy it had been Eugene's ambition to follow his older brother Donal into the Mill Hill Fathers to become a missionary priest. He therefore went to St Peter's College at Freshfield in Lancashire which was run by the Mill Hill Fathers and, after two years there, moved to Burn Hall in County Durham for a further year of study. However, he began to have doubts about his vocation and, following consultations with his spiritual director, decided that the priesthood was not for him.

The young Esmonde then sought another career that would give him travel and security. An Air Ministry advertisement for pilots for the Royal Air Force caught his attention and, on 28 December 1928, he began his RAF career. Following five years' service, including a spell with the Fleet Air Arm,† he became a pilot with Imperial Airways with whom he flew for a further five years. Then came a letter from the Admiralty in January 1939 offering him a commission in the Fleet Air Arm, which was now under naval control. This was followed by an offer of a commission as a lieutenant-commander on a 15-year regular service engagement. Esmonde accepted and re-enlisted on 14 April; after refresher training he took command of No. 754 Squadron‡ at Lee-on-Solent on 8 May. Just over a year later, on 30 May 1940, he was appointed to command 825 Squadron, which was equipped with Fairey Swordfish torpedo-bombers, which the squadron had operated since 1936. By May 1941

---

* Tovey was the Commander-in-Chief of the Home Fleet.
† Naval flying was under RAF control at the time and thus this branch was the Fleet Air Arm of the RAF rather than the Royal Navy.
‡ FAA squadrons numbered in the 700 range are second-line, or training, squadrons. Operational, or front-line, squadrons are normally numbered in the 800 range although there were many higher numbers issued during the war.

Esmonde's 825 Squadron was a highly efficient organization, superbly led, with tremendous morale and considerable operational experience.

In the afternoon of 24 May Admiral Tovey ordered HMS *Victorious* to change course for a position that would put them within about 100 miles of *Bismarck*, from where 825 Squadron would be launched in an air strike against the great battleship. Torpedoes dropped by Swordfish were unlikely to sink *Bismarck* but Tovey hoped that the German ship might be damaged sufficiently to slow its progress and allow the main body of his force to get closer and engage it. That night, with weather conditions worsening – there was a thirty-two-foot swell and a rising north-westerly wind – the decision was taken to fly off the Swordfish some 120 miles from their target. Thus, just after 10 p.m., with less than two hours of daylight left, Esmonde led nine aircraft of 825 Squadron off the deck of *Victorious*. Inevitably, should they return, the crews were going to have to find their carrier in the dark.

En route to find *Bismarck* the nine Swordfish prepared to attack the Town-class cruiser HMS *Sheffield* which had been misidentified as the target on the ASV (air to surface vessel) radar set in Esmonde's aircraft. Fortunately, *Sheffield* was correctly identified in time and no torpedoes were dropped. Shortly after the planes began to reform and climb away, the real target was spotted. It was about 10.30 p.m. By then the Swordfish did not have sufficient height to make a successful attack and the squadron, in formation, flew away from *Bismarck* to gain altitude. As they did so, *Bismarck*'s anti-aircraft armament opened up on them and even at a range of four miles one of the ailerons on Esmonde's aircraft was blown away.

In spite of the damage to his own machine, Esmonde led his eight remaining aircraft in to the attack, one Swordfish having been forced to return to *Victorious* with mechanical problems. Such was the intensity of the ack-ack fire coming up from *Bismarck* that the squadron's tight sub-flight formation had to be broken some four miles out from target. What the attackers did not know, and certainly were unlikely to believe, was that the German anti-aircraft fire-control equipment was unable to cope with the very slow attack speed of the Swordfish. The fire-control system was at its lowest possible setting but the shells continued to burst ahead of the approaching Swordfish. At one stage *Bismarck* even opened fire with its main 15-inch guns. Still the lumbering biplanes pressed on, their pilots displaying what one German officer described as 'suicidal courage'.

Eugene Esmonde's own attack was 'a perfect drop at 88 yards or so' after which he 'turned down wind to the left'. All eight Swordfish launched their torpedoes from different angles at a zigzagging *Bismarck*. One torpedo struck the ship, killing a chief boatswain – *Bismarck*'s first fatality – and injuring several others. The projectile had struck the ship's armoured belt just below the waterline, but no real damage had been sustained by *Bismarck*. A brief exchange of gunfire then took place between the German ship and HMS *Prince of Wales* but this was soon broken off as the light faded.

Six aircraft from Esmonde's squadron returned safely to *Victorious*; of the two machines that failed to return the crew of one were picked up from a lifeboat ten days later. During 25 and 26 May Esmonde's aircraft flew some reconnaissance missions and anti-submarine patrols, but this effectively ended their part in the *Bismarck* episode. Further air strikes by Swordfish would be carried out from the aircraft carrier *Ark Royal*.

For his part in the operation against the *Bismarck*, Eugene Esmonde was awarded the Distinguished Service Order. The captain of *Victorious* had described his leadership of the attack as 'skilful and gallant' and had commended his unbounded enthusiasm which inspired the whole squadron.

Bismarck was being shadowed by *Suffolk*, which was watching the German ship on radar. However, early on 25 May the battleship vanished from *Suffolk*'s screen and none of the other ships could find it. Efforts to find *Bismarck*, including searches by Swordfish of 825 Squadron, failed. The German ship was finally tracked down, some thirty-six hours after it had been lost, by a Catalina flying-boat of RAF Coastal Command, operating from Lough Erne in County Fermanagh. During the early evening of 26 May Swordfish from *Ark Royal* attacked and crippled *Bismarck* with at least one hit on its rudder.

Surface vessels were closing in for the kill, among them six destroyers, commanded by Captain Philip Vian. All were of the Tribal class with four of them – *Cossack*, *Maori*, *Sikh* and *Zulu* – belonging to 4th Destroyer Flotilla. Commander H.R. Graham was *Zulu*'s captain and his engineering officer was Lieutenant-Commander (E) John Witham Esmonde, brother of Eugene. Vian's destroyers attacked *Bismarck*, now without steering control and her speed greatly reduced, just before midnight as a howling gale blew up. The crippled battleship's crew fought to save her throughout the night but the arrival of the battleships *King George V* and *Rodney* at 8.30 a.m. was the last chapter in the *Bismarck* story. In a gun battle that lasted almost two hours, *Bismarck* was battered by the British ships. Orders were given to 'abandon ship' at 10.15 a.m. Shortly afterwards the pride of Hitler's navy turned over and sank below the waves. More than 2,000 of her crew of 2,200 went down with *Bismarck*.

John Esmonde was subsequently awarded the Distinguished Service Cross for his work as engineering officer of HMS *Zulu*. His captain commended his 'great zeal and efficiency' over a four-month period as well as his 'devotion to duty and coolness under fire' on the night of 26/27 May. His award was a tribute to the work of the engine-room staff who worked in terrible conditions, without knowing what was happening above them, and with almost no chance of survival should the ship be hit. In December 1943 John Witham Esmonde was appointed OBE. (By a remarkable coincidence another Esmonde brother was in the same area as Eugene was leading his squadron on their attack. His twin, James, was in a convoy heading from Britain as he returned from West Africa where he was a mining engineer.)

At the end of May Eugene Esmonde's 825 Squadron sailed on HMS *Victorious* to provide air cover for convoy W58X to Gibraltar. On 4 June the squadron's aircraft spotted and halted the German supply vessel *Gonzenheim*, which had been waiting to rendezvous with *Bismarck* off the Azores. The German crew scuttled their ship and were taken aboard *Victorious* which sailed on to meet up with Force H, which included the aircraft carrier HMS *Ark Royal*, and enter Gibraltar a week after the encounter with *Gonzenheim*. There, to his chagrin, Esmonde was ordered to transfer his squadron to *Ark Royal* while the latter's No. 820 Squadron transferred its Swordfish to *Victorious* which departed for Britain on 19 June.

Ark Royal and Force H's primary area of operations was in the Mediterranean with the emphasis being on the protection of convoys to the besieged island of Malta. Esmonde and his squadron now took part in a wide variety of air operations. As well as Malta convoy escort duties, the Swordfish took part in anti-shipping strikes while Esmonde himself led an incendiary attack on cork woods at Tempio on Sardinia on 24 August. The next morning he was flying over neutral territory leading a formation of all three Swordfish squadrons from the *Ark*. This mission came about as a result of a request from the British Consul in Valencia who wanted to put paid to the story that the Germans had sunk *Ark Royal*. Many claims had been made on German radio that *Ark Royal* had been destroyed and it was hoped that the flypast by the ship's squadrons over Valencia, and several other Spanish coastal towns, would convince the Spanish that the carrier was still operating. Other operations included a night-bombing mission, again over Sardinia, and a successful search for the crew of a downed Swordfish.

Ark Royal's tempo of operations continued in this fashion until November when the ship carried out an aircraft delivery mission to Malta. Thirty-six Hurricane fighters from Nos. 242 and 605 Squadrons, RAF were embarked on *Ark Royal* and the old carrier *Argus* and these were flown off the carriers to complete the trip to Malta on 12 November, at which point the two carriers and their escort turned for Gibraltar. The following day *Ark Royal* finally ran out of luck when she was struck by a torpedo fired by the German submarine U-81. That torpedo struck shortly after 3.30 p.m. and *Ark Royal* listed to 10 degrees almost immediately, with the list increasing to 12 degrees in minutes and then to 18 degrees about half an hour after the explosion. All non-essential personnel were ordered to leave the ship while strenuous efforts were made to save the aircraft carrier. At first these appeared to be successful but then, at 2.15 a.m. on 14 November, fire broke out in a boiler room and stopped salvage efforts for two hours. The list increased to 20 degrees and, by 4 a.m. had worsened to 27 degrees. Half an hour later it had reached 35 degrees and it was obvious that *Ark Royal* was finished. The order was finally given to abandon ship and the last 250 men slid down ropes to the destroyer HMS *Laforey*.

Except for the captain, the last man to leave the doomed carrier was Eugene Esmonde. Although given the opportunity of leaving with the main evacuation he had volunteered to stay on as one of the skeleton crew. Appointing himself catering officer, Esmonde arranged the supply of food and refreshments to the men who struggled to save their ship. He was the sole pilot aboard during the last hours of *Ark Royal*. After he left the ship he 'continued to see to the welfare of his men, including their spiritual needs in the case of fellow Roman Catholics by arranging for a local priest at Gibraltar to attend them'. His work on board the carrier and during *Ark Royal*'s death throes earned Esmonde a Mention in Despatches which spoke of his 'courage, enterprise and resolution in air attacks on the enemy'.

Esmonde and the bulk of 825 Squadron's crews were transferred back to Britain, travelling on board the battleship HMS *Nelson*, to the shore base at Lee-on-Solent where the squadron re-equipped with new Swordfish. By now the Irishman had commanded 825 for eighteen months with most of that time on front-line operations. Had he been serving in the RAF, with whom his flying career had begun, he would probably have been 'rested' at this stage with a non-operational posting. However, the Fleet Air Arm was short of pilots with Esmonde's experience and rank and this probably played a part in his continuing to command 825 Squadron.

After a short period of leave over Christmas, which he spent at home in Ireland at Drominagh, Esmonde returned to the task of re-building his squadron in readiness for whatever operational deployment the Admiralty might have in mind for it. In January 1942 he still had only six aircraft, although there was no shortage of Swordfish, and only two of his pilots and four observers had seen operational service; all six telegraphist/air gunners (TAGs) had been on operations. None of the members of 825 Squadron could have foretold that this part-trained unit, still only at half strength, was soon to be launched on an impossible mission, from which most of them would not return.

The sinking of *Bismarck* had removed a major threat to the Atlantic convoys but the Kriegsmarine still had a number of large surface vessels; these continued to haunt the minds of the Admiralty and of the seamen who braved the sea lanes between the United Kingdom and North America, and even further afield. These ships included *Tirpitz*, sister ship to *Bismarck*, as well as two other battleships, *Scharnhorst* and *Gneisenau*, the pocket battleship *Admiral Scheer* and the heavy cruisers *Prinz Eugen* and *Hipper*. The Royal Navy had to ensure that these ships were kept in port or, if they broke out, to protect convoys against them.

Scharnhorst and *Gneisenau* had slipped out of Kiel at the end of 1940 and sailed into the Atlantic where, over the next three months, they sank some 115,000 tons of Allied shipping before docking at Brest on 22 March 1941 for refitting. There they were joined by *Prinz Eugen* after the latter parted company with the doomed *Bismarck*. *Tirpitz*, *Scheer* and *Hipper* were in Baltic ports where they posed a major threat to Arctic convoys; *Lützow*, formerly *Deutschland*, was in dock undergoing repair.

Since the Admiralty's principal operational priorities in 1941 were the protection of the Atlantic convoys and of troop convoys from Britain to the Middle East, the boding presence in Brest of three major surface units of the German navy was a major headache. The ships were a threat to both Atlantic and Africa-bound convoys and added to the overstretching of the Royal Navy's resources. As a result of the navy's difficulties the RAF was called upon to deploy Bomber Command against the German ships. An Air Ministry directive of 29 April 1941 suggested possible air action against any future moves by the enemy vessels. This became Operation FULLER.

Two days later Bomber Command's supremo, the Irishman Air Marshal Sir Richard Peirse, issued a directive in which he stated that if the ships attempted to move then they would be attacked by surface vessels and aircraft by day, but that no aircraft would attack by night. Bomber Command later expended much effort in trying to bomb Brest and other French harbours by daylight and suffered considerable casualties in so doing. At this stage, however, the Germans were quite happy to keep all three ships at Brest as their presence there caused so much diversion of British naval and air effort. That changed in September 1941 when Adolf Hitler told the Kriegsmarine's commander, Admiral Erich Raeder, 'that all German battleships would be better employed guarding Norway from an anticipated ... Allied invasion of that country'. Raeder managed to talk Hitler out of that idea at that time but, having surfaced once, the idea was certain to come back again. And it did.

Convinced that the Allies intended to invade Norway,* Hitler delivered an ultimatum to Raeder and his staff to move *Scharnhorst*, *Gneisenau* and *Prinz Eugen* from Brest or have the ships dismantled with their heavy guns being moved to the Norwegian coastal defences anyway. In the face of such a threat, Raeder had little choice: the order was issued to begin planning the move of the ships from Brest to a German port from where they would later sail to Norway. The detailed planning of the move fell to Admiral Otto Ciliax, commanding the Brest Group, and began on 12 January 1942, shortly after Eugene Esmonde returned to Lee-on-Solent following his Christmas leave.

The German plan was to sail from Brest after dusk on a moonless night that would provide the maximum cover for the first stage of the voyage. Early February offered an ideal opportunity as there would be some twelve hours of darkness at that stage. With a full moon on 15 February, and the desired tide and current conditions prevailing from 7 February until 15 February, the final date was suggested by the meteorologists who forecast low cloud and reduced visibility on 11 February. That date was chosen for what eventually became Operation CEREBUS; *Scharnhorst*, *Gneisenau* and *Prinz Eugen* would slip their moorings at 7.30 p.m. and, with their escort force of destroyers and other vessels, sail through the night towards the English channel, entering the straits of Dover at about noon the following day. Sailing in darkness reduced the chances of detection by British ships or aircraft and allowed the opportunity to cover much of the route to Germany without being intercepted.

British planning for a possible escape from Brest and a dash through the channel by the German ships had been based upon a daylight sailing, even though the prime need for the cover of darkness made the plan as finally chosen the only logical one. However, the air aspects of Operation FULLER seemed to take account of a variety of possible German plans with regular daylight fighter patrols over the channel area supplementing Coastal Command's patrols over the bay of Biscay and the western French coast. ASV-equipped aircraft from Coastal Command also flew regular patrol routes designated STOPPER, off Brest itself, LINE SE, from Ushant to Ile de Brehat, and HABO, from Le Havre to Boulogne.

During early February aircraft of Bomber Command were deployed to lay mines along the possible routes of a German dash from Brest while three squadrons of

---

* Hitler's obsession with the invasion of Norway mirrored a similar obsession on the part of Winston Churchill.

Bristol Beaufort torpedo-bombers, with escorts provided by 11 Group of Fighter Command, stood ready to launch attacks on the three German ships. The Beauforts were seen by both senior naval and air officers as the principal weapon to be used against Ciliax's force. Remembering the *Bismarck* attack, and the damage wrought on the Italian fleet at Taranto by Swordfish torpedo-bombers, it was believed that the Beauforts could inflict sufficient damage on the enemy ships to leave them at the mercy of Royal Navy ships in a surface engagement. Almost as a postscript to the FULLER plan it was decided to add a force of Fleet Air Arm Swordfish to the attacking air units. This decision came from Vice-Admiral Bertram Ramsay at Dover. Ramsay shared the belief that the Germans would leave Brest in daylight and pass through the Dover straits in the darkness before dawn. That darkness would provide cover for the Swordfish, in conjunction with the Beauforts, to attack without a fighter escort. The Swordfish 'force' was to be Eugene Esmonde's 825 Squadron which was ordered to move to RAF Manston in Kent in readiness for the operation. Esmonde led his six aircraft to Manston on 4 February, flying through a blizzard to get there.

The Operation FULLER squadrons at Manston, including 825, adopted a daily routine of full readiness from 4 a.m. each day until dawn when the crews were stood down. This indicated that the Admiralty still believed that *Scharnhorst*, *Gneisenau* and *Prinz Eugen* would make their run through the Channel by night. Following the dawn stand-down, Esmonde's crews continued the training routine he had devised for them; he considered that it would be at least four weeks before the crews were up to normal operational standards. He had also developed a plan of attack should his Swordfish be called upon to engage the three German ships. This called for 825 Squadron to approach the targets from the front before splitting into two sub-flights when they were within torpedo range. The aircraft would then attack from port and starboard quarters at the same time in order to create the maximum confusion among the German gunners and minimize the effect of their fire.

Interestingly, fighter cover for Operation FULLER was to include another two Irish airmen: Group Captain Victor Beamish, the Cork-born commander at RAF Kenley, and Squadron Leader Brendan 'Paddy' Finucane, a native of Dublin, who was then the RAF's highest-scoring fighter ace and its most-decorated fighter pilot still engaged actively on operations. Beamish was to play a crucial role in the events that were beginning to unfold.

On 11 February Eugene Esmonde left Manston and the routine of training and preparation to travel to Buckingham Palace for the investiture ceremony at which he received his DSO for his part in the operations against *Bismarck* the previous year. That evening he was a guest at a dinner given by Admiral Somerville before returning to Manston. Across the Channel Admiral Ciliax had issued an order to his command to leave harbour for an exercise. This purported to be a night exercise between La Pallice and St Nazaire with the group returning to Brest the following day. In reality it was a cover for Operation CEREBUS: the breakout was about to begin, although it was known only to a very few senior officers.

The German ships were due to set sail at 7.30 p.m. but, just at that time, British bombers arrived over Brest and, for almost an hour, a stream of Wellingtons dropped their loads on the city; none of the ships was hit. The all-clear was sounded at 9.14 p.m. and Ciliax immediately gave the order for his group to slip anchor and depart. *Scharnhorst*, with Ciliax flying his flag aboard, led the group out of harbour, followed by *Gneisenau* and *Prinz Eugen*. After a short spell on a westward course the order was given for the change of course that would take the group to Germany. By midnight they were passing Ushant, sailing at best speed through a thin haze on a clear, starlit night. It was then that Ciliax advised *Scharnhorst*'s crew that they were making for home through the English Channel.

The Germans were unwittingly benefiting from a series of radar problems on the Coastal Command aircraft that were maintaining the standing patrols over the area. Two Royal Navy submarines, stationed off Brest to intercept the battleship should they attempt to leave, were also caught on the hop: one was too far away to see the ships while the other had moved offshore to recharge its batteries. (It would have been in position had the Germans sailed at their planned time.) Coupled with jamming of the British ground-based radar stations and weather effects on radar, plus the failure accurately to interpret some of the information that radar was revealing, Ciliax's ships were able to make their run undetected.

Two Spitfires of No. 91 Squadron did spot German naval activity the following morning but their reports were noted only 'with mild interest'. Since neither pilot was aware of Operation FULLER, which was shrouded in secrecy, nor knew anything about the anticipated breakout from Brest, they considered their patrol to be simply another routine reconnaissance over the Channel. German luck was holding.

It was 8 a.m. before any suspicion was aroused in British minds when a squadron-leader radar controller at RAF Biggin Hill recognized radar blips for what they really were: Luftwaffe aircraft escorting naval vessels moving at some 25 knots. The controller, Squadron-Leader Bill Igoe, knew of Operation FULLER, and reckoned that the three large blips had to be Ciliax's ships. A telephone message to 11 Group Headquarters was met with a blank reaction; the recipient had no idea what Igoe was talking about. The German luck was still holding.

A frustrated Igoe managed to speak to the officer commanding 91 Squadron and asked him to have a look at enemy fighters circling off the Somme estuary. Two aircraft were scrambled for this task. At much the same time, 10.20 a.m., another RAF officer at an airfield near Dover came to the same conclusion but could not get through to the naval headquarters at Dover Castle as both the GPO and secure 'scrambler' telephone lines were out of order. But two more aircraft were now in the air to carry out a reconnaissance patrol over the Channel. The two Spitfires took off from RAF Kenley and were piloted by Group Captain Victor Beamish and Wing Commander Finlay Boyd.

Both pairs of Spitfires spotted the German ships and identified them as major surface units. One pilot broke radio silence to make a report, but this message was not received in England, although the Germans picked it up. Beamish flew back at low level and tried to make an immediate report on landing but it took almost thirty minutes before he could get Trafford Leigh-Mallory, Air Officer Commanding (AOC) 11 Group, on the phone. By the time Beamish succeeded it was 11.35 a.m., an hour after the sighting had been broadcast by one of the pilots. Ciliax could not have asked for better luck than that which he was enjoying.

Even then it was 12.15 p.m. before Esmonde and his crews climbed aboard their Swordfish to attack the German ships. An escort of five fighter squadrons had been promised. Esmonde had been told by Admiral Ramsay that the decision to go was his and his alone; he was not being ordered to lead his squadron in a daylight attack. Indeed, he had

> originally volunteered his squadron for *Fuller* on the premise of a night sortie, and ... trained his men in the techniques necessary for such an attack. He knew only too well from personal experience what lay in store for his men now that it seemed certain to be a daylight attack.

Assured of the protection of the five fighter squadrons, however, Esmonde made the decision to go, having asked 'for the love of God' that the fighters be with 825 Squadron in time. And so, at 12.25 p.m., Esmonde led his six Swordfish off Manston's frozen grass runway and into the air and headed for Ramsgate and the rendezvous with the Spitfires.

At 12.32 p.m. ten Spitfires from 72 Squadron met up with Esmonde's planes over Ramsgate. Although Esmonde circled over the area for two more minutes, no more fighters appeared. At this point Esmonde could have called off the mission and no one would have blamed, or criticized, him. He had, after all, volunteered for a night attack and had accepted the daylight mission only on the understanding that his highly vulnerable biplanes would have five fighter squadrons – 60 aircraft – in support. But, instead of ordering his squadron back to base, Esmonde, with a wave of a gloved hand, led them over the channel to their rendezvous with Admiral Ciliax's force. Why did he choose to do so? His biographer, Chaz Bowyer, suggests that, since he had given his word to Admiral Ramsay that 825 Squadron would go in, he felt duty bound to carry out the attack as

> by his very nature [he] would have felt totally obliged to honour his word – honour and duty had been the lynchpins of the Esmonde family lineage and Eugene particularly exemplified those ideals throughout his life. His devout Catholic faith undoubtedly softened the all-too human fear of death and its aftermath. But, whatever his actual thoughts at that crucial moment, Esmonde's decision became instantly plain.

The Swordfish dropped down to a height of only fifty feet above the waves and made for their target at a speed of less than 100 m.p.h. Above them the ten Spitfires of their escort flew a weaving flightpath at some 2,000 feet altitude. As the Swordfish made their way across the Channel the missing escorts arrived at the rendezvous over Ramsgate some fifteen minutes late, and in two separate formations, before heading across the Channel and engaging enemy aircraft but without coming across 825 Squadron.

Esmonde's aircraft met their first enemy fighters when they were some ten miles out from Ramsgate. Two *staffeln* of Messerschmitt Bf109 fighters from Jagdgeschwader 2, *Richtofen*, pounced on the lumbering biplanes and raked them with cannon and machine-gun fire, causing damage to most of the Swordfish but no injuries to any of the crews. Before the Bf109s could come in for a second attack the Spitfires of 72 Squadron dived on them and began to beat them off. Having done so, the Spitfires returned to the task of escorting the Swordfish. At this time the Spitfire commander, Brian Kingcombe, spotted *Prinz Eugen* and, for the first time, realized what Esmonde's men were planning to do.

At 12.50 p.m. the German fleet was sighted as was the mass of fighters, Bf109s from Jg 2 and Focke Wulf Fw190s from Jg 26, in the air above it. As the Swordfish closed to within two miles of the battleships the German fighters swarmed in for the kill, having to lower their flaps and even their undercarriages to reduce their speeds to match those of their victims. Kingcombe and his Spitfires dropped to engage the 109s and 190s and to try to protect Esmonde's tiny force.

Down below a small flotilla of Royal Navy motor torpedo boats (MTBs) had just finished an attack on the German giants, each firing its two torpedoes in an vain effort to damage the enemy vessels. Now, with their torpedoes expended, the MTBs remained close by in case they might be needed to rescue the crews of the Swordfish. Esmonde had reached the outer screen of destroyers and E-boats and, already, his aircraft was trailing fabric torn by the fire of the German fighters. Still he flew on, through a blizzard of tracer fire and the huge, frightening spouts of water thrown up by the heavy armament of the German battleships. The other two aircraft of his sub-flight – they were attacking as planned in two sub-flights – followed close behind. As they bore in on their targets a further attack by the German fighters forced them to weave and dodge to avoid being shot down. Then they were back on a steady course, heading for *Prinz Eugen*.

Charles Kingsmill, flying the third machine in Esmonde's sub-flight watched his leader fly steadily on with tracer fire all around him. So intent was he on watching Esmonde's aircraft that he had no recollection of being aware of danger; and, apart from one fighter, hardly noticed the German aircraft. He did not take his gaze off Esmonde even when his own plane shook as cannon shells hammered into it. Then Esmonde's plane lurched upwards and Kingsmill lost sight of it.

It must have been at that stage that Esmonde's Swordfish was attacked by two Bf109s. The enemy fire set the tail of the Swordfish on fire and the TAG, William John Clinton, calmly crawled out along the fuselage and beat out the flames with his hands before returning to his position and resuming fire with his single machine-gun at the attackers. Then *Prinz Eugen*'s heavy guns blasted forth at the leading Swordfish, tearing away most of the port lower wing. Although the biplane dipped a wing seaward as it staggered from the force of the shell strike, Esmonde regained control, brought his doomed machine back on course and kept flying towards the huge warship.

Then the two Bf109s came in again from behind, their bullets killing Clinton and the Observer, Lieutenant William Henry Williams, and hitting Esmonde in the back and head. The aircraft's nose tipped up slightly and its torpedo was seen to fall away, presumably released by the dying Irishman. The battered aircraft fell towards the sea and simply disintegrated as it struck the surface. Fighters also brought down the other two Swordfish of the sub-flight and the captain of *Prinz Eugen* ordered a change of course that allowed his ship to avoid the torpedo fired by Esmonde.

All six Swordfish were shot down. Only five of the eighteen crew members survived, all but one of them being wounded, and were rescued by the waiting MTBs. Esmonde's last moments had been witnessed by at least three RAF pilots. When the sole unwounded survivor, Edgar Lee, returned to Manston, he was met by the station commander, Wing Commander Tom Gleave, who had watched the Swordfish depart, saluting each one as it passed him for he had seen in Esmonde 'the face of a man already dead' and had known that the biplanes of 825 Squadron would not return. Now Gleave sat down to write a report in which he noted:

> I discussed the operation with Lieutenant-Commander Esmonde prior to the squadron taking off ... His pilots and crews present at this meeting displayed signs of great enthusiasm and keenness for the job they were about to undertake, and it was no doubt due to ... Esmonde's leadership that such a fine spirit prevailed. Nothing more was heard of the squadron until the five survivors were brought ashore. The German battle-cruisers were undoubtedly protected by a terrific barrage of flak, and covered by one of the biggest fighter screens ever seen. Against this, the determination and gallantry shown by Lieutenant-Commander Esmonde and his pilots and crews is beyond any normal praise. I am of the opinion that Lieutenant-Commander Esmonde is well worthy of the posthumous award of the Victoria Cross.

Gleave's recommendation – the first time a RAF officer had recommended a naval officer for the VC – was endorsed by Leigh-Mallory and forwarded to the Admiralty for consideration. It was also supported by Admiral Ramsay whose recommendation became the citation for Eugene Esmonde's decoration. Concluding his recommendation Ramsay wrote that Esmonde's 'high courage and splendid resolution will live in the traditions of the Royal Navy and remain for many generations a fine and stirring memory'.

But Ramsay was also highly critical of the planning and operational errors that had led to the deaths of Esmonde and so many of his squadron. They had died in vain, for their effort had made no impression on the German ships, which did reach their homeland. No impression, that is, except to note the gallantry of the airmen who, in their antiquated little biplanes, had tried to take on the might of the Kriegsmarine and Luftwaffe and had died in so doing. Ciliax wrote that they were men 'whose bravery surpasses any other action by either side that day', reflecting Ramsay's comment that it was 'one of the finest exhibitions of self-sacrifice and devotion that this war has yet witnessed', and Gleave's succinct summary of the Swordfish crews as 'courage personified'.

There could be little doubt that Eugene Esmonde would be posthumously awarded the Victoria Cross and the official announcement appeared in the *London Gazette* on 3 March 1942. Two weeks later, on Saint Patrick's Day, his mother and two of his brothers – Owen, an officer in the RAF, and Patrick, an Army doctor – travelled to Buckingham Palace to receive the Cross from King George VI. It had been the king's suggestion that this posthumous investiture of an Irishman with the VC should take place on Ireland's national day; and the Esmonde family had decided that Eily Esmonde, although infirm, should be the one to receive her son's award.

Eugene Esmonde had lived a life in which duty was a paramount consideration. In a letter to his family in 1940 he wrote that 'I can think of no greater honour, nor a better way of passing into Eternity than in the cause for which the Allies are fighting this war.' Less than two years later, in the English Channel, he demonstrated that those words summarized his own devotion to duty and his outstanding personal courage, rooted in a deep faith.

Esmonde was the second Irish naval VC of the war. Both were posthumous awards and went to men who had a highly-developed sense of duty and were steeped in the traditions of the Royal Navy. Although there were fewer Irish members of the Royal Navy than of either of the other two services, they would account for three of the Irish VCs gained during the Second World War and for many other decorations and awards for gallantry and distinguished service. Irish seamen saw service from the Arctic to the Pacific, from the first days of war until the very end – when the third naval VC was won – and in the air above the fleet as well as on the surface and beneath the waves. In chapter Ten the story of the Irish seaman will be continued.

~6~

The bombers: war in the air, part I

IN THE SHADOW OF DEATH

In the years between the wars, proponents of air power had talked about the ability of bombers to deliver a 'knock-out blow' on an adversary.* When war began, however, it soon became clear to Britain's War Cabinet that the Royal Air Force's bomber squadrons were incapable of any such decisive strike against Germany. Since the French possessed only a small heavy bomber force – fewer than 200 machines – it was obvious that any Allied air attack on Germany would bring about swift and large-scale retaliation from the Luftwaffe. Thus, while Germany and Russia carved up Poland, the two Allied air forces desisted from any operations that would precipitate a major enemy air strike on their own territory.

By 1939 the RAF was divided into a number of commands: Fighter Command was responsible for the air defence of the United Kingdom itself; Bomber Command was tasked with strategic offensive operations against the enemy; Coastal Command's role was maritime reconnaissance, the protection of convoys within range of its bases, and operations against enemy submarines. There was also a large training organization which was expanded greatly in the days of the phoney war.

On 3 September 1939 there were 118,000 regular personnel in the RAF, with another 68,000 reservists. In the UK the service had a total of almost 1,500 aircraft with another 435 overseas. Against this Germany could deploy 3,600 first-line aircraft with 500,000 personnel; and another 500,000 personnel in anti-aircraft defences, which came under Luftwaffe control.

Bomber Command's full strength at the outbreak of war was thirty-three squadrons. Most of the aircraft were twin-engined types, including Vickers Wellingtons, Armstrong-Whitworth Whitleys, Handley-Page Hampdens and Bristol Blenheims. There were also single-engined Fairey Battles but ten squadrons of these aircraft, of 1 Group, had been flown to France on 2 September as part of the Advanced Air Striking Force (AASF), the air component of the BEF. The Battles were

* Such views were expounded by Trenchard in Britain, Mitchell in the USA and Douhet in Italy. The UK's Brooke-Popham Report on defence against the manned bomber had virtually accepted the bomber doctrine and Trenchard's comment that the 'bomber will always get though' was repeated in the house of commons.

supplemented by five squadrons of Blenheims, four of Hawker Hurricane fighters, and five of Westland Lysanders, the latter two types being intended for army co-operation.

It was the Fairey Battles of the AASF that were to gain the Royal Air Force its first Victoria Crosses of the war; one of those VCs was also to be the first gained by an Irishman in the conflict – Flying Officer Donald Edward Garland, from Ballinacorr, County Wicklow. Garland was one of four brothers, all of whom were to lose their lives in the course of the war. Although the youngest of the quartet, Donald was the first to perish.

When war broke out in 1939, Donald Garland was only twenty-one years old, having been born in Ballinacorr on 28 June 1918. As a young man it was his ambition to fly and, following his education at Cardinal Vaughan School in Kensington, he applied to join the RAF. On 12 July 1937 he was accepted for a short-service commission and undertook his elementary flying training at Hamble, after which he was confirmed in rank as a Pilot Officer on 3 September. He then progressed to No. 2 Flying Training School for his service training and graduated from there on 7 May 1938 to be posted to No. 12 Squadron which was converting from Hawker Hind biplane bombers to the new Fairey Battle light bomber.*

In 1939 Donald Garland was promoted to Flying Officer and was a member of No. 12 Squadron's B Flight when the squadron was told, in the closing days of August 1939, that it was to be posted to France. This transfer of the AASF was codenamed Operation PANTHER and was quickly carried out by all 180 Battles of the ten squadrons assigned to the AASF. Garland's squadron flew to Barry-au-Bac where it set up base in a small cornfield from which it flew its first operational mission on 17 September; this sortie was a reconnaissance overflight of the German border zone.

It was not long, however, before the Battle's inferiority to enemy fighters became all too clear. On 30 September five Battles of No. 150 Squadron were intercepted by German fighters while on a photographic reconnaissance mission over German territory. Engaged at first by AA guns they were also pounced upon by Messerschmitt Bf109 fighters, which shot down four of the five bombers and severely damaged the fifth, flown by the formation leader, Corkman Squadron-Leader William MacDonald (later Air Marshal Sir William MacDonald, GCB, CBE, DFC). The latter's skilful flying, jigging his aircraft around the sky to avoid the fighters, kept damage to his machine to a minimum, although the Battle was hit several times; MacDonald had already been injured by a flak splinter. He finally escaped the attention of the Germans after a fight lasting some thirty minutes. When he brought his plane, which had been hit more than forty times, in to land, a burst tyre caused the Battle to spin right around before catching fire. All three crew members escaped. Sergeant Frederick Gardner, who saved the life of the air gunner, Aircraftman Murcar, by putting out the flames which engulfed his clothing, was later awarded the British Empire Medal while MacDonald and

---

* The Battle was a monoplane, powered by a 1,030 h.p. Rolls-Royce Merlin engine, the same powerplant as the new Hurricane and Spitfire fighters. However, with a crew of three and a bombload of 1,000 lbs (maximum) the Battle was hopelessly outclassed by the contemporary Luftwaffe fighter the Messerschmitt Bf109. By the time war broke out the Battle was already obsolete.

Murcar received the Distinguished Flying Cross (DFC) and Distinguished Flying Medal (DFM) respectively. This was the first instance in the war of every member of one crew being decorated.

After this incident, offensive operational flights by the Battles were stopped. In December Donald Garland's No. 12 Squadron moved to a satellite airfield of Barry-au-Bac, at Amifontaine, although even practice flying was restricted considerably by the extremely cold winter conditions. This lack of flying added to the image of phoney war and it was not until March 1940, when a thaw set in, that a regular routine of flying began. The Battles were being allowed to fly night operations, dropping leaflets, over Germany. Once again the squadron engaged in reconnaissance flights over German territory, although these generally followed NICKEL leaflet raids.

On 9 April the Germans invaded Denmark and Norway; an Allied expeditionary force, including British, French and Polish elements, had sailed for Norway two days earlier. Although Hitler had completed his plans for the invasion of France, life remained quiet on the western front, and No. 12 Squadron's routine continued. However, that routine was shattered completely on the morning of 10 May when the Germans launched Operation SICHELSCHNITT (sickle cut), the invasion of France, Belgium, the Netherlands and Luxembourg; the neutrality of the latter three countries was ignored completely.

It was the afternoon of 10 May before No. 12 Squadron learned of the German attack and five aircraft were quickly sent out on a daylight-bombing mission, in spite of the Battles' shortcomings. Only one machine returned to Amifontaine; that the Battle was truly obsolete was being confirmed in tragic and dramatic manner by its encounters with Luftwaffe fighters. There were no missions flown by Garland's squadron the next day, but German bombers struck, with little effect, on Amifontaine.

Battles of No. 142 Squadron also flew operations on the 10th, taking off from Barry-au-Bac to engage columns of enemy troops on the road from Luxembourg to Dippach. Eight machines took off, but one was forced to return with mechanical problems leaving seven to carry out the attack. Of the attacking aircraft three were shot down by heavy fire from the ground. The pilot of another, Pilot Officer Walter Corbet, from Dublin, was wounded in the ankle, and his Scottish observer, Sergeant George Irvine, was killed. Corbet was later awarded the DFC for nursing his damaged aircraft back to base 'in spite of his weakened condition ... and saving the air-gunner and the aircraft'.

The Battle squadron sorties of 10 May had proved, yet again, that daylight operations in this aircraft were little short of suicidal. Although the word *kamikaze* had yet to enter the airman's vocabulary, it could easily have been applied to the Battle crews. What was to come for Donald Garland and his comrades of No. 12 Squadron was to underline the vulnerability of the outdated and outclassed Battles.

Early on the morning of 12 May, No. 12 Squadron's crews were summoned to an emergency briefing session. The invading German army had seized, intact, several bridges over the Albert canal on the first day of the assault. These bridges were vital to the Germans as they facilitated their move into Allied territory. Several attempts had been made by RAF aircraft to destroy the bridges, but these had failed in the face of intensive opposition from German fighter aircraft and anti-aircraft artillery on the ground. The purpose of No. 12 Squadron's briefing was to let the crews know that the squadron had been selected for a special mission – the destruction of the bridges at Veldwezelt and Vroenhoven.

Since the bombers which had already attempted to destroy the bridges had suffered so heavily, this was to be a mission for volunteers. As soon as the call for volunteers was made, every member of No. 12 Squadron stepped forward; each was eager to take the risks involved in trying to deny the bridges to the enemy forces. With everyone volunteering, the decision was taken to allow the six crews who were already detailed on the 'readiness' roster to be the strike force.

Those six crews and their machines were then designated as two sections, each of three aircraft, with each section attacking a bridge. Flying Officer Norman Thomas was selected to lead the section that would attack the bridge at Vroenhoven, which was of concrete construction, with Donald Garland leading the attack on Veldwezelt's steel bridge. Both section leaders opted for different tactics: Thomas intended to make a divebombing attack from high-level, while Garland opted for a low-level approach to his target.

By 9 a.m. all six Battles were fuelled, bombed-up and ready for take off. Just as the aircraft were preparing for take off, one of Thomas' section discovered a fault with his machine that left the plane unserviceable and forced him to abandon the mission, thus reducing that section to two aircraft; the second machine was flown by Pilot Officer T.D.H. Davey. There were no such problems with Garland's section and all three Battles flew away from Amifontaine to seek out their target. Ahead of No. 12 Squadron's machines, eight Hawker Hurricane fighters of No. 1 Squadron were acting as escort to the light bombers with the task of engaging any German fighters that attempted to intercept the Battles. That escort was to prove woefully inadequate.

As well as his own aircraft – P2204 'K' – Donald Garland's section included the Battles L5439, flown by Pilot Officer I.A. McIntosh and L5227, flown by Sergeant Fred Marland. The Irishman's crew was Sergeant Thomas Gray, observer, and Leading Aircraftman (LAC) L.R. Reynolds, who manned the Battle's single Vickers K rear-ward-firing machine-gun.*

Thomas and Davy reached their objective at Vroenhoven to be met by a curtain of anti-aircraft fire and considerable fighter opposition. Both made dive-bombing attacks from 6,000 feet, but both aircraft were hit. Thomas was brought down and captured, while Davey, after ordering his crew to bale out, succeeded in coaxing his damaged plane back to Allied territory. Their attack had caused some damage to the concrete bridge.

Meanwhile Garland's section, after a low-level flight under the cloud base at 1,000 feet, had reached Veldwezelt. Once again there was considerable opposition: the Germans had emplaced some 300 AA guns in a ring around the bridge area and there

---

* The Battle was also fitted with a .303 machine-gun in one wing which was fired by the pilot.

were also swarms of fighters in the area, from Jagdgeschwader (Jg) 27 (which was to become one of the leading German fighter squadrons of the war). The latter had pounced on the Hurricanes which had been intended to defend the Battles and these were left helpless as the RAF fighters fought desperately for survival.

From 1,000 feet Garland led his trio of aircraft in a shallow diving approach to the bridge. The bombing run had to be made through a storm of fire from the AA guns around the bridge. With such powerful defences it was almost impossible for the Battles to get through; it was as if they were flying into a wall of steel. McIntosh's plane was struck by flak before he could even begin his final run; the main fuel tank was punctured, fuel ignited and the aircraft began to blaze, forcing its pilot to dump his bomb load and try to bring the Battle down. Incredibly, McIntosh did manage to make a forced landing. He survived the crash but was then captured and made prisoner of war.

As Donald Garland's aircraft swooped for the bridge the intensity of fire inevitably told. The Battle was struck by enemy rounds, and the aircraft 'was blasted into the ground'. Garland and his crew perished as P2204 'K' fell to earth. Sergeant Fred Marland and his crew in the third aircraft also died as the German guns hit it repeatedly. Just after Marland released his bomb load the stricken Battle was seen to go into a sharp climb before winging over and diving into the ground.

As the smoke cleared, it could be seen that the Battles had achieved the impossible: the western end of the Veldwezelt bridge was badly damaged by bombing; the planes had carried out their mission although almost all the crew members had died in the process. The evidence was not conclusive but it did suggest 'that this damage had possibly been caused by Garland's cool attack'. It was, however, quickly repaired by the Germans.

Not only were the Fairey Battles hopelessly outclassed by 1940, but the tactics employed in the attacks on the bridges were seriously flawed. Too few aircraft were deployed against each target, and such was the strength of the defences that the attackers were bound to be overwhelmed. Yet the AASF did not have sufficient modern planes to attack and overwhelm targets. It would be some time before the RAF was able to do this in daylight operations on mainland Europe. In spite of this, the courage of the men sent against the bridges was in no doubt, and Donald Garland's cool and inspiring leadership was a vital factor in the little success that No. 12 Squadron did achieve.

A month later, on 11 June, the *London Gazette* carried the official announcement of the posthumous awards of the Victoria Cross to Garland and to Thomas Gray, his navigator; but no award was made to LAC Reynolds, the third crew member.

Almost exactly a year later Garland's mother, accompanied by her son Patrick, attended the investiture ceremony at Buckingham Palace, to receive the little bronze cross awarded to Donald – first of her four sons to die during the war.

Donald Garland had become Ireland's, and the Royal Air Force's, first VC of the Second World War.

Two of Renée Garland's other sons also died on active service with the RAF. The oldest son, Patrick James – named for his father Dr P.J. Garland, GMG – was turned down initially by the RAF which considered him to be too old for flying duties. Undeterred, Patrick Garland joined the Army, enlisting in the Irish Guards, from which he was commissioned into the Green Howards. Then, in the latter part of 1942, he transferred to the RAF for pilot training. He gained his 'wings' as a fighter pilot and was posted to No. 168 Squadron with which he flew many missions over France in 1944. Tragically he lost his life in January 1945, not as a result of enemy action but in a flying accident. He was the last of the four boys to die.

The next Garland brother, Desmond, also died while flying with the RAF. Having qualified for his 'wings' at the beginning of the war, Desmond was later discharged from the service on medical grounds. However, he was determined to make his contribution and enlisted in the Royal Army Service Corps (RASC) as a private soldier. His determination saw him succeed in obtaining a transfer back to the Royal Air Force and flying duties. He lost his life in a mine-laying operation over Dutch waters in September 1942.

The final brother, John Garland, who was the third-born, was rejected by the RAF as being medically unfit for flying duties. However, he was later commissioned into the RAF as a medical officer, but his ill health caused him to be discharged and he died of natural causes in March 1943. Dr and Mrs Garland had raised a family of four sons and one daughter, only to have war snatch all four sons. One can but guess at the pain suffered by the widowed mother and sister.

The Hurricanes of No. 1 Squadron that had escorted Garland and his comrades on their final mission had also been commanded by an Irishman, Squadron-Leader P.J.H. Halahan, who had been born in Dublin. Known as 'Bull' Halahan, his eight Hurricanes were engaged by twice that number of enemy aircraft but, in spite of the odds, six German aircraft were claimed as destroyed with Halahan being responsible for two of those. In November 1940 he and another officer attacked and shot down a Dornier Do17. Both incidents were included in the citation for his Distinguished Flying Cross which also referred to his 'excellent example to his pilots' and the fact that he 'was mainly responsible for the fine spirit of his squadron which, while under his command, has destroyed approximately seventy enemy aircraft'.

Donald Garland was not the only Irishman in No. 12 Squadron. Leading Aircraftman Robert Tod Tomlinson, from Dublin, was the observer in Battle L4949, piloted by Flight Lieutenant Bill Simpson. Two days before Garland's final flight, Simpson led B Flight against a strong German troop column on the Luxembourg-Junglister road. As Simpson released his bombs from a height of only thirty feet, the Battle was struck by enemy fire and was so badly damaged that the pilot was forced to look for a suitable area on which to belly-flop the aircraft. Such an area was found and Simpson put his stricken bomber down on it but, as the machine slid to a stop, flames leapt back from the engine compartment to ignite fumes and fuel in the cockpit. Simpson was engulfed in flames and unable to release himself. At that point, Tomlinson and Sergeant Edward Odell, the other crew member, fought their way through the flames to release Simpson's harness and drag the pilot clear of the burning aircraft. They had got him out and were rolling him on the grass to extinguish the flames that were burning away his flying kit when the flares and ammunition in the Battle began to explode. Soon after that, the fuel tanks exploded. Simpson was later awarded the DFC. For their rescue of the pilot both Tomlinson and Odell received the DFM. Odell returned to flying duties almost immediately but Tomlinson was hospitalized with burns to his hands. He was later promoted to Sergeant but was killed in a flying accident on 8 February 1941. Unusually for an Irish victim of the war, he was buried in his native Dublin.

As well as the Fairey Battles of the AASF, the air force sent twin-engined Bristol Blenheim bombers on operations against targets such as German warships and, after the invasion of France, other military targets in the battle area. Although the Bristol Type 142, from which the Blenheim was derived, had been faster than any fighter aircraft then in RAF service back in 1935 it, too, was showing its age by 1940 and, in common with the Fairey Battle and other types of aircraft then in service, was totally unsuited for daylight operations. But circumstances demanded that the Blenheim be used on such missions and this continued for some time. It should be said that its crews did not regard the Blenheim as obsolete at the time and Blenheim crews tended to look with sympathy at the Battle squadrons. The Blenheim was very popular with its pilots as it was a lovely aircraft to fly.

The first Distinguished Flying Crosses of the war went to Blenheim pilots, one of whom was an Irishman, Flight Lieutenant Ken Doran, of No. 110 (Hyderabad) Squadron. Although the announcements of the awards were not made until 10 October 1939, the decorations had been earned in the very first days of the war. On 4 September Doran led fifteen Blenheims in an attack on German shipping in Wilhelmshaven; Flying Officer McPherson had earlier flown a reconnaissance sortie over that port and Brunsbüttel. There can be little doubt that these were first gallantry decorations of the war for the Royal Air Force. Ken Doran's fifteen aircraft came from three squadrons – 107, 110 and 139 – and they took off in adverse weather conditions. The Blenheims crossed the North Sea through low clouds and made for Wilhelmshaven and the German pocket battleship *Admiral Scheer* and the cruiser *Emden*. Five of the bombers failed to find the target, but Doran led the remaining ten against the defences of the harbour to make low-level strikes against the two ships, both of which added their own anti-aircraft guns to the defensive fire being put up against the Blenheims. It was hardly surprising that half of the attackers were shot down by the AA defences; four of these were from the five 107 Squadron machines in the raid. The attack was pressed home, however, and at least three bombs fell on the *Scheer*; none exploded and the pocket battleship escaped even slight damage. *Emden* was damaged and there were casualties among the crew but this was a result of one of the stricken Blenheims falling on the cruiser rather than any RAF bombs hitting the ship. For his leadership on the raid Doran was recommended for the DFC. He was presented with his Cross by King George VI at a parade held at RAF Wyton on 2 November.

As the Blenheims led by Doran were attacking Wilhelmshaven, fourteen Vickers Wellington bombers were en route to Brunsbüttel at the mouth of the Kiel canal. Four of the Wellingtons found the targets to be bombed, but at least one bombed the neutral Danish town of Esbjerg, 110 miles north of their target, killing two civilians. Two Wellingtons were shot down, and among the dead was a pilot, Edmund Sorley, a man from south Armagh. Together with those lost from the Blenheims at Wilhelmshaven, Sorley was among the RAF's first casualties of the war. For the bomber squadrons such casualties were to become depressingly familiar.

Strabane man Douglas Cooper was also a Blenheim pilot with No. 110 (Hyderabad) Squadron when war broke out. He had fulfilled a childhood ambition to fly by joining the RAF in 1936 and learned his trade on biplanes. In January 1938 the Hawker Hind biplanes of No. 110 Squadron were replaced by Blenheims, and the new, fast monoplane bombers with retractable undercarriages occasionally caused embarrassment to some pilots who forgot to lower the undercarriage prior to landing. By September 1939, however, 110 Squadron was well acquainted with the Blenheim and, on the second day of war, took part in the RAF's first bombing mission of the war, that attack on German warships at Wilhelmshaven, from which one of the squadron's aircraft failed to return.

The raid on Wilhelmshaven set the pattern for 110 Squadron's operations in the early part of the war. Many of these were 'sweeps' over the North Sea, searching for German shipping to attack and sometimes drawing the unwelcome attention of German fighters as on 4 January 1940, when a sweep which included Flight-Lieutenant Doug Cooper was jumped by six Messerschmitt Bf110s. The Blenheims quickly dived to wavetop height to deny the Bf110s the opportunity of attacking from below, and a running fight ensued. The Blenheims escaped to return to base; a claim was later made that at least one Bf110 had been shot down and an artist's impression of the dogfight was issued in one newspaper. For his leadership on this occasion, Squadron Leader Ken Doran was awarded a Bar to the DFC he had earned on 4 September 1939.

(This episode had a happy sequence over fifty years later when Doug Cooper received a letter from Wolfgang Falck, the Austrian commander of his Luftwaffe attackers that day. Falck, who later rose to prominence in the night-fighter defence of the Reich, and Cooper have since met up on several occasions and have spent holidays in each other's homes.)

There was a break from the routine in February when Cooper was one of a number of pilots to fly Blenheims to Finland where they were being delivered to the Finnish air force. The return flight from Finland was made on board a Junkers Ju52 of Finnish Air Lines, which allowed the inclusion of an enemy type in the RAF men's log books. This operation was shrouded in secrecy at the time; tiny Finland was at war with its larger neighbour Russia which had a non-aggression pact with Germany.

Typical of the operations carried out by Doug Cooper's squadron at this time was a mission on 25 April when six Blenheims took off at 12.10 p.m. to bomb German transport ships in Granvins fjord in Norway. Three Blenheims, led by Cooper, attacked a troop transport in the fjord. Two of the remaining Blenheims also bombed targets, but the last plane was lost. In the course of the raid the RAF machines were pounced upon by German aircraft, and claims were made for the destruction of two enemy fighters, although the only German loss appears to have been a Dornier Do18 flying boat.

One of the other Blenheims on that raid on Granvins fjord was piloted by an airman from County Cork, Pilot Officer Robert James Hill, of Crosshaven, who was subsequently awarded the DFC for an attack on two Dornier flying boats as he was returning to his base,

> he encountered two Dorniers alighting on the sea, and ... resumed the attack with his front gun, several bursts being seen to hit the fuselage of one of them. While he was continuing his attack, the second Dornier attacked his aircraft but was beaten off and it eventually dived at the water, where its bows submerged. During this last phase Pilot Officer Hill was wounded in the face and hand but throughout the engagement he displayed great courage and initiative.

It would appear that Hill was, therefore, the man responsible for the destruction of the Do18 that day. Other enemy aircraft may have been damaged but the flying-boat was the only German loss. Robert James Hill recovered from his wounds to return to operational flying. He was killed on active service in March 1941.

When the Germans invaded the Low Countries on 10 May 1940, the Blenheims, still operating from England, were switched to operations over mainland Europe in support of the Allied ground forces. Since January 1940 a new command structure had been in place in France with the creation of the British Air Force France (BAFF), the commander of which had control of all air units in France. He could also call on 2 Group of Bomber Command for support; Doug Cooper's No. 110 Squadron was part of 2 Group.

For 110 Squadron one of its earliest operations at the request of BAFF was to attack a bridge at Tongres near Maastricht on 11 May. French reconnaissance aircraft had reported 'continuous traffic streaming from the town' over that bridge. Eleven of the squadron's aircraft took off from Wattisham in mid-afternoon and flew out over the North Sea and then across the Belgian coast en route to their target at 3,000 feet. Anti-aircraft fire began bursting around them near Recklein. This was a foretaste of the intensive flak over Maastricht where enemy fighters were also engaged.

Doug Cooper's Blenheim – L9217 – was the lead aircraft on the approach to the target. He recalled that the AA fire 'looked harmless, little puffs of black smoke that you could fly between' and that is what he did. Two aircraft were lost, one to a German fighter and the other probably to flak; three of the six crew members of the two aircraft survived. On returning to base at Wattisham, Flight-Lieutenant Cooper was surprised to find that his aircraft was the only one without bullet holes – leading the attack had some advantages. He was even more surprised on 28 May when he learned that he had been awarded the DFC for his part in the Maastricht raid. His observer, Sergeant J.S. Robertson, was awarded the DFM for the valuable photos which he had taken during the attack.

In total Doug Cooper flew eleven operations in May and amassed 620 hours and 45 minutes flying time, almost all of which was operational (he flew two non-operational flights). Most of the flights were over France, and all were in daylight at heights up to 8,000 feet. He was not always as fortunate as he had been over Maastricht: on 24 May, following an attack on German armoured vehicles on the Calais-Englebert road, his Blenheim was shot up very badly with 'a hole in the wing you could have jumped through'. The hydraulics had been shot away, so it was impossible to lower the undercarriage: a crash landing was inevitable.

Cooper had no fears about crash-landing his machine. In fact he 'had always wanted to try landing a Blenheim without the undercarriage [because] it looked so graceful'. He had, of course, watched as other pilots had done so, due to forgetfulness. And so he brought his crippled bomber in to land on its belly and found that the procedure 'was a piece of cake really'. Less than two weeks later, on 5 June, when taking off on a mission to support 51st (Highland) Division which was still in France in the St Valery area, his Blenheim crashed.

There were other Irishmen among the Blenheim crews in that first summer of the war. Sergeant George Anthony Gamble was a twenty-year-old Dubliner serving as an air gunner with No. 40 Squadron. In the Blenheim piloted by Flying Officer C.W. Bromley he also saw much action as the RAF strove to stem the German advance. On 14 June nine Blenheims of the squadron took off to attack enemy ground transport and a bridge over the river Eure. The squadron commander, Squadron-Leader Gerald Gleed, who had flown some dozen such missions since the opening of the German attack on 10 May, was flying one of two aircraft to be shot down while others suffered damage. Operations continued at a high intensity and on 27 June six aircraft set out for a photo-reconnaissance mission over Boulogne and Guines. Bromley was flying Blenheim R3811 as a section leader with Gamble as his gunner. In the course of the sortie the Blenheims ran into heavy anti-aircraft fire. Enemy fighter aircraft also engaged the British machines.

> On the return flight across the Channel the section was attacked by a formation of Heinkel 111s. Sergeant Gamble, although wounded in both legs, returned the enemy's fire and reported the tactics of the Heinkels until the intercommunications gear was shattered. It was largely due to his courage and determination that the section leader was able to withdraw safely with two aircraft.

Bromley force-landed his damaged aircraft at RAF Hawkinge in Kent. One Blenheim did not return from the operation; its crew were killed. Gamble was recommended for the award of the Distinguished Flying Medal which he later received. The citation for his medal also noted that, during an operation in May, when his bomber was attacked by an enemy fighter, Gamble's accurate reporting and steady fire allowed his pilot to take successful avoiding action; the attacking fighter broke off the engagement and appeared to be on fire.

His wounds took Gamble away from further operations. It was in June, also, that Doug Cooper was rested from operations and posted to Bicester on training duties. His role there was to convert pilots from their previous aircraft to Blenheims, and it was, in his view, 'probably the most dangerous time of the entire war'. Three months later he was sent to RAF Squire's Gate, at Blackpool, to train air gunners. This was an easier posting and, since it was possible for the trainee gunners to fire off a week's supply of ammunition by Wednesday, he was often able to fly across the Irish sea to Aldergrove and visit his fiancée. That routine ended when he was posted back to operational flying with No. 21 Squadron at RAF Watton on 20 February 1941.

Cooper's new squadron was also operating Blenheims, but many of its operations were now at night. On 12 March* the squadron was part of a bombing force sent against the German port of Hamburg, and this turned out to be 'a dicey one' with Cooper's aircraft believed lost for a time. His perception of flak that night proved to be much removed from that formed on daylight raids: 'I didn't like the flak at night [with] all these coloured lights coming at you slowly. And then, suddenly *whoosh* past you. It was more frightening than in daylight.'

As he approached the target at 10,000 feet that night, Doug Cooper saw an area of 'inky blackness' off to one side and decided to make for that patch of sky. Throttling back, he changed course for the apparent safety of the darkness when the sky suddenly cleared and became like broad daylight. The Blenheim had been caught in searchlights, and Cooper threw his plane into a dive 'for the deck' to escape the lights. Flak was bursting all around them and he reckoned that his rear gunner's eardrums were never the same again. But the Blenheim evaded the lights and the flak and completed its bomb run before turning for home.

Landfall over Britain was usually made over the Wash from where the aircraft of No. 21 Squadron would head for Watton. That night Doug Cooper was able to spot the Wash at the expected time but it never seemed to get any closer. What he had spotted was a reflection caused by some meteorological phenomenon and when, eventually, he crossed the coast he was an hour behind schedule. Back at Watton the aircraft was believed to have been lost but then it roared out of the night sky to land safely.

Doug Cooper's luck ran out on 1 July 1941 when Bomber Command sent 39 Blenheims and six Stirlings to various targets in north-west Germany. Six Blenheims of No. 21 Squadron flew against the Kiel canal but the raid was 'abandoned due to unfavourable weather conditions'. Of 45 bombers sent out that day, only six machines

---

* In *The Bomber Command War Diaries*, Martin Middlebrook and Chris Everitt do not list any Blenheims in the attacking force. The squadron's operational record book shows a raid by seven aircraft on Bremen that night followed by a raid on Hamburg the following night [AIR27/263].

bombed targets, and three aircraft, a Stirling and two Blenheims, were lost. One of the downed Blenheims was V6396, flown by Squadron-Leader Doug Cooper. His aircraft was hit by flak as he made a bombing run at 600 feet against a bridge. He ordered his crew to bale out and took to his own parachute, although wounded in one ankle by a shell splinter.

Doug Cooper was taken prisoner and given medical treatment for his wounded ankle by the gunners who had shot him down. Neither of his crew members survived; they had not been able to escape from the stricken Blenheim. For Doug Cooper that was 'the saddest experience of the war'. He was subsequently transferred to a hospital near Hamburg and from there to the first of five PoW camps in Germany or Poland where he was to spend the rest of the war.

In one sense Doug Cooper was lucky: becoming a prisoner meant that he lived to see the end of the war. Casualties in Bomber Command were so high – more than 50,000 airmen died and over 9,000 aircraft were lost – that the chances of survival were very low. Of the 125,000 men who served as aircrew in Bomber Command during the war nearly 60% became casualties. A total of 59,423 were reported killed or missing thus giving a mortality rate of 47.5%. Fatal casualties to aircrew numbered 55,500; another 9,838 became prisoners of war; over 4,000 were wounded on operations while a similar number suffered injury in flying or ground accidents in the UK. In all the RAF lost 73,600 personnel killed during the war, of whom, it can be seen, the bulk were from Bomber Command. The only fighting arm of any of the combatant nations with a higher casualty rate was the Kriegsmarine's U-boat service. Among the dead of Bomber Command were a number of Doug Cooper's fellow Irishmen.

One of those dead bomber crewmen was a man whose home was less than twenty miles from Cooper's. Andrew Woodrow Dunn was a Derryman who had also joined the Royal Air Force before the war. Dunn was a pilot as well, but he flew Armstrong-Whitworth Whitleys, one of the RAF's heavy bombers of the early-war period. Pilot Officer Dunn served with No. 77 Squadron, the first to be equipped with the Whitley Mark V. As with other Bomber Command squadrons the Whitleys of 77 were engaged in NICKEL raids in the early months of the war.

However, the Whitleys switched to their intended bombing role in the spring of 1940 and Dunn's squadron was involved in a number of 'firsts'; these included the first attack on an enemy land target, the first large raid on mainland Germany and, on the night after Italy declared war on Britain and France, the first attack on an Italian city.

In June 1940 aircraft from No. 77 Squadron were included in a bombing force sent against targets in the Ruhr valley, Germany's industrial heartland. Dunn was flying one of the squadron's Whitleys that night and, as he made his run in to the target, his aircraft was subjected to intense anti-aircraft fire over a period of fifteen minutes. Several hits were made on the Whitley but none caused serious damage to the bomber. Then a Luftwaffe nightfighter, identified as a Messerschmitt Bf109, attacked.

> The first attack disabled the inter-communication gear and also wounded the
> air observer, Sergeant Savill, and the wireless operator, Sergeant Dawson. The

rear gunner, Pilot Officer Watt, was unable to warn the captain of the enemy
fighter's second attack, but, by quick reaction and skill in aiming, he delivered
a good burst of fire at short range which destroyed the enemy

Although the Messerschmitt had been destroyed it had managed to inflict severe
damage on Dunn's Whitley before being downed by Watt. One of the Whitley's two
engines was knocked out in spite of which Dunn pressed on to the target and dropped
his bombs before setting course for home. With only one engine it was a slow journey
homewards for the stricken bomber, which was steadily losing height. For three and a
half hours Dunn struggled with the controls and the North Sea was crossed at only 400
feet. The two injured crew members played their part with Sergeant Savill navigating
the Whitley while Sergeant Dawson, operating his radio, managed to obtain a number
of homing bearings which were vital in plotting the bomber's return journey.

For his part Andrew Dunn 'displayed resolution, courage and determination in
piloting his badly damaged aircraft'. In spite of all the crew's efforts the Whitley was
not to return to its base. Dunn was forced to land the crippled machine in the sea off
the south coast but the crew was rescued speedily and taken to dry land. All were
subsequently decorated with Dunn, P.O. Montagu and P.O. Watt each receiving the
Distinguished Flying Cross while Sergeants Dawson and Savill received the
Distinguished Flying Medal.

Very few of those who flew on Bomber Command's early operations were still alive
at the end of the war. Death took a heavy toll of the bomber crews and on the night of
23/24 September 1940 it claimed Andrew Dunn and his crew. Dunn had taken off
from Driffield in Yorkshire at the controls of Whitley P5046, O-Orange, bound for
Berlin as part of a force of 129 Whitleys, Wellingtons and Hampdens. Bomber
Command had decided to concentrate its main force on the German capital that night
and this raid was, therefore, unique at this stage of the air war against the Reich.
Eighteen separate targets had been identified, including seven railway marshalling
yards, six power stations, three gasworks, an aero-engine factory and an aircraft parts
factory. Over a three-hour period 112 aircraft reported dropping their bombs from
heights varying from 16,000 down to 4,500 feet. However, target identification was
not easy as the ground was obscured by mist and searchlights also affected vision.

Three bombers were lost that night, one of each type involved in the raid. The lost
Whitley was P5046, Andrew Dunn's aircraft. Nothing had been heard from Dunn and
his crew, and no trace of the plane was ever found. The RAF presumed it 'to have
crashed into the sea' with the loss of all five crew members. It may well have been that
the events of that June night were being repeated and that Dunn was trying to bring
home a crippled bomber.

Berlin's records of that raid were removed by the local authorities, but it is believed
that most of the bombs fell around the Moabit area where one of the power-station
targets was located and there was some slight damage to the Schloss Charlottenburg.

With his aircraft lost without trace, neither Andrew Dunn nor any of his crew has
a known grave. However, Dunn's distraught family have commemorated him in the

family plot in Londonderry City Cemetery. The inscription on the headstone indicates that Pilot Officer Andrew Woodrow Dunn, DFC, was killed in action 'during the Battle of Britain' which would suggest to the casual visitor that he had served in Fighter Command. Had he done so, Andrew Dunn might have lived longer and may even have survived the war.

The death rate in Bomber Command was brought home to Sean Drumm by a chance encounter on a train. In 1943 nineteen-year-old Drumm, from the Midlands, had completed training as an air gunner at No. 12 Air Gunnery School at RAF Bishop's Court in County Down. After passing out from there he went on leave to visit relatives in London and arrived at Euston station as an air raid was in progress. At the end of his leave he travelled to RAF Silverstone in Northamptonshire (the modern-day racing circuit and home of the British Grand Prix) where he had been posted to join Bomber Command. (Alternative postings for air gunners included Coastal Command, Fighter Command and the overseas commands.) There he met the members of his future crew who, with the exception of Sergeant Bill d'Arcy from Waterford, were all Australians.

One day, as Sean Drumm was changing trains at Peterborough, he met two veteran air gunners in a railway carriage. Veteran is, of course, a relative term; these two young men were scarcely older than Drumm but were veterans by virtue of each having completed twenty operational missions. They were, therefore, two-thirds of the way through their operational 'tours' which lasted for thirty missions, or for 200 hours' operational flying.

Drumm noticed that both men showed signs of nervous exhaustion with nervous twitches of the mouth and pale complexions. In airmen's parlance they were 'flak-happy' and neither believed that he would survive to the end of his tour. The young Irishman tried to reassure them that the worst was over and that, after ten more missions, they could look forward to postings as instructors. Both remained despondent and indicated that they felt they had little chance of surviving their tours; they had been on a mission to Nuremberg just a few nights earlier in which Bomber Command had lost heavily. They saw Sean Drumm off to his train and, shaking his hand, suggested to the young Irishman that he should not be too anxious to get into a front-line bomber squadron. It was an upsetting meeting for Drumm, who had been looking forward to his first experience of action but had not fully appreciated the stern reality of the bomber war over Germany. He later discovered that both men were killed on their final mission. The scales were balanced against bomber aircrew surviving: of the fifty trainees who had passed through Sean Drumm's air-gunnery course at Bishop's Court, only seven survived the war. Drumm was fortunate to be one of the survivors.

The task of an air gunner was a dangerous, tiring and lonely one. He was vital to the defence of a bomber and he had to remain alert at all times, scanning the night skies for any possible attacker. He was lonely because of his position in the aircraft. Typically British heavy bombers, the four-engined Avro Lancasters, Handley-Page Halifaxes and Short Stirlings, carried a gunner in a turret on top of the aircraft's fuselage – the mid-upper gunner – and another in a turret at the extreme tail of the machine – the rear gunner. The mid-upper gunners manned twin Browning .303-inch machine-guns, while their tail-end comrades had four such weapons; later versions of the Halifax had four guns in the mid-upper position also. Lancaster mid-upper gunners often felt especially exposed as their turrets sat above the fuselage almost in line with the RAF roundel which, to many, seemed like an aiming mark for an attacker. There was also a nose turret with two guns which was normally manned, when necessary, by the bomb-aimer; this turret was eliminated in the later Halifax Mk III as it was seldom used, German nightfighters preferring not to try head-on attacks against the British heavies. In the latter days of the war some Lancasters mounted a pair of .50-inch machine-guns in the tail turret which provided a more formidable defence against enemy fighters.

Many bombers returned to base with wounded, dying or dead gunners in their turrets. On numerous occasions the gunners' alertness and quick responses were responsible for saving aircraft from destruction. Needless to say, a significant number of gallantry decorations went to air gunners and among the ranks of the decorated were many Irishmen. Some of those men saw most of their service in the bombing offensive against Germany, while others served in theatres such as the Mediterranean or the Far East. One of the Mediterranean-based airmen was Dubliner John Desmond Bingham, a garage-hand in civilian life, who had enlisted in the Royal Air Force in 1937 and trained as a wireless-operator. Bingham later retrained as an air-gunner and was awarded the DFM when he had notched up almost 100 missions.

Flight-Sergeant Bingham served with No. 69 Squadron which was based on the beleaguered island of Malta and was equipped, variously, with Beaufighters, Marylands, Baltimores and Mosquitoes. Its task was strategic reconnaissance of enemy ports and airfields in Sicily, Italy and Libya. When Spitfires were added to the squadron strength, these single-engined machines took over the reconnaissance tasks while the Baltimores engaged on shipping surveillance and anti-submarine patrols. These mission types meant that the squadron's aircraft ran a high risk of interception and its air-gunners were kept busy.

> As wireless-operator/air gunner [Flight-Sergeant Bingham] … displayed praiseworthy ability and determination. On numerous occasions, when his aircraft has been engaged by enemy fighters, he has used his guns to good effect. Flight-Sergeant Bingham has carried out 98 sorties, including raids over Germany and German-occupied territory as well as in the Middle East.

The squadron was later posted back to Britain and flew Wellingtons on night reconnaissance missions which included operations over Normandy on the eve of D-Day using flares to locate enemy troop movements. In September 1944 No. 69 Squadron moved to France and Belgium and continued its reconnaissance work until the end of the war.

Eric Dunlop was posted to the Middle East at first but was transferred to India before being assigned to a squadron in the Western Desert as he had been expecting.

Although he had begun training as a pilot he was subsequently remustered as a navigator and posted to a bomber squadron flying Blenheim Mk IVs. By this stage in the war, the Blenheim was showing its age, but there were still many of these machines operating in the Far East. In the Blenheim Mark IV the navigator sat in an extended glazed nose with his chart table along one side of the fuselage. He was also the bomb-aimer and had responsibility for a pair of rearward-firing Browning .303-inch machine-guns mounted under the nose; these were aimed through a periscope arrangement.

In India Eric Dunlop joined No. 60 Squadron and became navigator to an 'exceptionally fine pilot' called Sandy Webster, a Scot who had the DFC and Bar in contrast to his previous pilot, Murphy, who was Australian. The squadron was moved to Asonsol on the border of East Bengal and Bihar, 'about three or four hundred miles back from the Burma border' as a result of Japanese air superiority over Burma.

Shortly after their arrival at Asonsol one of the squadron's Blenheims, flown by Paddy Huggart from Kerry, was sent to bomb Akyab on the coast of Burma. On its way back to base the Blenheim was attacked by three or four Japanese fighters but managed to fight these off. Huggart was aided in this combat by the fact that the Japanese aircraft were more outdated than his Blenheim and even had fixed undercarriages. One of the fighters was shot down into the sea, and it was later learned that it had been flown by a senior Japanese officer. The Blenheim was badly damaged and was forced to make a wheels-up landing on its return to base.

However, Flying Officer Eric Dunlop did not encounter many Japanese fighters in his time over Burma. One of his most dangerous moments came in September 1942, when nine aircraft from Nos. 60 and 113 Squadrons – the latter was also based at Asonsol – were sent to raid the harbour at Akyab where two Japanese ships had just docked. As the bombers circled the harbour before launching their attack, the Japanese had time to prepare for them and anti-aircraft fire was heavy. Fighters also joined in and three bombers were lost; one of the ships was sunk. Dunlop believes that had the AA gunners been Germans his aircraft would not have survived either. Subsequently fighter escorts were provided for the bombers.

Eric Dunlop's first experience of AA fire was when his aircraft was sent on a mission against an airfield at Magwe. Flying in at about 12,000 feet,

> we were just coming into our bombing run and I saw these black puffs start to appear ... above me and beside me and behind me and through the glass where I was trying to aim the bombs. I just felt on edge but not unduly disturbed. I had an unhappy feeling that I was very exposed and that was very unpleasant but you're concentrating on the job and there's nothing much you can do about it. You have a slightly cold feeling but nothing else.

On other raids against Akyab Sandy Webster flew in at about fifty feet above the sea and at a speed of over 200 m.p.h. so that the attack was over very quickly.

There was the sight of red tracer and stuff flying around the place and big black puffs of smoke here and there and columns of water, splashes in the sea, but otherwise it was always very short.

Neither Japanese pilots nor anti-aircraft gunners were any match for the Germans in effectiveness in Dunlop's view. However, he considered the weather to be a significant enemy.

If you could survive the weather you were 30 to 40% sure of surviving the war in the Far East. That was my experience. From April to May the monsoon built up, that is the clouds built up into huge cumulus edifices going up to twenty, thirty thousand feet with terrific electric currents and terrific up currents and down currents and draughts, up draughts and, in fact, an aircraft really couldn't afford to get into one of those – it would probably be pulled apart. And you would get terrific rainstorms coupled with mountainous terrain and unless you knew your way around and [had] the experience to survive one monsoon, you could make a mistake. You had to be very careful not to crash into the hills in bad weather.

One aircraft loss that Eric Dunlop is certain was due to weather and terrain rather than enemy action caused the death of Sergeant Simon Eden, son of Anthony Eden, Churchill's Foreign Secretary, who was the navigator.

Eric Dunlop survived a total of over sixty missions in Burma and was decorated with the Distinguished Flying Cross in 1943.

Flying Officer Dunlop has completed a large number of operational flights over Burma. He has guided his aircraft, through extremely bad monsoon weather and over mountainous country, safely to the target and back, achieving excellent results. This officer has served as leading navigator/bomb aimer on many occasions and has also been the navigator/gunner on attacks against enemy shipping in a defended harbour. Throughout all these operations Flying Officer Dunlop has displayed great courage, thoroughness and good tactics both in his pre-flight planning and when faced with enemy opposition.

He subsequently went on to fly in Douglas C-47 Dakota transport aircraft.

The Mediterranean was the principal area of operations for Flight Lieutenant Derrick John d'Alton who was awarded the Distinguished Flying Cross for his work as a gunnery officer. Born in Kilkenny, d'Alton enlisted in 1939 to train as an observer and was commissioned in 1940. He showed a keenness to participate in operations whenever possible, although his duties did not require him to do so, and this set a first-class example.

On one occasion over Benghazi, his aircraft was attacked by enemy fighters. Two of the bomber's engines were put out of action, the hydraulics were rendered unserviceable and the intercommunications became useless. Displaying great coolness, Flight Lieutenant d'Alton gave his captain evading directions which enabled him to fly clear of the attackers. On the homeward flight, about an hour later, the aircraft was attacked by another enemy fighter. Once more, Flight Lieutenant d'Alton's commentary on the attacker's movements enabled his pilot to evade the fighter and fly on to base. This officer has always displayed great technical skill. He has suggested tactics in gunnery and formation flying which have been adopted and have resulted in the destruction of at least seven enemy fighters.

But it was the bombing offensive against mainland Europe that involved the largest number of air gunners. Among the Irishmen who performed this arduous task was Flying Officer Walter Bonar Kirkwood-Hackett, from Templeogue in County Dublin, who joined the RAF in 1940 and was commissioned the following year. As an air gunner Kirkwood-Hackett took part in many missions over Germany and occupied Europe, including raids on heavily-defended targets such as Berlin and Gdynia. He also flew on many raids on the Ruhr, including thousand-bomber operations and in a daylight raid on Milan in Italy. 'Throughout all these attacks Flying-Officer Kirkwood-Hackett ... displayed a most praiseworthy degree of courage and devotion to duty' which earned him the DFC. A similar award was made to Norman Beattie, from Drumcondra, who joined the RAF in 1940 and was commissioned in 1942.

Most air gunners were NCOs although some were either commissioned officers or were warrant officers. Michael George Clynes, from Edgeworthstown in County Longford, was a carpenter's mate in civilian life before volunteering for the RAF in 1940. Trained as an air gunner he gained promotion to sergeant and then to warrant officer and saw a considerable variety of service. Clynes took part in bombing attacks against Tripoli, Benghazi, Naples, Catania as well as other targets in North Africa and the Mediterranean area.

> He has also attacked some of the most heavily defended targets in Germany. On four occasions his aircraft has been attacked by night fighters and each time he has successfully directed his captain's evasive action. During these combats he has destroyed at least two enemy aircraft. Over a long period this warrant officer has set a splendid example of courage, determination and devotion to duty.

Michael Clynes was decorated with the Conspicuous Gallantry Medal (Flying).

Flight Sergeant James Hughes from Dublin (he was born in Leeds) was described as 'a most skilful air gunner' in the citation for his DFM. He, too, saw action over German targets that included Berlin, Hamburg, Essen and Kassel and, on two occasions, his accurate fire was responsible for repulsing attacks by German fighters. On a number of occasions, Hughes volunteered to fly with crews other than his own, demonstrating a keenness to participate in operational flying in spite of all the risks.

Joseph Chestnutt Barkley was born in Clare, County Tipperary, in 1913 but was living in Warwickshire when war broke out. A lorry driver in civilian life, he enlisted as an infantryman in the Royal Warwickshire Regiment and transferred to the RAF in 1941 where he trained as an air gunner. As a rear gunner he flew on many missions over Germany and his targets included Duisburg, Frankfurt and Hamburg and he also flew on operations against targets in Tunisia. The citation for his DFM described him as a gunner who 'always co-operated efficiently with his captain and crew, often in trying circumstances'. On one raid on Duisburg his aircraft was attacked by a night fighter which Barkley engaged. Hits were observed on the German aircraft which was probably destroyed. On other occasions his directions to his captain enabled the aircraft to evade fighters or anti-aircraft gunfire.

Joseph Moloney, from Roscrea in Tipperary, also received the DFM for his work as an air gunner. Flight Sergeant Moloney, who joined the RAF in 1941 at nineteen, was a veteran of many flights over Germany by the time he was decorated. On a mission to Cologne his bomber was intercepted by a Junkers Ju88 nightfighter which was driven off by Moloney's accurate defensive fire. En route to another target he made skilful use of emergency signalling when the aircraft's intercommunications' system was out of action and thus enabled the pilot to escape from a preying night-fighter and press on to the target. Moloney, who also took part in minelaying opera-tions, was regarded as an 'outstanding air gunner [whose] skill in the air and cheerful courage have enabled many missions to be successfully completed which would other-wise have been abandoned'.

There were many times when all the skill in the world, on the part of any crew member, was of no use to an aircrew. An aircraft could be struck by a flak shell and destroyed or badly damaged with the crew forced to make a crash landing or bale out by parachute. Or it could have the misfortune to meet a German nightfighter armed with *schräge Musik*, or jazz music, the ironic name given to an idea conceived by an armament technician, Paul Mahle, and consisting of a pair of 20mm, later 30mm, cannon installed amidships in the Messerschmitt Bf110, Junkers Ju88 and Heinkel He219 to fire forwards and upwards at an angle between 70 and 80 degrees. This allowed the nightfighter to approach a bomber from behind and below and fire upwards into the engines or fuel tanks. Many bombers were lost to this weaponry before the RAF became aware of it and began fitting ventral armament to its bombers. The first use of *schräge Musik* was on the night of 17/18 August 1943 during a Bomber Command raid on Peenemunde. For the crews of such stricken aircraft it was a case of either death or spending the rest of the war as a prisoner.

Warrant Officer Denis Murnane was one who survived being shot down to become a prisoner of war. Although he had started training as a pilot, he developed snow blindness and slight double vision while training in Canada and was remustered as a bomb aimer and was eventually posted to No. 51 Squadron, based at Snaith and equipped with Handley-Page Halifaxes. Murnane's aircraft carried out twenty missions before being shot down by anti-aircraft gunfire on its twenty-first mission, a daylight operation. They had only two encounters with nightfighters.

The first one ... the Germans had a plane [we] called the Black Widow which had two Oerlikon cannon [a *schräge Musik*-equipped] pointing up ... and the pilot had a sight which would give him the plane and he would fire and these two Oerlikon cannon ... would literally blast a plane out [of the sky]. And fortunately, at the very last minute, our rear gunner spotted him and it was a very dark night, it was just lucky he did see him, and the pilot just managed to swerve and the guns went out just where we'd been just a couple of seconds beforehand. But it damaged the aircraft, we came back with a damaged turret and one of the engines; the magneto was shot out so we had to make a forced landing at an American base in the south of England which we delighted in. We'd never seen so many cigarettes, and chocolate bars and food for about six months previously.

The second engagement was just an ordinary nightfighter with machine-guns. He did a pass at us and missed. Another plane spotted him and I think he must have damaged him because he broke off the engagement.

There were other dangers over the target area apart from the defences. Since Bomber Command aircraft were individually navigated they did not arrive over the target in a tight formation as the American daylight bombers did. RAF tactics brought the bombers to their targets in a lose gaggle and the gunners had the task of watching the sky for other aircraft with which it might be possible to collide.

As you can imagine you'd have about five hundred aircraft all going in in the space of twenty minutes and all heading for the same target. There were a few collisions, some were fatal. We had one Halifax came back one night and they'd fifteen feet of their wing missing where they'd been sliced by another bomber which, of course, crashed because its wing came off completely.

On one raid several aircraft were brought down by the build-up of ice on their wings. This was a mission against a synthetic-oil refinery at Opland, about midway between Leipzig and Berlin and the distance necessitated the fitting of an additional fuel tank to each aircraft.

The real problem with that [raid] was that it was an absolutely moonlit night and we were expecting a lot of nightfighters and we didn't see any. But the big problem was ice and we lost quite a lot of aircraft that night through icing up and weight forced the planes down. We got back and we were astounded ... to hear other pilots and crews in the squadrons reporting attacks by nightfighters and we never saw a nightfighter the whole way.

The constant factor that faced every aircraft on every raid against a defended target was the anti-aircraft gunfire. Doug Cooper had noticed early in the war that this looked harmless in daylight but frightening at night. Denis Murnane felt that aircrews could get used to it.

The first time you see it, it's fairly shattering, but I think you, sort of, get used to it. You feel the bumps as the air shocks rock the plane as you're going in but the worst moment is going up on the target when you have to go in as straight and level as possible and, literally, everything is coming up at you. You see the tracer coming towards you, you see the bursts, and I would say anybody who said they weren't frightened were either madmen or great liars. I must say I always felt scared. You did have a few that really terrified the guts out of you ... especially the day we were shot down, we realized we just had to get out, the whole wing was on fire. That was pretty shattering.

That came, as we have seen, on the crew's twenty-first mission, a raid on Cologne on 2 March 1945. There were two raids that day on the city of Cologne, now virtually in the front line of the ground war: the first raid was carried out by 703 aircraft with 155 machines in the second operation. These were the final RAF operations against Cologne which was taken by American forces on 6 March. Denis Murnane's Halifax was shot down in the first of those raids and was one of nine aircraft lost; six Lancasters and two Halifaxes were lost over the target while another Halifax crashed in Belgium. This was the only daylight mission which Murnane's crew had undertaken and, as they approached their target,

We were hit by what we called predicted flak. They pick you up on radar and operate on that and the first bursts came just behind us and we continued on to the target and the next burst, just as we were dropping the bombs, hit [one of] the starboard engine[s]. It went on fire and the pilot did the usual exercises of feathering his prop, which ... meant he turned it so that it faced into the wind and stopped it windmilling, switched off all fuel and turned on the fire extinguishers. But the fire was too big, so we all had to jump.

The tension of the moment was eased slightly by the sight of one crew member making the sign of the cross before he went through the escape hatch. A Scot, the man had long professed to be an atheist but now proved the old adage that there are no atheists in the height of battle.

Denis Murnane was fortunate to survive the parachute descent as his rig would not open at first. He discovered that the release wire had been cut and thought, 'My God, some bastard's sabotaged this', but the parachute finally opened when he removed his flying gloves and extracted a split pin. The canopy looked like a lace curtain and the Dubliner realized that his pack had been hit by a piece of shrapnel. On that fateful March day that parachute saved Denis Murnane's life not once but twice.

For two days he managed to evade capture but was spotted while hiding in a haystack and taken prisoner by two Luftwaffe groundcrew. The flight engineer was also captured that day, and both men spent the night on the floor of a Cologne hospital before being taken to an interrogation centre at Frankfurt from where he was later sent to a prisoner-of-war camp and where he learned that the only member of his crew not to survive had been the pilot who had remained at the controls to allow the others to escape.

In common with other bomber crew members the survival rate for air gunners was low. Sean Drumm's experience indicated that as few as 14% of gunners could hope to survive their tour of operations. He was one of the fortunate few who did survive. By the end of the war he had completed thirty-two missions with No. 630 Squadron, based at RAF East Kirkby in Lincolnshire. This squadron was formed out of B Flight of No. 57 Squadron on 15 November 1943 and it flew Avro Lancaster Is and IIIs.

East Kirkby played an important role in the latter stages of the war and its two squadrons, Nos. 57 and 630, flew operations against targets in Germany, France, including the southern coast, Belgium, Holland, Norway, Poland and Czechoslovakia. Many of the missions flown over France were carried out to support Allied ground forces immediately before and after the invasion of Europe in June 1944. During his tour of duty Sean Drumm served as mid-upper and tail gunner at various times. Before any mission he recalled that the atmosphere on the station was 'tense' while he emphasized the single word to describe the atmosphere afterwards: *'tense'*.

In the air it was very cold and 'frostbite was a hazard'. During the early stages of the war, aircrew had relied on thick woollen clothing and sheepskin flying jackets and lined boots to keep warm but electrically-heated flying suits were subsequently developed. But these could be dangerous and were 'sometimes a cause of burns' so that some aircrew chose not to use them.

> A lot of our missions were at low level where cold wasn't a problem but at eighteen to twenty-thousand feet on a long flight on a winter's night it was very cold. These heated flying suits were developed and I tried one on. They were all talking about it as if you'd got a first-class suit from London. Mine went on fire. I looked down and there were sparks coming from the flying boots. I got out quickly and got the suit off. I wouldn't wear one again, nor would anybody else. We used to dress in long johns and vests and overalls and then a thick brown inner suit and an outer suit followed by the flying boots.
>
> You had to try not to sweat when you were in the plane. Sweat would freeze at high altitudes into little chunks of ice. This affected the gunners most. The tail turret was the coldest and myself and the mid-upper gunner used to take turn about between the two turrets. When you got back from a long flight you were like the hunchback of Notre Dame; it took you a couple of hours to straighten up afterwards.

The exposed tail turret was an extremely cold location and this was exacerbated as gunners on No. 630, and other squadrons, were ordered to remove the central perspex panel from the turret's glazing. This was intended to improve the gunner's night vision: no matter how carefully it was cleaned and polished the perspex scratched and, in night-time conditions, distorted greatly the tail gunner's field of vision.

During the missions that Sean Drumm flew, his Lancaster, L-Love, was attacked six times by German nightfighters and engaged by anti-aircraft fire on many more occasions. On each occasion, however, the pilot, Flight-Lieutenant Hoare of the Royal Australian Air Force, brought the machine back to base. In the summer of 1944 most of their missions were flown to support the Allied armies in their advance in France, but there was a return to traditional targets in the autumn, when No. 630 Squadron was ordered to attack a German naval base at Bergen in Norway. The Kriegsmarine's U-boats had been forced to leave the ports on the west coast of France, and Bergen was one of several Norwegian ports being used by the submarines. U-boat pens in the port were being enlarged, and many German technicians, as well as a large labour force, had been sent there. Bergen had been bombed at the beginning of October by aircraft of Nos. 6 and 8 Groups; on the night of 28/29 October it was the turn of No. 5 Group which had not flown any operations since the 23rd. A total of 237 Lancasters, including No. 630 Squadron, and 7 Mosquitoes was despatched on the raid.

> We were instructed not to go below 8,000 feet. If the cloud base was obscuring the target we were to jettison the bombs in the sea and return to base. Two aircraft were flown by Norwegian crews. They knew the area and would go in first. When we got to Bergen the cloud base was almost ground level. The Norwegian crews disobeyed instructions and attacked below cloud. Both were shot down. The remainder of us closed into box formation to ward off attacking Focke-Wulf 190s and we landed at Kinloss in Scotland.

As well as the two aircraft manned by Norwegians, one other Lancaster was lost. The Master Bomber had tried to bring the attacking force down below 5,000 feet but, finding the target still obscured, had ordered the mission to be abandoned after forty-seven aircraft had dropped their bombs. No damage was caused to the U-boat pens although four bombs hit their roofs. Around the harbour area almost ninety houses were destroyed or damaged, but no civilians were injured, indicating that the residents had probably been evacuated. In the town centre, however, more houses were hit, fifty-two civilians and two Germans were killed and Bergen's historic Engen Theatre, the oldest in Europe, was destroyed.

Shortly after this raid the Lancasters of No. 630 Squadron were back over Norway. This time the target was Trondheim and one of 630's machines failed to return. One other Lancaster and a Mosquito were also lost. Sean Drumm subsequently learnt that the two air gunners he had met at Peterborough were killed on this raid, which would have been the final mission of their tour.

Another target for No. 630 during November was the Dortmund-Ems canal, which was struck at the beginning of the month and then almost three weeks later. There had been an earlier raid on the canal in September. The damage caused by the raid at the beginning of November was repaired by the Germans and so No. 5 Group was ordered to strike again. Once again considerable damage was caused by the bombing which was carried out at such low level that Sean Drumm recalls the bombers being flung up in the air by the force of the explosions. Interrogated by the Allies after the war, Albert Speer, the German Armaments Minister, admitted that it was the raids on the Dortmund-Ems canal, as well as those on the German railway system, that produced the most serious setbacks for German industry at this stage of the war.

Sean Drumm took part in a raid on another target that Speer subsequently acknowledged caused a major setback to Germany. This was an attack on the synthetic-oil plant at Brüx in Western Czechoslovakia on the night of 16/17 January 1945. Lancasters and Mosquitoes from Nos. 1 and 5 Groups participated and one Lancaster was lost from a force of 231 machines. During this raid L-Love was damaged by enemy fire and its hydraulics were shot away. The aircraft was forced to make a wheels-up landing at Woodbridge in Suffolk, a USAAF base with a very long runway that would allow damaged aircraft to get down. There was scarcely enough fuel left in the tanks to create the risk of a fire. After the landing the crew of L-Love were given a meal and in the canteen they met the crew of another damaged machine from RAF Upwood near Peterborough. From them Sean Drumm discovered that the two air gunners he had met in Peterborough had perished in the raid on Trondheim in November.

L-Love's pilot 'was highly offended' to learn that the Americans had no intention of salvaging the Lancaster. He made a plea to an American officer, saying that the station commander at East Kirkby wanted the Lancaster back, but to no avail. The Americans were adamant and a bulldozer shoved L-Love off the runway and began the process of reducing the plane to scrap. Its crew had to 'endure the humiliation of going home on railway warrants'.

Raids such as that on Brüx were carried out to support the Red Army's advance on the Eastern Front. During the winter of 1944/45 Sean Drumm and the crew of L-Love made many long trips to targets in eastern Europe.

> The Eastern Front struck fear in us. We'd all heard stories that some crews were shot down and never heard of again. They'd crashed or parachuted behind the Russian lines. We'd all been told that if we were forced down in the Russian area that we should say 'Inglesi' or 'Britanski' and we'd be all right. But many of these Russian soldiers had no idea what that meant, they were from central Asia and one airman looked like another to them, and they were shooting them.
>
> The other big worry was the length of the mission. Sometimes we'd get back to base with just enough fuel in the tanks to fill a bloody cigarette lighter. You can see from my log book that we were sometimes up for as long as eleven hours. My longest trip was eleven hours and thirty-five minutes.

As well as the missions to the Eastern Front there were further raids over the industrial heartland of Germany, the Ruhr valley, which also proved to be a terrifying experience for Allied airmen. The Germans had strengthened the anti-aircraft and searchlight defences with equipment that had been brought back from other fronts:

to describe it is almost impossible today. It was like Armageddon. At night the sky would be lit by massed searchlights and bursting shells, the ground a mass of flashes from falling bombs.

But Sean Drumm survived the war to remain in the Royal Air Force for many years afterwards. His survival story includes no spectacular escapes from doomed aircraft and he was certainly one of the lucky members of Bomber Command.

Another lucky Irish air gunner, also based at East Kirkby, was Patrick O'Reilly who was assigned as tail gunner to a Lancaster piloted by a South African. O'Reilly considered his pilot to be an extremely arrogant man and felt that it was not going to be a happy crew. He did not realize that he was to be the only survivor from that crew. O'Reilly's aircraft took off from East Kirkby on a daylight navigational exercise over the British Isles during which the navigator had to guide the pilot to certain landmarks, each of which had to be overflown at a specified time. In the tail turret O'Reilly maintained the same level of alertness as he would have done on an operational flight since there was always the possibility of a German intruder engaging the Lancaster. It was as he swung his turret from side to side to scan the sky that O'Reilly noticed that one of the engines appeared to be on fire. He immediately notified the pilot over the aircraft's intercom. He was told brusquely that the pilot and flight engineer would deal with the problem.

Shortly afterwards O'Reilly realized that the engine fire was getting worse: the Lancaster's fire extinguishers seemed to be no match for the conflagration. Once again he called up the pilot. This time he was told that the matter was under control and that he should mind his own business and stick to his job as a tail gunner. A worried O'Reilly continued to observe the burning engine: the situation was worsening as the flames were licking along the wing towards an internal fuel tank; a further attempt to acquaint the pilot with the seriousness of the situation met with further rebuff.

The Irishman decided that he had taken enough. He informed the pilot that he intended to bale out of the Lancaster if the latter was going to take no action. There was no positive response and the Irishman turned his turret through ninety degrees, opened the door at the back and dropped out some 10,000 feet over the English countryside. As he drifted down the Lancaster exploded and pieces of the stricken aircraft fell past him on his journey to the ground. None of the other crew members survived.

While Sean Drumm and Patrick O'Reilly lived to see the war end, another Irish air gunner from No. 630 Squadron was to be among the 1,020 airmen from East Kirkby who were to die in service. Flying Officer Albert Edward 'Bertie' Truesdale, from Newry in County Down, was the wireless operator/air gunner on Lancaster Mk I, LL950, Y, flown by Pilot Officer Ronald Bailey which took off from East Kirkby at 10.18 p.m. on 21 May 1944 for a minelaying operation in Kiel bay. It was one of 70 Lancasters and 37 Halifaxes that were carrying out similar operations over the Frisians, Heligoland, and the Kattegat as well as Kiel bay.

As the Lancasters approached the enemy coast they were picked up on German radar and nightfighters were scrambled to intercept. Hauptmann Eduard Schröder, commanding Nr 12 Nachtjäger Geschwader, was one of the pilots ordered aloft. Until January 1944 Schröder had been flying Junkers Ju88s on nightfighter missions from Grove in Denmark but had converted to Messerschmitt Bf110s and was now operating from Jagel. Schröder was ordered to fly into southern Denmark and patrol the central Jutland area as this was a regular route back to England for Bomber Command. At much the same time the Lancasters were dropping their mines in their target areas. All the aircraft laid their mines without interruption from German aircraft. In the normal Bomber Command fashion the aircraft turned to make their homewards journeys, flying as individuals rather than in a formation.

At 2 a.m. on 22 January a German radar station picked up Bertie Truesdale's Lancaster and passed the information to Schröder together with a course on which he could intercept the bomber. The Bf110 made contact with the Lancaster, and it is believed that its attack damaged one of the engines, forcing the British machine to lose height. In the area of Give the bomber was engaged by anti-aircraft guns, and a hit was claimed by the Luftwaffe flak gunners. About two kilometres further on an engine was seen to fall from the plane, landing in a field near Doerken, some five kilometres north of Give. The remainder of the Lancaster fell in a field near Vesterlund, causing an explosion that was seen twelve kilometres away.

The crash was witnessed by a local schoolteacher, Karl Neilsen Vester: 'At that time, I lived in the house at the end of the school and I got up to see if I could see any searchlights. Suddenly I discovered a little fireball in the western sky and I wondered what it was, but suddenly everything was enveloped in flames. I saw the plane coming in a curve and thought it would crash in the schoolyard.'

The Lancaster's fuselage came down in a field about 600 metres from the school. There were no survivors as the machine exploded on impact. Some twenty minutes later German soldiers from the next village of Thyregod arrived at the crash site and cordoned it off. The aircraft was still blazing and its ammunition was exploding at intervals.

Schröder landed his Bf110 at Grove rather than his base at Jagel, and it may be that his aircraft had suffered some damage from his engagement with the Lancaster. Within a few weeks the villagers had placed a wooden cross on the crash site, replacing this with a permanent stone monument in May 1945. Each year since then a service of remembrance for the crew of Lancaster LL950 Y has been held on 22 May, for which the village closes and the entire population attends the service to pay respects and tribute to the airmen who perished there in 1944.

Another airman from Northern Ireland to lose his life in 1944 was Flight Lieutenant Granville Wilson, DSO, DFC, DFM, of No. 7 Squadron. Wilson died as a deputy Master Bomber during a raid on Emden. To improve the effectiveness of its bombers, the RAF had created a Pathfinder Force to lead the way to and accurately mark targets. This force included some of the most proficient airmen in Bomber Command. Other highly experienced pilots were employed as Master Bombers. Theirs was a daunting task as they had to remain over the target for the duration of a raid and guide the efforts of the attacking force. Needless to say, the Germans would make a special effort to try to down the bomber that was cruising about all night, if this was at all possible.

Granville Wilson was acting as deputy to the Master Bomber on a daylight raid on Emden, the first since June 1942, on 6 September 1944. The attacking force was provided with a fighter escort, at first of British Spitfires and then of US Mustangs, but it was a flak shell that struck Wilson's Lancaster. The twenty-three-year-old pilot was killed instantly, as were his navigator and bomb aimer; the other five crew members were able to escape from the stricken aircraft which was the only one of the 105 Halifaxes and 76 Lancasters sent against Emden to be shot down that day. This was the last raid on Emden by Bomber Command. The town was seen to be in flames and local reports note that some vessels in the harbour were sunk.

Flight Lieutenant Granville Wilson is buried in Sage War Cemetery near Oldenburg while the other two crew members who perished are commemorated on the Memorial to the Missing at Runnymede.

Another Irishman to perish on similar duties was Anthony Loftus-Tottenham of Mullingar who served with the Royal Australian Air Force in Bomber Command. One of a number of members of his family who joined the British and Australian forces (see chapter Two) Tony Tottenham was only eighteen years old when he joined the RAAF in early 1942. After training as a pilot he was posted to England where he served in Nos. 463 and 467 Squadrons of Bomber Command. Both squadrons were RAAF units and operated Lancasters. Tony Tottenham flew a total of thirty-four missions as pilot and captain of a Lancaster and was recommended for the Distinguished Flying Cross when he brought his badly-damaged Lancaster home from a raid on Brest. At the end of his tour he could have accepted a posting as an instructor which would have allowed him to rest from operational flying but instead he volunteered for target photograph work which was an extremely hazardous duty. It was while flying on such duties that he was shot down and killed over Calais on 26 September 1944. He was just two weeks past his twenty-first birthday. Once again the local inhabitants stepped in to provide a memorial to the crew of the bomber. At first they removed the remains of the airmen from the crashed aircraft and concealed them from the Germans, before interring them in their local churchyard. The graves continue to be treated with reverence by the local people. Tony Tottenham is also remembered each year in the Anzac Day service in Balmoral, Australia where he joined up in 1942.

There is another memorial to Tony Tottenham in north London. For a time during his tour of operations he flew Lancaster S-Sugar which was to survive the war and a total of over 100 missions. Today S-Sugar is preserved in the Bomber Command Hall of the Royal Air Force Museum at Hendon and on its engine nacelles are printed the names of crew members: one of the names, on the port outer nacelle, is that of P.O. Tottenham, DFC.

Tony Tottenham did not live long enough to receive his Distinguished Flying Cross. This was presented to his family by King George VI in late-1946. Present at the Investiture were his father (who had survived a Japanese prison camp in spite of his age) his mother and his sister Barbara; all three were in uniform on the occasion.

From the first missions of September 1939 until the last days of war in August 1945 Irishmen were to be found among the crews of the RAF's bomber aircraft. They suffered their share of the highest death toll in any branch of the Allied forces and those who survived were, in later years, to see the strategic value of their efforts not only questioned but criticized and, on occasion, condemned. What is often not remembered is that Bomber Command's offensive was supported by the Allied leaders and by the overwhelming majority of the British public at the time. Those airmen did the job that was asked of them and they need have no personal regrets about that. It was dangerous, it was frightening and it was often the only way of taking the war to the Germans. As the American General Sherman once said, 'War is hell and you cannot refine it.' The truth of that statement is reflected in the bombing offensive of the Second World War.

~7~

Irish chaplains at war

IN THE NAME OF GOD

The role of chaplains serving with the forces, whether in peace or war, has often been questioned. Some would see a contradiction in their doing so, describing it as being contrary to Christ's teaching of the rejection of war in his Kingdom. Yet Christ also advised his followers to 'render unto Caesar' and we find St John the Baptist baptizing Roman soldiers while telling them not to abuse their power. The interaction of Christian clergy with serving soldiers can, therefore, be described as a very old tradition.

The word 'chaplain' itself derives from the 'Cappellani', the guardians of the *cappa* – cloak – which was a relic of St Martin, bishop of Tours. Martin, a soldier who tore his cloak in half to share it with a beggar, is the patron saint of chaplains. Aside altogether from arguments about the morality of war, chaplains to the forces, and their religious superiors, would assert that there is a moral duty to provide pastoral care to the serviceman, especially when he is in danger of death; and to provide the comfort of the last rites to him should he be killed, or mortally wounded on the battlefield.

The Great War had wrought a considerable change in the role and perception of the army chaplain that was due, in some measure at least, to the way Catholic chaplains had carried out their duties. Until 1836 there had been no official appointment of Catholic chaplains, and thus the first war in which Catholic priests ministered to servicemen with official approval had been the Crimean War. In order to administer the sacraments of penance, Eucharist and Extreme Unction – the last rites – to soldiers, Catholic priests often risked their own lives in the battle zone. During the Great War they had gone regularly into no man's land to give the last rites to dying men. One of the most famous chaplains of the war had been the Irish Jesuit priest Father William Doyle, MC, who lost his life while helping the wounded of 16th (Irish) Division during the disastrous battle of Langemarck in August 1917. The example of men such as Willie Doyle inspired other denominations and caused a debate within the Anglican communion in the post-war years on the nature of the sacraments. In the Second World War all denominations were ministering to all combatants in much the same way.

In action the chaplain, or padre as he was often called by the soldiers, would be at a field ambulance – mobile hospital – section where the wounded were being received from the regimental aid posts (RAPs), although with an Irish battalion it was more common for him to be found at the battalion's RAP. He was always ready to go forward to minister to soldiers in need. Chaplains were also to be found at the casualty clearing stations (CCSs).

During the Second World War many Irish clergymen, from all the major denominations, served as chaplains to the Royal Navy, Army, Royal Air Force and Dominions' forces and were active in all theatres of war. Some went to sea in ships escorting Atlantic convoys, or faced the dangers of shell, mortar bomb and bullet with the front-line infantry, or, in one case at least, flew on operations over Germany. At all times they provided guidance and comfort to men of all religious persuasions, and even to those with no particular beliefs. After the war several chaplains rose to eminent positions in their own churches, some chose to continue ministering to servicemen and others returned to the everyday life of a local curate or minister.

Irish chaplains went to France with the BEF in 1939 and were then involved in the *blitzkrieg* campaign of 1940. The first British gallantry decoration of the war to a clergyman was the award of the Military Cross to Father Thomas Duggan, who had been on the staff of St Finbarr's College, Cork, when war broke out and had volunteered his services as a chaplain. Father Duggan had undertaken such a role in the Great War and was taken prisoner in the German spring offensive of 1918. In 1939 his request to return to the Army was rejected initially as, at almost fifty, he was over age, but he persevered and was accepted for the Royal Army Chaplains' Department. He was then assigned to 151 Infantry Brigade, a Territorial Army formation, part of 50th (Tyne Tees) Division, composed of three battalions – 6th, 8th and 9th – of the Durham Light Infantry; the division moved to France at the beginning of February 1940.

When the Germans launched Operation SICHELSCHNITT in May 1940, the battalions of 151 Brigade were soon in action. In common with the remainder of the BEF they were soon on the retreat to Dunkirk. It was during this period that Father Duggan earned the Military Cross. A regimental aid post had been established at Moeras, into which the wounded were brought for treatment. As the medical staff laboured to help the injured German shells fell around the RAP. In spite of the danger Father Duggan moved among the wounded men to minister to them, give the last rites where necessary, and provide words of encouragement to both wounded and medical staff. He was an invaluable source of morale for everyone and the recommendation that he be decorated spoke of '[h]is coolness, energy, courage and example' as being 'outstanding'. Lord Gort, C-in-C of the BEF, approved the immediate award of the MC to Father Duggan.*

Father Duggan's age finally caught up with him and he was relieved of his appointment with 151 Brigade and posted to Northern Ireland as Senior Chaplain to the Forces where

---

* Awards fall into three categories: Immediate, Operational or Periodic. An Immediate award is as its title suggests; an Operational award is made for gallantry or outstanding service in a specific operation, e.g. the attack on *Bismarck*, or the battle of El Alamein; and a Periodic award is given for gallantry or outstanding service over a sustained period.

the influence of this Nationalist Irish priest did much to counter the anti-British views of the Rt Rev Neil Farren, bishop of Derry, who refused to become Vicar-Delegate to British Troops in Northern Ireland, but willingly accepted that responsibility for American troops when they arrived in Northern Ireland.

Father Duggan was subsequently appointed an Officer of the Order of the British Empire (OBE). After the war, he became a missionary priest and was sent to Peru where he engaged in another war, against the poverty of the people of that country. He ended his days there, dying in Lima in December 1961 at the age of seventy-one.

By a remarkable coincidence, the third clerical gallantry award of the war also went to an Irishman, the Revd Richard Newcombe Craig, a Dubliner and a priest of the Church of England, ministering in Derby, who also received the Military Cross. Mr Craig was with the doomed 30 Brigade which included two motor battalions – 2nd King's Royal Rifle Corps and 1st Rifle Brigade – and which arrived in Calais on 23 May. The brigade had been formed only a month earlier on 24 April to be the motor brigade of 1st Armoured Division.* When 30 Brigade embarked in England it had orders to land somewhere in France and to help with the defence of Boulogne, where 20 Guards Brigade had arrived from England on 22 April. Boulogne was now under heavy attack by the Germans. But 30 Brigade was not to move from Calais: on its arrival there it found the port held by a London TA battalion, Queen Victoria's Rifles,† which had arrived only a day earlier, and a strong ring of German troops, supported by tanks, around the town. A German attack was about to be launched on Calais and so Brigadier Nicholson, commanding 30 Brigade, realized that his task would now be to defend that town rather than attempting to move to Boulogne; such a move would have proved impossible due to the enemy cordon. Reinforced by some tanks and artillery, 30 Brigade prepared to do his best in an uneven struggle.

As the Germans moved in on Calais, bombing and shelling the town, many soldiers were killed or wounded and it became clear that there were not enough medical officers to cope with the injured. On learning this, the Revd Craig, who had been offered but refused the opportunity to embark on a vessel leaving for England, volunteered to assist with the wounded. Enlisting the assistance of some straggler personnel, he established an aid post near Calais Docks station where

> without a medical officer for three days, he organized the dressing and evacuation of some 300 wounded who otherwise might have been without care. On

---

* Motor brigades provided mobile infantry for armoured divisions and were usually composed of battalions of the rifle regiments, King's Royal Rifle Corps (KRRC), also known by its pre-1881 designation of 60th Rifles, and the Rifle Brigade (RB). The full-dress uniform of rifle regiments is a very dark, or rifle, green and thus such regiments were known as Green Jackets. In the amalgamations of the 1950s and 1960s the title Royal Green Jackets was given to a new regiment formed from the Ox and Bucks Light Infantry, the KRRC and the RB

† Queen Victoria's Rifles, formerly 9th London Regiment, was a TA battalion of the KRRC. Officially, the battalion was part of 30 Brigade but it had not joined the brigade prior to departure for France.

the afternoon of May 25th he learned that six badly wounded men were lying on the dunes, under enemy sniping fire, unable to get away. Without hesitation he called for four volunteers, drove an ambulance himself to the spot nearby, and with his volunteers crawled to the men, and rescued them, driving back under fire. All six wounded were dressed and placed on a ship under the direction of this very gallant chaplain.

Such was the confusion of those days that no war diaries exist for 30 Brigade's headquarters, 2nd King's Royal Rifle Corps or Queen Victoria's Rifles. There is, however, an account of the experiences of 1st Rifle Brigade in that battalion's records, and it includes a reference to a 'Padre who[m] no one had ever seen before' and details how that padre organized an aid post in the railway station and 'drove an ambulance nearly all day on Saturday'. Without waiting for calls for help the padre drove to wherever 'the shelling was heaviest and asked for wounded'. The writer was, of course, witnessing the Revd Craig in action.

The Green Jackets were unable to escape from Calais as a brigade and thus most went into captivity when the Germans, fighting from street to street, finally overcame the defenders of the port. The Revd Craig was among those who were taken prisoner. A Catholic chaplain, Father Vincent Gallagher, SJ, was also taken prisoner after being wounded. However, the War Office reported him as being missing, presumed killed as no news was heard from him for some time. It was later established that he was in a PoW camp where he spent the next four years. Given the opportunity of repatriation through an exchange of prisoners in 1943, he elected to remain in captivity and allowed a married man to be repatriated in his place.

The Chaplains' Department of the BEF was a unified structure with an Anglican Deputy Chaplain-General and a Catholic as his assistant. This assistant had been the Principal Chaplain (RC) to the Army, Monsignor John Coghlan, a native of Castlepollard, County Westmeath. Together with a Staff Chaplain, Father Basil McCreton, Monsignor Coghlan was based at rear Headquarters, BEF near Arras.

The German breakthrough in mid-May threatened that rear HQ which was ordered to pull back to the Boulogne area on 15 May. It took nearly a week for Monsignor Coghlan and Father McCreton to make the journey, along refugee-packed roads which were sometimes strafed by German aircraft. In the course of the withdrawal to Boulogne, Coghlan and McCreton visited military hospitals and gave spiritual comfort where they could.

On the night of 23/24 May rear HQ was evacuated from Boulogne to England but Monsignor Coghlan and his staff remained in France, true to the tradition that the chaplain's place was with the soldiers facing danger. They moved from the Boulogne area to Bergues, some eight miles from Dunkirk, where they attached themselves to an Advanced Dressing Station (ADS). As well as ministering to the wounded, of all denominations, they also assisted the medical officers when they could and buried the dead. A party of Belgian and French nuns who joined them also helped; some of them were trained nurses.

This work continued over the next several days while refugees, HQ elements of various formations and service troops moved through their positions back to the docks and beaches at Dunkirk. As the first of the fighting troops began withdrawing through the area on 28 May, it became clear that the campaign was almost over. The following day enemy shells began to fall on Bergues and demolition parties of Royal Engineers started the task of destroying anything of military value. Then came the order to evacuate on the night of 29/30 May.

Coghlan's party tried to embark at Dunkirk docks but failed since the harbour was blocked by wrecks. They decided to make for the beaches. Off-shore, about three miles away, were ships which were firing at the attacking German aircraft. The area was battered, Dunkirk was covered in a shroud of smoke and thousands of soldiers awaited evacuation from the beaches. Little ships, some of them weekend pleasure craft, were ferrying men from the beaches to the larger vessels offshore. The beaches now represented the chaplains' party's only chance of escaping from France. On those same beaches only days before another chaplain, the Benedictine priest Father G. Hobson-Matthews, had died, becoming the first British chaplain to lose his life in action in the war; Father McCreton had met Father Hobson-Matthews in Bergues as the Benedictine made his way to Dunkirk with 1st Division's artillery.

The first of the little ships that spotted Monsignor Coghlan's party was unable to take them all on board and so they waited for another boat, an overloaded cutter, which ferried them out to HMS *Impulsive*. Although damaged in the embarkation, *Impulsive* limped its way across the channel to dock at Dover that night. Monsignor Coghlan was subsequently made a Knight Commander of the Order of the British Empire for his gallantry during the battle for France;* Father McCreton was award-ed the Military Cross.

As the three armed forces expanded in the early days of the war there had been a call for clerics to provide chaplaincy services to the large numbers in uniform. The response from the Irish churches was excellent, but Irish chaplains also came from many parts of Britain where they had been serving before the war; this was especially true of the Catholic clergy, some of whom were from monastic orders. In the after-math of Dunkirk, the Army, which had the greatest proportion of service chaplains, found the experiment of a unified chaplains' department had produced too unwieldy an organisation and reverted to the earlier system. This found Monsignor Sir John Coghlan, as he had officially become, once again in the post of Principal Chaplain (RC) at the War Office.

By the summer of 1940 the only elements of British ground forces that were direct-ly engaged in combat with an Axis army were those of the Western Desert Force in Egypt. The conflict that began in North Africa in June 1940 was to last almost three years and, once again, Irish chaplains would play their part. However, it was to be some time before the campaign in North Africa built up and, in the meantime, the war

---

* Monsignor Coghlan was ordained for the diocese of Meath in 1913 and served as a chaplain in France, Flanders and Mesopotamia during the Great War. After the war he remained in the Army and served in Germany, Malta, Shanghai, Egypt and Britain.

in Europe continued on the sea, especially on the convoy routes, and in the air. The war at sea brought the Royal Navy to the river Foyle to establish an escort base, HMS *Ferret*, at Londonderry. Sailors, especially Catholics, based there were to meet one of the most remarkable chaplains of the war – Father Willie Devine, MC.

Father Devine, a native of Castlederg in County Tyrone, was already over fifty when war broke out in 1939. Born in 1888, he had been ordained for the diocese of Derry at Maynooth College in 1912 but almost immediately was sent on loan to the archdiocese of Melbourne in Australia. When war broke out in 1914, Australia and New Zealand began raising an expeditionary force, the Anzacs,* to go overseas to support Britain and France. Father Devine volunteered to serve as a chaplain with the Australian Imperial Force (AIF), the Australian element of the Anzacs. He was commissioned in May 1915 and was promoted to captain on 1 July of that year. In February 1917 he sailed for the western front in France. There Father Devine was awarded the Military Cross and the Croix de Guerre. Between the wars he served as a curate at home in Ireland, then, again, in Melbourne, was a missionary in China, where he taught at a university, and was recalled finally to Derry in 1932. He also found time to write a history of 48th Battalion, AIF. When war returned to Europe he was a curate at Sion Mills, near Strabane in his native Tyrone, and he began to provide a chaplaincy for the crews of ships operating from the Londonderry naval base. This was formalized into an official naval chaplaincy, although it was not until 1944 that the Admiralty permitted Catholic priests to hold permanent commissions in the Royal Navy. Interestingly, the ending of this piece of religious discrimination, possibly one of the last surviving vestiges of the penal legislation of earlier centuries, came about after the appointment of Admiral Sir Andrew Cunningham as First Sea Lord. The Dublin-born Cunningham came from a Presbyterian family.

Father Willie Devine, affectionately known as 'The Major' to his fellow priests of the Derry diocese, proved to be a remarkably popular and effective chaplain. One former Wren recalled him as 'a very imposing figure' whose smart appearance, with highly-polished shoes, made him look the epitome of the military chaplain. He went to sea with ships of the Londonderry Escort Force and shared all the risks of convoy protection duties, whether from the conditions of the North Atlantic or the attentions of the Kriegsmarine's U-boats or surface vessels and the Luftwaffe's aircraft. As escort groups prepared to leave Derry for their seagoing tasks, Father Devine would try to see that all Catholic sailors should attend confession and receive the Eucharist before sailing. He applied the same rule to himself whenever he went to sea as he told a fellow priest. Initially Father Devine had his own memorable (and unorthodox) methods of ensuring that the men in his care did attend confession by inviting them into a room and then refusing to allow them to leave until they had made confessions.

Willie Devine ministered at the Derry base until 1943 when, with the battle of the Atlantic turning in favour of the Allies, and a massive naval build-up in the Mediter-

* Anzac; from the initials of Australian and New Zealand Army Corps. The AIF provided the larger portion of the corps with the balance coming from the New Zealand Expeditionary Force (NZEF).

ranean in preparation for the invasion of Sicily, he was posted to North Africa where he was based at Algiers. After the conquest of Sicily the Allied armies invaded Italy and Father Devine moved to Taranto from where he assumed responsibility for the east coast of Italy, along the Adriatic. Once again he endeared himself to all ranks prompting the historian of Royal Navy chaplains to describe him as 'an elderly very charming Irishman'.

Another Catholic chaplain who earned the respect and admiration of all who encountered him in North Africa and Italy came from the kingdom of Kerry. Daniel Kelleher, affectionately known as Father Dan, was to earn the Military Cross for saving the lives of wounded soldiers under the shadow of Monte Cassino. Born in 1909, Father Dan Kelleher was serving in the archdiocese of Liverpool when he volunteered for service with the RAChD and was commissioned on 26 March 1941. In September of that year he was posted to the Middle East where he served with Support Group, 1st Armoured Division in the recently-formed Eighth Army. He remained with 1st Armoured Division until after the final battle of El Alamein when he was hospitalized for a time in Palestine.

Returning to Eighth Army he was attached to 1st Argyll and Sutherland Highlanders in 154 Brigade of 51st (Highland) Division with whom he served throughout the Sicilian campaign and the early months of the Italian campaign. Then, in December 1943, he came home, in a spiritual sense, when he was transferred to 1st Royal Irish Fusiliers in the Irish Brigade of 78th (Battleaxe) Division.

Dan Kelleher's rich Kerry accent caused a problem for the battalion's adjutant, Captain Brian Clark. The English-born and educated Clark 'couldn't understand a word' of what Father Dan was saying at first, but that problem quickly disappeared. One of the new padre's first tasks with this most Irish of the Irish Brigade's battalions was to organize the celebration of Christmas. Father Dan celebrated midnight Mass, to which all officers, irrespective of their religious affiliations were invited, and the band of the Irish Guards, then visiting Italy, added to the overall sense of occasion. Strictly speaking,

> Father Dan was the RC padre for the [Irish] Bde, but he was attached to the Faughs and he belonged to us! Whichever Bn was in the lead Dan would be with them. He seemed to be quite fearless and once told me that dying did not worry him as it would indicate that he had done what was required of him on earth and therefore the Almighty had a use for him elsewhere.

Father Dan's spiritual and physical support of the soldiers under his care became a legend in the Irish Fusiliers. His work was summarized succinctly by John Horsfall when he wrote:

> If church services were compulsory our men still went because they wanted to. Fear, resolution, comradeship – all went hand in hand in this, but above all they knew, or soon discovered, that they could not cope on their own without

the Divine power to help them. Later, especially with our famous padre Dan Kelleher, these services were uplifting in the highest degree for men who had been badly shaken in battle. When Dan was displeased he could promise Hell to those who performed indifferently and disgraced the Holy cause they were fighting for.

As the Irish Brigade fought its battles and skirmishes throughout an Italian winter Dan Kelleher came to know the men to whom he was ministering, and they came to know him. He was respected and loved by Catholic and Protestant alike, Irish and Sassenach, and some of his greatest admirers were men who might have worn Orange sashes and marched to the beat of a Lambeg drum at home. He made no distinctions among the soldiers on the basis of denomination and he showed a tremendous example of courage and devotion to duty. This was nowhere more apparent than in late March and April 1944 when the Irish Brigade took over positions around Monte Cassino.

Jack Broadbent, the subaltern commanding the mortar platoon of 1st Royal Irish Fusiliers, had his mortars dispersed among the battalion's four companies and it was his practice to visit them. Broadbent had

> great regard for Father Dan, and what a very brave man he was ... at Monte Cassino ... I used to visit my mortars out with the Companies. I on occasions went with him. He would walk calmly along, soft hat and stick, even when shells were falling nearby. On one occasion I left him with the remark that there was 'no need to stick one's neck out and have one's head blown off by shells, a different matter to take risks when it was necessary.

Jim Trousdell joined the Faughs as a young officer at Cassino and soon found Father Dan to be both a friend and an inspiration in dangerous times.

> At Cassino I remember being caught in a burst of shellfire, lying flat on the ground, trying to get some cover. Father Dan was nearby and although he had also taken cover he was not particularly perturbed, lying there resting his chin on his hand looking around to see what was going on. There were other occasions in the following weeks when I was glad to have Father Dan nearby, his presence was a great morale booster when spirits were low and the going was tough.

And it was on an occasion when the going was very tough that Father Dan showed the full extent of his courage. On the evening of 6 April 1944,

> the night that Cairo village received Evensong from the German guns and while every living soul in that heaving rubble lay flat and prayed, a figure walked calmly among the shellbursts carrying a dying man in his arms to shel-

ter. No-one grudged Father Daniel Kelleher, The Kerryman, that MC and he probably got a ghostly pat on the shoulder from old Saint Benedict himself, peering down from Heaven to see what we were making of all his architecture. The Church Militant or Triumphant? – who can say?

Father Dan had taken himself out into an inferno of shellfire to help wounded soldiers and assist the stretcher-bearers. Brian Clark, the Faughs' adjutant, wrote the citation that brought a Military Cross to the padre:

> Rev Kelleher was at Battalion HQ in the Caira area when heavy shelling was reported in Caira village causing several casualties to one of the platoons.* The Rev Kelleher immediately raced to the village, which was under very heavy shelling. He found the wounded men and assisted the stretcher bearers in their work, carrying wounded in his arms at great personal risk, to the shelter of a ruined building.
>
> He comforted the badly wounded men and assisted the overworked stretcher bearers in applying bandages to their wounds.
>
> His cheerfulness and practical assistance undoubtedly saved the lives of two men and gave fresh proof of his unfailing devotion to duty.

Cassino finally fell to the Allied forces in May after some of the toughest fighting of the Italian campaign. At the beginning of June the city of Rome was liberated by American soldiers of General Mark Clark's Fifth Army as the Irish Brigade moved northwards up the Tiber valley. However, there was a lull in fighting in the brigade's area about a week later and so it was possible for its commander, Brigadier Pat Scott, an Irish Fusilier, and Father Dan to arrange an audience with the pope, Pius XII, for a representative party of the brigade. This was held to be an excellent idea by all denominations in the brigade and the pope concurred.

A party of 150 officers and men arrived at the Vatican on 12 June at 8.45 a.m. and, following the Pipes and Drums, they marched up the Vatican steps to be led by officers of the Noble Guard to the audience chamber. Following the audience with Pope Pius, the Pipes and Drums played a selection of Irish tunes before Father Dan celebrated Mass for the visiting party, which was far from being entirely Catholic. In fact one warrant officer of 2nd London Irish Rifles even wore his Orange sash into the Vatican, making that sash unique in the history of the Orange order as the only one ever to have been blessed by a pope. After Mass the Pipes and Drums beat retreat on the steps of St Peter's and this was enjoyed immensely by the many Irish priests present. According to Brigadier Pat Scott, he asked the pipers to play some requests for the priests, with the 'Boys of Wexford' being the most popular tune. Some of the Irish priests present were to join the Allies as chaplains as the Italian campaign progressed, some serving with the British Eighth Army, including the Irish

---

* The forms Cairo and Caira appear to have been used for the name of this village.

Brigade, and some with the American Fifth Army. Among those men were Fathers
Louis Madden, of Achonry, and Kevin McCabe, of Kilmore, who became known as
Father Dan's curates in the Irish Brigade. Both had been in the class for ordination
at Easter 1944 and had, of course, no way of travelling home to Ireland. They joined
Eighth Army, 'through Dan Kelleher's intervention', as it was engaged between
Florence and Bologna. Subsequently other priests from the Irish College, including
Father Sean Quinlan and Father John Shortall, served with the Irish Brigade in post-
war Austria.

In the words of Colin Gunner, Father Dan was 'the Willie Doyle of our war'. His
calm courage and his generous nature made him unforgettable. He was a very down-
to-earth priest who could enjoy a drink with his soldiers or their officers and was not
averse to joining in a game of cards. When the Irish Brigade was returning to Italy
after a spell in Egypt Colin Gunner shared a cabin with Al McLennan, a Canadian
officer serving with the Royal Irish Fusiliers. After dinner a game of poker was under-
way which Gunner soon quit after losing 'the few shillings' he had left. Just then
Father Dan entered the cabin and asked if he could join in. He took Gunner's place
and the latter dozed off, waking at intervals to see that, while others were coming and
going in the game 'the Church and Canada were the real antagonists'.

> The breakfast gong was sounding when I climbed down to wash and saw glee-
> fully that Father Dan sat like Humpty Dumpty on a heap of notes and coins
> while the exponent of Canada's national game glumly wrote out a cheque. Dan
> pocketed all, and as fit and fresh as when he first sat down, strode off to his
> breakfast kipper. While I scraped away in the mirror, I heard an explosive colo-
> nial oath and the blood-curdling vow: 'That's the last time I ever play with a
> goddam priest!' Events since have confirmed my belief that seminaries run a
> pretty intensive course on games of chance, or perhaps the psychology of the
> confessional helps.

In the final year of the Italian campaign Father Dan continued to minister to the
soldiers of the Irish Brigade with the same disregard for his own safety as he had
always shown. In December 1944 the brigade was high in the northern Apennines as
part of Fifth Army. The Allies were still hoping to push forward although the weather was unfavourable. In a series of actions there were many casualties, among them,
on 10 December, Fusilier Victor Webb of the Faughs.

Hit, among other places, in the throat, Webb was left for dead by the medics who
believed that his wound was fatal. His closest friend in his section, a Catholic, decided to fetch Father Dan to give Victor the Last Rites, even though he was not a Catholic. When the chaplain arrived, he knelt down to talk to the wounded fusilier and
asked him how he felt. Getting a response he then offered Webb a swig of water which
helped to clear some of the blood from his throat after which Dan Kelleher calmly
picked Victor Webb up and carried him to safety and medical attention.

I may add that I owe my life to Father Dan Kelleher [who] carried me back to the First Aid Post where I was treated by the doctor before being put on a stretcher and tied to a mule then taken to an ambulance, finishing up in 31 General Hospital. My wounds were such that the war was over before I arrived back to the Irish Fusiliers in Austria.

There were many who had reason to be grateful to Father Dan, 'that wonderful man of God' as Colin Gunner described him. He continued to serve the Irish Brigade until its disbandment in Austria after the war and then chose to remain in the Army. In 1956, while he was serving with the Berlin Brigade, the Almighty finally decided that there was work for Father Dan elsewhere. He died in a traffic accident in the former German capital on 15 June. His remains were repatriated for burial in his beloved Kerry. Such was the esteem in which Dan had been held in the Royal Irish Fusiliers that many former members of the regiment subscribed to the building of a school as a memorial to him in the hills of northern Burma where his brother, Father Jeremiah, was serving as a Columban missionary.

Father Dan Kelleher was not the only member of his family to serve as a chaplain to Irish soldiers. Jeremiah, three years Dan's junior, was already a missionary in Burma when war came to that country with the Japanese invasion in 1942. The Japanese onslaught brought about a reinforcement of the tiny British force in Burma, so small that it did not even merit the title army. Among the reinforcements was 1st Royal Inniskilling Fusiliers; the battalion was flown into Magwe aerodrome in Burma from its peacetime base in India and was then lorried to Prome to join 1st Burma Division.

It was at Prome that the Inniskillings and Father Jerry Kelleher first came into contact. Father Kelleher had arrived there with Kachin troops having been permitted by his Columban Superior to serve them as a chaplain.

> In granting permission, the Superior made it clear that it was granted only to serve Kachin troops – his mission, as the Columbans had no responsibility for British or Indian troops. He left in January 1942 and after a delay, while they sought authority from Delhi, which probably never arrived, the British authorities at Maymyo appointed him to a chaplaincy.

The Kachins – who were strongly pro-British – were serving as garrison troops, defending rear areas, when the Inniskillings arrived on their way to the front. The battalion had no chaplain at all and, on learning this, Father Kelleher decided that he had a greater duty of spiritual care to the Irishmen than to the Kachins. He approached the Inniskillings' commanding officer, Lieutenant-Colonel Ralph Cox, MC, a Catholic Belfastman, and offered to serve his battalion as a chaplain. The offer was accepted with no hesitation. The soldiers of the battalion were delighted to learn that they had a chaplain. One Wexfordman who had asked Father Kelleher for private confession told him that when the CO told us that there was a Catholic chaplain in this benighted country I could not believe it and when he said that you were Irish I felt that God had dropped you down from heaven for the Inniskilling Fusiliers. That was tremendous for me; it was worth joining the Army for that alone.

The battalion's first action was to try to hold a Japanese breakthrough. They were then in action around Prome itself before it was evacuated on 1 April. Rearguard action then followed as 1st Burma Division fell back to the oilfields at Yenangyaung, which it had orders to destroy. The Japanese were striking northward on a parallel line to try to reach the oilfields first. During the course of the retreat, Colonel Cox was killed by strafing fire from a Japanese aircraft on 10 April.* Only fifteen minutes before that, he had received Holy Communion from Father Kelleher. His successor as commanding officer, Major Samuel McConnell, was killed in action just over a week later, struck down by a sniper's bullet. As the battalion retreated there were many anxious moments as Japanese aircraft attacked them, as on the occasion that Colonel Cox was killed, or when ground forces opened up with machine-guns and mortars. Jerry Kelleher was close to death on a number of occasions: once, while travelling on a truck, men on either side of him were killed by machine-gun bullets.

The battalion reached Yenangyaung on 17 April to find that the oilfields had been destroyed by Chinese troops. Even at night Father Kelleher could read his breviary by the light from the blazing oil wells. By now the British troops were in a precarious position, being isolated and already cut off to the south and to the north by an arc of enemy posts; the Japanese had encircled Yenangyaung and set up road blocks. A break-out through the enemy positions at Yenangyaung was decided upon, with 13 Brigade making the effort. Two Indian battalions were to advance to the slopes of a ridge after which the Inniskillings would leap-frog through and occupy the ridge.

There followed what Viscount Slim later described as 'a brutal battle', fought in a temperature of 114 degrees, with no water, amid the destruction of the oil-fields and with a blanket of black smoke overhanging everything. On 18 April the division 'fought doggedly over ridge after low ridge' with the Japanese defending in suicidal fashion, holding each position until the last soldier lay dead. Eventually, as Slim wrote, 'a detachment of Inniskillings struggled through to the Pin Chaung' where they were ambushed by Japanese troops who had pretended to be Chinese. The attack was halted.

The following day B and C Companies made an advance towards Twingon village but were forced to withdraw. It was during a subsequent enemy attack that Major McConnell was killed; the attack was thwarted. Finally, pressure from the Chinese allowed the division to break out of their encircled positions. Only 114 members of the battalion reached India. Jerry Kelleher was one of the survivors of Yenangyaung. In the course of the battle he collapsed from heat-stroke and was left behind the retreating troops in an area already overrun by the Japanese. But a young officer from

---

* Colonel Cox's father had also commanded a battalion of the Inniskillings.

a tank regiment risked his own life to bring Father Jerry from danger and then placed him in a tank; the armoured vehicle then fought its way through a Japanese road-block to safety with enemy bullets pinging off the armoured skin.

Subsequently Father Kelleher was evacuated by ambulance to Mandalay where he was placed on a river steamer that had been pressed into service as a hospital ship. On the journey northwards to Myitkyina, he ministered to the other sick on board. Arriving at Myitkyina on 2 May he met another Columban priest, Father James Cloonán, and began to assist Father Cloonan with his ministry to troops and refugees in hospitals in the area. Father Cloonan had already been working at full stretch at Myitkyina and had been meeting train-load after train-load of wounded soldiers 'giving the last sacraments to men who had not seen a priest since the terrible campaign began'.

As the British began evacuating the area, taking the sick and wounded out by air, the two priests decided to stay with the Kachins rather than go to India. Father Kelleher remembered that he had gone to the army 'only to minister to Kachin troops, so I decided to remain behind with Jim Cloonan'. They remained at their posts and Father Kelleher changed from his chaplain's uniform into a soutane but Father Cloonan kept his uniform on and was badly beaten by Japanese troops when the two men were taken prisoner on 7 May. They were interned in Rangoon jail until liberated in 1945. Many years later, while working in the Philippines, Father Jerry was to tell a Japanese nun, who suggested that he must have suffered a lot from her country's army, that he had been treated very well in captivity.

The Japanese advance was finally fought to a standstill on India's borders and the battles of Imphal and Kohima in the Naga hills in 1944 marked the turning point of the war in Burma. These were among the bloodiest battles of the war in the Far East and fighting was close and intense as the Japanese laid siege to both Imphal and Kohima. Their intention was to use the huge supply depot at Imphal to re-provision their troops for the advance into India, but the small garrisons held out tenaciously until reinforcements finally helped to turn the tide of battle. At Garrison Hill, Kohima, on the night of 22/23 April the Japanese made a determined attack and succeeded in penetrating part of the perimeter. During the fierce fighting that followed an Anglican chaplain, David Edmond Rice, a Dubliner by birth, organized stretcher parties.* The Revd Rice led the bearers throughout a period of four hours during which he was exposed to enemy grenades, mortar- and small-arms-fire. Over eighty wounded men were brought to safety during and immediately after this action.

> Throughout the next day, without any rest, he undertook to act as stretcher-bearer himself, carrying the wounded down a difficult path from the hill 500 feet above the road with untiring energy and cheerfulness. On the night of May 27th-28th, 1944 when the battalion was again heavily attacked in the

---

* David Rice was a cleric of the Church of England who had been serving in Derby before the war; he returned to that city. Interestingly, Revd Richard Craig, who won the MC at Calais, also ministered in that city and both men at some time were chaplains to battalions of the Durham Light Infantry.

same positions for five and a half hours, Captain Rice displayed the same high qualities. His conduct was an inspiration and an example to all.

Another Irish chaplain who served in Burma died during the campaign: Father John Hayes served with 36th Division, commanded by the redoubtable 'Front-Line Frankie', Major-General Francis Festing, later Field-Marshal Sir Francis. Father Hayes was a Jesuit and thus was often referred to as the Willie Doyle of Burma. He was an outstanding chaplain who was loved and respected by all the soldiers with whom he came in contact. A Limerick man, he was appointed as a chaplain in July 1941 and was selected for overseas service in 1943.

Assigned to 36th Division at Poona in India, Father Hayes served with them in the fighting in Burma for almost all of 1944.

> It was a tough assignment, but the asceticism which for so long had moulded his character stood every test and strain. In their Chaplain the men saw a strong, fearless man of God fired by an intense passion to win all he could for Christ. Affectionately, they dubbed him 'Battling Hayes'. Hardship and priva-tion found him always cheerful; weariness and fatigue seemed strangers to him; if he felt any fear of wounds or death he never gave sign of it; his coura-geous conduct through the long months of fierce jungle fighting was an inspi-ration to every officer and man who witnessed it. General Festing ... resisted every effort to have him transferred from his divisional command. The General being a Catholic, he appreciated the sources of his Padre's tireless energy and indomitable courage.

A fellow officer of 36th Division, also an Irishman and a former student of Belvedere College, wrote of John Hayes' style of ministry:

> To one and all he was known as 'Battling Hayes', utterly devoid of any fear. It was only on the express order of General Festing that he took his batman to act as escort when on his rounds. No matter where one went, more especially in the height of battle, there one would find Father Hayes, in his peculiar dress: Gurkha hat, battle-dress blouse and blue rugger shorts. It was common to see him walking along a road, known to be infested with the enemy, without any protection of any kind, happy in the thought that he was doing his job ... Nothing mattered: monsoon, rain, heat, disease, the enemy: his one thought was to be among his flock, doing all he could to help them. Nothing was too much trouble, and the further forward a Unit was, the greater his delight in going forward to celebrate Mass.

Father Hayes' first active service with 36th Division was in the Arakan, on Burma's western coast, in early 1944. This was hard fighting with the division being committed to help stop a Japanese advance; it was followed by a rapid air transfer to the main Burma front. The division took part in the fighting for Myitkyina and then pushed on to the Irrawaddy. It was on the banks of that great river that Father John Hayes died, not from Japanese shot or shell but from illness. On 28 December 1944 he was evacuated to the CCS at Katha where he was diagnosed as suffering from typhus. Although the disease was taking its normal course, Father Hayes requested the last rites on 6 January. He must have sensed that his end was near: pneumonia set in and his condition worsened steadily until, on Sunday 21 January 1945, he died. Writing to his mother after his death, General Festing described Father Hayes as

> an exemplification of all that a Catholic Priest and army chaplain should be. He was a tireless worker, and if any man worked himself to death, it was he. Your son was an undoubted saint and he died fortified by the rites of Holy Church. May he rest in peace.

Festing's assessment was supported by another Catholic chaplain in 36th Division. Father Clancy, from County Clare, in a letter to Father Hayes' Provincial.

Gallantry in such adverse conditions was not the sole preserve of Catholic chaplains. We have already seen how Richard Newcombe Craig earned the MC at Calais in May 1940; this achievement was paralleled by another Dublin-born clergyman, Reginald Worrall Leadbetter, of the Church of Ireland. The Revd Leadbetter was serving in North Africa with 6th Grenadier Guards in early 1943 when he won the Military Cross during the battle for the Mareth line.

During a night attack on the Horseshoe feature near Wadi Bou Remli on the main road to Mareth on 16/17 March, the Revd Leadbetter's battalion, in what was to be their first experience of battle, advanced into a minefield in the darkness and suffered very heavy casualties from anti-personnel mines. These were the vicious S-mines that sprang several feet into the air to explode at head height and fill the surrounding area with their deadly packing of shrapnel. Mortar- and machine-gun-fire added to the ordeal of the Grenadiers who, in spite of their suffering, went on to take all three of their objectives. But the human cost was high and

> The padre undertook the duty of collecting wounded both in darkness and daylight from the mined areas. He carried out his self-imposed task with complete disregard for his personal safety and with the utmost bravery ...

There was little doubt that Leadbetter's actions saved many lives as well as reducing the suffering of the wounded generally. In the nightmare that overtook the Grenadiers an improvized ambulance service was organized by the Revd Leadbetter. The battalion's war diary records how the MO, Captain A. Winder, the chaplain and the medical staff 'were doing magnificent work under trying conditions of shell and mortars falling all around them but never actually hitting the RAP'. It proved impossible to consolidate the battalion's gains and a withdrawal had to be ordered.

A few days later Padre Leadbetter directed the removal of the dead from the minefields and his 'inspiring example, energy and personality' played an important part in the successful completion of this most unpleasant and dangerous task. The level of danger can be gauged from the fact that about 720 mines had to be lifted in order to remove 69 bodies from the mined areas where the victims had fallen.

Within two months of the Horseshoe battle the campaign in North Africa had come to an end. It had lasted almost three years and had involved many Irish servicemen and a number of Irish chaplains. Most of the chaplains had served without gaining any special distinction, as was the case with the majority of chaplains throughout the war, but they had always been available to the soldiers to whom they ministered. The only Irish regiment to serve throughout the entire campaign was 9th (Londonderry) HAA Regiment, Royal Artillery* which had, as its chaplain, a Church of Ireland minister, the Revd Louis Crooks, of the diocese of Derry and Raphoe.

Louis Crooks earned the admiration and respect of all in the regiment, irrespective of denomination. When 9th Regiment was posted to Palestine for a short period in the summer of 1942 he organized trips to see many of the historic locations of the Holy Land and these were enjoyed by Protestant and Catholic soldier alike. (He also helped to organize audiences with Pope Pius XII in Rome in 1944.) On one memorable occasion, early in the regiment's time in Egypt, Louis Crooks organized a church service to be held in the canteen tent. He was dismayed, on arriving to prepare for the service, that no-one was present and he went out to order any soldier whom he saw to go at once to the canteen for the service. One of those who found himself in the tent was Paddy Moynihan, a Cork Catholic and a former seminarian. Spotting Moynihan, another soldier asked him why he was in the canteen as Catholics did not have to attend Anglican services. Moynihan's reply was that 'in the Army you always obey the last order, but I'll complain later'. Needless to say, no complaint was ever made.

Louis Crooks continued to serve as 9th Regiment's chaplain throughout the Italian campaign and until the war ended in 1945. When the regiment arrived in Egypt in November 1939, its first home was the tented camp at Sidi Bishr on the eastern outskirts of Alexandria, an unprepossessing location. One day a group of soldiers were sitting in their tent when a padre appeared and asked where he might find the chaplain. The newcomer was a Catholic padre, Father McBrearty from Sligo, who was to minister to the regiment's Catholics. He had sought directions from a quartet of Protestant soldiers, two of whom were from Donegal and who recognized his accent immediately. One of those gunners, George Lapsley, volunteered to take Father McBrearty to his destination but asked that, whenever he would visit Sidi Bishr again, he should also call on the men he had first met. From then on Father McBrearty never failed to visit his Protestant friends.

Among other Church of Ireland ministers who served as chaplains in North Africa were Cuthbert Peacocke, from Down but later to be Louis Crooks' bishop in Derry and Raphoe; Godfrey MacManaway, also from the Derry diocese; and Arthur Butler, from Connor, who later also became a bishop. The latter had a memorable experience

---

* 8th King's Royal Irish Hussars also served in North Africa but was withdrawn soon after the battle of El Alamein and sent to Cyprus.

when serving as Senior Chaplain with 1st Division in Tunisia after the North African campaign had ended. The commander of 1st Division was an Irishman, Gerald Templer, who decided that the Allied victory should be marked with a divisional service of thanksgiving. Rather than leave the planning of the service to his Senior Chaplain, Templer sent for Butler to discuss all the details. This was not a problem until it came to the choice of the final hymn, for which Templer wanted 'Be Thou My Vision', also known as the 'Hymn of the Irish Church'.

Butler pointed out to the general that the hymn was not to be found in English hymnals, it certainly was not in the small Army hymnals and it was doubtful if any of the bands had the music. Templer's reaction to the latter comment was to tell Butler to 'get it'. The chaplain thought that there was one very musical chaplain who might know the music and could possibly write it out from memory but the man was some 200 miles away. That did not deter Templer who told Butler to set off immediately and obtain the music of the hymn. Fortunately, the chaplain did know the music and could write it down and so Arthur Butler was able to return to Templer with it. The thanksgiving service for 1st Division went ahead with 'Be Thou My Vision' as its final hymn. Arthur Butler's 400 miles round trip must have been one of the more unusual tasks carried out by an Irish chaplain in the course of the war.

The Presbyterian Church was also represented in North Africa. David Henderson, a member of the congregation of First Derry Presbyterian Church, who had enlisted in 1937, was posted to North Africa where he became a chaplain to the famous 7th Armoured Division, the Desert Rats. On 25 April 1941 he was called to attend to wounded soldiers of 25 Heavy Anti-Aircraft Battery, detached from 9th (London-derry) HAA Regiment, who had been injured when a Heinkel He111 bombed their gun-site at Mersa Matruh. Tommy Porter, from St Johnston in County Donegal, had been driving into the site when the raider appeared and he sustained severe abdomi-nal injuries. Padre Henderson was at Tommy Porter's side when he died in the MDS eight hours later and subsequently conducted the burial service. The 'Derry Boys' of 25 Battery found it a consolation that a native of their own city laid to rest the Battery's first fatal casualty of the desert war.

David Henderson was later to witness a fellow chaplain, and personal friend, die in similar circumstances. On 23 June 1941 the Revd E.J. Dodge, another of 7th Armoured's padres, was killed by an exploding bomb in the Western Desert, just as he was preparing to return to the Nile delta for a much-needed rest. This was to become David Henderson's most vivid memory of the war. After the war he remained in the Royal Army Chaplains' Department and rose to become the Army's Deputy Chaplain General.

The Allied forces involved in the North African campaign later saw action in Italy where, once again, Irish chaplains showed outstanding devotion to duty. Father Dan Kelleher's story has been told earlier in this chapter but before Father Dan joined the Irish Brigade in Italy another Irish Catholic chaplain won the Military Cross with 2nd Royal Scots Fusiliers at Minturno. Limerick-born Father Patrick Bluett was a priest of the diocese of Middlesbrough and, on 24 November 1943, he was visiting his charges in the area of Alfedena. He met Corporal Vincent Vokes, an Intelligence Corps NCO attached to the Scots Fusiliers and a Catholic, who was on observation post duty and trying to locate a German self-propelled gun that had been harassing the battalion area. The priest asked Vokes if he could have a look through the binoculars with which the latter was studying the surrounding area. After a while Father Bluett observed that there was an Italian flag being flown back to front in a house on ground below them.

Handing the glasses back to Corporal Vokes, Father Bluett indicated the house with the flag and the NCO trained his glasses on it. He was then able to identify the muzzle of an 88mm gun; the house was concealing a Tiger tank and the flag had been an attempt to camouflage the muzzle brake as it protruded from the building. The priest's realization that the flag was the wrong way round had foiled the Germans' deception measure. As he radioed back the co-ordinates of the tank, Corporal Vokes advised Father Bluett to leave the area as 'there's going to be killing here'. In fact, the priest had, unintentionally, exceeded the chaplain's brief not to become involved in combat.

As he left the observation post area, Father Bluett learned that the battalion's forward company, based in Alfadena, had been cut off and had suffered casualties who could not be evacuated until dark because the open ground around the position was being swept by enemy fire. Father Bluett resolved to go forward to give what assistance he could and set off in his vehicle for Alfadena.

> The way to the company was down a forward slope across the open; after he had gone a short distance the enemy shelled and machine-gunned his route. Undeterred by enemy fire, he made his way to the company and administered to the casualties such comfort as he was able and then returned over the same route in daylight. His action and disregard of danger had a most invigorating effect on the company and greatly assisted in sustaining its high morale during the period for which it was isolated.

The Methodist Church is the smallest of the four major denominations in Ireland but it also made its contribution to military chaplaincy. Fred Rea had gone to Rhodesia as a missionary before the war and became a chaplain to the forces in mid-1941. Eventually he served with 6th South African Armoured Division in the Italian campaign where he was attached to the Engineers and Signals Corps. The Division arrived in Italy in April 1944, after a year's training and preparation in Egypt. After the liberation of Rome it took part in Eighth Army's advance in the Tiber valley and was subsequently transferred to Fifth Army, the American element of 15 Army Group, also known for a time as Allied Armies Italy.

> Crossing the Arno, the men had their first baptism of fire. Fred speaks of the accuracy of the enemy shelling. 'A dozen shells fell all around us. We dropped flat, another lad and I, side by side. Suddenly he cried out, 'I've had it!' He had

been shot through the lungs. A Cape Coloured stretcher bearer was killed, another had his leg blown off and a third was wounded in the mouth. In another encounter one man got a direct hit, only his belt and revolver were found. His companion had his legs blown off and was blinded.'

Such were the worst experiences of a front-line padre. In the fabric of his life, such periods of absolute horror were interwoven with the everyday and the almost banal. Fred Rea also ministered to civilians and spent much time with the Division's wounded in hospitals as well as working on educational programmes. He found soldiers asking him if their own appointments with death had been fixed by God, a question with which most padres were familiar, and he responded by telling them that 'the final choice is God's, but he does not make the choice by an arbitrary decree ordained from birth'. For those who had kept that final appointment, he wrote letters to their families, and sometimes received printed memorial leaflets in return.

That final year of war in Italy was one of great frustration as the chances of victory in 1944 slipped away. The winter months were spent in cold and wet conditions with the constant danger of death from an ever-active foe. It was difficult to sustain morale and the role of the chaplains assumed extra importance. Then, in the final days of the war, the Division was on the move again, in the last great Allied offensive in Italy. Moving off in mid-April, 6th South African Armoured advanced quickly and, in seventeen days of small-scale fights and ambushes, lost 106 men killed and 500 wounded. Fred Rea and George Daneel, another chaplain, held a thanksgiving service at Monza; the occasion was tinged with sadness for the memory was ever present of the 500 men of the Division who had died and the more than 2,000 who had been wounded.

Fred Rea's painstaking work was rewarded with the award of the MBE 'for inspiring devotion to duty, outstanding courage beyond the call of duty, and for his consistently magnificent example in disregard for personal safety.'

While Army padres could share the dangers of the front-line soldier and their naval colleagues also had the opportunity to sail with those to whom they ministered, the Royal Air Force's chaplains were confined to serving on the ground. All that is except one chaplain who decided that he could only come to a true understanding of what the aircrew in his pastoral care were enduring if he shared their experience. And so Father W. Pollock came to take part in a bombing raid on the heavily-defended German industrial city of Essen.

Some years after the war, using the pseudonym Hamilton-Pollock, Father Pollock wrote of his experience in a heavy bomber over the Ruhr. The priest had spent many sleepless nights as he struggled with his conscience over the question of insinuating himself into the crew of an operational bomber. Chaplains were not allowed to fly on operations but that did not allow the Irishman to square his conscience. In the end it was the taunting of a fellow-Irishman, a lapsed Catholic whom he called O'Reilly in his book, which made his mind up.

After one debriefing O'Reilly approached the priest and suggested that he might like to come on an operation some night.

> The question really went home. The fact that he had never accompanied the men on a bombing raid had been worrying the chaplain. True he could hide behind his Roman collar and chaplain's badge and say that he was not allowed to go. Chaplains were not supposed to fly on operations, and if they were captured by the enemy they would lose their Red Cross privileges ... What must those lads think, coming back night after night, after such ordeals, to find the chaplain sitting comfortably in the operations room? 'Oh, we are all right, fellows! The padre will wave us good-bye and greet us when we come back – yeah, but you won't find him coming.'

The mission on which Father Pollock planned to go was cancelled and so he found himself in O'Reilly's plane bound for Essen a day later than he had at first intended. Since taking the priest on board an operational aircraft was against the rules, Father Pollock thought that the pilot most likely to co-operate with him was O'Reilly himself, as the Irishman was inclined to flout the rules. Thus it was that, following a visit to a local parish priest to make his confession, Father Pollock borrowed some flying kit, removed his badges and boarded O'Reilly's bomber, C-Charlie.

As the bomber lifted off its English runway the priest looked for his little chapel and wondered if he would ever again set eyes on it. Then he turned his attention to the crew and especially the pilot whom he found to have a different character when at the controls of his aircraft. O'Reilly was serious in his airborne role as captain of the bomber and the responsibility of command seemed to rest easily on his shoulders. Pollock was also able to see how each crew member fitted into a professional team, each individual concentrating on his particular task so that, save for the roar of the plane's four engines, there was little to hear.

The flight to the target took several hours, which gave the priest more than enough time to appreciate that special brand of anxiety experienced by bomber crews. He was reminded of the visions of hell described in Butler's *Lives of the Saints* as he gazed down on the target area.

> This was no vision, this was a bird's eye view of hell let loose. There were the flares dropped by the path-finders, the flak that was coming up from down below, and right there in front hundreds of search-lights converging together like illuminated sticks on a witch's broom. Those search-lights are trouble. 'Father,' consoled the renegade O'Reilly, 'if you are picked up in one of those you've had it.'

O'Reilly had scarcely uttered the words when the aircraft shuddered as it was caught in the blast of an explosion. The blast was the destruction of another bomber that had blown up as it was hit by a flak shell. By then C-Charlie was making its final run in to the target and the bomb-aimer was directing its approach. As he uttered the words 'bombs away',

> C for Charlie shot up into the skies as if the weight of the bombs had been holding it down ... 'Now for home,' said O'Reilly, dodging in and out of searchlight beams, 'and look out for enemy fighters on the way back.'

As soon as C-Charlie touched down Father Pollock went to his chapel to offer a prayer of thanksgiving for his safe return. He then went to the crew debriefing, where he mentally contradicted O'Reilly's assertion that the mission had been 'a piece of cake'. The Irish pilot was subsequently reprimanded for allowing the chaplain to fly with C-Charlie's crew that night while the Commanding Officer approached the priest and told him that he had been wrong to go on the mission:

> 'If anything had happened to you we would all be in trouble.' Then with a grin he put out his hand to shake, and in a quiet voice said: 'Off the record, Father, I'm glad you went. The boys will appreciate it.' When the de-briefing was over, Father Hamilton went to his chapel to celebrate Mass ... It was a Mass of thanksgiving. He put in an intention at the 'Commemoration of the Dead' for the crews of five planes that had not returned and for all the German people of Essen who had died that night.

Samuel Eaton, who had volunteered for service with the RAChD in 1939 was called up for service with the RAF in 1941 and, after some training, was posted to RAF Halton where he found that there was also an Irish Catholic chaplain. From Halton, the Revd Eaton went to North Africa and then to Italy.

> After the liberation of Rome I was posted there [and] discovered that there was a Presbyterian church in Rome at the time; it was actually a Church of Scotland church. I got in touch and a small canteen was opened there and a lot of my boys in the RAF came there; you were able to get lovely homemade buns. The pastor came to meet this Irishman he had heard about. That was me and he invited me to meet his family which I did. When I arrived the first thing he did was show me a photograph album and the first picture was of Assemblies' College in Belfast with Professor Paul and himself in it.
>
> I asked Pastor [name forgotten] if it would be possible to meet the Pope and he said that it should be. He arranged an audience and a lot of my boys wanted to go with me but I was only allowed to have four accompany me. So I met Pope Pius XII and he spoke in several languages. I will never forget how he finished: 'God bless England, God bless her king, and God bless you'.

From Italy, Samuel Eaton was posted back to North Africa. Shortly before the war in Europe ended he was sent to India where he worked at a number of air bases. The war ended with the atomic bombing of Hiroshima and Nagasaki in August and Sam Eaton found himself selected for a posting to Japan. He did not want to go there and was pleased when his congregation's second request for his return was accepted by the Air Ministry two days before he was to leave for Japan. Instead he was able to board a ship that would take him home.

For most chaplains to the Royal Air Force the war passed with much less excitement than that experienced by their counterparts in the Army. However, there were many occasions on which they were called out to crashed aircraft and to minister to badly-injured airmen in hospitals and thus it would be both inaccurate and unfair to imply that their war was any easier than that of an Army chaplain. They also had the task of burying dead airmen and of informing next-of-kin of the death of a loved one. Samuel Eaton did this on many occasions:

> one of my tasks was to bury dead airmen. Whenever I performed a burial an official photographer was always present and he took pictures of the service. Afterwards it was my duty to write to the deceased's family and enclose a photograph of the service. Some of them wrote back to thank me.

Such a simple act of Christian charity sums up the role of the chaplain, whether he served on land, at sea or in the air. The chaplain brought comfort, a listening ear, a friendly word and smile to the fighting man. He was the link with the better side of human nature and a reminder of the promise held out in the Christian faith that was shared by all those Irish fighting men, for there were no non-believers in the front line. Perhaps the words of the Soldiers' Prayer are the best summary of the nature of the chaplain's work.

> Heavenly Father, by whose grace Thy servants are enabled to fight the good fight of faith and ever prove victorious ... Help us to think wisely, to speak rightly, to resolve bravely, to act kindly and to live purely. Bless us in body and in soul and make us a blessing to our comrades ... Let the assurance of Thy Presence save us from sinning, strengthen us in life and comfort us in death.

~ 8 ~

Irish doctors at war

FAITHFUL IN ADVERSITY

The largest of the medical services of Britain's three armed forces, the Royal Army Medical Corps (RAMC), was formed in 1898 from the Medical Staff and the Medical Staff Corps. Medical services in the Army were organized on a private and regimental basis until the Crimean War, but the shock applied to the Army's administrative system by the Crimean experience led to the speedy development of a more regular system. The creation of the RAMC can be said to have been the culmination of that development. The Royal Navy also developed a medical system which took account of its needs as a seaborne service, while the newly-formed Royal Air Force soon created its own Medical Branch.

Seventeen members of the Royal Army Medical Corps have won the Victoria Cross – although four of those awards were actually gained before the creation of the corps – with eight of the VCs being awarded in the Great War. By contrast, only one VC was awarded to the corps during the Second World War although, as we shall see, there ought to have been at least one other.*

On the outbreak of war in September 1939 there was already a considerable number of Irish doctors serving in the RAMC, some of whom had achieved high rank. (An Irishman, W.P. MacArthur, became Director General of Army Medical Services.) Others were serving as Medical Officers (MOs) to infantry battalions, armoured regiments and artillery regiments or on the staffs of field ambulances, which were battlefield hospitals, or general hospitals. The declaration of war helped many doctors decide that their duty lay in serving the Allied cause and so there was a rush of applications to join the RAMC. Among those who joined up at that stage were two men who would have distinguished careers as Army doctors: Desmond Whyte, a native of County Down, and Alfred Denis Parsons, from County Westmeath. Parsons was the first of the two to see action.

Parsons, better known as Andy, had qualified from Trinity College, Dublin, in 1937. He had worked at the Derbyshire Hospital for Women and in a hospital in the

---

* The award, which was posthumous, was made to Lance-Corporal Henry Eric Harden, a medical orderly, with 45 RM Commando for his actions in saving lives under fire on 23 January 1945.

Channel Islands before signing on as a ship's doctor in the Merchant Navy. In late 1939 he left the MV *Glenogle* on volunteering for military service with the outbreak of war. A spell with 14 General Hospital, a Territorial Army unit, gave him his first taste of life as an army doctor; he went to France with that unit to join the BEF. At the beginning of May 1940 Andy Parsons was transferred to 164 Field Ambulance in 13 Brigade of 5th Division. Destined to become the most widely travelled division in the British Army during the war, as a result of which it was dubbed the 'Cook's Tour Division', 5th Division was commanded by a Corkman, Major-General Harold Franklyn. As with all infantry divisions, there were three brigades, each of three battalions, as well as the various supporting elements such as artillery, engineers, signals and transport. The senior brigade of 5th Division was 13 Infantry Brigade which included 2nd Cameronians, 2nd Royal Inniskilling Fusiliers and 2nd Wiltshires, thus laying claim to being a Union brigade with one Scottish, one Irish and one English battalion. The fortunes of war would make Andy Parsons the MO of the Inniskillings on the retreat to Dunkirk.

Until the German attack on the Low Countries on 10 May 1940, life in 164 Field Ambulance was little different from that of peacetime, and the doctors were able to enjoy some social life, including eating well in local restaurants. The field ambulance had set up its Main Dressing Station, from the personnel of ambulance headquarters, and two Advanced Dressing Stations, one from each of the two companies. Fifth Division was not in the front line when the German strike occurred. A month earlier, when the Germans invaded Norway, 15 Brigade was detached from the division for service in that country and the remainder of the division was ordered to move south to the Arras area to become a War Office reserve. When Operation SICHELSCHNITT was launched, the BEF commander, General Lord Gort, VC, obtained the return to his command of 5th Division. However, it took the division four days to reach its assigned position along the river Dendre, its journey made doubly difficult by congestion caused by the numbers of refugees and troops on the roads. One of the enduring memories of the civilian refugees was the sight of mattresses strapped to the roofs of cars.

No sooner had 5th Division got into position than it was ordered to move forward to Hals on the river Senne where its task was to help cover I Corps' withdrawal from the line of the river Dyle. The BEF had left its prepared positions, the Gort Line, to move forward to bolster Belgian resistance, but the Belgian army was crumbling and in retreat. Nor was it taking time to demolish bridges over the river Maas (Meuse) and the Albert canal. A change of plan was called for and 5th Division was redeployed. On 17 May the Inniskillings made their first contact with the enemy; over the next twelve days there were many more contacts in a situation that was confusing not just to the ordinary soldier but also to his officers. Andy Parsons' field ambulance reached the little village of Petit Ennetières, near Seclin, on the evening of Sunday, 19 May, where Parsons was called upon to deliver a baby,

> in a little shop near the centre of the village. In the back room I found a
> woman lying on the bed, obviously in strong labour, a dirty-looking handy

woman, and a crowd of interested spectators. The baby was born almost at once without any necessity for advice or help from me.

The following day 164 Field Ambulance suffered its first fatal casualty. Tragically it was as a direct result of British action, the type of loss that has become known today as a 'friendly fire' incident. It happened soon after breakfast when,

> Basil, Toby and I were sitting sunning ourselves in a field by the roadside. Suddenly there was a terrific roar and three fighters with British markings flashed over the roof-tops with their machine-guns pouring out tracer bullets. We soon heard that they had riddled one of our ambulances and killed the driver. This was our first casualty … We tried to take the charitable view that they were captured aircraft flown by Germans.

It was on 29 May that Captain Andy Parsons had his first experience under fire with the Inniskillings, who had lost their Regimental Medical Officer. The Athlone man had been asked to take over that morning. By this stage 5th Division was engaged in a desperate rearguard action to allow II Corps to withdraw to Lille and thence to the river Lys, thus allowing the creation of a defensive perimeter to cover the evacuation of the BEF from Dunkirk.

Thoughts of strategy were far from Andy Parsons' mind as he set up a Regimental Aid Post (RAP) in a Belgian farmhouse near Hoogestadt that Wednesday evening. Hardly had the RAP been established than enemy shells fell on and around it; on entering it Parsons found two badly shocked soldiers, one of whom had part of a foot blown off and his blood was spreading over what had been a white floor. Neither man could speak coherently. But the scene outside the house was even more ghastly:

> I will never forget what I saw when I came out into the street. Seven or eight men were lying on the cobbles, one of them blown to pieces with his intestines hanging out on the ground, another with both legs blown off and a third with one leg amputated at the groin.
>
> I had a horrible impression of khaki and crimson against the grey background of the cobble stones, and all around were dead white faces and groans and helpless struggles. Over all was a foul stench of burnt flesh and powder.

That stench of burned flesh and cordite pervaded the air as Parsons struggled to do something to help the wounded. His medical supplies at that moment were a single dressing and a bottle of disinfectant, and he had no recourse other than to get the wounded onto a truck and drive at high speed for Hoogestadt with shells falling around the road. But, first, he had to perform an emergency operation:

The man who had lost his leg at the groin had the other one completely shattered below the knee and a compound fracture of his thigh. Thinking that the
leg was just hanging on by a small piece of flesh, I borrowed a clasp knife from
a fusilier and started to cut it off; but it appeared that there was more flesh
than I had thought. The man started to scream. I was glad when it was
finished, and I did not know whether I had done right or not, but it seemed
urgent to get away from this place as quickly as possible.

Several of the wounded were dead by the time the truck reached its destination.

After their rearguard action the Inniskillings finally reached Dunkirk on 31 May.
The battalion's strength had been reduced to 11 officers and 204 men from its original overall strength of more than 700 all ranks. Captain Andy Parsons reached the
beach in darkness and recorded how, every few minutes, an aircraft would swoop
along the beaches and machine-gun the men the pilot knew to be there in the darkness. Shells were also falling among those waiting for evacuation. The Inniskillings
moved to the mole, where soldiers were gathering to embark. Most waited stoically,
but some tried to push their way to the front of the queue, often taking advantage of
stretcher cases to do so: Parsons noted that some stretchers were carried by at least six
men with several more holding the wounded man's kit.

The MO's greatest fear was that the mole would be strafed by German fighters as
soon as daylight came, and that most of the troops waiting for ships would be killed
as there was no cover of any description. In the darkness there was still the shellfire to
endure but, in the course of a five-hour wait, only two shells struck the mole. After
one of those strikes, Parsons saw 13 Brigade's Methodist padre being stretchered past;
it was clear from the man's face that he was dying and the MO later heard that the
chaplain had expired.

Andy Parsons was eventually evacuated on the cross-channel steamer *The Maid of
Orleans*. There followed a period of service with the home forces with all the frustra-
tions of peacetime soldiering, including form-filling in the shape of regular returns. It
was not long before Andy Parsons applied for an overseas' posting, and this finally
came at the beginning of 1941. After a course in tropical medicine at Liverpool he
travelled north to the Clyde to board an aged vessel, the *Nea Hellas*, for the long voyage to Egypt, via South Africa.

For a time Andy Parsons served in Egypt and in Syria – in the campaign against
the Vichy French – in a field ambulance, but he now wanted to be a battalion medical
officer and was eventually posted to 2nd York and Lancaster Regiment, which was
destined for Tobruk. However, a severe case of jaundice put him in hospital and cost
him his posting to the York and Lancs. On his discharge from hospital, he was posted
to 63 General Hospital outside Cairo, where he was general duty officer on an
orthopaedic ward:

The chief recollection with which it has left me is the sight and sound of a large
number of maimed men in pain. There was the huge Australian with a leg

amputated above the knee, who wept every time his dressing was done until I started giving him an anaesthetic; there was the boy with the severed sciatic nerve who lay with his face buried in his pillow (I was to think of him often later on, and wonder what I could have done to ease his lot.) There was the nineteen-year old gunner ... who had an infected compound fracture of his thigh-bone; could he have been saved if his leg had been taken off earlier? I don't know, but I do know that the weeks of suffering that he went through could have been avoided by an amputation, as at the worst it would have hastened the end. There were men who had had their feet shattered by mines.

Hanging around a base hospital doing a job that he considered light work 'made me feel ashamed of my youth and physical fitness' and prompted Andy Parsons to go to Headquarters, Middle East in Cairo where he requested to be posted as a regimental medical officer. As a result he was posted to 1st Buffs, the motor battalion of 8 Armoured Brigade in 10th Armoured Division. He joined the battalion at No. 5 Camp, Khatatba on 19 March 1942, three days after it began to reform as a motor battalion. The Buffs were one of the Army's oldest regiments, the 3rd Foot in days gone by. Their title recalled that they had once been commanded by a Colonel Howard as had another regiment, later the 19th Foot; the pair were identified by the colour of their uniform facings – thus the Buff Howards and the Green Howards, with the senior regiment abbreviating its name to the Buffs. The regimental recruiting area was east Kent, and their full title was The Buffs (Royal East Kent Regiment). Even in that south-eastern corner of England, however, the regiment managed to include Irishmen in its ranks, and so Andy Parsons would not have been the sole son of Erin in the battalion which was training for its part in Eighth Army's offensive at El Alamein.

On 23 October 1942 the final battle of El Alamein began as General Montgomery's Eighth Army opened up its assault on the Italo-German Panzer Armee Afrika. Eighth Armoured Brigade had already seen action in the desert war, and Parsons' battalion had to undertake a strenuous training programme on joining it. During that period the battalion had been dive-bombed by German aircraft and three men had been killed with two others wounded; one of the dead had been a senior officer.

After the retreat to the Alamein line in early-July 8 Armoured Brigade, then part of XXX Corps, had seen action in the battle of Alam Halfa, in which an attempted advance by Field-Marshal Erwin Rommel's forces had been repulsed by Eighth Army. Thereafter, Montgomery's command prepared for its own offensive against the Axis army. On the night of 21 October the brigade moved up to its battle positions. Its task was to pass through three gaps in the minefields for which it deployed in three armoured regimental groups. Each group included a motor company of 1st Buffs and Andy Parsons was assigned to C Company with the Staffordshire Yeomanry Regimental Group. (The MOs of the brigade's Royal Horse Artillery and light anti-aircraft regiments were to accompany the other two groups.)

As part of 10th Armoured Division the battle plan envisaged the tanks of 8 Armoured Brigade penetrating gaps made by XXX Corps in the northern sector of the line and pushing through into the open desert to engage the enemy armour. At 10 p.m. on the night of 23 October, following a bombardment by over 800 guns, Eighth Army launched its attack. Two hours later 8 Armoured Brigade reached its start line in front of the Miteiriya ridge on an area of the front held by General Freyberg's 2nd New Zealand Division.

The New Zealanders' attack was successful; by dawn, the division had reached its objectives, with the exception of the left of their line where they were just short of the objective. There was, however, no possibility at that stage of the division exploiting further. The tanks of 10th Armoured Division were to pass through the New Zealanders but had to make and mark their own paths through the minefields. By 5.30 a.m. on 24 October the Staffordshire Yeomanry's tanks were reaching the crest of the Miteiriya ridge where they ran into an unexpected minefield and the attention of enemy anti-tank guns which prevented them from crossing that obstacle. Other regiments of the brigade found themselves blocked also and this had an effect on the units waiting to move up, resulting in congestion and considerable confusion.

Captain Andy Parsons' C Company had moved up behind the ridge. There he found that a number of New Zealand casualties had been lying for most of the night without medical help; many were severely wounded. Ignoring intense shell and mortar fire, Parsons

> collected about a dozen severely wounded men from an area exposed to direct small-arms fire in the middle of a minefield. He would not have failed in his duty had he devoted himself to casualties nearer to hand and less exposed to fire. Throughout the twelve days of the Alamein battle he repeatedly recovered wounded men from forward slopes under fire, who must otherwise have lost their lives.

Those twelve days left an abiding impression on the Athlone man. He recorded in his diary his thoughts and feelings on seeing the many burned-out armoured and soft-skinned vehicles that littered the battlefield. Among them were vehicles from the armoured regiments of 8 Armoured Brigade: the Staffordshire Yeomanry lost eleven tanks on their first day in battle and a further ten on 25 October; this from a regiment that had started the battle with a complement of 43 tanks. Other regiments had suffered as badly with the Notts Yeomanry losing ten tanks on the first day and suffering heavier casualties than the other regiments of the brigade. The anti-tank guns of 1st Buffs had also endured heavy casualties as they fought for two days and nights in 'an inferno of fire' as they strove to help their armoured comrades through the corridors in the minefields.

Throughout it all the MOs of the brigade excelled in their efforts to help the wounded. In spite of the 'disgusting mixture of sights and smells; twisted blackened metal and burned bodies with their characteristic yellowish look lying in grotesque attitudes among the wreckage or on the grey sands', the doctors tended the wounded. They were kept busy as the brigade had taken a severe battering in its first two days

in the battle and reinforcements of men and tanks on 26 and 27 October were subjected to dive-bombing attacks from German aircraft. On several occasions Andy Parsons
and his colleagues had narrow escapes from enemy shells or bombs. Then 1st Buffs
were pulled out of the front line to rest and re-organize for three days before being
deployed further to the north.

Captain Parsons took upon himself the task of searching for identity tags among
the dead. This was a task that was often stomach-churning, especially when the dead
were tank crews who, often, were either cooked in their vehicles or torn to pieces by
shell fragments ricocheting inside the tanks. He noted that 'the smell of burning
rubber and over-cooked flesh' dominated the scene:

> Burnt bodies are greasy and unpleasant to the touch. In most cases I had to
> turn them over to search in shirt pockets for paybooks and letters, which were
> often soaked in melted fat. Some of the men were wearing identity discs, but
> often the string which held the disc in position round the man's neck had been
> burnt and when two or three bodies were lying together there was no way of
> telling which body was which – not that it mattered; all I wanted to know was
> who was definitely dead. I found one disc by burrowing into the mixture of fat
> and sand on which the body was lying.

And there was a further hazard: some bodies had been booby-trapped by the
enemy; such incidents were more common as the Panzer Armee began to retreat. Ten
days into the battle Parsons came across the corpse of a soldier of a highland regiment;
an area around the Scot's body had been marked off with mine tape by the engineers
to indicate the danger of a possible booby trap. But he began to realize that the battle
was going in the favour of Eighth Army when he saw that the Germans were starting
to abandon their own dead on the battlefield; this was contrary to their normal practice – which was also the normal Allied practice – of burying the dead as soon as
possible. In Parsons' words it was 'a cheering sight to see the grey-clothed bodies just
lying there on the white sand'. While searching abandoned enemy positions for
anything that might prove useful, he and another officer, John Spence, came across one
body that was a 'peculiarly disgusting sight'. A German soldier lay 'with all the top of
his head blown off and his face surmounted by just the empty cranium. He was
swollen and yellow and crawling with flies.' Even worse was the sight, encountered
the following day, 5 November, of 'a dead German boy, naked from the waist down,
lying in a heap of excreta. He had been hit in the head, I suppose while he was relieving himself.'

The battle of El Alamein ended on 4 November when Rommel ordered his troops
to withdraw, abandoning several Italian infantry divisions as they did so. In the
pursuit that followed, 8 Armoured Brigade was probably Eighth Army's most successful formation. Now part of 1st Armoured Division – its original parent formation,
10th Armoured Division, had been withdrawn after El Alamein – the brigade reached
Mersa Matruh, 120 miles from Alamein, on 7 November, and 1st Buffs entered the

town that afternoon. The following day Allied troops landed in French north-west Africa in Operation TORCH; the Axis forces were now to be subjected to a pincer movement.

Eighth Army's advance into Libya was to take it to Tripoli, the last city of the Italian empire which fell to British troops on 23 January 1943. Just four days before that the Panzer Armee had fought a delaying action on the Homs-Tarhuna line, and 8 Armoured Brigade was in action before Tarhuna, with 1st Buffs attracting heavy enemy shellfire. Andy Parsons went forward to the area of heaviest shelling to see what he could do for casualties. He placed one badly-wounded soldier in a jeep and set off to drive the man to the RAP. En route he came across another shelling incident in which the commander of 7th Armoured Division, Major-General A.F. (John) Harding, had been seriously injured; one hand had been almost severed. As an ambulance was nearby, Parsons saw to it that the wounded soldier was placed safely on board for the remainder of his journey. Then, oblivious of the continuing fire, he went to tend to Harding, got some plasma and set up a drip. In his own account Parsons noted that sometimes 'I persuade myself that he would have died if he hadn't had blood plasma immediately he was hit'. Others were convinced that he had saved Harding's life: 'there is little doubt that his calm skill saved a valuable life'.

Three days later in the Tarhuna Pass, four men were killed by heavy mortar fire from close range. Others were injured and, after dressing their wounds, Andy Parsons crawled out on to a forward slope, in full view of the enemy mortarmen and under direct fire, to rescue a soldier still believed to be alive.

On 25 January, west of Zavia, Parsons again showed total disregard for his own safety as he worked with wounded while shells fell all around. Others took cover, but the calm Irishman's dedication to his task again saved several lives.

For his work over a period of almost eight months Captain Andy Parsons was awarded the Military Cross. The citation included the comment that:

> the personal bravery and determined initiative of this officer have been responsible for the saving of a great many lives. On every occasion he was to be found at the spot where casualties were most likely to occur, and it is due to his complete disregard of danger, the calm skill and speed of his work, and his devotion to duty under fire that so many men owe their lives...
>
> It is in fact not possible to speak too highly of the sustained and unselfish courage of this officer in saving life throughout eight months of nearly continuous periods of action.

Andy Parsons continued to serve throughout the remainder of the North African campaign, which came to an end in May 1943 when General Alexander signalled to Winston Churchill that his 18 Army Group were now 'masters of the North African shores'. The next objective for the Allied armies in the Mediterranean was the island of Sicily, conquered in a brief campaign that began on 10 July 1943. Then it was on to mainland Italy, where the first Allied troops went ashore on 3 September. Italy surrendered to the Allies but that did not end the war as German troops had moved into the peninsula and, on Hitler's orders, prepared defences north of Naples. So stubborn was that German defence in a land which, with its mountainous spine and many lateral river valleys, was ideally suited to defensive warfare that the decision was taken to land troops behind the enemy lines in an effort to create a pincer that would force the Germans out of their mountain positions and lead to the liberation of Rome. Thus was born Operation SHINGLE, launched on 22 January 1944 when British and American troops of Fifth Army's VI Corps landed unopposed at Anzio, some sixty miles behind the Gustav line and less than forty from the Italian capital.

But the aim of Operation SHINGLE was not achieved. Instead of moving quickly inland, General Lucas, commanding VI Corps, decided to wait and see, thus allowing German troops to be rushed to the area and ensure that the Allies did not advance inland. The soldiers of VI Corps were to remain in the confines of the Anzio bridgehead for four months, and it was there that the war ended for Andy Parsons. Still with 1st Buffs, but now in 18 Brigade, Parsons arrived at Anzio in late-February.

Once German forces established themselves around the perimeter of the Allied bridgehead they maintained a constant bombardment of shell- and mortarfire into the Allied positions and there were many casualties. Medical Officers were kept very busy but a convention developed that MOs of either side would treat wounded men. Furthermore, both sides respected the Red Cross and this allowed wounded to be collected and moved in daylight. It was during one such expedition to move a wounded man that Andy Parsons was himself wounded. On 15 April he was about to move Corporal Anderson, a signaller, from the RAP back to a dressing station. The wounded man was placed on a stretcher and

> Sergeant Davis took hold of one end of the stretcher and said to one of the stretcher-bearers, Private Worsfold, 'Come on, mate. Give us a hand', and they started off up on to the roadway preceded by another stretcher-bearer, Private Haggis, waving the Red Cross flag. They were up on the roadway when suddenly I thought that perhaps I should go up too, just to see that everything was all right. As I was getting near the top of the slope from the wadi to the roadway, I could see that Sergeant Davis and Worsfold had put the stretcher on to the jeep, and they were coming back towards me. Richardson was getting ready to drive off.
>
> Then everything went black for a fraction of a second. I felt an explosion taking place, it seemed to me, inside my thigh. I thought that I had got a direct hit with a two-inch mortar bomb. I was lying on the ground and I looked down towards the wadi and I could see on the slope just five yards below me a crater, which I think from its size must have been made by a 105 mm shell.

Andy Parsons had been struck in the right thigh by a splinter from the shell that tore open the thigh along its entire length and damaged his sciatic nerve. His injuries were such that he was evacuated from Anzio and then, after hospital treatment, was sent back to the United Kingdom. His active war had ended, although the scars of that war would remain with him for the rest of his days.

While Andy Parsons was suffering the rigours of life in the Anzio beachhead, another Irish doctor of the Royal Army Medical Corps was preparing for one of the most difficult and memorable operations of the war. Desmond Whyte was serving with 3rd Indian Division in India, but the title of that formation was intended to hide its real role: in reality this was Special Force, the long-range penetration troops under the command of Major-General Orde Wingate. Special Force, which included six brigades, is better known as the Chindits, from the divisional badge of a Chinthe, that mythical beast, part-lion, part-dragon, which stands as guardian to the entrance of every Burmese temple.

Born on 20 September 1914, Desmond Whyte was the son of a Dublin woman, whose brother had served in the RAMC in the Great War in the early stages of which he had been wounded. At Queen's University, Belfast, where he studied medicine, Whyte had been a colour-sergeant in the Officers' Training Corps and so already had an inkling of what service life might be like. On the declaration of war, less than three weeks before his twenty-fifth birthday, he volunteered and was accepted for the RAMC. His first appointment was as MO to 9th Worcesters, the regiment in which his older brother Norman had been commissioned. After service in the UK he was posted for a short period to Palestine and then to India.

At that stage in the war there was no threat to India and life in the sub-continent was very much in the peacetime style although Desmond Whyte used some of his time to learn Urdu so that he could serve and work with Indian soldiers. Then, on 7 December 1941, the Japanese attacked the US Pacific Fleet base at Pearl Harbor in Hawaii and also launched an attack on Malaya,* then a British possession. The peacetime routine of India was shattered.

Japanese troops also landed in Thailand on 8 December and, at the end of the month, pushed into Burma. British forces in Burma were thinly spread and too few to stop the invaders; they were also unprepared for jungle warfare as the pre-war military wisdom had ruled out fighting in the jungle. In this respect the Japanese provided an eye-opener and an object lesson which the British were to learn well:

> We underestimated the Japanese. It had been believed that the Japs' eyesight was bad, the entire race that is, and that they would not be good at fighting, or at flying aeroplanes. We were stunned by the news of the Jap attack on Pearl Harbor.

Desmond Whyte was working in Calcutta when the Japanese made their first incursion into Burma. Early in 1942, as the enemy 'were marching right up through

---

* The attack on Malaya occurred at much the same time as the Pearl Harbor raid although the intervention of the international date line between Hawaii and Malaya means that the records show that Malaya was attacked on 8 December 1941.

Burma' he was approached to become MO to the TMB Legion, an Indian unit with European officers. His proficiency in Urdu was obviously a factor in his being offered this posting. By 20 May the British, Indian, Burmese and Gurkha troops had completed the 900-mile retreat to India at a cost of over 13,000 dead (against Japanese losses of some 4,500 dead), and but for a thin stretch of the border area between India and Burma the Japanese held all of the latter country. The arrival of the monsoon in May made things difficult for both attackers and defenders as well as disrupting the organisation and training of Desmond Whyte's new unit. However, when the weather settled down that training resumed, including jungle warfare, and

> in late 1942 we moved down south away from Tripura. We marched light, all equipment had to be man-carried and so we were lightly armed. There was no transport. We went down river in the direction of Chittagong, but not as far south. We had virtually no air support.
>
> We engaged the enemy and besieged them and ultimately drove them off. This was the first victory for the Allies in that area. The Japs escaped, they slipped away with their wounded at 3 o'clock in the morning, a defeated force, never to return.
>
> This was an important little action. We learned a lot of lessons.

The attacking force had found problems with its wireless equipment and communications were very poor but much of this was due to weather and atmospheric conditions. Casualty evacuation had been another problem with no means of rapidly evacuating wounded from the fighting area. A detachment of the Baluch Regiment had taken out the wounded. Many soldiers had suffered from malaria, the victims of which included Desmond Whyte. His work with the Legion had also earned him a Mention in Despatches.

There followed a period of treatment for the malaria and recuperation, during which he heard about the formation of a special force:

> This was a 'secret' organisation. I presented myself, volunteered for this, and was accepted. Then I met this small individual, a very strong personality and [with] deep convictions such that he invariably ended any speeches with a biblical quotation. He was sincere.

This was Orde Wingate, who had developed the concept of long-range penetration behind the enemy lines in Burma and had, by this time, carried out the first Chindit expedition – Operation LONGCLOTH – during which the Chindits had marched about 1,500 miles and caused serious damage and disruption to Japanese transport and facilities. Although many in the military hierarchy were opposed strenuously to his concept of long range penetration, Wingate had some very enthusiastic supporters, including Winston Churchill, in whose eyes the Chindit leader was 'a man of genius and audacity', as well as the American generals George Marshall, the US Army's Chief of Staff, and Hap Arnold, the US air supremo: the latter pair saw Wingate as one of the few British generals prepared to take on the Japanese. While LONGCLOTH had inflicted casualties and damage on the Japanese it had also proved that British troops could fight in the jungle, as a result of which it simultaneously raised morale among British troops while depressing Japanese morale.

In the wake of LONGCLOTH Churchill took Wingate with him to the QUADRANT conference in Quebec where the support of the Allied Combined Chiefs of Staff for a further, but more ambitious, Chindit campaign was obtained. In the paper he presented to the Combined Chiefs and to Churchill and President Roosevelt, Wingate accurately predicted the strategy that the Japanese would adopt in 1944 and how Chindit operations could affect that strategy. The Chiefs of Staff decided that six brigades would be allotted to Wingate's scheme.

The creation of Wingate's force for 1944 meant the breaking up of the British 70th Division, previously 6th Division, which had been transferred from North Africa. Wingate's new force, codenamed 3rd Indian Division or Special Force, was formed on his return to India from Quebec. The Chindits were to have the support of the American No. 1 Air Commando, which meant that they could be flown in for their next operation in Burma. The Air Commando included 100 WACO CG-4A gliders; a similar number of light aircraft, made up of Stinson L-1s and L-5s; 20 Douglas C-47 Dakota transports; 12 UC-64 Norseman utility transport aircraft; 20 B-25 Mitchell bombers, 30 P-51 Mustang fighters; and six Sikorsky helicopters, the Allies' first combat deployment of rotary-winged aircraft.

The training programme for the soldiers of Special Force began in earnest in the late summer of 1943. Training took place in central India and was tough and vigorous, with airdrops, river crossings – in daylight and in darkness – and punishing marches through jungle while carrying heavy packs. Those who were unfit were weeded out, and there were some fatal casualties, including the drowning of a number of soldiers in the Gangan reservoir. Once behind the enemy lines the basic operating unit of the Chindits would be the Column; each battalion provided two numbered columns.* The final training exercise was organized in December. By now Desmond Whyte had been appointed as the Senior Medical Officer, with the rank of major, to 111 Brigade which was to be commanded by a fellow-Irishman, Brigadier W.D.A. Lentaigne, DSO, better known as Joe to his fellow officers.

Desmond Whyte had learned much from his previous experience behind enemy lines, and he was re-assured that casualties would be airlifted out by the L-1s and L-5s. The Chindits were to operate from 'Strongholds' in the jungle which were to provide the hub of operations and within which were to be airstrips capable of operating light aircraft, although C-47s might also take off and land from these. Speedy attention in a hospital with good facilities would therefore be available for the wound-

---

* The numbering of columns usually had some relevance to the battalions which provided them: 45th Reconnaissance Regiment was divided into 45 and 54 Columns; 4/9th Gurkhas into 49 and 94 Columns and 3/4th Gurkhas into 30 and 40 Columns; 1st Cameronians provided 26 and 90 Columns, the Cameronians having been the 26th and 90th Regiments of Foot.

ed and for those who suffered from serious illnesses, such as peritonitis. During operations in the jungle the Chindits would be supplied by airdrops every five days. They would live on American K-rations, which were thought to be excellent, while equipment and supplies would be carried by mules and ponies. The animals had been muted by having their vocal chords removed so that they would make no sounds to alert the Japanese. However, the ponies died 'one by one, they couldn't stand it, but the old mules were wonderful, they were very tough'.

The SEXTANT Conference in Cairo in November 1943 agreed that Wingate's 1944 Chindit campaign, codenamed Operation THURSDAY, would go ahead, and on 18 January 1944 the final details of the operation were agreed. With the exception of 16 Brigade, the Chindits – 9,000 men in all, with 1,100 animals – would fly in to small jungle clearings by glider after a night-time flight over 7,000-foot high mountains. It was to be a spectacular plan, fraught with difficulties and danger, but the soldiers of Special Force were inspired by Wingate's dynamism and determined to take the fight to the Japanese.

Late in January 111 Brigade moved into Assam and waited through the following month near Imphal while staff officers studied maps and intelligence reports and 16 Brigade began its march in to Burma. It was then that the brigade learned of Wingate's plan to fly them in to their jungle destination and fresh plans had to be made for the movement by air. On 6 March 111 Brigade began to fly out from Tulihal and to the clearing codenamed Chowringhee, after Calcutta's main street. This was a last-minute change of plan as it had been intended to fly Lentaigne's brigade in to the Piccadilly clearing, but it was believed that the Japanese knew of this plan as aerial reconnaissance photographs showed the landing area to be obstructed by teak logs. (There was a simple explanation: the logs had been dragged there to dry out by Burmese foresters in the normal course of their work.) The brigade move was complete by 8 March without any serious Japanese reaction. From Chowringhee, 111 Brigade was to destroy the railway south of Indaw to prevent enemy reinforcements reaching that town; an element of the brigade under Lieutenant-Colonel Jumbo Morris, drawn from 4/9th Gurkhas and known as Morrisforce, was detached to move eastwards to the Bhamo road. At the same time, two other battalions of the brigade, 2nd King's Own Royal Regiment and 1st Cameronians, were diverted to Broadway where the fly-in was smooth and successful. This left Lentaigne with 111 Brigade Headquarters and 3/4th Gurkhas. The reduced formation was to cross the Irrawaddy and rendezvous with the King's Own and Cameronians on 24 March. At this stage 111 Brigade's plans began to go awry.

When the force reached the Irrawaddy, the Air Commando flew in gliders with rubber boats and outboard motors to facilitate the river crossing. However, the mules refused to swim the river and hours of coaxing only succeeded in getting a small number of the beasts to make the crossing. Lentaigne therefore decided that 40 Column, part of 3/4th Gurkhas, would not cross at all but would march eastward to rendezvous with Morrisforce while Brigade HQ and the remainder of 3/4th Gurkhas – 30 Column – completed the crossing and met up with the other two battalions. As if that were not bad enough the next airdrop to Brigade HQ and 30 Column went badly wrong and it took most of a day to collect the supplies after which the soldiers were completely exhausted.

There had, however, been one aspect of the operations that proved successful, and a morale-booster. When the brigade reached the Irrawaddy and the gliders came in, it was decided to evacuate two sick Gurkhas by air. This was done by snatching the glider into the air, a technique developed by the Americans:

> ... once the glider landed ... in the ordinary course of events it was written off. But our American friends had worked out a plan some time before the invasion into Burma whereby it was possible to attach a loop to the front of the glider. That loop was hung on two poles that were fifteen-feet high, each with a little bulb at the top that they would light at night; by day they didn't need them [There was a third bulb on the actual glider.] You now had two poles sticking up with a light on top of either, and the loop was hung across the top of that – the bottom part of course being attached to the glider. And the specially-equipped Dakota had a great hook sticking out from the back with a very strong spring drum. And, I actually watched this, we'd load our wounded in, the plane would come down, make two or three false runs and then, to your great relief, the glider would be suddenly hooked, rather like a salmon in a way, and it would go off.

The pair of Gurkhas who were evacuated in this way from the east bank of the mighty Irrawaddy were not seriously ill; but Lentaigne had decided to use this novel method of casualty evacuation as a demonstration of how quickly sick and wounded could be removed from the fighting zone. It went some way to easing Desmond Whyte's concerns about this subject, based on his previous experience. So, also, did the use of the Stinson light aircraft which could land on very short strips of ground to take out one or two casualties.

In spite of that demonstration of efficiency, 111 Brigade failed to show any efficiency in the execution of its intended operations. Wingate's original plan anticipated Lentaigne's brigade taking Indaw which would then become a stronghold garrisoned against Japanese attacks. The brigade ought to have demolished the main railway line south of Indaw to prevent the enemy using it to move reinforcements up to the town. Instead a track which appeared to be derelict was blown up.

As the brigade continued its weary march to meet up with the King's Own and the Cameronians, it became clear to some of the officers that Lentaigne was suffering from strain. He, and most of his command, were also suffering from the shortage of adequate food.

> We were living on five-day drops but we were always on short rations. Sometimes the enemy drove us off, sometimes the rations didn't arrive. We were burning up eight thousand calories a day but the ration was much less than this [and] so we were burning up our own fat from early on.

1 (**Clockwise from top right**) Tony Tottenham DFC, Royal Air Force, shot down and killed two weeks after his twenty-first birthday. 2 Veronica Tottenham with her two eldest daughters, Joan and Barbara, all of whom joined the Women's Auxiliary Air Force. 3 Major Harold Tottenham, who rejoined the Army on the outbreak of war by falsifying his age. He was taken prisoner at the fall of Singapore and met his son Nicholas, a soldier in the Australian forces, in the prison camp. Major Tottenham survived the war, as did Nick. 4 Joan and Tony Tottenham.

Top right: 5 Corporal Jimmy Barnes, 2nd London Irish Rifles, who was recommended for a posthumous Victoria Cross for knocking out an anti-tank gun during the battle of Cassino. The VC was not awarded. **Bottom right: 6** Second-Lieutenant Reginald Bryan Woods, Royal Ulster Rifles, from Malahide. He quit his studies at Cambridge to join his older brother's regiment and was mortally wounded at Arnhem in 1944 while commanding the mortar platoon of 2nd Parachute Battalion.

Bottom left: 7 Father Dan. Reverend Daniel Kelleher MC, Catholic chaplain to the Irish Brigade. He was decorated for his courage in rescuing wounded under heavy shell- and mortar-fire at Monte Cassino. His brother, Father Jeremiah, a Columban missionary in Burma, attached himself to 1st Royal Inniskilling Fusiliers as their chaplain. **Top left: 8** Captain Niall Hogan, Royal Army Medical Corps. A capable and effective medical officer, he was recommended for a Mention in Despatches, which was rejected because his CO regarded him as an irreverent individual.

9 (above): The torpedomen from HMS *Jamaica* who sank *Scharnhorst* at the battle of North Cape on 26 December 1943. On the right is Petty Officer J.O. Mahony, from Midleton, Co. Cork. *Jamaica*'s Torpedo Officer was another Cork man, Lieutenant-Commander Paul Chavasse, DSC, from Castletownshend. 10 (below): Lieutenant-Commander Eugene Esmonde VC, DSO, who led No. 825 Naval Air Squadron against the German ships *Scharnhorst*, *Gneisenau* and *Prinz Eugen* in the Channel Dash of February 1942.

11 (above): Lancaster L-Love of No. 630 Squadron is 'bombed up' for a raid. Sean Drumm is seated third from left.   12 (below): Second-Lieutenant John Duane, 2nd Royal Inniskilling Fusiliers, (centre) on his first day with his new battalion near Dungannon, Co. Tyrone.

13 (above): A Medical Officer gives a drink to a wounded soldier at an Advanced Dressing Station during the battle of El Alamein. 14 (below left): Lieutenant-Colonel Desmond Whyte DSO, who was recommended for the VC for his outstanding gallantry with 111 (Chindit) Brigade during the siege of the Blackpool block in 1944. The then Major Whyte was awarded the DSO instead. 15 (below right): Captain Andy Parsons MC, who saw active service in France, North Africa and Italy before being wounded at Anzio and invalided home. His MC was awarded for a series of incidents from El Alamein onwards and the citation was one of the longest of the war.

16 (above): Flight Lieutenant Brendan Finucane DFC** at the controls of his Spitfire, days before his twenty-first birthday. At the time the photograph was taken, Brendan Finucane had already scored 24 victories. 17 (below): Wing Commander Victor Francis Beamish DSO, AFC on right of photograph.

18 (above): Hurricane fighters of RAF Fighter Command take off during the battle of Britain. Victor Beamish flew a Hurricane at this time. 19 (below): Sergeant J.B. Currie, of No. 77 Squadron, pictured beside the 'tally' on his Whitley bomber of 29 bombs and a swastika. The bombs represent raids and the swastika the shooting-down of an enemy aircraft, which was carried out by Currie, an air gunner. Sergeant Currie came from Ireland.

20 (above): HMS *Jamaica* in heavy seas in late 1943 while on Russian convoy escort duties. Paul Chavasse was the Torpedo Officer on board *Jamaica* and fired the torpedoes that sank *Scharnhorst*. 21 (below): An X-craft or midget submarine. It was in a similar vessel that James Magennis won his Victoria Cross in the Johore strait, off Singapore, in July 1945.

22 (above): HMS *Ark Royal* lists to starboard after being struck by a torpedo in the Mediterranean in November 1941. Eugene Esmonde was one of the last to leave the stricken carrier. **23 (right):** James Magennis VC, who planted mines on the hull of the Japanese cruiser *Takao* in the Johore strait in July 1945. His VC was the penultimate of the war and the last Irish VC to be won. He was the only person from Northern Ireland to be awarded the VC during the Second World War.

24 HMS *Formidable* minutes after being struck by a Japanese kamikaze bomber in May 1945. The carrier was back in operation within hours.

25 Soldiers of 6th Royal Inniskilling Fusiliers advance near Catenanuova in Sicily in July 1943. The battalion was part of the Irish Brigade in 78th (Battleaxe) Division.

26 Soldiers of 2nd London Irish Rifles, supported by a Sherman tank of 16th/5th Lancers and a 17-pounder anti-tank gun, during the battle of Cassino.

27 (above): Officers and men of 56th Reconnaissance Regiment who were decorated for gallantry in the Tunisian campaign. Fourth from left is the commanding officer, Lieutenant-Colonel Kendal Chavasse, who was awarded the DSO. Colonel Chavasse was a native of Castletownshend, Co. Cork. He earned a Bar to his DSO at Termoli in Italy in October 1943, the only DSO and Bar to be awarded to the Reconnaissance Corps. 28 (below): Major John Duane MC, 2nd Royal Inniskilling Fusiliers, who was awarded the MC for his outstanding leadership of the battalion's battle patrol in Italy. Major Duane was a native of Co. Galway.

Clockwise from top: 29 Third Officer
Elizabeth Beresford-Jones (*née*
Chamberlain), Women's Royal Naval
Service. **30** Brenda Graham in Red Cross
uniform in Italy. An Irish harp can be seen
on the tunic and a shamrock is discernible
below the Order of St John cross on the
right sleeve. **31** Maeve Boyle who served
with the WRNS in her native Derry,
photographed on her first day in the service.

32 (above): A group of Wrens based at HMS *Ferret*, the Royal Navy's shore base on the river Foyle. Most are Irish. Maeve Boyle is second from left in the back row. 33 (below): Reconciliation - a group of former adversaries lay wreaths on an Alpine memorial to those who perished on both sides during the Second World War. One of those laying the wreath is Strabane man Doug Cooper DFC, while Wolfgang Falck, with whom Cooper's squadron engaged in combat over the North Sea in 1940, looks on.

34 An anti-submarine training school was established at Derry and Wrens were important members of the staff. Maeve Boyle is the second Wren from the left in the middle row. The photograph includes a number of other Irish Wrens. 35 (below left): Memory. A family photograph of Pilot Officer Bertie Truesdale, from County Down, who died when his Lancaster was shot down on 22 May 1944. 36 (below right): Rest in peace. The grave of P/O Bertie Truesdale

We were carrying a seventy-pound load per man, including a groundsheet,
rations, spare socks if you had them – socks and boots were very important for
healthy feet – and we wore green clothing with no badges of rank.

The rendezvous with the other two battalions was made on 24 March; the King's
Own and the Cameronians had clashed with some Japanese patrols but had met no
serious opposition. Next day a column blew up the railbridge over the Ngane chaung;
Lentaigne completed plans for the brigade's further operations; and a welcome drop
of supplies was received. But another event that day was to change events completely
for the Chindits generally and especially for 111 Brigade. The news of that event was
received in a signal that night: General Orde Wingate had been killed in an air crash;
Lentaigne was to be flown out immediately to assume command of Special Force.

Wingate's death was a disaster for the Chindits. Lentaigne had never been enthusiastic about Wingate's concept of long-range penetration, and his choice as successor
to Wingate was a strange one, especially as Major-General Symes, who had commanded 70th Division and had remained with Special Force as Wingate's second-in-
command, was available to step into the breach. Colonel Jumbo Morris was promoted
temporary brigadier but, as he was away with Morrisforce, Major Jack Masters, the
Brigade Major, was appointed to command the greater part of 111 Brigade; he
remained in his major's rank, however.

Masters' last experience of command had been at company level before the war
and his combat experience was limited: in the war, he had seen action in Iraq and Syria
while, before the war, he had fought on India's North-West Frontier. He was now to
lead 111 Brigade in a campaign that lacked the guiding inspiration of Wingate and in
which that brigade was to suffer intensely. In common with Lentaigne and Morris,
Masters believed that Wingate's tactical doctrine, of striking at Japanese prepared positions, could lead to casualties that were disproportionate to the damage inflicted.
Instead, Masters believed that the enemy should be forced to attack the Chindits on
ground and times of the latters' choosing and in circumstances that would permit the
Chindits to disengage whenever they chose – 'in order to engage elsewhere'.

Masters failed to take Indaw and Bernard Fergusson's 16 Brigade suffered heavily
as a result. In early April 14 and 111 Brigades were ordered to leave the Indaw area and
march to the support of 23 Brigade, a Chindit formation that had been held in reserve
and was committed to harassing the Japanese forces thrusting towards Dimapur and
Kohima. That order was rescinded when US General Joe Stilwell, whose Chinese forces'
advance on Myitkyina had been baulked, accused his British allies of failing to pull their
weight. Masters' men then carried out a number of small operations against the
Japanese but there were no spectacular raids, nor was much destruction achieved. On
23 April the brigade was ordered to move north to establish a block north of Hopin in
the railway valley; other brigades were to move north also in support. The overall aim
was to continue the stranglehold on the road and railway to Mogaung.

Moving in two bodies, 111 Brigade marched through thick jungle up the Meza
valley towards Hopin. It was exhausting work and the shortfall in the calorific value

of the rations was becoming ever more obvious to Desmond Whyte. Malaria was also a problem for the doctors with the brigade.

Evidence of the brutal ways in which the Japanese treated the captured was found on the line of march one day when a dying man was found crucified to a tree, both wrists pinioned to the tree by bayonets. Such treatment was barbarism enough, but it had been made even worse by tearing open his stomach, presumably with a bayonet, and pulling out his intestines. He had been left with his feet dangling just above the ground but when discovered most of his lower legs had been gnawed away by jackals. The unfortunate man could barely speak.

> He asked us to shoot him, for Christ's sake. We didn't do that but I had suffi-
> cient morphine to give him an injection that eased his passing. It was the most
> humane thing I could think of. Then we buried him. But the jackals were
> always around and, well, I don't need to elaborate.

At last, the soldiers of 111 Brigade sighted Lake Indawgyi and, beyond that, an area of flat land which would take a day to cross. That crossing was made in battle formation with no interruption from the enemy. Masters had made his decision about the location of the block – by the ridge that ran between the Namyang and Namkwin chaungs. It was not an ideal site, as Masters admitted himself, since it was too close to Japanese front-line troop positions and would quickly draw their attention to it. At force headquarters Derek Tulloch, the BGS (Brigadier General Staff) who was imbued in the Wingate doctrine, tried to prevent the establishment of the block but was overruled by Lentaigne. And thus the Blackpool block was set up.

> Within forty-eight hours, at night, the enemy attacked from the north-east, and
> there was very unpleasant fighting. We had our barbed-wire emplacements
> down by then and the enemy retired before dawn, having sustained very heavy
> casualties. The enemy came back in greater numbers the following night and
> broke through in several places. That was repulsed.

When the sun came up the following day there was the ghastly sight of Japanese dead and dying hanging on the barbed wire. The sight of the bodies was unpleasant enough, but the heat, coupled with the fact that it was now the monsoon season and the early rains had begun, filled the air with the smell of putrefaction as the corpses rotted on Blackpool's perimeter.

Inside the perimeter conditions were very bad for the besieged Chindits. Even before the block had been established, the soldiers had been 'worn down physically'. As the days passed, their condition worsened:

> We were all full of malaria, we were under suppressive treatment with a view
> to keeping the malaria in check … Jungle sores; you'd get a small scratch, it
> would begin to ulcerate. Leechbites, which were ever present, would go septic.

The jaundice, infective jaundice, began to make itself felt; and there were the usual bowel complaints which were very unpleasant and very wearing.

Masters had believed that he was placing his command in a position from which it could harass the enemy in the region, although he recognized that the opposite could happen. The latter turned out to be the case as the Japanese launched the ferocious attacks on Blackpool described by Desmond Whyte. An airstrip was constructed for C-47s, using bulldozers and graders flown in by glider. Field guns were flown in to give the block artillery support and an answer to the Japanese 105mm guns that were bombarding Blackpool with shellfire which Masters likened to continuous drumming; Bofors light anti-aircraft guns were also flown in. Two battalions from the Broadway stronghold – 2nd King's Regiment (Liverpool) and 3/9th Gurkhas – arrived to strengthen the defences but of the anticipated 14 Brigade and the West African Brigade there was no sign. Casualties were evacuated in the C-47s as they flew out from Blackpool, but Desmond Whyte and his medical staff still had their hands full:

> Lack of sleep was probably the worst problem, that and the insufficient food. We were [still] living on K rations … and, of course, the K ration was not designed for this sort of warfare. It was a temporary, emergency, ration, and we were living off our own fat, on the downgrade.
>
> By the time we got to Blackpool our physical condition was far from ideal, but morale was high. We believed we were the élite, that's what kept us going. But how sad to watch close colleagues, friends … just the flame of life gradually flickering, and you'd awaken after three or four hours when the alert was sounded, and your friend was dead beside you. The flame of life had gone. That was very sad.

At one stage Masters was flown out of Blackpool in a light aircraft to meet Lentaigne and General Joe Stilwell to discuss plans, but no relief was available for 111 Brigade at Blackpool and Masters flew back to his command. On 22 May an enemy advance against the block began from the south east. Masters deployed one battalion to meet the enemy and delay his progress while he held the remainder of the brigade inside the block. This was the stage where, he felt, the arrival of 14 Brigade could give the Chindits a signal victory.

But 14 Brigade did not appear and the Japanese gained positions around the Blackpool perimeter that prevented the C-47s flying in at all. Masters sent a signal to Lentaigne asking permission to abandon Blackpool. On the night of 23/24 May the bombardment continued, increasing in ferocity just before dawn when, as daylight began, Japanese infantry penetrated the perimeter. By now the rain was incessant.

Desmond Whyte's Main Dressing Station had not been immune from attack. Wounded men had been killed by shellfire on the night of 22 May; two days later Desmond reported that he had forty-five serious cases in the MDS with no more space available, just minutes before two direct hits took the lives of many of those casualties.

At one point Major Whyte was wounded in the back but continued to work after treatment. He recalled that his only thought at the time was that 'Henley days are over'.

As the battering continued, Whyte remained a picture of calm professionalism amidst the death and destruction that surrounded him. He was, as Masters described,

> the man who, above all others, had kept the brigade going ... but Desmond has not dashed out and rescued one wounded man under fire, he has only saved two hundred over a hundred days, calm and efficient and cheerful while shells blast the bodies to pieces under his hands.

Finally the order was given to abandon Blackpool. Even as the brigade prepared to leave the block Desmond Whyte's casualties were still suffering: one man whom he had been fighting to save for twenty-four hours was hit again in the same spot and died. There were soldiers so badly wounded that they could not be moved. These men were of particular concern to Desmond Whyte. He asked Masters to come with him to the MDS. The doctor showed his commander nineteen men on stretchers, each with horrendous injuries: one had his stomach cavity blown away; another had no lower limbs or hips; yet another had lost his face. Some of the nineteen were conscious: 'At least, their eyes moved, but without light in them.'

Desmond Whyte's predicament was simple. None of the men would live more than two hours and they were already full of morphia. Thirty others could be saved, if they could be carried. As the two men talked, two of the wounded soldiers died. But if they were left behind at the mercy of the Japanese they would be treated with sadistic brutality, as had been the case with the officer found crucified to the teak tree. Masters made his mind up quickly and told Desmond Whyte that he did not want the casualties 'to see any Japanese'.

There was no more morphia to spare but Masters told Whyte to give what he could to those 'whose eyes are open'. Then he walked away, telling the doctor that the stretcher-bearers were to move in five minutes. Thus was Desmond Whyte, a man who had dedicated his life to saving lives, forced to end the suffering of the badly wounded men. Masters described the next few minutes succinctly. 'One by one, carbine shots exploded curtly behind me. I put my hands to my ears but nothing could shut out the sound.'

The few surviving mules were pressed into service to help carry the wounded as 111 Brigade quit the scene of its seventeen-days' travail and, suffering the added pain of defeat, began the journey to Lake Indawgyi in the rain. Four days later the brigade reached the lake where RAF Sunderland flying boats and American light aircraft flew the wounded and the sick out, some 600 men in total.

The remainder of the brigade then began to move northwards on the orders of Stilwell under whose command they had now been placed. But it was a weakened 111 Brigade that began the march to Mogaung. Whyte informed Masters that many men were close to death from exhaustion and lack of proper food, as well as the strain of operations and lengthy exposure to the conditions of the jungle, especially during the monsoon season. His advice was confirmed by the number of cases of what would normally have been mild conditions that had dramatic effects: men died from the exertions of even a short patrol, or from a chill, while a cut finger could lead to death in a matter of days. And still there was no relief.

Even in such condition the Chindits continued to operate, and to fight. On 9 July Major Jim Blaker, of 3/9th Gurkhas, led his company in an attack on a well-defended Japanese position. When the attack was held up, Blaker charged on, inspiring his soldiers to follow his example. Although he was fatally wounded, the Gurkhas routed the Japanese. Masters commended Blaker for the Victoria Cross, which was awarded immediately.

The brigade commander was to write another VC citation, for Desmond Whyte. This was supported by the four battalion commanders who had witnessed Desmond's efforts in Blackpool and subsequently.

> Major Whyte ... was in command of Blackpool Medical Dressing Station from the 7th to the 24th of May 1944.
>
> ... the fortress was under continual attack by enemy infantry, mortars, machine-guns, artillery and aircraft. The garrison suffered numerous casualties, all of which passed through the Medical Dressing Station. The [MDS] was hit several times by shellfire and patients killed. Continuous rain made conditions for patients and doctors bad. There was a chronic and continual shortage of all medical stores. Evacuation of a proportion of casualties was carried out from an airstrip; on at least two occasions under enemy fire. Major Whyte supervized the evacuation.
>
> Throughout this period Major Whyte showed complete disregard of his personal safety and gave a superb and sustained example of cheerfulness and courage. He treated patients in his [MDS] and went out on shell and machine-gun swept slopes to collect and treat them.
>
> On [25 May 1944], when Blackpool was evacuated, he organized the evacuation of wounded, including stretcher cases. During the evacuation twelve patients and stretcher bearers were killed in the immediate vicinity of Major Whyte, who carried on as if nothing was happening.
>
> From the 25th to the 29th May 1944, Major Whyte organized the carriage, movement and treatment of 180 wounded men, mostly without equipment, blankets or cover of any kind, with inadequate medical equipment, over 18 miles of muddy mountain track in continuous pouring rain, without food.
>
> This officer's continuous courage and cheerfulness was an inspiration to the wounded, many of whom would have succumbed but for him and the other Brigade Medical Officers.

In spite of this recommendation, Desmond Whyte was not awarded the Victoria Cross, receiving instead the Distinguished Service Order. Masters described this downgrading as 'not good enough'.

When the Chindits were withdrawn from Burma to recover, Wingate's concept was allowed to die; the force was disbanded and the various battalions were either returned to normal operations or broken up. The soldiers had expected to train for further Chindit operations and many were disappointed that this did not happen.

Desmond Whyte, in common with all Chindits, had a period of recuperation before moving on to other duties. In his case this involved volunteering for parachute training after which he joined 44th Indian Airborne Division. The division was destined not to go into action,* plans for its deployment being made redundant by the dropping of the atomic bombs on Hiroshima and Nagasaki, and it was disbanded in October 1945. Thus the end of the Chindits' second expedition also marked the end of Desmond Whyte's active service in the war, but he had seen more action in that time than many saw in the entire war and his DSO was small reward for the magnificent work he had carried out under such trying circumstances.

Andy Parsons and Desmond Whyte were among a large number of Irish doctors in the wartime RAMC. A number of others were also decorated for their service, although there were many who served without such distinction coming their way. That is not to say that their service was any less valuable; they worked with skill among the wounded and dying, and some died while doing so. For the survivors the experience of having been a front-line doctor in wartime helped to make them even better doctors in civilian life; the pressures of civilian hospital work could rarely throw up any circumstances that matched the pressures they had dealt with in wartime.

Niall Hogan, a native of Dublin, was working in a Lancashire hospital when war broke out. He decided to join up and chose the RAMC. In his own words he thought that military service 'would be fun'. His first posting to an active service area was in November 1942 when he went with First Army to French north-west Africa in Operation TORCH, whose strategic aim was to place the Italo-German forces in a nutcracker with Eighth and First Armies being the arms of the device: Eighth Army was now advancing westward after its victory at El Alamein; First Army was to move eastward.

Whatever the strategic aim of the planners there were more mundane matters to be dealt with on the ground. First Army's soldiers were coming ashore in Algiers and concentrating in makeshift accommodation there, many of them in the Jardins d'Essai, a large area which was about half the size of Dublin's Phoenix Park. The presence of so many soldiers created a serious hygiene problem, and Hogan, with a dentist called Humpherson, was given the task of turning a major health hazard into something more acceptable to the medical authorities. In Niall Hogan's own words the area was 'a shithouse' and he devised a plan for latrine trenches which would be used for a twenty-four period. After an individual soldier had used the latrine he was expected to cover his personal contribution – shovels were provided – and the latrine lines were policed by soldiers detailed for that purpose and stationed at each end of the lines. After twenty-four hours' use the latrines were filled in, 'Foul Ground' signs placed on the site, and new latrines dug. Thus Hogan ensured that the Army's normal sanitary

---

* One of the division's brigades – 50 – made a parachute drop in May 1945.

discipline was enforced. The area Assistant Director Medical Services was so impressed with Hogan's work that he suggested to the Irishman's commanding officer that a Mention in Despatches might be appropriate. However, the CO regarded Niall Hogan as a rather irreverent individual – who claimed to have consumed the entire stock of medicinal brandy on board the troopship which brought him to Algeria – and so no recommendation was made.

Probably the first Irish doctor to be decorated for Army service in the war was a native of Mullingar, Lieutenant John Graham Lord, who earned the Military Cross on 29 May 1940, the very day that Andy Parsons had his first experience of action at Hoogestadt. Lord's unit, an anti-tank regiment of the Royal Artillery, was engaged by German tanks that day, and one of its guns was in action near the RAP. In the fighting that followed, the gun was overwhelmed by the strength of the enemy armour and all the detachment* members were wounded. Lord attended to each man at the gun position as soon as he was injured. Inevitably he was also under the same heavy fire but this did not deter him from helping those casualties, treating their wounds at his RAP and then evacuating them in his MO's truck under heavy machine-gun fire.

Another early recipient of an award was Colonel Arthur Beveridge, OBE, MC, a Dubliner, who served with the North-West Expeditionary Force, the doomed Allied force that was sent to Norway in 1940. Beveridge, a Great War veteran, was awarded the Norwegian Military Cross and the Sword of King Haakon for his bravery and devotion to duty during that short campaign. Describing his service under trying conditions in the Namsos area from 15 to 20 April 1940 as 'conspicuous and zealous', the citation went on to note that 'he had been indefatigable in his [successful] efforts to cope with the medical arrangements', at times working while bombs fell around him, or roads were being machine-gunned.

A number of senior Irish RAMC officers were decorated for their service in the Middle East. Colonel George Frederick Allison, MC, a Monaghan man, was appointed Deputy Director of Medical Services for No. 18 Area in the Canal Zone of Egypt in December 1940, having arrived in the Middle East as the Officer Commanding 27 General Hospital which he had commanded since its formation at Goodwood House in Surrey on 7 January of that year.

When he assumed his post as DDMS Canal (No. 18) Area there was one hospital under his command and he oversaw the expansion to eleven hospitals and five prisoner-of-war hospitals. As well as supervising the provision and organisation of these facilities he also made his vast experience available to the newly-appointed commanders of each of the hospitals. Promoted Brigadier on 14 December 1941, Allison's work earned him a knighthood. He was appointed Knight Commander of the Order of the British Empire. The citation stated:

> During operations in the Western Desert, Brigadier Allison was very fully occupied in organising the reception and evacuation of casualties, and it was large-

---

* In the Royal Artillery a gun is manned by a detachment, rather than by a crew.

ly due to his powers of organisation and the high standard of his work that these receptions and evacuations were carried out so smoothly.

Allison subsequently prepared notes on the work of his command which were used in the preparation of the medical history of the war. In his time in the post he had to deal with a wide range of medical problems, including a typhus epidemic, but all were met with a wide array of skills from his staff and a determination to overcome the difficulties arising from climatic conditions and from factors such as the overcrowding of prisoner-of-war camps which occurred from time to time.

Galway-born Brigadier Robert Fowler Walker, OBE, MC, another Great War veteran, was made a Commander of the Order of the British Empire (CBE) for his work as Deputy Director of Medical Supplies in the Middle East. Walker was responsible to the Director of Medical Supplies for the many and complex medical plans needed to suit the myriad of operations carried out in that difficult theatre. Each planned operation demanded a medical plan based on the general staff's assessment of anticipated casualties from which the medical staff and the adjutant-general's staff then estimated transport needs by calculating the probable percentages of fatalities and of wounded, whether lying, sitting or walking. Of course, each plan also had to take account of the climates in which the troops would be fighting, and this was especially true in the Middle East. The detailed planning then involved the quantities and types of medical stores needed, including drugs, chemicals, clothing and other medical equipment, as well as the transport required for the terrain.

The citation for Walker's CBE noted that:

> this officer's foresight, judgement and careful calculation based on his specialized knowledge have covered medical results in evacuation and nursing of casualties, which have brought nothing but praise from the highest authorities.
>
> His keenness, loyalty, devotion to duty and entire application to these many difficult problems have been an example to all.

Allison and Walker were the highest-ranking Irish medical officers in the Middle East but they were not alone in the higher echelons of the medical service. Colonel Douglas Bluett, a native of Delgany, County Wicklow, was appointed an OBE for his work in the Western Desert where he commanded 14 Field Ambulance until 28 May 1942 when he became Assistant Director Medical Services, the chief medical officer of a division. In his earlier role, Bluett was considered 'quite imperturbable under fire and an example to all ranks', while his field ambulance was regarded as a 'model ... in every way'. His promotion to ADMS came just before Rommel launched his major offensive against Eighth Army on the Gazala line and he then became embroiled in the chaos and horror of the battles of late-May and June which led to Eighth Army's withdrawal, first to Matruh and, subsequently, to El Alamein. Bluett remained at his post until the day before Tobruk fell – 21 June – when he was ordered to another assignment. During those hectic weeks 'his work in co-ordinating reception and evacuation of thousands of casualties under circumstances of extreme difficulty and danger was beyond praise'.

Another OBE went to Lieutenant-Colonel Theobald Denis Phelan, a Clonmel man, who commanded a field ambulance attached to an armoured brigade of Eighth Army. Phelan consistently showed a 'very high degree of vision, foresight and initiative – the results of which have been manifest in the work of his unit', which enjoyed a reputation second to none in Eighth Army and had a superb medical record; the ratio of deaths to battle casualties dealt with by the MDS was 'most unusually low'.

Lieutenant-Colonel Robert James Valentine Pulvertaft, a Dublin-born Fellow of the Royal College of Physicians, was yet another Irish doctor to be appointed OBE for his work in the Middle East. Pulvertaft was not, however, engaged in the front line, nor in the planning of medical services, but, as a pathologist at Westminster Hospital in civilian life, he was appointed pathologist on the staff of the 1,200-bed No. 2 General Hospital on his arrival in Egypt in September 1940. Subsequently, in June 1942, he was appointed to take charge of the Central Pathological Laboratory in Cairo, a post which he combined with the duties of Deputy Assistant Director of Pathology for the Middle East. He was later promoted to Assistant Director.

A man with an enquiring mind and a keen interest in research, Pulvertaft studied the treatment of infected wounds with chemotherapeutic substances. This work was brought to the attention of the War Wounds Committee in Britain which considered it to be of real value,

> especially his laboratory research into the substance now known as Penicillin. By most industrious and painstaking investigations and experiments he has added considerable knowledge to the development of this substance. The introduction of Penicillin into war surgery will undoubtedly revolutionize the treatment of septic wounds.

Seldom has a more accurate prediction been made: penicillin was a revolutionary drug and it helped many casualties to survive who would otherwise have died of septicaemia and other complications. Pulvertaft, who also assisted the British Council in Egypt, certainly deserved his award.

Below the grade of Officer in the Order of the British Empire is that of Member (MBE) and a number of these awards also went to Irish doctors. Among them was Major Julius Cecil Summ, from Clones, who was working with a forward brigade during the battle of El Alamein and the subsequent advance where he was 'an inspiration to the officers and men of [his] unit ... [and] directly responsible for maintaining the morale of the unit at a high level during many difficult times'; and Major Peter Joseph May, from Dun Laoghaire, who commanded a motor ambulance convoy which did sterling work in moving casualties from forward clearing stations to railhead or hospital ship port. At all times 100% of his vehicles were available for use, no mean feat when it is remembered that they travelled almost 200,000 miles in less than two months.

The Military Cross also went to a number of Irish doctors in addition to Andy Parsons, whose story has already been told. Fellow recipients of this gallantry award included Major Terence Reginald Wilson, a Dubliner, Captains Kelvin Francis Patton from Mullingar, John Stuart Martin from Robinstown, County Meath, Stephen Martin Patrick Conway, Basil Ernest West Aldwell and Aiden Asquith Byrne, all from Dublin. Both Martin and Aldwell earned their awards in the Sicilian campaign, while the others were won in North Africa.

Captain Byrne gained the MC in the break-out from the crumbling Gazala positions in June 1942 when his ambulance car ran into a British minefield in the dark. Byrne went forward to help extricate the patients from the vehicle and then marked a way out of the minefield along which the injured were then brought to safety. Conway's MC was won on 28 October 1942, during the battle of El Alamein, when the young MO spent more than three hours making journeys to help the wounded in a position that was under such intense shell- and machine-gun fire that everyone else was forced to take cover in their armoured vehicles or in slit trenches.

Major Terence Wilson was serving with First Army in Tunisia when he won the Military Cross in early 1943. He established an Advanced Dressing Station in a gully near St de Ksar Mezouar and organized a system of casualty evacuation that was so efficient that all recoverable casualties were back on an operating table in Beja within three to four hours, a factor that saved many lives and meant that a large proportion of casualties were spared the necessity of limb amputation.

Ernest Basil West Aldwell was with an infantry battalion in Sicily in July 1943 when he won the MC for his work over a period of at least a week. On 13 July Aldwell worked in the open under heavy fire for long periods while, on 20 July, in the Cardone area he worked with the wounded after bringing up water and additional stretcher-bearers. Although he had been hit himself by a piece of shrapnel he would not leave his post until another MO came up to relieve him.

John Stuart Martin was with a battery of 17th Field Regiment, Royal Artillery which was in action south of Bronte in Sicily on 9 August 1943 when he won his MC. That evening the road between the battery's positions and Bronte was shelled and mortared with devastating accuracy as the Germans were stiffening their resistance to cover the evacuation of their forces from the island to mainland Italy. 'Unfortunately no alternative positions were available and consequently a number of casualties were suffered.' Realizing that this would be the case, Captain Martin rushed to the area where shelling was heaviest and, in spite of the danger to himself, attended to the wounded. He undoubtedly saved some lives while his calmness had a steadying effect on those around him.

In September 1943 Allied forces invaded mainland Italy. It was not long before they discovered just how tough fighting in Italy could be with a series of river valleys running down from the mountainous spine of the country. The initial impetus of the advance was soon slowed down as the Germans fought doggedly to make each river obstacle a purgatory for the Allies. It was at one such river crossing that Captain Leslie Joseph Samuels, from Dublin, won the Military Cross. Already an experienced MO, Samuels had regularly shown complete disregard for his personal safety.

During the attack across the River Trigno on October 27 1943, he tended the wounded under very heavy fire for five hours and there is no doubt he saved many lives.

During this time he supervized evacuation across the river under continual enemy shellfire.

His cheerfulness and courage under the worst conditions have been an inspiration and example to all.

A Military Cross went to Captain Frank Pantridge, MO with 2nd Gordon Highlanders in the Singapore campaign. Pantridge had graduated in medicine from Queen's University, Belfast and then, on 1 August 1939, became a house physician at the Royal Victoria Hospital from where, with a number of his colleagues, he went to the recruiting office at Clifton Street to join the RAMC. None of the group was accepted immediately because they lacked hospital experience, and they were obliged to wait until April 1940 to be called up. After training Pantridge was posted to Singapore where, on disembarking, he 'felt as though I was enveloped by a hot, wet blanket', a feeling that he was to endure for the next five years. He also encountered the 'indescribable and unforgettable' smell of Singapore. After an altercation with the commanding officer of the military hospital at Tanglin, Pantridge was punished with a posting to 2nd Gordon Highlanders at Selerang barracks.

The life of a medical officer in Singapore followed a virtual peacetime routine for some eighteen months after Pantridge's arrival on the island. In spite of the news from Britain, North Africa and the Soviet Union, the war had little effect on those based in Singapore. There was talk of a threat from Japan, but the Japanese were dismissed as being militarily insignificant, their infantry useless and incapable of using rifles, their airmen being handicapped by the supposedly bad eyesight of their nation, and their ships of such design and construction as to be useless in action. Thus, as we have already noted from Desmond Whyte's account, there was complacency in the Far East which was rudely shattered when the Japanese attacked Pearl Harbor on 7 December 1941.

The Gordons were deployed to man coastal defences at Pengerang, on the southern tip of Johore, although part of the battalion remained on Singapore island. Pantridge thus had to commute between the two locations and while doing so one day 'in the first week of December' he saw the battleship HMS *Prince of Wales* and the battle-cruiser *Repulse* with their escort of destroyers sail from Singapore.* Two days later, the two capital ships, without air cover, were sunk off Malaya by Japanese bombers. In his book *An Unquiet Life*, Pantridge expresses the belief that the Brewster Buffalo fighters of No. 453 Squadron, Royal Australian Air Force, could have reached the area before *Prince of Wales* was attacked and that, since the Japanese bombers had no fighter escort, the Buffaloes could have saved the day. But a communications failure

---

* Force Z, the nucleus of the Royal Navy's Eastern Fleet, actually left Singapore at 5.35 p.m. on 8 December 1942.

meant that Tim Vigors, the Irish commander of No. 453 Squadron, was not asked to provide air cover.

At much the same time as they struck at the US Pacific Fleet in Hawaii, the Japanese were also landing at Kota Bahru on Malaya's east coast. Having taken Kota Bahru and its airfield in two days, the Japanese began a rapid advance down the Malayan peninsula using the jungle to avoid Allied defences on roads. The 2nd Gordons at Pengerang were now serving in a redundant role and were switched to northern Johore where the battalion was brigaded with two Australian battalions, 2/29th and 2/30th. With neither air nor naval support the brigade was told to set up road blocks to hold the Japanese by day before retreating by night to set up a fresh road block ready for the next encounter.

The brigade's first encounter with the enemy came when an ambush was set up in the Gamass Gamet Yongpong area; the main part in this action fell to 2/30th Australian Battalion. Japanese soldiers on bicycles, followed by trucks and tanks, crossed over a bridge that had been mined in preparation for the ambush. As the foe passed over the bridge it was blown and concealed machine-guns on either side of the road opened fire, as did mortars. Pantridge watched from a bank some ten feet above the road as 'arms, legs and other bits of bodies [came] flying past me'.

The Gordons and their Australian comrades were to operate in this fashion for a week or more. It was an exhausting time for the soldiers, and Frank Pantridge described how he felt a curious sensation 'as if I were walking on air' due to the lack of sleep. At dawn the troops would dig in and invariably Japanese aircraft would strafe the new positions. There was also the danger of snipers who had tied themselves to trees; the non-combatant doctor abandoned his revolver in favour of a Thompson sub-machine-gun. When the aircraft attacked, Pantridge recalled,

> [w]e quickly learned to keep down or to get on the right side of a tree. I had a much exaggerated fear of the whine of ricocheting bullets since one had taken the skin off one buttock. It hardly mattered that I was unable to sit down. There were very few opportunities to do so. The thuds and slams of the mortars were treated with much respect. If one landed in front and then one behind, the Japanese were getting the range. It was time for quick movement.

As the retreat continued there was concern about leaving wounded men behind, a concern that was justified when the fate of a number of Australian and Indian prisoners became known: some 200 men were beheaded by Japanese troops, who then ran over the bodies with their vehicles before soaking the corpses with petrol and burning them. Frank Pantridge was determined to ensure that his wounded were moved back as quickly as possible and 'that those who could not be moved would never suffer at Japanese hands'.

Pantridge was unsparing in his efforts for the wounded. In his autobiography he says little about his own work while praising that of others, especially his senior NCO, who 'was completely fearless' and who was later awarded the Distinguished Conduct

Medal. But Pantridge himself was awarded the Military Cross for his courage in the field. That courage continued after the fall of Singapore when the gallant Belfastman did much to ease the suffering of his fellow prisoners of war and was regarded by many as the sole reason for their survival.

The survivors of Singapore had already spent two years in prison camps when Allied forces landed in Normandy in Operation OVERLORD on 6 June 1944. During the early days of the fighting on the beachhead a Dublin doctor distinguished himself in his care for the wounded. Captain Gordon Spencer Sheill was awarded the MC for his devotion to duty on 8-10 June 1944

> at Haute Longueville, [where he] was in charge of the Regimental Aid Post. Casualties were heavy and many units were passing wounded through for attention. In difficult conditions and without regard for his own safety, Captain Sheill attended Allied and enemy wounded alike, often in the face of intensive aerial bombardment or artillery and mortar fire. His quiet efficiency and skill were without doubt instrumental in the saving of many lives, and his unflagging energy and cheerfulness throughout these difficult operations were an inspiration to officers and men alike.

As the Allied armies continued their advance across Europe there were many similar examples of devotion to duty by doctors of the Royal Army Medical Corps. One of the most outstanding came during Operation PLUNDER, the crossing of the river Rhine in March 1945. One of the crossing points for Field Marshal Montgomery's 21 Army Group was at Rees where the assault crossing began on the night of 23 March with the supporting fire of some 3,500 artillery pieces. There was strong German resistance in the area and, on the morning of the 24th, when Major Patrick Esmonde, a younger brother of Eugene Esmonde, VC, DSO, a senior medical officer, crossed with a reconnaissance party about 500 yards from the town, fierce fighting was still taking place nearby. Mines had been located in the neighbourhood but there were no Royal Engineers available to clear the deadly devices from the proposed site of Esmonde's Casualty Clearing Station.

Anxious to get the CCS into operation as soon as possible, Esmonde decided on a risky method of ensuring the area was clear of mines. He filled his own jeep with sandbags, to cushion any blast, and drove the tiny vehicle around in ever-increasing circles until he had covered the entire site of the CCS. He thus made certain, to the best of his ability, that the area was free from mines, and the CCS was soon set up. Over the next few days, sharp fighting continued around Rees, which was under direct enemy observation, and the CCS came under fire from shells and mortars as well as rifle fire.

Although some of his own personnel were wounded in this fire, Paddy Esmonde continued to organize the treatment and evacuation of the wounded who were ferried across the Rhine in amphibious DUKWs. In this way, Esmonde saved the lives of many wounded soldiers. He was awarded an immediate Military Cross for his courage.

Of the three services, the Army had the largest number of doctors and other medical staff and so there were more Irish doctors in the Army than in the Royal Navy or Royal Air Force. Doctors in the other two services worked under very different conditions to those of the RAMC, but this did not prevent a number of them receiving gallantry awards. Among those awardees three Irish names are to be found.

Operation JUBILEE was the title given to the Dieppe raid in August 1942 in which a large-scale amphibious operation was launched in daylight 'against a coast defended by units of the most highly trained and most formidable army in Europe'. The bulk of the 6,000 soldiers involved were Canadian and they suffered heavily in the fighting during which three VCs were won, two of them by Canadians. The troops who landed on the beaches at Dieppe were transported by ships and landing craft of the Royal Navy. Among the latter vessels was HM LCF (L) 2 – Landing Craft, Flak (Large) – on board which the Medical Officer was an Irishman, Surgeon Lieutenant Miles Patrick Martin, a native of Dun Laoghaire.

The German opposition to the landing was fierce and furious with coastal batteries and aircraft attacking the Allied fleet and landing troops. LCF (L) 2 was subjected to such heavy fire that the ship's captain was killed and the vessel was disabled and lay only a few hundred yards from the German coastal artillery positions. All the other officers on board had also been injured and, as the landing craft's situation became even more perilous, Martin took command of the stricken vessel. Satisfied that the landing craft could take no more offensive action and that it was doomed, he ordered the crew to abandon ship.

Surgeon Lieutenant Martin spent thirty minutes in the water before he was picked up. During that time he had been under machine-gun fire. After his rescue he was transferred to HMS *Calpe* where, in spite of his own ordeal, he immediately offered to work with the ship's medical officer in tending to the wounded on board, of whom there were about 300 cases. All of this time *Calpe* was being shelled and bombed. For his efforts at Dieppe, Miles Patrick Martin was subsequently awarded the DSO.

While naval medical officers and their RAMC counterparts can go into action with their ships or units, the same is not true for their RAF colleagues who must wait on the ground while the crews of fighters, bombers and other aircraft endure the actions and suffer casualties. It was normally when the aircraft returned to base that the air force MO went to work. On occasions that work could start in the blazing wreckage of a crashed machine as was the case with Flight Lieutenant Simon Theodore Winter, a Dublin-born doctor who had been commissioned into the RAF's Medical Branch in 1941 and promoted to Flight Lieutenant in 1942. In July 1943 a Short Stirling bomber, returning from an operational mission, was attempting to make an emergency landing but crashed whilst doing so and burst into flames.

> Flight Lieutenant Winter, who was the medical officer on duty, immediately proceeded to the scene. Regardless of his own safety, he assisted the crew to escape and entered the burning fuselage in a vain endeavour to release the mid-upper gunner who was trapped upside down in his turret.

Winter suffered burns to the head and face in his heroic effort to save the trapped gunner but, in spite of his own injuries, he attended to the needs of the injured crewmen whose escape he had already assisted. Only then did he seek assistance for his own burns. His 'high courage and devotion to duty' earned him the award of the MBE.

The George Medal was instituted on 24 September 1940 to be awarded for acts of gallantry that did not merit the George Cross, instituted on the same day, which was considered the civilian VC. It was this medal that was awarded to Squadron Leader Joseph Aidan McCarthy, MB, CHB, BAO, who had been commissioned in the Medical Branch of the RAF in September 1939. A native of Berehaven, County Cork, McCarthy had qualified from University College, Cork and he won his GM in circumstances similar to those in which Winter earned his MBE:

> One night in May 1941, the pilot of an aircraft attempted to land with the undercarriage retracted. The aircraft crashed into the main bomb dump and then burst into flames. Group Captain Gray and Squadron Leader McCarthy immediately went to the scene of the accident, and between them succeeded in extricating two members of the crew who were trapped. Squadron Leader McCarthy suffered minor facial injuries caused by burns, but, despite this and the strain to which he had been exposed, he would not retire to his quarters until he was satisfied that everything possible had been done for the comfort of the injured. Both Group Captain Gray and Squadron Leader McCarthy displayed great bravery in the most appalling circumstances.

Almost all the doctors featured in this chapter were decorated for gallantry, but there were many more Irish doctors who served in the medical branches of the forces who received no distinctions. Nonetheless their work was valuable and often made the difference between life and death for a wounded sailor, soldier or airman. Their skill and attention to duty were always appreciated by the fighting man.

9

Irish fighter pilots: war in the air, part II

SOMEWHERE AMONG THE CLOUDS ABOVE

In 1990 the fiftieth anniversary of the battle of Britain was marked by church services, air displays and parades as well as by special features in the media. A national service of commemoration was held in London in the course of which the flags of all the nations represented in Fighter Command in 1940 were displayed. At the principle airshow to mark the anniversary the RAF's freefall parachute display team, the Falcons, dropped with each member of the team having, attached to one leg, the weighted flag of a nation which had provided pilots for Fighter Command in those distant days. Many who watched both occasions were surprised to note that, along with the flags of the United Kingdom, Poland, France, Australia and the USA was the tricolour of the Republic of Ireland. For, fifty years earlier, there had been neutral Irishmen in the cockpits of the Spitfires and Hurricanes that fought the Luftwaffe in the skies over southern England.* And neutral Irishmen, with their Northern Irish comrades, continued to serve in fighter aircraft throughout the war.

The best known of all Irish fighter pilots was the Dubliner Brendan Finucane who became the RAF's top scoring 'ace'. Born in Dublin on 16 October 1920, Brendan Eamon Finucane was educated at Marlborough Street and Synge Street elementary schools and then at the O'Connell School, run by the Christian Brothers of Ireland. A devout Catholic who took his religious duties seriously, he was also academically strong and a gifted sportsman. In addition to boxing, rowing and swimming, the young Finucane also played rugby and captained O'Connell's First XV in his last year at the school. It was on the rugby pitch that his gifts of leadership first became apparent.

Finucane's family had a long tradition of service in the British forces: his grandfather had served in the 25th Foot, the King's Own Scottish Borderers, while other ancestors had been officers in various regiments, including the 88th Foot, the Connaught Rangers. However, Brendan's father, Andrew Finucane, an accountant by profession, had marched to a different drum and followed the example of his former mathematics' teacher, Eamon de Valera, with whom he fought against the British in

---

* In his biography of Brendan Finucane, Doug Stokes notes that there were eight Irish fighter pilots in the battle of Britain.

April 1916. (In spite of this, Andy Finucane applied to join the Royal Air Force in 1939 at the age of 44; his English-born wife prevented him from donning air force blue.)

After leaving school, Brendan Finucane followed his father into accountancy, working in Dublin for some time. When his father, now a company director, went to England to open a new office in London the family followed, moving to live in Richmond on the outskirts of the capital in November 1936. Brendan went to an office job in central London, but his mind was on other things.

For many years he and his brother had holidayed with his father's sister in Southampton, and there the young Brendan had developed a love of aeroplanes; his aunt's home was not far from the home of the Supermarine company, which was to build the famous Spitfire fighter. There was no opposition from Andy Finucane when his son told him that he wanted to apply for a short service commission in the Royal Air Force. In the summer of 1938 Brendan was accepted for pilot training and was sent to 6 Elementary and Reserve Flying Training School at the end of August.

Flying training did not come easily to Brendan Finucane, who was not a 'born' pilot. However, a determination to succeed created an impression on his instructors and carried him through his course. He took between four and five hours more dual-controlled instruction than his fellow trainees before going solo for the first time and finished his basic course with a grading of 'average'. After earning his wings he was posted to a technical unit at RAF Henlow in Bedfordshire where he made several applications to be posted to a fighter squadron. On 27 June 1940, Pilot Officer Brendan Finucane finally was posted to No. 7 Operational Training Unit for a two-week Spitfire conversion course before joining a fighter squadron. On 12 July he completed his course and received a posting to No. 65 Squadron, which was based at Hornchurch in Essex. The Spitfires of No. 65 Squadron were soon moved to Rochford, near Southend but were forward-based across the Thames estuary at Manston in Kent, flying there at first light each day.

On 25 July Finucane became operational but his first sortie was an anti-climax: flying a well-worn Spitfire, N3128, he developed a coolant leak, his cockpit filled with vapour from the glycol condensing on the aircraft's hot engine and his radio stopped functioning. As he landed, his machine suffered undercarriage damage from a hollow on the grass airfield, and he came to a halt with the wheels up and a dead engine. It was hardly an auspicious beginning.

Pilot Officer Finucane was issued with a new Spitfire on 1 August and it was in this machine, R6818, that he shot down his first enemy aircraft eleven days later. This was the day that the Luftwaffe changed its tactics and made a maximum effort to destroy Fighter Command on the ground and in the air. The new German tactics involved co-ordinated attacks on the radio direction finding, or radar, stations that gave early warning of attacks and on the airfields in south-east England. This was to be the prelude to *Adler Tag*, Eagle Day, in which the surviving aircraft of Fighter Command would be drawn into a large-scale air battle and destroyed. The way would then be clear for the invasion of England. Manston was to be in the front line of this new phase of the battle of Britain; it would earn the soubriquet of 'Manston-in-the-dust' after becoming the most-bombed airfield in England.

On the morning of 12 August No. 65 Squadron was scrambled at 11 a.m. and had climbed to 26,000 feet ten miles out to sea from North Foreland within thirty minutes. There the squadron broke into sections to dive on a gaggle of twenty to thirty Messerschmitt Bf109s some two thousand feet below them. Finucane tried to engage a Messerschmitt which was attacking Ken Hart, one of his section, but was forced to take evasive action as he came under attack himself. In doing so he lost a lot of height and had to climb back to 20,000 feet to rejoin the mêlée. He then found himself in a favourable tactical position, being both above and behind a formation of a dozen enemy fighters:

> He got the tail-ender with a burst from 250 yards down to 50 yards, seeing it pour grey smoke and dive towards the Channel; he landed back at Manston at 11.45 a.m. where the kill was confirmed by Sergeant Orchard who saw it continue straight down into the Channel.

The squadron had scarcely touched down before a new order to scramble was received. As the Spitfires raced down the runway, Luftwaffe bombers arrived overhead to attack Manston at low level. Only one Spitfire was unable to get off the ground; the remainder, including Finucane's, did so successfully and were soon engaged with the attackers. On this occasion the Irishman chased a Bf109 through cloud and out to sea. He fired a long burst from 1,000 feet away and the Messerschmitt dived sharply, trailing smoke. Some 200 feet above the waves Finucane broke away as another 109 tried to pounce on him. He avoided that machine and was able to fire a short burst at another 109 that was turning just under the cloud base. The first machine he hit was claimed as probably destroyed, the second as damaged.

At armament practice camp during his training days one of his instructors had noted that Finucane would always get as close as possible to the target in order to maximize the chances of hitting it. That tendency was now being put into practice for real and would become the Irishman's hallmark. On 13 August he claimed another Bf109 which he engaged at ranges closing from 300 to 75 yards at a height of 19,000 feet. The Messerschmitt went down in flames, and yet another machine was damaged when Finucane hit it with a burst from 200 yards. Two Bf109s destroyed, two probably destroyed and one damaged was a formidable record for a new fighter pilot and was all the more creditable for being achieved in two days' operational flying.

On 28 August No. 65 Squadron was sent north to RAF Turnhouse, near Edinburgh, to rest from the rigours of constant action and to replace losses. Six days later Brendan Finucane was promoted to Flying Officer. On 9 September he was praised in a confidential report: 'I have great hopes of this officer. He is keen and intelligent and shows likelihood of becoming a very efficient leader. Is being trained as a leader and is learning quickly.'

Although its pilots did not know it at the time, the move to Turnhouse marked the
end of No. 65 Squadron's part in the battle of Britain. Finucane was able to hone his
aerial fighting skills with a practice dogfight with one of the squadron's Polish pilots,
but, generally, this was a time for recuperation from the stresses of lengthy combat
flying. At the beginning of November the squadron transferred to Leuchars in Fife,
where it remained for three weeks before moving south again, to Tangmere near
Chicester in West Sussex. The short dark days of winter meant that there was little
flying for the pilots of Fighter Command who found themselves almost helpless as
German bombers pounded British cities in the night blitz. Tackling the night bombers
effectively was a task for special fighters, twin-seaters fitted with airborne interception
radar (AI), rather than the single-seat Spitfires.

But the Germans were still trying to make some daylight sorties over Britain and
patrols were mounted over the south coast to intercept these intruders, which were
frequently single aircraft. On 4 January 1941 Finucane was leading a section of three
Spitfires at 7,000 feet over Selsey Bill when they caught a German raider just before
10 a.m. The German, flying a Messerschmitt Bf110, spotted the British fighters and
tried to evade them, turning for France as he did so. Finucane dived on the twin-
engined intruder and pursued it for fifteen miles across the channel, finally bringing it
down into the water on his fourth attack.*

On 19 January Finucane and Sergeant Orchard intercepted a Junkers Ju88 off the
Isle of Wight and, after a low-level running battle, brought the German bomber down
some five miles off the French coast.† However, the Ju88's rear gunner was an accurate shot and had scored several hits on Finucane's Spitfire as the Irishman pressed
home his attacks at close range. As a result his hydraulics system was damaged and he
was forced to make a wheels-up landing at Tangmere. He was soon back in action
and, on 5 February, shot down a Bf109 over France during a sweep in the St Omer
area in which No. 65 Squadron flew with Nos. 610 and 302, the other two squadrons
making up the Tangmere Wing. This sweep was an offensive operation by Fighter
Command and was a foretaste of things to come. By now Finucane had destroyed four
enemy aircraft, shared in the destruction of a fifth, had probably destroyed a further
two and had damaged another. His reputation as a fighter pilot was increasing all the
while.

On 15 April Finucane increased his score to five enemy aircraft destroyed when he
shot down a Bf109 over the channel. By now No. 65 Squadron was stationed in
Lincolnshire, at Kirton-in-Lindsay, as part of 12 Group of Fighter Command (it had
previously been in 11 Group). With Nos. 266 and 402 Squadrons, 65 carried out a
sweep over Boulogne. It was on the return flight, about midway between Calais and
Dover, that Finucane pounced on the 109 from 14,000 feet. He followed the Messer-

---

* The Bf110, or Zerstörer, was designed as a long-range fighter. It proved unequal to the task and was
deployed as a fighter-bomber as on this occasion. The aircraft finally found its true *métier* as a nightfighter
later in the war.
† The Junkers Ju88 was one of the most versatile and successful aircraft designs of the war. It served as a
bomber, reconnaissance machine, nightfighter and dive-bomber among its many roles.

schmitt right down to the surface, pulling out from his dive as the enemy machine went straight in.

It was Finucane's last mission with No. 65 Squadron. The day before he had been promoted to Flight Lieutenant and appointed to command a flight of No. 452 Squadron, also at Kirton-in-Lindsay. No. 452 was a Royal Australian Air Force unit, the first of a number of RAAF squadrons to be formed in Britain for operations in Europe. With his new Australian comrades, Finucane was to become a household name both in Britain and Australia. And he was about to receive his first decoration: as he left No. 65 Squadron his commanding officer made out a citation for the Distinguished Flying Cross; he also endorsed Finucane's logbook with an 'exceptional' rating. The Irishman had come a long way since those first days struggling to come to grips with the skills of flying.

The citation for the DFC was published in the *London Gazette* on 13 May. It noted that Finucane

> has shown great keenness in his efforts to engage the enemy and he has destroyed at least five of their aircraft. His courage and enthusiasm have been a source of encouragement to other pilots of the squadron.

The fact that he had shot down five enemy aircraft put Finucane in the 'ace' category but it hardly indicated that he would soon become the Royal Air Force's top fighter pilot; there were many pilots with either DFCs or DFMs.*

Moving across the airfield to No. 452 Squadron, Flight Lieutenant Finucane took command of A Flight and found his new Australian comrades to be in marked contrast to the RAF pilots with whom he had been familiar heretofore. Australians tended to have a more relaxed attitude to matters concerning discipline and service etiquette than did their British counterparts. Used to the ways of a Royal Air Force squadron, which still had a core of pre-war regulars, Finucane took some time to adjust to the easygoing Australians. They even had a different nickname for him at first, calling him Finney in contrast to the Paddy by which he had been known in No. 65. But the Paddy nickname was adopted quickly by the Australians; and so, too, was Brendan Finucane, who was to become almost an Australian national hero.

Throughout late April and May, Finucane had the task of training all of No. 452 up to operational standard. The fact that he was responsible for the full squadron was a result of a flying accident in which Finucane collided with the commanding officer's aircraft from behind and cut off most of the latter's fin and rudder. (The accident happened because the squadron was flying old Spitfire Mk Is and Finucane had the only machine with a metal rather than wooden propeller, which made his aircraft slightly faster. At the time of the collision the squadron was flying in a very tight formation.) As part of his training programme Finucane carried out practice dogfights

---

* The Distinguished Flying Medal was awarded to NCOs as their equivalent of the Distinguished Flying Cross.

and found the Australian pilots keen to learn. He was also responsible for the ground crews' training, which he felt, was not progressing well enough. Calling all the NCOs into the A Flight offices, Finucane let them know how he felt about their progress and told them plainly that he expected improvements. He got what he wanted. On 2 June 1941 the squadron was declared day operational by Fighter Command. Eight days later its new Australian commanding officer, Bon Bungey, arrived. Then, on 11 July, No. 452 Squadron flew its first circus operation.

Fighter Command's 11 Group had begun the practice of flying sweeps, or circus operations, over France in February 1941 and such operations were to be the main task of the Command.* This policy was initiated by Operational Instructions 6 and 7 which stated that

> The German Air Forces in Occupied territory have by day been comparatively undisturbed by offensive action on our part. The initiative has been entirely theirs until recently, to be as active as and when they pleased ... As a result of our circus operations to date the Germans have now started putting up standing patrols and these show signs of increasing with each operation ... The object of these attacks is to force the enemy to give battle under conditions tactically favourable to our fighters.
>
> ... the object of circus operations, from a fighter point of view, is to destroy enemy fighters enticed up into the air, using the tactical advantages of surprise, height and sun.

In fact, the nature of the operations often surrendered at least two of those tactical advantages: surprise was rarely achieved. At times the Germans would not rise to the bait, or, alternatively, they would be up at a great altitude and obtain the advantage of height. Small groups of bombers – sometimes even a single machine – were used as the bait for these missions, flying in to attack a selected target while many squadrons of fighters supported them; those aircraft were escorted by other fighters at an even higher altitude.

Most of Fighter Command's heavy losses in 1941 were as a result of these sweeps with the greatest toll falling on the escort squadrons. The sweep offensive was a reversal of the battle of Britain situation, with the RAF making the same mistake as the Luftwaffe had made in 1940 when Göring had given in to the pleas of the bomber pilots for closer fighter protection. Fighters left to wait for attackers were always tactically disadvantaged. At the end of June 1941 the sweeps were stepped up by Fighter Command as a result of the German invasion of the Soviet Union. A new strategic

---

* Although the circuses were the main element of Fighter Command's offensive operations there were other types of operation, each with its own distinctive codename: *Ramrods* were missions escorting bombers where the main aim was to destroy the target; *Fighter Ramrods* involved escorting cannon-armed fighters against ground targets; *Roadsteads* were missions escorting bombers against ships at sea or in port; *Fighter Roadsteads* were the same type of mission without bombers; *Rodeos* were fighter offensive sweeps without bombers; *Rhubarbs* were harassing operations by small numbers of fighters taking advantage of cloud cover; and *Intruders* were missions operated by night-flying squadrons.

imperative had been created: the need to keep German aircraft committed against the RAF in the west and reduce the pressure on the Soviet air arm.

The operation on which No. 452 was blooded on 11 July was Circus 44, a diversion for Circus 45. A single Blenheim bomber was the decoy, protected by the fighters of three wings, a total of eight squadrons as one of the wings, from Kenley, was still incomplete. The Australian squadron together with Nos. 65 and 266 Squadrons made up the wing from 12 Group; the other two wings were from 11 Group. Having refuelled at West Malling, the 12 Group wing crossed the Channel to make landfall on the French coast near Dunkirk. No. 266 was in the lead, flying at 17,000 feet, with 452 at 18,000 feet and 65 at 19,000 feet as the top squadron.

Over Poperinghe the wing split into fours as it made its way to Cassel. Action was joined five miles west of Lille with anti-aircraft guns opening up on the fighters and enemy aircraft coming in to intercept them. The leading German machine overshot Finucane, who cut in on the inside of his opponent's turn and followed him in his dive. Having closed to within 150 yards, Finucane fired a short burst at the Bf109 and saw the pilot bale out. He had achieved the first combat victory for No. 452 Squadron. He was also the only member of the squadron to have engaged an enemy aircraft. One of 452's pilots was shot down; he later managed to evade capture and made his way back to England.

On 21 July the squadron was moved to Kenley, south of London, to complete the wing there alongside Nos. 602 (City of Glasgow) and 485 (New Zealand) Squadrons; all three squadrons operated Spitfires. The routine of the summer weeks had been indicated by that operation of 11 July; by the end of that month the Kenley wing had flown ten circuses, on seven of which they provided close escort to bombers and thus had little opportunity to engage in fighter-to-fighter combat as their principal duty was to stay with the bombers.

Brendan Finucane's next combat success came on a mission in the early morning of 3 August. At about 7.30 a.m. some five miles west of St Omer he shot down a Bf109 from a range of 200 yards at a height of 14,000 feet. In the same combat he scored hits on a second 109, damaging its tail unit and sending the machine into a vertical dive. The first 109 was confirmed as destroyed; the second was probably destroyed. Six days later he had another series of successes over the Gosnay-Béthune area. On this occasion Finucane downed one Bf109 with a four-second burst from 100 yards and shared in the destruction of two other aircraft, one of which he hit in the tailplane with a three-second burst from 25 yards and the other with a five-second burst from 100 yards. By the end of August he had shot down a further six Bf109s with yet another probable. In one case, on 16 August, Finucane had closed to within ten yards of his opponent as his gunsight had failed; he shot off the 109's tail unit with a three-second burst.

A Bar to Finucane's DFC was awarded on 9 September, followed by a second Bar on 26 September. These two awards were direct results of his successes in combat over the summer months. In the citation for the first Bar it was noted that since July he had destroyed three enemy aircraft and assisted in the destruction of another two. He was said to have been largely responsible for the fine fighting spirit of the unit.

This award clearly covers the period between 11 July and 9 August during which Brendan Finucane shot down three Bf109s, shared in the destruction of two and had probably shot down a sixth machine. The citation for the second Bar noted that he had destroyed a further six enemy aircraft, of which three were shot down in one day and two in a single mission on another day. The three were downed on 16 August, including the one hit from ten yards' distance, while the two were destroyed on 27 August. Mention was also made of how Finucane's 'ability and courage have been reflected in the high standard of morale and fighting spirit of his unit'. The citation concluded by noting that his personal score of enemy aircraft destroyed stood at fifteen.

Brendan Finucane was not the only pilot in No. 452 Squadron to achieve success in that summer of 1941. August proved a particularly successful month for the squadron with 21 victories and three probables. Of these Finucane had been responsible for seven of the victories, had shared in two and had two of the probables. Both Finucane and the squadron were to achieve considerable fame in Britain, and further afield, as a result of their achievements. That fame arose when a leading war correspondent hailed the Irishman as the RAF's leading fighter ace. Although the claim was premature – he was 23rd on Fighter Command's list in August, jumping to 8th in September – the reputation stuck. On 23 September the *Daily Mail* carried the headline 'Spitfire Finucane shoots down 20 Nazis'. His reputation was further enhanced on 11 October when the Irishman was awarded the Distinguished Service Order, days before his twenty-first birthday, although the award did not appear in the *London Gazette* until ten days later. The citation noted that

> Recently during two sorties on consecutive days Flight Lieutenant Finucane destroyed five Messerschmitt 109s bringing his total victories to at least 20. He has flown with this squadron since June 1941 during which time the squadron has destroyed 42 enemy aircraft of which Flight Lieutenant Finucane has personally destroyed 15. The successes achieved are undoubtedly due to this officer's brilliant leadership and example.

Not only had Finucane's achievements made his a household name in Britain as the RAF's most outstanding fighter pilot but he also drew special praise from Prime Minister Winston Churchill. On 9 October 1941 the premier suggested – in a note to the Chief of the Imperial General Staff, General Sir John Dill, himself an Irishman – that the time was ripe to create an Irish Brigade in the Army, 'also an Irish Wing or Squadron of the RAF ... The pilot Finucane might be a great figure.' Although an Irish Brigade was formed in the Army within weeks of Churchill's suggestion, there was no parallel Irish Squadron or Wing in the Royal Air Force, even though Churchill had even proposed a name for it – Shamrock. Finucane's aircraft had long been decorated with a shamrock just forward of the cockpit.

Instead of being posted to command an Irish squadron, or wing, Brendan Finucane continued on operations with his Australian comrades, including a circus on 12 October against the docks at Boulogne during which Finucane shot down a Bf109F, although his wingman, Sergeant Chisholm, DFM, was shot down. Then, on 13 October, he destroyed two 109s and damaged another during another circus, this time to Arques. In the course of that operation the squadron accounted for seven enemy aircraft destroyed and three damaged. Finucane's personal score was now 24½ enemy aircraft destroyed. It would be some time, however, before he would add to that tally.

That evening Finucane fractured his right heel after a night out with some of his comrades in London. He spent his twenty-first birthday in hospital and it was to be many weeks before he returned to operational flying. In the meantime, on 25 November, he went to Buckingham Palace with his mother and his brother Raymond, now a sergeant air-gunner with No. 101 Squadron, to be invested with the DSO and the two Bars to his DFC by King George VI.

Early in the new year of 1942 he was passed fit for flying duties and returned to Kenley where the station commander was another Irishman, Victor Beamish. At the end of January Beamish promoted Finucane to the rank of Squadron Leader and posted him to command No. 602 (City of Glasgow) Squadron of the Kenley Wing. An Irishman commanding a Scottish squadron produced the sight of Finucane's personal Spitfire being decorated with both the lion rampant of Scotland and the shamrock of Ireland.

The City of Glasgow Squadron was based at Redhill, a satellite airfield of Kenley where his new command soon got to know Finucane well and to develop respect for him. His biographer, Doug Stokes, quotes a number of ground personnel who were impressed by the new CO's attitude. One man who remembered him with respect and admiration was Joe Parker, a flight mechanic on A Flight, who told Stokes that Finucane re-organized the morning NAAFI break at dispersal points so that the men did not have to queue. Another groundcrew man, Alex Davis of B Flight, recalled how, when the squadron paraded to meet its new CO, Finucane told them to break ranks and gather around him informally. Thus was the ice well and truly broken and the new 'boss' received in favourable light from the day of his arrival.

For the first few weeks of Finucane's command at Redhill, weather conditions precluded flying: heavy snow in January was followed by freezing rain, which left the airfield waterlogged, and then by more snow and ice. It was not until 12 February that the squadron was called upon for operational duties. This was in the 'Channel Dash' of the German capital ships *Gneisenau*, *Scharnhorst* and *Prinz Eugen* from Brest to Norway, the operation in which another Irish flier, Eugene Esmonde, gained a posthumous Victoria Cross as he led his squadron of flimsy Swordfish biplanes against the mighty German ships and their massive air escort.

At 11.30 a.m. that day Finucane's squadron was ordered up on a Roadstead operation, an attack on shipping. No one knew the exact nature of the operation and, in fact, it seemed to change, as the first order was to escort Beaufort torpedo-bombers. This was cancelled and another task was allocated but the controller was not certain which squadron Finucane's Spitfires were to escort. The Dubliner led his squadron into the air and they were midway to their rendezvous point on the south coast when a signal was received telling them to return to base.

There seemed to be no clear idea of what was happening and the pilots were told that they could go to lunch. During the meal No. 602 was ordered to be ready for operations at fifteen minutes' notice. Just after 1 o'clock came the signal to scramble and, within minutes, the Spitfires were in the air. The Kenley Wing did not find the Beauforts that they were to escort and headed out over the channel. Spotting two armed enemy merchant ships, Finucane led his squadron down to attack them with both cannon and machine-gun fire. Shortly after this attack they swooped on two warships, thought to be destroyers, which opened an intense fire on the fighters.

Not until later did Finucane and his pilots learn the full story of that February day. At the subsequent inquiry Finucane was called as a witness on 19 February, the fourth day of the inquiry. The following day he was back on operations when he and another pilot flew across the channel and strafed a ship in Dunkirk harbour. They spotted two aircraft taking off from the German airfield at Mardyck but then lost sight of them and dropped to sea level. Only two minutes later two German fighters attacked the pair of Spitfires. These were not Messerschmitt Bf109s but the new Focke-Wulf FW190s, the Luftwaffe's latest fighter and a machine that, with a top speed of 418 m.p.h., was about 50 m.p.h. faster than the Spitfire VB, the current model in service with the RAF. Although the Spitfire VB was more manoeuvrable than the FW190, and could turn in a tighter circle, the new German fighter had the overall advantage.

This was the first occasion on which Finucane met the FW190, and it was almost his last. On the Germans' first pass Finucane's wingman, Dick Lewis, an Australian, managed to get some hits on one of the 190s, but the Focke-Wulfs came in for another attack. As they did so Finucane tried to get into a firing position but his opponent had the advantage and opened fire first. A burst of machine-gun fire passed over Finucane's Spitfire, but a second burst struck the plane's fuselage, wings and tailplane. A piece of damaged fuselage was driven into Finucane's right thigh and he was forced to dive to sea level to try to make his escape home. He let Lewis know what had happened and the Australian took up position behind Finucane to drive off the Germans as they made six more attacks from behind. The final attack was made with the two FW190s approaching from opposite directions, but Lewis managed to shoot one down and the other soon gave up the chase.

The wounded Finucane managed to nurse his damaged fighter back to Kenley, where he lost consciousness on landing. He was later operated upon to remove the piece of fuselage from his thigh and was subsequently sent on sick leave. On 10 March he returned to the squadron and three days later he led them on Circus 114 to the marshalling yards at Hazebrouck, where he shot down a FW190 and shared in the destruction of another. Subsequently there was dispute about the claims submitted by RAF pilots for this operation – ten aircraft destroyed – and post-war research into

German records suggests that the Luftwaffe admitted the loss of only one machine that day; that was a 109 that made an emergency landing after sustaining battle damage. It seems highly unlikely that a pilot as experienced as Finucane would have made a claim that he could not justify and, in fact, he had a practice of not claiming a 'kill' if he had not seen the machine crash. In his combat with the FW190 Finucane had clashed with the German at 23,000 feet and fought him down to 8,000, where he fired the burst that sent his opponent into the ground. His second combat began at 20,000 feet and he subsequently reported that the Spitfire VB could turn twice as well as a Focke-Wulf FW190 at those heights.

On Saint Patrick's Day the commanders of Fighter Command's Nos. 10 and 11 Groups were notified by Sholto Douglas that the sweep offensive over France against the Luftwaffe was to be resumed. Once again the strategic imperative of supporting the Soviets by weakening the German fighter force in the west was an underlying reason for this decision. But Douglas was concerned about the loss rate in Fighter Command; he wrote:

> Owing to the drain on our fighter resources particularly for overseas, there is still need to avoid heavy wastage due to operations such as those covered by this directive. The difficulty of regulating operations to ensure low wastage rates is realized, but so far as possible these operations should be so planned and conducted that the losses sustained by our fighters are not normally greater than those inflicted on the enemy.

On 25 March, a beautiful spring morning, Finucane took A and B Flights of No. 602 Squadron up on a practice flight that took them out across the channel. Before long the pilots realized that this 'practice flight' was really Finucane looking for action. On reaching the French coast the Irishman took the squadron down almost to sea level and flew down the coast at Cap Gris Nez with the German anti-aircraft gunners desperately depressing their barrels in an effort to engage the British fighters. Such a practice flight was not unusual with Finucane: he believed that it was good battle inoculation for his pilots and was well aware that the anti-aircraft guns had very little chance of hitting aircraft flying below them at 350 m.p.h.

Further Circus operations led to further 'kills' for Brendan Finucane: on 26 March in Circus 116A – referred to as Ramrod 17 in No. 11 Group's reports – he destroyed another 190; on 28 March he shot down a 190 and a 109 and shared another 109 while, on 2 April, he damaged a further 190.

His fame was spreading. When the squadron returned from operations on 26 March they found a press group waiting for Finucane. Laela Laid of *Life* magazine and the photographer Oswald Wild were there to prepare a feature on the Irishman, which duly appeared and served to enhance his reputation. But, on 28 March, there was tragic news: Victor Beamish, the station commander at Kenley, had failed to return from a fighter Rodeo. On learning of this Finucane took his squadron up again that evening to carry out a search for his fellow Irishman. It was in vain. No trace was ever found.

Following Beamish's death, a senior officer at Kenley had Finucane's claims for 28 March, a Bf109 and a FW190 both destroyed, downgraded to probably destroyed in each case. It seems that not everyone was pleased with the publicity that the young Irish ace was receiving. Stokes notes that veterans to whom he spoke were convinced that this officer had a strong personal dislike of both Finucane and No. 602 Squadron, and one former pilot told how he had been asked to downgrade a 'kill' achieved by Finucane.

At the end of March 1942, however, Brendan Finucane was the top-scoring fighter 'ace' still on operations. The only man ahead of him, 'Sailor' Malan, was non-operational. With 29½ kills Finucane was only 2½ behind Malan and the next-highest-scoring ace, Bob Stanford-Tuck, with 29 kills, had been shot down and taken prisoner in January. Finucane was also the most decorated of the RAF's aces at this time. Between then and his death in July Finucane accounted for another two enemy aircraft destroyed, one of which was shared, bringing his total to 31, and two probables as well as four damaged. There were other victories that would have taken his tally higher, but these had either not been claimed by him, or had been attributed by him to others, or had been downgraded.

It was rare that Finucane misread a situation, but one of the few occasions on which he did occurred on 13 April when his squadron was bounced by higher-flying 190s over Cap Gris Nez. The 190s had dropped from over 30,000 feet when Finucane led 602 on a diving attack on fifteen 190s below them. But, once action was joined, Finucane read the combat situation in masterly fashion and controlled his aircraft, which he had ordered to fly in a defensive circle. As attacks were made he directed the tactics of his pilots and turned into many attacks himself to engage the enemy. Between attacks he would order pairs of aircraft to break and head for home. Finally, he led his own section out, diving to sea level and heading for home. The defensive battle had lasted fifteen minutes but, thanks to Finucane's excellent leadership, 602 sustained no losses. That battle was one of Brendan Finucane's finest achievements.

On 17 May 1942 the Air Ministry released a press bulletin (No. 7011) in which Finucane was credited with another FW190 destroyed and which claimed that his overall tally had risen to 32 kills, putting him a par with Malan. The publicity surrounding the young Irishman continued to grow. During the blazing warm days of June 1942 he led the Kenley Wing on a diversionary sweep for Circus 191, during which he probably destroyed a Focke-Wulf FW190, and then on Circus 193 to Le Havre which was his last sweep with No. 602.

That night No. 602 held a party to celebrate Brendan Finucane's promotion to Wing Commander, the youngest in that rank in Fighter Command. He was to move to command the Hornchurch Wing and left Kenley on 21 June.

The Hornchurch Wing was beginning to convert to the latest version of the Spitfire, the Mark IX, which was a match for the FW190 and put the RAF pilots back on a more even battleground. As wing leader at Hornchurch, Finucane adopted the standard practice of marking his aircraft with his own initials – BE-F – as well as with the shamrock. He continued to fly with his squadrons as the wing leader's responsibility was for the operational effectiveness of his squadrons, a role he took very seriously. In the first week of his command he led his squadrons on Circus 195, two fighter ramrods, two rodeos and two practice flights. Adverse weather prevented operational flying in early July, but this restarted on 12 July with a fighter rodeo followed by Circus 198 that afternoon. Circus 199 followed on 13 July and, next day, there was a low-level fighter Roadstead to Ostend.

On 15 July Brendan Finucane led his squadrons on a fighter Ramrod to strafe a German army camp at Étaples. It was to be his last flight. The Spitfires of No. 154 Squadron led with Finucane at their head. They crossed the channel at wavetop height and made landfall at Le Touquet. As they crossed the French coast a burst of machine-gun fire from the ground struck Finucane's Spitfire. His wingman, the Canadian Alan Aikman, broke radio silence to let his leader know that his radiator had been hit. Finucane acknowledged with a thumbs-up sign and made an immediate turn for the channel and Hornchurch. White vapour was streaming from the damaged radiator. Aikman followed, strafing the machine-gunner on the ground as he headed out to sea. About ten miles out to sea from Le Touquet Finucane called to Aikman that his engine was overheating. He ditched the stricken aircraft in the channel. Before the Spitfire struck the water, Aikman saw the Irishman jettison his cockpit canopy and heard him say, 'This is it, Butch,' just before he removed his flying helmet.

Although Finucane did everything correctly in ditching his machine, the Spitfire was a difficult aircraft to land on water and it disappeared in a wall of spray and water, before its nose plunged downwards and the plane sank instantly. Finucane did not get out of the stricken plane. It is possible that he was thrown forward and knocked unconscious on the gunsight as he had the habit of flying with his harness loose in order to have more freedom to scan the skies; but he did tighten it when going into combat. As Doug Stokes comments, 'The question must remain unanswered.'

Although Aikman remained over the site of Finucane's ditching for ten minutes, and radioed a mayday, there was no sign of oil or debris on the surface and the Canadian had to turn for home as his fuel was running low.

Sholto Douglas wrote to the Finucane family:

> Your son's courage, skill and powers of leadership were a great inspiration to the Fighter Command, including myself. His influence among his fellow pilots was remarkable for one of his age. We shall all miss him greatly. He was the beau ideal of the 'fighter boy'.

This was the same Sholto Douglas who, in his memoirs, referred to Finucane as 'a rather wild Irishman', something he patently was not. Doug Stokes, with the evidence of over one hundred aircrew, paints a picture of a different man – a consummate professional and a born leader who inspired confidence and trust in those around him. But even Stokes, a balanced biographer, reverts to stereotype with an introduction headed 'The Fighting Irishman' and the suggestion that it was the 'Gaelic restlessness in his nature' that drove him and would have prevented him ever sitting at a desk again. But, as with so many other Irishmen – and servicemen of other nationalities – Finucane was driven by a sense of duty and a belief in what he was fighting for and it is not difficult to think of him in an ordinary job again had he survived the war. But survive he did not and his passing added another hero to the RAF's pantheon and to the many Irish who gave their lives for freedom. The extent of Finucane's fame can be gauged by the fact that a telegram of sympathy on his death was received from two of the Soviet Union's leading fighter pilots, Ivan Kholodar and Eugenyi Gorbatyuk.

Finucane had served under the command of another remarkable Irish fighter pilot, Victor Beamish, and the paths of the pair had crossed with Eugene Esmonde on that dark February day in the English channel when the man from Tipperary had flown to his doom. Before the year was out all three were dead, their lives ending, by some quirk of fate, in that same strip of water that separates Britain from mainland Europe. Finucane was the last of the trio to die, with Beamish's demise occurring on 28 March 1942, not long after Esmonde's last mission.

Victor Francis Beamish was born in Dunmanway, County Cork, in September 1903, an area where Beamishes had farmed since the eighteenth century. His father, however, was headmaster of the local school rather than a farmer. The Beamish family had first come to the province of Munster as planters in the reign of Elizabeth I and, after the earl of Desmond's rebellion, three Beamish brothers were given grants of some of the earl's land. A pattern of settlement was being repeated, as the original Beamishes had come to England from Normandy: the family name had been anglicized from the French Beaumais.

When Victor was nine years old, the family moved first to Dublin, where his father became a schools' inspector, and then, three years later, to Coleraine in County Londonderry. Victor, whose education had started at Dunmanway Model School, moved to Coleraine Academical Institution in 1915 when his father became the schools' inspector for County Londonderry. It was from Coleraine that Victor joined the Royal Air Force, at his second attempt, in 1921. In 1920 he had joined the Boys' Wing at Cranwell, the RAF College, but had been removed, after only a day, by his aunt, Ellen Ross Beamish, who lived in London.

At Cranwell, Beamish was a good student, doing well academically and at sport and demonstrating a flair for leadership that gained him rapid promotion to flight cadet under-officer. He was also learning to fly, beginning on the Avro 504K and progressing to the Bristol Fighter on which Beamish went solo for the first time. He qualified as a pilot in September 1923 and went to No. 4 Squadron at Farnborough in Hampshire. In February 1925 he was promoted to Flying Officer and took a further step on the promotion ladder in December 1928 when he became Flight Lieutenant Beamish. By that time he had served in India but, after crashing an aircraft in May 1926, he was posted home and became a pupil instructor at the Central Flying School.

With a posting to Canada, where he formed and led the Royal Canadian Air Force's aerobatic display team, and his promotion to Flight Lieutenant, Beamish seemed set for a successful career in the RAF. However, he was invalided out of the service as a result of tuberculosis in 1933, which appeared to spell the end of his career. The resourceful Beamish managed to rejoin the RAF in 1936 as a civilian adjutant at Aldergrove in County Antrim. He was later restored to his commission and returned to flying duties, albeit this was unofficial at first, and took command of the Meteorological Flight and No. 2 Armament Practice Camp at Aldergrove. In 1938 he was awarded the Air Force Cross for his work in establishing the flight.

Beamish was commanding No. 504 Squadron soon after war broke out, having turned down a staff appointment. He made an excellent job of leading 504 and was described as 'having the gift of leadership with an Irish charm, and very friendly'. Nonetheless he was a tough taskmaster and imposed high standards on his pilots; but he never asked them to do anything he would not do himself.

At the end of May 1940 Beamish was appointed to command RAF North Weald in Essex. This was a job that was principally ground-based but Beamish did as much flying as he possibly could. He had a Hurricane of No. 151 Squadron allocated as his personal aircraft and he flew over the coast of France, meeting enemy aircraft in action for the first time on 7 June. Eleven days later, Beamish made his first claim when he engaged a Heinkel He111 over Cherbourg; the bomber was classified as 'probably destroyed'. The fighters had been patrolling over the channel when they spotted three He111s attacking shipping. When Beamish attacked and badly damaged his victim the other two Heinkels jettisoned their remaining bombs and fled.

Over the next nine months at North Weald, Victor Beamish was involved in eighteen aerial combats in which he claimed enemy aircraft destroyed, probably destroyed or damaged. He claimed four 'kills': two Bf109 fighters destroyed over the channel on 30 June; a Dornier Do17 bomber destroyed east of Orfordness on 12 July; and Junkers Ju87 dive-bomber shot down over Shellhaven on 6 September. His probables included that first He111, as well as two others over London in September during the battle of Britain; a Junkers Ju88 over Chelmsford on 18 August; four Bf109s; a Bf110; a Junkers Ju87; and an Italian Fiat Cr42 over the east coast on 11 November. He shared one 'damaged' Bf109 as well as three others on his own and a Dornier Do215.

These results show that Beamish was not content to stay on the ground during the battle of Britain. Frequently, he took off in his own Hurricane after the station's squadrons had scrambled and joined in the aerial battles. This was a dangerous practice as he had no wing man to cover him: Fighter Command had adopted the practice of having its aircraft fly and fight in pairs with the two machines of each pair providing mutual cover, a tactic adapted from the Luftwaffe.

Now aged thirty-seven, twice as old as some of his pilots, Beamish flew an incredible 126 fighter sorties during the battle of Britain. Although he certainly shot down a number of enemy aircraft, the exact figure cannot be ascertained, as he would never make a claim unless he was absolutely positive that the enemy machine had gone down. Nonetheless, he was decorated with the DSO in July 1940. The citation noted that he took over command of an RAF station after two squadrons there had been intensively engaged in successful fighting operations over France for thirteen days and personally led them on many patrols against the enemy. In June 1940 during an offensive mission over France six Messerschmitt '109s were destroyed, two of them by Wing Commander Beamish himself, and twelve driven off. One day recently he assisted in the destruction of a Messerschmitt 110 while leading the escort to a convoy* and three days later he shot down a Dornier 17. This officer's outstanding leadership and high courage have inspired all those under his command with great energy and dash.

The battle of Britain had not begun when Beamish was awarded his DSO. As the summer of 1940 moved into early autumn the Luftwaffe onslaught reached a new intensity and the pilots of Fighter Command, Churchill's famous 'Few', fought to exhaustion as they strove to repel the German attacks. Beamish played a full and active part in these operations, and several of his claims were made in September, including the Ju87 dive-bomber that he destroyed on 6 September. In one combat, on 15 September, which was the heaviest day of fighting in the battle, Beamish flew twice and, on the second occasion, he probably shot down a Heinkel He111. The reason this particular aircraft was a probable was that Beamish went so close to it in his attack that oil from its damaged engines smeared the cockpit canopy of his Hurricane and a piece of debris from the Heinkel struck his wing. Three days later he claimed a Bf109 as a probable and this was followed by another of the single-seat fighters on 27 September; this was Beamish's last combat in the German daylight bomber offensive.

Although the Luftwaffe had abandoned its daylight bomber operations in favour of nocturnal raids on Britain, the German fighters were not quiet and continued to mount offensive missions against Britain. Some of these were carried out at low level and were known as 'tip-and-run' raids. Fighter Command was kept busy throughout October and November until active operations all but ceased in December.

One of the 'tip-and-run' raids was mounted against Beamish's own North Weald station on 29 October, and Beamish took off through a hail of bombs and cannon- and machine-gunfire from the attacking Bf109s. Five men died on the ground that day and one Hurricane pilot was killed as his aircraft lifted off the ground.

On 8 November Beamish was awarded the Distinguished Flying Cross. The citation noted his 'exceptional keenness in his engagements against the enemy' and his inspiring 'coolness and courage'. One day earlier he had a close brush with death when he took off on a solo patrol over the Thames estuary and caught up with No. 249 Squadron shortly after they had attacked a Luftwaffe force that was bombing a convoy. On the day's third patrol, Beamish left the formation to fly solo for a time, as was his practice, but as he returned to join the other aircraft he flew into the tail of Ginger Neil's Hurricane. Neil's machine lost its tail unit and Beamish's propeller was

---

* This was not the Bf110 listed as 'probably destroyed' in Appendix B of Stokes' biography of Beamish. That machine was intercepted more than a month after the announcement of his DSO in the *London Gazette*.

destroyed. The Irishman managed to make a forced landing at Leeds Abbey, near Detling, where his Hurricane struck an obstruction pole, causing yet more damage to the machine. Fortunately, the collision had occurred at some 18,000 feet and this allowed Neil to escape with his life. The younger man was able to bale out but not before the stricken Hurricane had descended to 4,000 feet. The incident is an indication of how much strain Beamish had endured. As a master of formation flying he was less likely to make such a mistake than were many of his younger colleagues but mental and physical exhaustion must have taken their toll after so many months of active flying duties.

In early 1941 Fighter Command adopted its offensive sweep strategy and the first Circus was flown on 10 January. Beamish took part and later spoke about the mission in a BBC broadcast at the beginning of February. This was a carefully-scripted description and Beamish told how his formation provided fighter cover for a bomber force. Although he described a formation attack on German flak ships, he had dived alone on these vessels. En route back to base he shot down a Bf109, which two of his pilots saw crash in the sea, although it was claimed only as a probable.

On St Patrick's Day 1941, Victor Beamish was posted to a staff job at Headquarters No. 11 Group with the rank of acting Group Captain. Although he was not happy in such a job, he was able to draft tactical notes in which he emphasized the lessons learnt in the circus operations. He also continued to fly, using a Hurricane and, later, a Spitfire based at Northolt, in which he would visit operational stations. Not surprisingly, Beamish even managed to fly on operations, including Circus 68 on which he claimed another Bf109 as a probable. Finally, he managed to persuade the authorities to return him to the command of a fighter station. This was RAF Kenley where he resumed his practice of flying operationally when he took up his command there on 25 January 1942. By then he had been awarded a Bar to his DSO.

The citation for the Bar noted that Beamish had carried out 71 operational sorties between October 1940 and March 1941.* During that time he had definitely destroyed one enemy aircraft, had probably destroyed three more and damaged several others. His 'courage and devotion to duty' were praised, as was the 'magnificent example' he had set. He was now one of the RAF's most decorated fighter pilots; and one of the most decorated Irish servicemen of the war.

In February 1942 Beamish flew a patrol to check if *Scharnhorst*, *Gneisenau* and *Prinz Eugen* were heading for the channel. Having established that they were, he flew back to Kenley and then tried to pass the news on to 11 Group HQ. He has been criticized for doing this: as a former staff officer, who had been involved in drawing up the plans for action in the event of the three ships breaking out of Brest, he knew the contingency plans for such an eventuality, and it has been suggested that he ought to have broken radio silence to report what he saw. However, another pilot who did break radio silence did so in vain, as his transmission was not picked up. With the radio sets fitted to the Spitfire it was unlikely that any message from Beamish, or

---

* The October date was incorrect, as he had been commanding RAF North Weald from June 1940.

anyone else, would have reached Britain. Climbing to transmit might have improved the chance of getting through, but it also raised the chances of being shot down. There was no real alternative to flying back fast and low, which is exactly what Beamish did; even then he had difficulty persuading others of what he had seen. A radio message could so easily have been ignored even if it had been received.

Circus operations resumed in March 1942, although they did not become official policy until 17 March. Beamish took part in these early operations and had his first engagement with a FW190 on 9 March during Circus 113. In a combat with a section of 190s, Beamish shot one of the German aircraft down. In the course of further operations he caused severe damage to a ship in Le Havre and, on 26 March, he destroyed another FW190 as well as a Bf109. These were to be his last claims.

On 28 March 1942 Beamish was flying with No. 485 Squadron of the Kenley Wing on a fighter rodeo over the Calais area. At 19,000 feet he spotted a force of about 50 to 60 Bf109Fs and FW190s and turned his wing in to meet them. In the ensuing battle he lost his wingman, and although another pilot, Reg Grant, moved in to cover him, the latter's radio was out of action. With Grant unable to warn him of an impending attack, Beamish was jumped by a 190, which inflicted considerable damage on his Spitfire before being shot down by Grant. Beamish was probably injured and was last seen heading for England, with smoke trailing from his aircraft. He was spotted entering a cloud layer at about 12,000 feet.

Victor Beamish was never seen again. In his wartime career, he had destroyed eight enemy aircraft, probably destroyed thirteen and damaged another five. That is a remarkable record for a man who was almost as old as the fathers of most of his fellow pilots and who could so easily have spent his time safely behind a desk. But seeking safety was not the style of Victor Beamish, who preferred the excitement of action in the air and who even claimed that he wore his best uniform only for shooting down Huns. (When he went to Buckingham Palace for an investiture he did so in an old uniform; he sat beside King George VI at lunch in the old uniform.)

Finucane and Beamish were undoubtedly the best-known Irishmen in Fighter Command, but they were not the only Irish pilots. John Ignatius Kilmartin, a Dundalk man, also fought in the battle of Britain and was awarded the Distinguished Flying Cross in October 1940. At that time he had destroyed twelve enemy aircraft and it was noted that 'His dash and determination, with clear thinking, combine to make him a magnificent leader'.

Kilmartin, who had been educated at Presentation College, Bray, had served in the Shanghai Light Horse Volunteer Corps as a trooper before joining the RAF in 1937. He was promoted to Flying Officer in 1939 and made acting Flight Lieutenant in July 1940. His score of enemy aircraft destroyed later rose to fourteen.

Flying Officer R.F. Smythe, who was born in Killiney, Co. Dublin, was also awarded the DFC for his service in operations over Britain. In July 1940, while leading his section over the south coast, he broke up a formation of six Bf109s and personally destroyed one. By the time he was awarded the DFC, he had shot down six enemy aircraft to join the ranks of the 'aces'.

Patrick Peter Colin Barthropp, a native of Dublin, was educated at Ampleforth College and was commissioned into the RAF at the age of nineteen in 1939. In August 1941 he was promoted to Acting Flight Lieutenant with No. 91 Squadron. The squadron had formed at Hawkinge in January 1941 when No. 421 (Reconnaissance) Flight was renumbered as 91 Squadron. Its principal tasks with its Spitfires included shipping reconnaissance and gathering intelligence on the movements, tactics and markings of enemy aircraft. By the summer of 1941 it had become a fighter squadron carrying out shipping patrols and weather reconnaissance. Barthropp was awarded the DFC in September 1941, having:

> carried out one hundred and fifty operational sorties, many of them over enemy-occupied territory. Throughout, Flight Lieutenant Barthropp has displayed a fine fighting spirit, frequently attacking enemy aircraft, troops and other targets on the ground. He has destroyed at least two, probably destroyed another, and damaged three enemy aircraft.

The DFC was also awarded to Flight Lieutenant Patrick Joseph Thomas Stephenson for his service in the battle of Britain and the subsequent operations against targets in France. Born in 1918 in Dublin, Stephenson was living in Hull when he joined the Royal Air Force Volunteer Reserve in 1938 to receive pilot training. He was commissioned in 1940,

> and took part in the Battle of Britain. Later, as Flight Commander, he participated in operations, assisting in the sinking and damaging of several ships in the Channel. During his tour of duty he has destroyed five enemy aircraft and has completed many patrols and escorts. On numerous occasions, Flight Lieutenant Stephenson has led the squadron, displaying fine leadership, skill and courage.

Two brothers from County Antrim both flew fighters with the Royal Air Force. Stuart and Tony Lovell were born in Ceylon, where their father was a tea planter, but they returned to live in Northern Ireland after Lovell senior's death in 1923. In spite of the family's straitened circumstances, both boys were sent to Ampleforth. On leaving Ampleforth, Stuart decided to follow in his father's footsteps and went to Ceylon and the tea industry. His younger brother, Tony, joined the Royal Air Force as soon as he left school with the aim of taking a short-service commission. In the longer term it was Tony's plan to enter the religious life, either as a priest or a monk.

Tony Lovell trained in the same group of pilots as Al Deere and joined No. 41 Squadron as a Pilot Officer in October 1938. The squadron, based at Catterick, was still equipped with Hawker Fury biplanes but began converting to Spitfires in January 1939. Although the 'baby of the squadron' Tony Lovell matured considerably during

1939, and his fellow pilots felt that he was an 'above-average fighter pilot on Spitfires when war was declared'.

Tony's first action was in December 1939 when he was scrambled to pursue a Heinkel, which made off towards the sea. His first claim was over Dunkirk in May 1940 when he shared the destruction of another Heinkel. 'It was also reported at this time that he caused another German bomber to crash by chasing it at low level along the French beaches when in fact he was out of ammunition.'

During the battle of Britain, No. 41 Squadron was based at Hornchurch, from where Tony Lovell had his first clash in that conflict. On 28 July he encountered the German ace, Werner Molders, known as *Vatti* (Daddy) to his comrades, over Kent. Molders had the better of Lovell and damaged his aircraft badly enough for the Irishman to have to force land at Manston, with a slight wound to his thigh. However, Molders was then engaged by 'Sailor' Malan and forced to crash land at his own base in France; the German was also wounded in the legs.

On 15 August – *Adler Tag* to the Luftwaffe – Lovell was among the Fighter Command pilots who fought off the only large-scale German raid on the north of England. In this engagement he shot down a Messerschmitt Bf110 and damaged another. Returning to Hornchurch, he was with No. 41 when it was scrambled on the afternoon of 5 September to reinforce units already preparing to meet waves of German bombers approaching the Thames estuary. The enemy aircraft were en route to bomb Thameshaven, and the Spitfires of No. 41 did not have sufficient time to climb high enough to dive on the bombers. Instead, the squadron split in two, and one half went for the escorting fighters while the other, including Tony Lovell, made for the bombers.

> For 30 minutes there was a mad mêlée, with aircraft and pilots falling out of the hazy sky all over South Essex. On the ground, confusion reigned as anti-aircraft and searchlight batteries, ARP and police, infantry and gunners, reported and cross-reported the events of the moment.
>
> In the fifteen minutes from quarter to half-past three alone, the searchlight unit at South Benfleet noted an unidentified plane crashed in the sea; a crashed Spitfire at Wallasea Island; a crashed Spitfire at South Benfleet; a crashed Hurricane at North Benfleet; a crashed Spitfire south of Nevendon; and a crashed Hurricane at North Fambridge.

Tony Lovell was among those shot down but he baled out of his stricken aircraft to land safely at South Benfleet. No. 41 Squadron had lost a quarter of its strength in thirty minutes. Lovell was back in the air the following day, when he shot down his first Bf109. Nine days later he shot down another 109 over Kent. The German pilot was Herbert Tschoppe, who subsequently reported Lovell's chivalrous conduct. As Tschoppe descended unconscious, Lovell flew in circles around him to protect him and, when the German recovered consciousness, he saw the Irishman salute him: he, of course, thought that he was being saluted by an Englishman. In spite of his injuries, Tschoppe was able to return the compliment before coming to earth in a tree.

In November 1940, Tony Lovell was awarded the DFC. When 1940 came to an end he was a fighter ace with nine enemy aircraft to his credit. In September 1941 he was given command of No. 145 Squadron at Catterick and, later that year, received a Bar to his DFC. His squadron left for the Middle East in February 1942, the first Spitfire squadron to deploy to North Africa, but Lovell resigned his command before the squadron saw any action. As he was only twenty-two years old at the time, it is possible that he was unable to handle the administration and enforcement of discipline necessary in an operational squadron.

Resigning his command did not appear to do Tony Lovell's career any real harm, as he was then posted to the beleagured island of Malta to command No. 1435 Squadron. Malta was under severe pressure from enemy air attacks, and the fighter defences were kept busy, both fighting off raids and providing cover for incoming convoys. Tony was in action over the Santa Marija convoy of August 1942 in Operation PEDESTAL. By the end of 1942 he had added another eight enemy aircraft to his score and been awarded the DSO for his outstanding leadership.

In early 1943 Lovell was promoted to Wing Commander and led various Spitfire wings in the defence of Malta and in offensive operations against Sicily. He was still only twenty-three. Later that year the Allies invaded Sicily and then Italy, to where Tony Lovell transferred as Wing Commander (Flying) with No. 322 Wing of the Desert Air Force* with whom he first fought in the Italian campaign; he later commanded No. 244 Wing. One of his Wing's tasks was the protection of US Army Air Force bombers operating from Corsica for which he was awarded the US Distinguished Flying Cross.

Operating in tactical support of the ground forces, Lovell's wing built up an expertise in such operations. Aircraft were on call from a ground controller with the forward troops and were able to respond quickly to any call for support. The system used was called 'Rover David', or cab rank, and was similar to that later used in Normandy.

Rome fell to the Allies in June 1944, and Tony Lovell took the opportunity to have an audience of Pope Pius XII before taking some leave, which he spent on retreat in a Dominican monastery. War had not changed his attitude or his religious beliefs: Tony Lovell continued to be a devout Catholic who went to confession each time he shot down an opponent. While others would have rejoiced at the destruction of an enemy, Lovell was concerned with the soul of his opponent and worried that he may have sent an unprepared man to meet his Maker.

Until the end of 1944, Tony Lovell was engaged on active operations. He was then posted to be Chief Instructor at the RAF's fighter Operational Training Unit at Ismailia in Egypt. While there he learned that he had received a Bar to his DSO. The citation noted that 'his courage, his flying ability and his tactical knowledge have been an inspiration to all who have flown with him and of a quality seldom, if ever, equalled'. His record also made Tony Lovell Northern Ireland's most decorated fighter pilot of

---

* The North African title was retained for the tactical air component in the Italian campaign.

the Second World War. With Bars to both the DSO and DFC, he also ranks with Finucane (DSO, DFC and Bar, Mention in Despatches) as the most decorated fighter pilots from either side of the border.

In August 1945 Tony Lovell returned to the UK as an instructor at the School of Air Support at Old Sarum in Wiltshire, where he was killed in a flying accident two days after VJ Day. His Spitfire failed to gain height after a slow roll on take-off and hit high ground beyond the end of the runway.

> Tony Lovell was a very complicated character. Shy and reserved, formal and meticulous, he seems to have held himself apart but not aloof. He would join in if invited but was unlikely to start a party off his own bat. There was also an element of the daredevil in him, and a streak of competitiveness, but his risks appear always to have been calculated ones. In character he was very far removed from the popular image of the gung-ho fighter pilot.
>
> There is little doubt that he was a very highly skilled pilot indeed. His element was the air; and in battle he had an instinct for impending danger. He was personally responsible for the destruction of some 21 enemy aircraft.

Stuart Lovell, the older of the two brothers, was a very different character. He was on his first leave from Ceylon in five years when war broke out and decided to join the RAF. In July 1941 Stuart was posted to Kidlington, in Oxfordshire, for flying training and, on 20 September, he was commissioned 'for the emergency' in the RAFVR. Next day he married Alicia Montagu, of Portstewart, who had been Tony's best teenage friend.

During the course of his operational training on Hurricanes, Stuart crashed one of 55 OTU's aircraft through his own carelessness. In December 1941 he was posted to No. 263 Squadron, one of the only two in the RAF flying the twin-engined Westland Whirlwind fighter, which was armed with four cannon in the nose. He did not become operational on Whirlwinds until 30 May 1942. Almost a year later he was posted to No. 257 Squadron, which was operating Hawker Typhoons. Promoted to Flight Lieutenant on 20 September 1943, he transferred to No. 183 Squadron, also on Typhoons, as commander of B Flight on 29 October.

He took another pilot with him on a 'Rhubarb' on 3 November, but abandoned the mission some five miles off the French coast as the cloud base was 2,000 feet and German light anti-aircraft fire was extremely effective up to that height.

On 29 January 1944, a Saturday, Stuart Lovell was one of six pilots who took part in a raid on Brittany, led by the squadron's CO. The aircraft took off from their base at Predannack in Cornwall shortly after 10 a.m., crossed the French coast at the Ile Vierge and made for the fighter base at Guipavas, near Brest, which operated FW190s. At Guipavas the Typhoons strafed the watch office and dispersal huts, and brought down the infirmary's chimney, before heading eastward for Lorient. Seeing no aircraft at Lorient, they then made for Vannes but low cloud forced them north to the coast and St Brieuc. There they strafed gun positions and fuel tankers before making for Morlaix.

As the Typhoons turned for home, Stuart Lovell and his wingman broke away and

> returned to fly low and fast over Guipavas, this time from the south-west, right over the heavy flak battery at St Hudon, to the south of the airfield boundary, firing as they went.
>
> The storage building in Stu Lovell's path was 20 ft high or more. His propeller tore a semi-circular chunk out of the roof and the Typhoon crashed on the dry fuel compound and exploded. A column of black coal dust shot into the air.
>
> On the airfield, the Germans hastily established a cordon around the burnt-out remains of the cockpit, engine and one wheel. To a French carpenter working on the base, there appeared to be a body in the wreckage.

The attack that cost him his life was typical of Stuart Lovell. He was outgoing and had been slapdash in his earlier years, and some of his colleagues on No. 183 Squadron remembered him as 'something of a pain in the buttocks by virtue of his predilection for beating up the huts at Predannack at very low level'. Their greatest concern arose from the knowledge that he was short-sighted.

Stuart Lovell was buried with full military honours by the Germans in Kerfautras cemetery, Brest, where he lies to this day. There were many other Irish pilots who died in action or who perished in flying accidents. One such was the pilot of a Hawker Tempest of No. 501 Squadron, which was deployed on anti-V-1 patrols over southern England in the summer of 1944.* Paddy Faraday was the wingman to Bill Polley, also an Irishman but from Northern Ireland, and they were on a routine standing patrol when Faraday died:

> My number two was a man called Faraday. One particular night we were up [and] he crashed. He said his engine had cut, and [I] and the ground control told him to check his petrol-tank and check various things. But he went into the ground. They told him to bale out and he didn't bale out. He had plenty of height. Something happened; he just didn't bale out because his harness wasn't even unlocked.
>
> His sister came across to the funeral. The service was in a [Catholic church] quite close to RAF Bradwell Bay, and his sister told me that he was the fourth brother, they came from southern Ireland, she had lost during the war. I thought that was absolutely remarkable and it just shows the number of people who joined up from southern Ireland. And that Paddy Faraday was the fourth member of her family to have died during the war. It was very, very sad.

---

* The V-1 was the first cruise missile. Rocket-powered, they were launched from sites on the continent against a general area and fell to the ground when their engines cut out. The Tempest was the RAF's fastest fighter at the time and could catch a V-1 in a dive.

After the defeat of its daylight offensive in the autumn of 1940, the Luftwaffe turned to bombing at night. The first night raids were launched on 7 September and these continued until May 1941 with London as the principal target. Intercepting night bombers was a much more difficult task for Fighter Command as its pilots simply could not see their targets with the naked eye. However, the radar stations on the ground could spot the attacking bombers and the RAF had been experimenting with an airborne radar – known as AI, for airborne interception – and these had been fitted to a number of Bristol Blenheim Mk 1F nightfighters. But the Blenheim's performance in the fighter role was restricted and a new and better aircraft was needed. This was the Bristol Beaufighter, a large twin-engined fighter carrying AI Mk IV as well as four 20mm cannon and machine-guns. On 10 January 1941 the RAF brought its first Ground Control Interception (GCI) stations into operation and eleven of these were operational by April. The GCI stations allowed the controller, who had a plan view of both fighter and target, to direct the fighter towards a target until it was close enough to use its own radar. As the fighter closed on the target, it was often possible to see the enemy bomber and bring fire to bear on it. Needless to say, these developments were secret at the time and the public was told that nightfighter pilots improved their night vision in a number of ways, one of which was by eating carrots.

Perhaps the most famous of all nightfighter pilots was John Cunningham, known as 'Cat's Eyes', who became a national celebrity in the blitz period. Although of obvious Irish descent, Cunningham was not an Irishman, but there were a number of successful nightfighter pilots who were Irish-born.

Among those Irish night 'aces' was Wing Commander C.H. Appleton, born in Ballincollig, County Cork, who received the DSO for 'gallantry and devotion to duty'. Appleton took command of a nightfighter squadron in February 1941,

> and by his sound organisation, drive, energy and high skill in flying has enabled it to attain a splendid record in night fighting. While under his inspiring leadership the squadron has destroyed at least 45 enemy aircraft at night and damaged many others. He has personally destroyed two and damaged two enemy aircraft.

Michael Kinmouth, born in Newport, County Tipperary, joined the RAF from Dublin and achieved 'ace' status on night operations before his untimely death in November 1942. He was awarded the DFC for his 'great skill, courage and devotion to duty' and was responsible for the destruction of five enemy aircraft.

In January 1942, Flight Lieutenant Ernest Cassidy, of No. 249 Squadron, was awarded the DFC when his squadron was based in Malta. Cassidy had been involved in night operations, both in Britain and Malta, since the outbreak of war and had destroyed two enemy bombers at night.

> In a recent engagement on a dark night, Flight Lieutenant Cassidy displayed great tenacity when severely damaging two enemy aircraft. It is considered

likely that one of them failed to reach its base. This officer has shown considerable dash and initiative. He has set a splendid example.

A native of Dublin, Cassidy had moved to live in Hampshire where he was educated at the Salesian College in Farnborough. He was commissioned in 1938 and promoted to Flight Lieutenant in November 1940.

Wing Commander Charles Michael Miller received a Bar to the DFC in February 1941 and went on to win a second Bar. Born at The Curragh, County Kildare, he was educated at Cambridge where he learned to fly with the University Air Squadron and was commissioned into the RAFVR in 1938. He was awarded the DFC in January 1941. His second Bar was awarded after he took command of a squadron.

> Since Wing Commander Miller took over command of the squadron six enemy aircraft have been destroyed and two damaged. Wing Commander Miller completed a large number of night operational patrols during this period, many of them in adverse weather, and personally destroyed two enemy aircraft. He has displayed great enthusiasm and keenness which have been an inspiration to all who serve under him.

Whether flying by day or by night, Irishmen played an important part in the work of RAF Fighter Command throughout the war. The names of men such as Finucane and Beamish have ensured that that part will never be forgotten but it is important that the many others who also flew in fighters should also be remembered.

10

Minelaying, convoys and midget submarines, the naval war, part II

RUMOURS OF WAR

In chapter Five the role of a number of Irish members of the Royal Navy was considered, including the part played in naval actions in the early part of the war by two Irishmen who won posthumous Victoria Crosses – Edward Stephen Fogarty Fegen and Eugene Esmonde. Both men were possessed of a strong sense of duty that led them to take actions that would cost them their lives. That was the ultimate test of leadership – that they were prepared to take such risks. Such men were a key factor in ensuring that the wartime navy operated at maximum effectiveness and their leadership was frequently a source of inspiration to their fellow officers, petty officers and ratings.

A strong sense of duty was also a paramount consideration in the lives of two brothers from West Cork who served throughout the war in the Royal Navy. Evelyn and Paul Chavasse, from Castletownshend, were regular naval officers and both were highly decorated by the end of the war. Their older brother, Kendal, served in the Army and earned a DSO and Bar as well as a Mention in Despatches. Paul Chavasse was the first member of his family to be decorated in the Second World War. He had joined the Royal Navy as a cadet in 1922 and his first ship was the battleship *Benbow* in 1925. Later he specialized in torpedoes and this was to play a significant part in his wartime service, although his first decoration would come while serving on a minelayer.

On 2 November 1939 Lieutenant-Commander Paul Chavasse was serving on HMS *Princess Victoria*, a railway ferry converted for minelaying duties, commissioned into the Royal Navy at Elderslie Dock, Glasgow, on that day. The following day the ship left Glasgow and sailed down the Irish sea, rounding Land's End at 5 p.m. on 4 November. It had encountered adverse conditions, and a moderate south-south-westerly gale became a westerly gale once Land's End was rounded; three-quarters of the 'young and inexperienced ship's company' was incapacitated by the gale.

Three hours later the ship's starboard engine broke down, and thereafter the racing of the port engine in the heavy sea forced the captain to reduce speed to such an extent that the vessel had almost no steerage way. It took forty-five minutes to turn its bow into the sea to reduce the motion of the ship sufficiently for the engineers to effect repairs. Eventually the *Princess Victoria* arrived at Portsmouth, where the engine defects were rectified. The ship then sailed back to the Clyde.

At Greenock 240 mines were transferred from *Princess Victoria* to HMS *Plover*. While this operation was being carried out, two mines that had been cut by the clearing sweep drifted ashore close to a main road near Clock Point. These two explosive devices presented a danger to anyone in the area and Paul Chavasse with Chief Petty Officer F.J. Snowling volunteered to make the mines safe. This they did 'with great coolness, in pitch darkness on a rocky shore, when neither of them had ever previously performed this unpleasant task'. The captain of HMS *Princess Victoria* commended both men for their actions and Paul Chavasse was subsequently awarded the Distinguished Service Cross.

Paul Chavasse had followed his older brother Evelyn into the Royal Navy in 1922. Evelyn Chavasse joined in 1920 at the age of thirteen when he went to Osborne and Dartmouth as a cadet. When war broke out, he was serving on the staff of the Commander-in-Chief, East Indies in Colombo

> preparing for war, and conducting the operations when war came. It was a tedious business, and we had the thankless and almost impossible task of searching the vast areas of the Indian Ocean, with a handful of overworked cruisers and aircraft, for occasional German surface raiders that preyed upon our shipping.

On 4 December 1941, three days before the Japanese attack on Pearl Harbor, Evelyn Chavasse embarked on the troopship *Awatea* at Colombo for the long voyage home. The ship sailed via Durban and Capetown and then crossed the Atlantic to Trinidad, passing close to New York before heading for Britain. Off the coast of New York *Awatea* had a narrow escape from a German torpedo which, it was believed, 'was intended for Winston Churchill who was that day due to arrive in New York'. Finally, in January 1942 the troopship arrived in Liverpool.

At the Admiralty Chavasse learned that his next appointment was to be as First Lieutenant on a cruiser; this, he was assured, would give him the best prospects of promotion to commander. This was not what he wanted, and he asked to be given any ship, 'however old, small and dilapidated, provided I was given command'. His entreaties were answered and he was appointed to command HMS *Broadway*, which proved to be both old and dilapidated, being one of the ancient four-funnelled destroyers given by the United States to Britain in return for leases on British naval bases in the western Atlantic. Broadway had previously been the USS *Hunt* and was far from being an attractive ship. She also possessed a disconcertingly low freeboard, so that her decks were awash even in a moderate sea; on one occasion two sailors were swept overboard and drowned. But she was fitted with an up-to-date Type 271 radar set and with the latest anti-submarine weapon, the Hedgehog, so called because of its spiky appearance with twenty-four 'bristles' pointing forward at an angle of 45 degrees.

> On each bristle was planted a bomb, and all 24 bombs were fired off in rapid succession and fell into the water in a neat circle about 200 yards ahead of the

ship. If you had made a good shot, one or more of them would plunge down on to the U-boat with a bang, and punch a neat hole in it. If you missed, there would be a sad silence, but the U-boat would not realize it had been shot at. You could then have another go.

This weapon obviously had great advantages over depth charges dropped from the stern (which we also carried), and as far as I know, Jerry never tumbled to the idea of our lobbing bombs *ahead* at them, instead of making the old-fashioned type of attack, in which the attacking ship had to pass, with noisily threshing propellers, over the U-boat, giving it a very good chance of dodging, before the depth charges were dropped. With the Hedgehog or the [later] Squid, they never knew what hit them.

Following completion of a refit, *Broadway* left port to test the Hedgehog on Mucking Flats and to embark ammunition at Sheerness. The ship almost immediately gave problems with her engines and steering gear, the latter causing her captain to suggest that should Noah's Ark ever be discovered on Mount Ararat it will be found to have 'the prototype of *Broadway*'s steering gear'.

From Sheerness, *Broadway* sailed north at 20 knots through the area of the North Sea known as E-boat Alley, where his brother Paul's ship had been sunk by a mine. As his ship rounded the north of Scotland, Evelyn Chavasse suffered seasickness for the first and last time during the war, although no one else on the ship knew.

So we came to Londonderry and I prepared to embark on my new duties, for I had been appointed, not only in command of HMS *Broadway*, but also as Senior Officer of an Escort Group whose duties would be to shepherd convoys across the North Atlantic.

Convoy escort duties were generally routine operations with little excitement, but they were vitally important to the Allied war effort. If the Allies were to lose the battle of the Atlantic, then the war itself would be lost; 'so while the little ships ... protecting the trade routes, could not bring Germany to defeat, we would, if we were beaten, bring the Allies defeat'. Londonderry was to be the most important escort base in that battle, and Evelyn Chavasse's escort group played an important part in the battle.

That escort group was Canadian but, as the Royal Canadian Navy was unable to bring it up to full strength, about half its ships were British. It was also under the operational control of the United States Navy but the strategic command of the British Commander-in-Chief, Western Approaches in the eastern Atlantic. In the western Atlantic the strategic command was that of the US Navy, which devolved it to a Canadian admiral. To add to the cosmopolitan nature of this set up, Chavasse had been born and bred in what had become neutral Éire. During the time that Escort Group C2* was commanded by Evelyn Chavasse there was dispute as to whether it

---

* Evelyn Chavasse also had the American designation of CTU 24.1.12, indicating that he was Commander, 12th Task Unit, 1st Task Group, 24th Task Force, United States Navy. He never came under command of Commander 1st Task Group but received orders from Commander 6th Task Group.

belonged to the Londonderry Escort Force or the Newfoundland Escort Force; he never learned the outcome of this debate.

In April 1942 Chavasse left Londonderry on his first convoy escort trip across the Atlantic. Until he was promoted to another job in July 1943 he commanded C2 Group on some twenty convoys, most of which were trans-Atlantic but with an occasional trip to Gibraltar.

> It was my job to dodge U-boats, not to look for them; and with the help of intelligence from home, and our own skilful operators of radar and high-frequency direction-finding (H/F D/F) on the spot, I became such an artful dodger that I was astonished to be told, on arrival at St John's Newfoundland on a January day in 1943 that I had been awarded a DSC. I suppose that I was given this for successfully running away from the enemy.

The object of every escort commander was summed up in the phrase 'The safe and timely arrival of the convoy'. It was the task of the escort to defend the convoy from attacking U-boats, but not to go seeking U-boats and leaving the merchant ships unprotected. Evelyn Chavasse, therefore, received his DSC for carrying out his job effectively. But the experience of his first trip was far from auspicious.

One evening, as Chavasse was having supper in the wardroom, a signal was received from the Admiralty warning of the presence of a U-boat fifteen miles directly ahead of the westbound convoy. He ordered *Broadway* to come alongside the commodore's ship and signalled the information to him; the latter agreed to have the convoy make an emergency turn 45 degrees to port. Unfortunately it was a misty evening and half the ships in the convoy failed to see the commodore's light signal (made to maintain radio silence) and continued on their original course while the remainder made the turn. The escort tried, fruitlessly, to bring the convoy together again, but when dawn broke there were two half convoys and two half escorts with several miles of ocean in between. The one piece of good fortune was that the U-boat warning had been a false alarm and no enemy submarine appeared to take advantage of the confusion.

Radio silence had to be broken, and this led to the discovery that the lost part of the convoy was well astern of the first part:

> Again I had a chat with the Commodore (who was of course responsible for the navigation of the convoy), and we agreed on a bold plan. I did not want to reduce our speed to allow the others to catch up, as we should have had almost to stop for them to rejoin in time. And so the half convoy, after careful instruction by the Commodore, carried out the most magnificent manoeuvres I have ever seen. By flag signal from the Commodore's ship, those twenty or thirty half-empty merchant ships, of all sizes and shapes, quite untrained in this sort of thing, made a turn together of 45 degrees to starboard, a second turn together of 45 degrees to starboard, then a third, then a fourth. They were then

steering back towards Europe, and just at the moment we had calculated, the other half convoy hove in sight dead ahead. When the Commodore judged we were at the right distance, he repeated the previous manoeuvre, and in four stages, made his second turn of 180 degrees, and fetched up just one mile ahead of the other bunch. We then reduced speed for a few minutes and our lost sheep steamed neatly up into position and, not far from Newfoundland, the convoy was reunited.

Thereafter Chavasse and his escort group settled into the routine of convoy duties. As each westbound convoy set off on its journey across the Atlantic it was escorted from its various ports in the UK by a local escort of trawlers that took it to a rendezvous with the Ocean Escort six miles off Oversay on the Island of Mull. But that Ocean Escort would already have been busy and active:

A day or two before our final departure, with butterflies now fluttering wildly in my stomach, we would slip down the tortuous River Foyle from London-derry to Moville, and go out to sea to spend the intervening time on a strenu-ous programme of day and night exercises in the Irish sea, carrying out dummy attacks on our own submarines, gunnery practices, signal exercises etc. On the last day we would fill up our fuel tanks off Moville, leave our last bags of mail in the tanker, and have a quiet night in bed. Early next morning, probably while it was still dark, we would slip quietly out of harbour and steam the short distance to the invariable dawn rendezvous with the convoy ... Then started the long business of forming the Convoy into ten or a dozen columns, for which there had been no room in the narrow waters of the North Channel; collecting the convoy papers which had come in the Local Escort from the conference at Liverpool, making them up into packets and shooting each packet by line to each ship of the Escort – a tedious business – so that all my ships should know the exact position of every ship in the convoy, what her cargo was and many other domestic details; signalling to the Commodore, or shouting to him by loudhailer my policy and dispositions for day and for night; telling him the up-to-the-minute U-boat intelligence; and a dozen other details of organisation. When he had finally got his ships into their proper places, and all my butterflies had flown away, we settled down to our long slog across the Atlantic.

The westbound trip across the ocean was usually slower than the return journey since the wind was generally against the ships. Even the eastbound convoys travelled at most at about nine or ten knots. It could take up to two weeks to make the easter-ly crossing which often finished with several days of dense fog. And all that before any U-boats entered the equation. Although Evelyn Chavasse made most of his crossings without suffering attacks by German submarines, there were a number of occasions on which U-boats engaged ships under his protection. One of those engagements left

him with the memory of a particularly heartrending decision. A westbound convoy
had come under attack by a pack of U-boats in the north Atlantic:

> My Escort Group was whizzing around like maddened bluebottles keeping the
> devils down. Successfully so far, nobody sunk. Two supporting aircraft had
> depth-charged a U-boat and blown her to the surface. One of my ships, which
> had been having fun and games with another U-boat astern of the convoy,
> raced up to rejoin, and passed close to the first U-boat, obviously in distress
> and about to sink, with her crew on deck waving frantically to be rescued. Our
> chap promptly signalled to me by R/T asking my permission to pick up the
> Germans. This was the second, or perhaps third, most ghastly moment of my
> life. I had clear evidence of a further U-boat threat ahead of the convoy, and
> the safety of the convoy was my job. I needed *all* my escorts around the
> convoy. I deliberately condemned those Germans to death, and said No.

The safe arrival of the convoy had to take priority and it did so even when those
in peril were Allied airmen. On one westbound convoy, beset by U-boats, the escort
had support from aircraft based on Iceland; their very northerly route took them close
to that country. Although no ships had been sunk, there were plenty of U-boat threats
ahead.

> Then one night I got a signal from Iceland that one of our aircraft ... had
> ditched in high seas, and could I spare an escort to go and rescue them? Again
> I had to put on the black cap, and say Sorry, No. Our own chaps. One day I
> shall know perhaps if I was right.

Those aircraft were a valuable asset to the convoy escorts and their presence
deterred many U-boat attacks. However, even with aircraft operating from Iceland,
North America, Northern Ireland, and elsewhere in the UK, and the Azores, there was
still an area in mid-ocean where the U-boats were safe from aerial observation and
attack. That remained the case until May 1943 when light aircraft carriers, known as
MAC (merchant aircraft carrier) ships, carrying a handful of planes, came into service
and began to operate as part of the convoy escorts. Until that point in the battle of the
Atlantic the advantage had generally been with the Germans, with March 1943 being
one of the worst months ever for shipping losses. By the end of May the pattern of the
convoy war had changed and the Germans were forced on to the defensive, to such an
extent that Admiral Karl Dönitz ordered his boats out of the deep ocean and effectively conceded the battle of the Atlantic to the Allies. During that month thirty-seven
U-boats were sunk in the Atlantic; Evelyn Chavasse's C2 Group was involved in, or
responsible for, the sinking of five of a pack of six U-boats that attacked Convoy
HX237.

In early May 1943 Convoy HX237 sailed from Halifax, Nova Scotia, to
rendezvous with C2 which sailed from St John's, Newfoundland, on 6 May. Although

the Escort Group was short of some ships,* it was supplemented by the aircraft carrier HMS *Biter*, and by three Home Fleet destroyers, *Opportune*, *Obdurate* and
Pathfinder. Although the captain of *Biter* at first refused to place his carrier and the
escorting destroyers in the centre of the convoy he was later ordered to do so by the
Admiralty. From then on, those vessels also came under the Irishman's command. The
first contact had already been made with a U-boat and the presence of the carrier was
to prove invaluable:

> *Biter* ... became quite invaluable, and in spite of frequent foul weather ... and
> sometimes very foul weather, she never once refused a request of mine to fly
> off aircraft on a sortie. Her contribution consisted of a series of superb feats of
> sea-plus-air-manship in the most difficult conditions imaginable, and not a
> single aircraft was damaged. We were now a co-ordinated team with *Biter*'s
> aircraft scouring the seas all around the convoy, *Biter*'s destroyers, with their
> thirty knots plus, streaking out ... to put the fear of God into any U-boat the
> aircraft spotted and forcing it to dive and go blind, and my own little team,
> perhaps a little more experienced in these matters, providing the final close
> protection of the convoy.

At much the same time as the carrier came into the convoy, it became clear that a wolf-
pack† was gathering to the north of HX237. Searches by Swordfish from *Biter* detected several submarines on the surface, most of which chose to fight it out with the
aircraft, but dived rapidly whenever any of the destroyers came into view. One
Swordfish pilot was injured in an engagement with a U-boat. As the convoy came within
range of shore-based aircraft from the Azores, these were also ordered to operate under
Chavasse's directions and increased greatly the protective zone around HX237.

Over a period of five days the convoy's escorts fought a running battle with the U-
boat pack. RAF aircraft, from the Azores, and *Biter*'s Swordfish, claimed to have
damaged several submarines with depth charges. Then an aircraft spotted wreckage
ahead of the convoy as well as survivors in a liferaft who were picked up by one of the
corvettes; they came from a ship which had sailed ahead of the convoy and been
torpedoed for its troubles. On 12 May a Coastal Command Liberator reported a
surfaced submarine which was attacked and damaged but a follow-up search by ships
proved unsuccessful. Then a Swordfish, making its way back to *Biter*, reported a U-
boat on the surface a mere six miles ahead of the convoy. Evelyn Chavasse immediately told the convoy commodore to turn his ships 90 degrees to port and, since
Broadway was the closest, and fastest, of the close escort, raced off to engage the
submarine, ordering *Lagan* to follow at her best speed of 20 knots.

---

* The group included *Broadway*, the sole destroyer, *Lagan*, a River-class frigate, the corvettes *Primrose*,
Morden, *Drumheller* and *Chambly*, of which the latter three were Canadian, the trawler *Vizalma* and a tug.
† At this stage of the war the wolfpack was the favoured U-boat tactic for attack. Once a convoy was spotted, by aircraft or submarine, a group of U-boats would be ordered to converge on the merchant ships. The
numbers of attackers made things much more difficult for the escort ships.

The U-boat had dived but the shadowing aircraft had dropped smoke markers to indicate its position and led *Broadway* to that spot. As the destroyer reduced speed there was a firm contact by Asdic.*

> The hunt was on … For once the weather was good.
>
> My first attack (by Hedgehog) missed. *Lagan* came trundling up, obtained contact and likewise missed. There followed a prolonged hunt, and I still have a rather crumpled photocopy of the original plot of *Broadway*'s movements: a most extraordinary document. U-89 (I didn't of course know her number then!) had dived to a depth of about 400 feet. She was a wily bird and … twisted and turned like a snake in ecstasy. *Lagan* and I shared the hunt and between us we held her, and if one of us lost contact, the other regained it. Finally the lot happened to fall on *Broadway*. A salvo of bombs from our Hedgehog soared beautifully into the air (memories of Mucking Flats!), splashed in a neat circle 250 yards ahead of us, and then, after the usual anxious pause, we were at last rewarded with a lovely bang. We had hit her fair and square.

U-89 had indeed been sunk, although Evelyn Chavasse was not certain immediately that this had been the case. He sent *Lagan* back to the convoy but remained in the area for over an hour until he was able to pick up positive proof that the submarine had gone to the bottom. Wreckage and debris, including part of an electrical control panel, a cotton singlet embroidered with a German eagle and swastika, and a sock with the owner's name tape, were enough to prove that the 'crew of U-89 were now lying in 1700 fathoms. May they rest in peace.'

The sinking of U-89 was the first to be achieved with Hedgehog, and it was to provide a morale booster for escort ship crews. Early next morning a Sunderland attacked a U-boat to the starboard of the convoy; HMCS *Drumheller* made Asdic contact, depth-charged the boat and immobilized it. Finally, *Lagan* sank the boat, which was U-456. The battle was over as the survivors of the wolfpack retreated from the convoy. *Biter* and her destroyers were ordered to go the aid of another convoy and HX237 finished its voyage without further interruption.

For his work in shepherding HX237 across the Atlantic to safety Evelyn Chavasse subsequently received an operational award of the DSO. Commodore Simpson, Commodore (Destroyers) Western Approaches, wrote that the recommendation was for

> good services during an A/S hunt on 12th May, 1943, which, after several setbacks, resulted in the destruction of an enemy submarine. Lieutenant-Commander Chavasse has been favourably commented upon on several occa-

---

* Now known by its American name, sonar, this was an underwater detection apparatus similar to radar that dated from the First World War and was an acronym of Allied Submarine Detection Investigation Committee.

sions in the past for his keenness and enthusiasm and it is evident that the result of his zeal has been to keep his ship's company in a high state of efficiency.

Simpson's recommendation was supported by the Commander-in-Chief, Western Approaches who noted that Chavasse's control of his escort group and co-ordination of H/F D/F intelligence and excellent use of aircraft 'all contributed to the safe and timely arrival of the convoy with relatively light losses and considerable loss and damage to the enemy'.

Convoy HX237 was also Evelyn Chavasse's swansong in HMS *Broadway*, which was paid off in June 1943. He was given a short leave that allowed him to go home to County Cork on leave, where his father had died on 9 May; his wife was at the family home where she had been looking after her father-in-law. On 30 June Evelyn Chavasse was promoted to Commander and given command of another escort group – 4th Escort Group – of American-built ships. These were new Captain-class frigates (destroyer escorts in the US Navy) and Chavasse was appointed captain of HMS *Bentinck*. The group was based in Belfast and, with the temporary withdrawal of the U-boats, was engaged in escorting convoys through the Bay of Biscay where Dönitz's force was now concentrating its attentions.

The Royal Navy also had the task of escorting convoys to Russia. Some of these came across the Atlantic from North America and were shepherded around Norway by British ships, while others originated in the United Kingdom. Dubliner David McCaughey was a loader on a 4.7-inch gun on the Tribal-class destroyer HMS *Ashanti*, which saw service in the Arctic convoys. In the summer of 1942 the Arctic convoys were suspended for a month while warships were diverted to the Mediterranean for Operation HARPOON, a convoy to Malta. On 27 June the Arctic convoys resumed when PQ17, with thirty-six merchant ships, left Iceland for Russia. *Ashanti* was one of the escort force for this ill-fated convoy.

I presume the merchant ships ... were stacked full of tanks and ... aeroplane parts. We were supposed to be greeted by the Russians. They were supposed to send aircraft out to meet us, about three or four hundred miles out. They never appeared, of course, but why they didn't appear I don't know.

[The threat to us was from] torpedoes and very, very brave enemy pilots who flew out from Norway, you know, five hundred miles out and five hundred miles back. They hadn't got a hope in hell once they were hit. They were down in the sea and, of course, you couldn't stop to pick them up because there were submarines as well. There was a lot of ships lost [to] torpedoes. So you had nothing but admiration for these people who you could hear sometimes over the ship's radio, they'd shove it on, where these fellows were calling for help and so on. But they'd had it, I'm afraid.

PQ17 was threatened by enemy aircraft, flying from Norway, by submarines, and by major surface units of the Kriegsmarine. Intelligence sources on German intentions were normally quite good as the Government Code and Cypher School (GC and CS) at Bletchley Park were decrypting quickly the German naval signals sent by Enigma. But this was one of those occasions when a delay in decrypting Enigma occurred. This was coupled with problems with Coastal Command surveillance as a result of an aircraft accident. Thus the fog of war had descended on PQ17.

The greatest worry for the Admiralty was that the German battleship *Tirpitz* would break out of Norway to attack the convoy. It was believed that the pocket battleship *Scheer* was at sea, and that *Hipper* and *Tirpitz* were moving north from Trondheim. This was the situation when the delay in decrypting Enigma signals occurred and Coastal Command surveillance was interrupted. It appeared that PQ17 was about to come under attack by *Tirpitz* and the other German ships. In fact, *Scheer* and three escorting destroyers had run aground and were out of the picture. But *Tirpitz* was the greatest threat and, believing her to be preparing to strike at the convoy, Admiral Sir Dudley Pound, First Sea Lord and Chief of Naval Staff, ordered the convoy to scatter on 4 July. 'As history shows [*Tirpitz*] hadn't come out at all, or it had only come out about a hundred miles or thereabouts. And they scattered [the convoy] and the Germans had a field day.'

Tirpitz did not sail until 5 July and, as David McCaughey suggested, returned to port almost immediately. But the damage had already been done. German submarines and aircraft, of which over 260 were concentrated in Norway to attack convoys, were able to pick off single ships. Twenty-three ships were sunk and many of the others damaged as they struggled the last 800 miles to their destination, virtually unescorted. The fate of those whose ships went down was grim.

> You didn't really last more than two to three minutes [in the water]. We were pulling people out and they were just as stiff as boards, if you could get a hold of them. You [often] couldn't get a hold of them because they were frozen, your hands were frozen. So it wasn't a pleasant afternoon's fun.

After the destruction of PQ17, the Arctic convoys were suspended until September 1942. In the meantime, HMS *Ashanti* was to move to the Mediterranean where David McCaughey would take part in another of the war's most memorable convoy actions.

There were still Atlantic escorts to be carried out but these were not as fraught with danger as had earlier been the case. Even so, Evelyn Chavasse's 4th Escort Group found itself engaged in an action against a wolfpack on a westbound convoy, ONS20, in October 1943. It was during this engagement that Chavasse had to give the order not to rescue German sailors from a stricken submarine. Later that same day, however, the ship, which had requested permission to rescue the submariners, was able to effect the rescue of the crew of another U-boat, U-841. But it remained 'a sad Sunday' for Evelyn Chavasse. Aircraft also joined in the action and the U-boats eventually broke off and ONS20 reached Canada safely with the loss of one merchant ship.

In December 1943 Chavasse was given the task of escorting convoys from Britain through the straits of Gibraltar to Naples. These fast troop convoys were 'the dullest job in the world' and were described as tramlines by those who carried them out. Such duties were the work of 4th Escort Group until Evelyn Chavasse handed over command to Commander Garwood in June 1944. On leaving the group Chavasse had only one more month of seagoing duty in the war, and that was to be spent on a luxury yacht. HMS *Philante* was the personal yacht of the millionaire aviation pioneer Sir T.O.M. Sopwith who had presented the vessel to the Royal Navy, which used it as a training headquarters ship for Western Approaches Command. For a brief time Evelyn Chavasse conducted the training of escort groups, including those exercises which he had himself taken part in when based in Londonderry. On one occasion *Philante* carried Northern Ireland's prime minister, Basil Brooke, and his wife to Rathlin Island, and the premier subsequently wrote a letter of appreciation to the Flag Officer Northern Ireland, Admiral Bevan. The latter was obviously amused by Brooke's commendation of Chavasse and wrote: 'Considering that you are a neutral, I think this praise from the PM of NI is very well deserved and most unusual!'

Evelyn Chavasse's next posting was to Derby House in Liverpool, the headquarters of Western Approaches Command, from which was waged the battle of the Atlantic. He spent the final months of the war on the Commander-in-Chief's staff in 'a horrible dungeon' that was to have such a detrimental effect on his health as to bring his naval career to a premature end.

By the time Evelyn's seagoing service had come to an end, his younger brother Paul had earned a Bar to the DSC he had been awarded in 1940. His service in HMS *Princess Victoria* ended when that vessel struck a mine on 19 May 1940. The ship was returning from a mine-laying operation in the North Sea.

> I had left the bridge at midnight and went to my cabin. I removed my sea boots and coat, just keeping on my trousers, high neck sweater and inflatable waistcoat. I then got onto my bunk. When we were mined, I struck the deckhead with some considerable force and was knocked unconscious. I do not know how long I was out. When I came to, my first thought was to blow up my inflatable waistcoat. This I could not do. I will never know whether the valve was defective or I was being stupid from the blow on my head. Probably the latter as we had tested the valve often enough. Anyway, it was as well I could not blow it up as the ship had turned over and I had to swim down to get out; I could not have done this with an inflated waistcoat.
>
> When I got to the surface I could not make out why I was swimming so badly but I eventually got hold of a large piece of wood with a large nail in it. I saw that part of the oil on the water was on fire as it had been ignited by the calcium flares attached to some life buoys.

After some thirty minutes in the water, Paul Chavasse was rescued by a destroyer that had been in the vicinity when his ship hit the mine. He had swallowed some of the oil and 'was soon as sick as a cat' in spite of a restorative brandy. When the destroyer berthed at Grimsby in the morning, the Senior Naval Officer there informed

Chavasse that he was the senior survivor. Of a ship's complement of 130 officers and ratings, thirty-one had drowned and about fifty were hospitalized.

After sick leave he was posted to HMS *Vernon*, a shore establishment, prior to joining one of four new fast minelayers that were being built at that time. These were vessels that were to be capable of crossing the North Sea and back under cover of darkness in one night and were to be called *Abdiel, Manxman, Welshman* and *Latona*. During this period of shore service Paul Chavasse became acquainted with that form of parsimony that is peculiar to bureaucracy. He completed a claim for his lost belongings – the very clothes he had been wearing when rescued had been destroyed by oil – and he went to considerable lengths to ensure that the claim was as accurate as it was honest. When the cheque finally arrived from the Director of Naval Accounts, it was less than a third of what he had claimed:

> I wrote to DNA asking why the claim had been so drastically cut as I thought I had a very honest claim. DNA replied to the captain of HMS *Vernon* saying that I was to be informed that the bases on which claims were assessed was confidential.

The first of the new minelayers to be completed was *Abdiel* to which Paul Chavasse was appointed as First Lieutenant and Mining Officer. While sailing to Scotland for acceptance trials and working up, *Abdiel* was ordered to dump her complement of practice mines and make for Portsmouth at full speed to load live mines. At Portsmouth the mines were loaded and the ship sailed with an escort of several K-class destroyers commanded by Lord Louis Mountbatten in HMS *Kelly*. The flotilla made its way to the coast of Brittany where *Abdiel* left the escort some twenty-five miles from the port of Brest to lay mines outside that harbour. In Brest harbour the German battleships *Scharnhorst* and *Gneisenau* were alongside, having recently docked following a raiding operation against British shipping. When the minelayer rejoined the escort, Mountbatten signalled to the captain that 'Samuel White were to be congratulated on their minefield'. *Abdiel* had been built by Samuel White, to whom, technically, she still belonged, as she had not completed her acceptance trials. Even so, she flew, proudly, the white ensign.

Shortly after this operation, *Abdiel* was ordered to the Mediterranean and sailed through the Straits of Gibraltar to Malta and thence to Alexandria, becoming the first British ship for some time to travel by that route. The minelayer had hardly arrived at Alexandria when it was ordered to sail for Crete with troops on board. At this stage of the war, British troops were being evacuated from Greece but Crete was being reinforced. Two days after *Abdiel* sailed from Alexandria there was a reversal of policy with the decision to evacuate Crete from Suda bay on the north coast of the island.

The evacuation of Crete proved a very expensive operation for the Mediterranean Fleet, which had lost, or had had damaged, so many ships that its Commander-in-Chief, the Dublin-born Admiral Sir Andrew Cunningham, ordered an end to the attempt to extricate troops from the island. However, there were many soldiers still on Crete and General Freyberg implored Cunningham to bring them to safety. Thus another night's evacuation was agreed to; this was to take place from Sphakia, in the south of the island, on the night of 31 May–1 June.

Only a handful of ships were available for this task: the cruiser *Phoebe*, on which Vice-Admiral King flew his flag, *Abdiel*, and the destroyers *Hotspur*, *Jackal* and *Kimberly*. *Abdiel* left Crete 'without nearly as many men as we could have carried'. Many of the soldiers seemed to prefer becoming prisoners of war rather than enduring the dangers of evacuation. One New Zealand officer, however, impressed Paul Chavasse with his determination and courage. The man, a Maori, had had both arms broken but had endeavoured to make his way from Suda bay over the hills to Sphakia. The trip was not without incident. Although the Germans believed the evacuation to be over, and there were, as a result, fewer enemy aircraft about, Chavasse suddenly saw an aircraft diving at *Abdiel* from astern and gave the order 'hard a-starboard'. The plane's bombs missed the ship, but if the order had been for a turn to port or straight ahead *Abdiel* would have been hit. When the evacuation was complete, over 50,000 men had been rescued from Crete: two destroyers and four transport ships were lost to air attack, as *Abdiel* so nearly was. As the ships made their way back to Alexandria, the anti-aircraft cruisers *Calcutta* and *Coventry* were to join them to provide protection against enemy bombers. However, a hundred miles out from Alexandria the cruisers were spotted by two Junkers Ju88s, which dived out of the sun to bomb the ships. *Coventry* had a narrow escape but *Calcutta* was not so lucky; the second Ju88 scored direct hits with two bombs and the cruiser went down in minutes. *Coventry* picked up 255 survivors before returning to Alexandria.

Back at Alexandria, *Abdiel* returned to her normal mine-laying duties before being deployed to carry men and supplies into the besieged port of Tobruk in Libya. Tobruk, surrounded on land by German and Italian forces, could only be supplied by sea and the endurance of the Australian garrison was already becoming one of the almost-legendary stories of the war:

> We were loaded up by Egyptian labour. We used to take ammunition, food and a few troops, and brought back others. We left Alexandria at 1600. For the first one and a half hours we had air cover. Then the bombing used to start. At first this was high level bombing. Occasionally there was a raid by low level bombers. I used to run a sweep stake on the time of the first bomb. I never won! Tobruk was not easy to find in the dark. There was only one navigation light which the Germans used to move about from time to time. When we found Tobruk, we had to thread our way between three booms. These booms had been laid for small two-funnel destroyers, all of which had been sunk. Taking a ship the size of *Abdiel* through the booms was no easy task. Because of danger from acoustic mines, we could only use low power. Once inside, there were no jetties so we had to land our stores on wrecks and it was a

matter of going flat out to get our stores out on time. I remember our Surgeon Lieutenant used to get into rugby clothes! All the time we were being shelled by an Italian battery of three 6-inch guns, this we called Bardia Bill. We had to be under way by 0200. On one occasion we had not unloaded all the stores in time so we threw them overboard for collection by the army. Once outside the booms we had to go slowly because of mines in deep water. We could then open up to full speed but were always bombed till we got under our own air cover.

Many ships were lost during the operations to support the garrison of Tobruk and among them was *Abdiel*'s sister ship, *Latona*, which was sunk during its first run.

At the end of 1941 *Abdiel*'s service in the Mediterranean came to an end when she was ordered to Singapore. The island with its great naval base fell to the Japanese before *Abdiel* reached there, and the minelayer was then employed on duties in the Indian ocean before returning to Britain, via South Africa, where Paul Chavasse bade farewell to her. For his work on board *Abdiel* he earned a Mention in Despatches for his dedication while the ship was involved in the evacuation of Crete and the resupply of Tobruk.

Paul Chavasse was not the only Irishman involved in operations at Crete and along the coast to Tobruk. Derryman Billy Jarvis was a member of the crew of the cruiser HMS *York*, which ended its days in Suda bay. (See above, pp 48-9.) Jarvis may have been evacuated by HMS *Abdiel* as he recalled walking over the mountains to the south coast of Crete to escape from the German invaders. Soon after his return to Alexandria he was posted to another vessel, which was in dramatic contrast to his previous ship. He was now to be a crew member on board HMS *Cricket*, a small gunboat that had been built for service in China and which was being used to shell the Via Balbia, the main supply route from Tripoli and Benghazi for the enemy forces besieging Tobruk, as well as running men and supplies into Tobruk.

The smaller ship was more like a family. It was so small you had to live like a family. Even getting into a bunk you had to be lifted up and put in sideways. You couldn't turn once you got in, it was so small. The facilities on it were very basic. It was just an old barge of a thing, but I suppose it did its job. Every time we fired the six-inch gun the deck split, that's how old it was. But we seemed to be nearer the hard core, if you could call it that, of the war with taking these men up and getting in close [to] shore, and all this.

After Billy Jarvis joined its crew, *Cricket* did about six trips to Tobruk and, on one occasion, she was detailed to pick up a raiding force of Australian troops and drop them behind the enemy lines. The gunboat was to wait offshore and collect the raiders when they had completed their task:

The gunboat couldn't get inshore, the water was too shallow, so we had to row them and then, when they got ashore, the whalers – the boats that had brought them in – had to lay offshore. There were men detailed off to stay ashore to give these fellows covering fire. Three of us were to do it.

It was pretty nerve-wracking, and while we were walking up and down this beach we heard the gunfire and explosions from inland. We thought this was the boys doing their stuff. Of course, as the time wore on we got more and more – I was going to say nervous but, to tell you the truth, it was scared. We got more and more scared and I kept looking out to make sure the boat was waiting on us, and, suddenly, out of nowhere, this hand came round my mouth. I nearly collapsed. It was the boys coming back and they thought this was a good joke.

One of them had been shot through the head – the temple – and the bullet went in one side and came out the other. Going back down to Mersa Matruh, he was sitting smoking on the upper deck, [with] the two patches of sticking plaster on each side of his head. So, he must have been very lucky.

But I'll tell you, it was pretty scary, somebody coming up behind you and you standing there waiting for something to happen. You didn't know who it was. That night I didn't need any castor oil, let me put it like that.

Cricket met its end as part of the escort to a small convoy to Tobruk. The greatest danger on such missions came from enemy aircraft and it was German dive-bombers that wrote *finis* to the gunboat. The vessel's anti-aircraft defences consisted of a number of captured Italian weapons, a Lewis gun and two Oerlikon cannon.

That's what we had to fight off these Stukas ... You just had to make do with what you had. It wasn't a very big convoy. It was just three or four ships and we were supposed to be supporting them. I was cook of the day and I had got the dinner all ready and was taking it up to put it in the galley and we heard the four warning shots from one of the other vessels. This was a signal that there was enemy aircraft about. I looked up and the sky seemed to be filled with Stuka dive-bombers. They started and they attacked us all in turn, and that went on from about 11 a.m. until about three in the afternoon.

They were very brave men, no doubt about it. They aimed their aircraft at the target and they had a contraption on the wings of these Stukas, which created a most awful screaming. It was like a demented banshee. The noise of it penetrated your brain. It's indescribable, but it was awful – the bombs exploding, guns banging and this screaming noise. And then, when they reached a certain level, they released the bombs and pulled up out of the dive and the bomb went on.

At about three in the afternoon this fella came down and, just before it, I remember seeing one of these planes coming along at water level and I don't know if I'm imagining it, or was imagining it, but I could see puffs of smoke coming from his guns and I could see the shells hitting the water in front of where I was standing. I was sure that was our lot. They dropped this bomb and it came down, went through one of our whalers, and exploded underneath the ship. And it blew us right out of the water.

We came down like a piece of wood that you shove into the water – it goes down under, you push it down, and it bounces back up. It blew the whole bottom out of the gunboat and there were seven men killed. One man, in particular, was blown over the side, and just before we'd left on that trip he'd got a letter from home to say that his wife had given birth to their first child. The last I saw of him, or any of us saw of him, he was being carried away. We couldn't stop to pick him up.

As if by some miracle, the gunboat was still afloat and able to make headway. In spite of continued bombing and machine-gunning, *Cricket* was able to get back to Alexandria.

They blew the whole bottom out of her, but because she was so wide, that's what saved us. And they still kept coming back and machine-gunning and bombing. I honestly don't know how we ever got back to Alexandria but we did. That was more or less the end of my war in the Middle East. It was really rough, really rough; not what we thought it would be, like you would read in the *Wizard* or the *Hotspur*. It was dirty, it was terrifying and I wouldn't want to go through it again.

The coastal runs to Tobruk were often terrifying experiences for the crews of the ships involved. Great risks were taken to sustain the garrison of the Libyan port, and the fact that Tobruk held out until relieved by Eighth Army in late-1941 was due to the efforts made by the Royal Navy. Similar efforts, with similar risks, were made in escorting convoys to supply the island of Malta. The most famous of the Malta convoys was that known on the island to this day as the Santa Marija convoy, as it arrived in Grand Harbour, Valetta, on the morning of 15 August 1942, the feast of Santa Marija and Malta's national holiday. The convoy's British codename was PEDESTAL:

This was a do-or-die effort. If we hadn't got something through, especially fuel, they were going to have to pack up Malta. It was a terrible convoy – I mean, the losses were dreadful. We got four ships in, amongst whom was the *Ohio*, which has gone into history now because the skipper got the George Medal.* Funnily enough, about two years later† I anchored alongside the *Ohio* which was sunk [but] was half-showing over the water in Grand Harbour. This was prior to the invasion of Sicily.

---

* *Ohio*'s Master, Captain D.W. Mason, was actually awarded the George Cross.
† This was really less than a year later, as David McCaughey indicated that it was prior to the invasion of Sicily which took place in July 1943.

David McCaughey was serving on HMS *Ashanti* as part of the escort force to PEDES-TAL. The accuracy of his assessment of the importance of this convoy is confirmed by the priority given to it by the War Cabinet. Ships of the Home Fleet were made available to strengthen the escort force for PEDESTAL by the straightforward expedient of not running a convoy to the Soviet Union in August even though the Red Army was retreating towards Stalingrad and the Caucasus before the might of Germany's summer offensive.

From the Home Fleet, the battleship *Nelson*, the aircraft carrier *Victorious*, the cruisers *Kenya*, *Manchester* and *Nigeria* with eleven destroyers were added to a battle squadron that already included two fleet carriers, *Eagle* and *Indomitable*, the battleship *Rodney*, six cruisers, the anti-aircraft cruiser *Cairo*, twenty-four destroyers, an ocean-going tug, two fleet oilers and an escort of corvettes. In addition, another carrier, *Furious*, was to fly thirty-six Spitfires into Malta under cover of PEDESTAL; *Furious* had a further eight destroyers to accompany her. The main body of the escort joined the convoy of fourteen merchant ships off the mouth of the Clyde on 3 August. Vice-Admiral E.F. Syfret, who flew his flag in *Nelson*, used the run to Gibraltar to make the convoy practise manoeuvres, including emergency turns, to a high standard of proficiency.

From Gibraltar, where most of the escort ships took on fuel, the convoy passed into the Mediterranean on 10 August. It was the following day before the Germans learned of its presence and soon German aircraft were shadowing the ships. Just after noon, *Furious* began flying off her Spitfires for Malta and then, at 1.15 p.m., U-73, which had slipped through the destroyer screen, fired four torpedoes at *Eagle*. The carrier went down in less than ten minutes, but 900 of her crew of 1,160 were rescued. Those of her aircraft then in the air landed on the other carriers. *Furious* turned for Gibraltar that evening, her task completed.

The pressure on the convoy intensified next day with German and Italian aircraft from Sardinia, Sicily and Pantellaria striking at the ships from all directions. Italian aircraft dropped a new weapon, the *motobomba FF*, a torpedo that circled in the water and that was intended to confuse its targets. For almost two hours, bombers, torpedo-bombers, dive-bombers and fighter-bombers attacked the convoy and the merchantman *Deucalion* was damaged, to be sunk later by a torpedo-bomber. *Victorious* had a bomb fall on the flight deck, but it broke up without exploding and no damage was done.

Submarines took over the attack in the afternoon but caused no damage to the convoy. One Italian submarine was rammed and sunk by a destroyer after being forced to surface by depth charges. Then the aircraft came back in the evening and some 100 machines again attacked from all angles and directions. The destroyer *Foresight* was so badly damaged that she had to be sunk later. But the main fury fell on the carrier *Indomitable* which took three hits on her flight deck from armour-piercing bombs and was thus unable to continue flying operations. As the bombers finally flew off for home, having lost many of their number to British fighters and AA fire, the convoy was twenty miles west of the Skerki channel, the point at which Malta convoy escorts usually turned for Gibraltar, leaving their charges to a local escort from Malta. Thus Syfret now turned his battleships and carriers, but left Force X, the cruisers and twelve destroyers, to continue with the convoy.

At this stage, things began to go horribly wrong for PEDESTAL. As the ships changed formation to negotiate the swept channel in the shallow waters of the Skerki Bank, submarines struck again. One Italian submarine, *Axum*, scored a triple success with hits on *Nigeria*, the flagship, *Cairo* and the tanker *Ohio*. *Nigeria* was forced to turn for Gibraltar and Rear-Admiral Burrough transferred his flag to *Ashanti*, David McCaughey's ship. *Cairo* was so badly damaged that she had to be sunk. The loss of *Cairo* and *Nigeria* increased the woes of the convoy. They were the only two ships that had the radio suites needed to control the escorting fighters that were being sent from Malta to cover the convoy. The lack of direction ships led to the withdrawal of the Malta-based fighters and, as darkness approached, the bombers came back. Some twenty Ju88s bombed and torpedoed the merchantmen, sinking two vessels, *Clan Ferguson* and *Empire Hope*, and damaging *Brisbane Star*. The latter, however, managed to continue on its way.

Then *Kenya* was hit by a torpedo, although the cruiser was able to stay with the convoy, which, at 12.40 a.m. on 13 August, was attacked by a new foe as German E-boats and Italian MTBs launched torpedo attacks. These lasted all the way down the Tunisian coast from Cap Bon to Kelibia and damaged *Manchester* to such an extent that her captain decided to scuttle his ship. Five stragglers were also torpedoed although one, *Rochester Castle*, was later able to rejoin the convoy. But the other four ships sank – *Almeriya Lykes*, *Glenorchy*, *Santa Elisa* and *Wairangi*.

With daylight the bombers returned and the merchantman *Waimarama* was blown up and sank, while *Ohio* was hit by a crashing Ju88 but continued on her way. Fighters from Malta were now overhead but could not prevent enemy aircraft getting through. Another wave arrived in mid-morning and crippled the merchant ships *Dorset* and *Rochester Castle*, while *Ohio*'s engines were stopped by near misses. *Rochester Castle* was still able to make headway and Admiral Burrough left a pair of destroyers with the crippled ships as what was left of the convoy steamed on for Malta.

Burrough's ships, too, were due to turn for Gibraltar and did so at 4 p.m. on 13 August. The local escort from Malta, four minesweepers and seven motor launches, then took over to see the three surviving ships of the convoy into Grand Harbour that evening. *Dorset*, *Ohio* and *Brisbane Star* were still en route, all three badly damaged and *Ohio* under tow from the destroyer *Penn*. HMS *Bramham* remained with *Dorset* but to no avail: that evening German bombers struck again, completing the destruction of *Dorset*. *Ohio* sustained more damage and two minesweepers, *Rye* and *Ledbury*, came to assist, finally shepherding the crippled tanker into Grand Harbour on the morning of 15 August. *Brisbane Star* had also made it and thus five of the original ships of the convoy had reached Malta.

The price paid was horrendous and it was small wonder that David McCaughey described the experience as terrible. PEDESTAL had endured seven sustained air attacks, three submarine attacks and two E-boat attacks. But the cargo that was brought in –

32,000 tons of food and supplies, plus *Ohio*'s fuel – was sufficient to maintain the island for about two months.

Fortunately the Italian fleet had not attacked the convoy, although five cruisers had put to sea. Two were damaged by a British submarine and the threat of air attacks brought the others' mission to an end.

David McCaughey remained in the Mediterranean for some time before being sent back to Britain for officer training. On commissioning he was sent to the United States to take command of a Landing Craft, Infantry (LCI) and returned to North Africa. He took part in the invasion of Sicily, Operation HUSKY, in July 1943 and the landings in Italy by Eighth Army at Reggio in September. HUSKY was his first experience of amphibious operations and his landing craft hit the beach harder than it should have; the vessel was beached. As the beach was being shelled, the crew were ordered off and David McCaughey was wounded in the leg. He was later evacuated to Malta but was fit enough to rejoin his LCI for Operation BAYTOWN, the landings at Reggio. Subsequently he took part in a number of commando-type landings on the Italian coast before returning to Britain, whence he was to take part in the largest military operation of all time: OVERLORD, the invasion of France. The naval prelude to the landings was codenamed Operation NEPTUNE.

The war in North Africa had come to an end in May 1943 and the Royal Navy played a vital role throughout. In November 1942, as Eighth Army began its pursuit of the Italo-German army after the battle of El Alamein, Allied forces were landing far to the west – in French north-west Africa – in Operation TORCH. Paul Chavasse was a member of the planning staff for TORCH. He was involved in one exciting incident when the admiral decided to take his flagship, HMS *Bulolo*, a former liner, into Algiers at first light after the initial landings. As *Bulolo* moved in, she was attacked by an enemy aircraft.

> She was met by a hail of shell. I took an Oerlikon and fired it with great joy. We brought the aircraft down. My Admiral threw his hat into the air and it landed in the sea! However, as a result of a signal, a replacement was put in the next aircraft coming out and he got it 24 hours later!

There was also the opportunity for a family reunion. Paul Chavasse's older brother, Kendal, was commanding 56th Reconnaissance Regiment, which was among the early units to land and the two brothers were able to meet at the harbour. As the light recce cars were being hoisted ashore, a wire rope parted, casting a LRC into the water. It was quickly retrieved, but Kendal Chavasse's regiment needed to move rapidly to Tunisia and there was no time to have the car repaired. He told Paul that he could have the vehicle if he wanted it. The offer was accepted and arrangements made for mechanics to work on the LRC. Unfortunately, the vehicle was ill-fated: a bomb landed on it the next day.

From Algeria, Paul Chavasse was posted back to the UK, arriving at his home in England on Christmas Eve, to the surprise of his wife and the delight of his son. He

also brought sixty bananas with him, a rare luxury in wartime Britain. His new posting was to the cruiser HMS *Jamaica* as First Lieutenant and Torpedo Officer. It was
while serving on *Jamaica* that he earned the Bar to his DSC.

Jamaica was employed on escort duties with convoys to Murmansk in Russia.
These 'were most wearing and usually took about 13 days'. On one occasion, the
vastly different attitude of the Soviet forces to their personnel was brought home to
British personnel in Murmansk. A British soldier of the RASC detachment stationed
in Murmansk took pity on a badly-shod Russian soldier, the soles of whose boots had
worn away completely, and gave the man a new pair of boots from a consignment
intended for the Red Army. The following day a Soviet officer reported to the British
admiral in Murmansk that one of his men, and one of the admiral's, had stolen a pair
of Red Army boots. The admiral told the Russian that it was a regrettable incident
and that he would investigate it. A day later the Russian was back to report that 'We
have shot our man. And yours?'!

In April 1943 Hitler approved the move of the battlecruiser *Scharnhorst* to northern Norway to reinforce the naval elements available for attacks on the convoys
running to north Russia. Two months before *Scharnhorst*'s move, Admiral Dönitz had
obtained Hitler's permission to take personal responsibility for choosing when to
commit his heavy surface vessels against the Arctic convoys. These were suspended by
Britain between May and November 1943. In the latter month the German naval staff
woke up to the possibility that the British might risk running convoys to Russia even
in the depths of winter when there was little daylight in the northern latitudes. The
Kriegsmarine's Northern Task Force, and the U-boats, were alerted to be ready to
operate against any convoys. The presence of major German surface units in
Norwegian waters compelled the Royal Navy to keep capital ships in home waters
and this, in turn, eased some of the naval pressure on Japan. Even when *Tirpitz* was
crippled and *Lützow* was recalled to Germany, the presence of *Scharnhorst* was
enough to tie down major Royal Navy vessels.*

When the Germans realized that the convoys had resumed, the Northern Task
Force was placed on full alert. In late December convoy JW55B was spotted by U-
boats and Luftwaffe aircraft as it sailed for Russia. On 22 December *Scharnhorst* was
ordered to be ready to sail at three hours' notice and permission was sought for the
ship to intercept the convoy. This was eventually given and, late on Christmas Day,
the giant ship slipped anchor in Altenfjord and made for the open sea. Her mess decks
were still festooned with Christmas decorations. Heavy seas meant that the destroyers that should have operated with *Scharnhorst* were unable to keep station with her;
the big German destroyers were not as good in heavy seas as the British destroyers.
The battlecruiser was effectively on its own but the Germans believed that there were
no heavy ships in the covering force for the convoy. In this they were seriously mistak-
en. Admiral Sir Bruce Fraser was at sea in his flagship, the battleship HMS *Duke of*

---

* *Gneisenau* had been burned to a hulk after being hit by RAF bombs in Kiel shortly after the Channel Dash
of February 1942.

York, accompanied by *Jamaica* and four destroyers. There was also a cruiser covering force of HM Ships *Belfast*, *Norfolk* and *Sheffield*. In addition Convoy JW55B, and homeward-bound convoy RA55A, each had escorts of ten destroyers and a number of smaller vessels.

Scharnhorst was outgunned by *Duke of York*; the latter mounted ten 14-inch guns against the German's nine 11-inch guns. The British force also had an 8-inch cruiser and three 6-inch cruisers, all of which were torpedo-armed, as were the destroyers. Paul Chavasse was *Jamaica*'s Torpedo Officer. The cruiser was commanded by Captain Hughes-Hallett, who had relieved Captain Storey. Admiral Fraser kept *Jamaica* with *Duke of York* while Vice-Admiral Burnett's cruisers were deployed about three miles ahead:

> This was St Stephen's Day and was very dark with a strong gale blowing and there was a high sea ... A radar echo was reported by one of Burnett's cruisers, and shortly afterwards we got one ourselves. At 0200 *Scharnhorst* was illuminated by star shell from the *Duke of York*.
>
> Then a shooting match started between the *Scharnhorst*, *Duke of York* and *Jamaica*. Our broadside consisted of twelve 8-inch guns, each broadside weighing over half a ton. They were fitted with tracer, so were most spectacular.

It was completely dark by this time, which was soon after 4.30 p.m. *Jamaica* was stationed astern of *Duke of York* and the two ships opened fire at the same time:

> However, our little 6" shells cannot have made much impression on *Scharnhorst*'s enormous armour. This gun action was most exciting and *Scharnhorst*'s shooting good. We were near missed several times. Of course a single salvo of his heavy stuff would have put us out. However we were lucky though a lot fell uncomfortably close. Some of his stuff burst on impact with the water, this caused an unpleasant number of splinters to fly. Others, the armour piercing stuff, burst deep. One of these fell just clear abreast B turret. This put up a column of water 100-150 [feet] high which fell on the bridge and simply soaked us. It was an amazing scene, calm sea, very dark night with these frequent blinding flashes from gun fire and shell burst.

Scharnhorst was fighting for her life and her captain was using his speed as well as his guns as a weapon. Although hit several times, the German ship's speed was not reduced and she began to draw away from her pursuers. *Jamaica*'s guns were outranged although the heavier weapons of *Scharnhorst* could still hit the British cruiser:

> I thought it would be over quickly as *Scharnhorst* continued to draw ahead. Of course, all guns were under radar control. Suddenly the range started to drop. She had received a chance lucky hit, and we received the signal from the

C-in-C 'Close and attack with torpedoes'. We had a poor torpedo arrangement, only three torpedo tubes each side. I missed with the starboard tubes,
but got two hits with the port tubes. These put her down. The safety fork off
one of those torpedoes is among my proudest possessions.

The British destroyers had made the first torpedo attack, having slowly worked
their way ahead in the darkness to manoeuvre into a position from which they could
strike. They did this 'with amazing guts' in spite of the hurricane of fire from
Scharnhorst. As a result of this attack the German ship slowed down, and *Duke of
York* and *Jamaica* were able to regain contact and another gun battle ensued. Then
Jamaica's captain received the signal to engage with torpedoes:

> We closed her bows on at very high speed. She was not the blazing hulk that
> the BBC broadcast made out. She was a powerful ship, still firing furiously but
> very much reduced in speed. Somehow or other she did not seem to like our
> close attention and blazed away furiously even with their close range weapons.
> These latter looked like streams of red tennis balls pouring out of her side.
> However I think that they must have been rattled as their marksmanship was
> poor and most of the stuff went over our heads. Anyway I got two torpedoes
> into her guts which exploded with the most glorious crashes. When the smoke
> cleared away we saw her lying on her side. She sank shortly afterwards.

Paul Chavasse understated his own part in the sinking of the *Scharnhorst*. There
had been technical problems at the critical moment that Chavasse was able to overcome and it was this application of 'enterprise and skill' that led to the award of a Bar
to the Distinguished Service Cross that he had earned on HMS *Princess Victoria*, some
four years earlier.

> This officer performed the duties of Torpedo Officer with efficiency and
> success. When ordered to torpedo the enemy he was faced with an unexpect-
> ed problem owing to the action plot and Type 272 radar having been put out
> of action by blast. As the enemy was only visible intermittently, it was neces-
> sary to obtain the data on which to fire torpedoes from the gunnery Fire
> Control table in the T.S. Lieutenant Commander Chavasse coped with this
> situation with coolness and speed.

The giant German ship slid below the icy-cold waters off the North Cape and with
her perished most of the crew. Of the 2,000 men aboard, only thirty-six were rescued.
Most died in the cold waves. *Scharnhorst* had been carrying prize crews as she had
intended to capture the convoy and, as the admiral was changing, there were two sets
of flag staff aboard. Thus ended the battle of North Cape, 'the last ever battle to be
fought at sea between major units, without the participation of either aircraft or
submarines'.

One of Paul Chavasse's most vivid memories of the battle was of a magnificent display of the Aurora Borealis, the northern lights, as the shells roared through the darkness, the Royal Navy ships closed in, and *Scharnhorst*'s life ebbed away.

Fraser's ships put in at Murmansk that night, before sailing back to Scapa Flow where Paul Chavasse left *Jamaica* to join the battleship *Anson* as Torpedo Officer.* It was not a posting that he had wanted, but it had the consolation that *Anson* had 'a strong southern Irish element' with Vice-Admiral The O'Moore, second-in-command of the Home Fleet, Edmund McCarthy, a Dubliner, as Captain, Frizelle, a Meath man as First Lieutenant, and Chavasse himself as Number Two and Torpedo Officer. St Patrick's Night 1944 was a pleasant occasion at Scapa Flow.

In his time on *Anson*, Paul Chavasse took part in two minor operations with Woolworth carriers whose aircraft attacked German vessels in a Norwegian port. Then came an order that the battleship was to sail to Portsmouth to have additional ventilation fitted for operations against the Japanese in the Far East. At this point Paul Chavasse was moved to his final wartime appointment, the command of the Operation Division (Mining), which was responsible for all mines, whether laid by surface vessels, submarines or aircraft of the Fleet Air Arm or Royal Air Force. A war that had started with a close association with mines ended in like fashion and the youngest of the three Chavasse brothers had added to an illustrious collection of decorations in that family: Kendal had earned a DSO and Bar – the only such double award to the Reconnaissance Corps – while Evelyn had a DSO and DSC and Paul had a DSC and Bar. Both Kendal and Paul also received Mentions in Despatches.

Harry Barton, who was at sea on the day that war broke out and who had subsequently been involved in a number of actions and convoy escorts, had then been given a shore job in Scotland. When his period of shore duty ended in early-1944, he was posted to the aircraft carrier, *Formidable*, built by Harland and Wolff of Belfast. The carrier was undergoing a refit in Belfast when Lieutenant-Commander Harry Barton joined it and

> It was full of Orangemen in cloth-caps and they were hammering her and burning her in hundreds of selected places. The flight- and hangar-decks were covered with cases of aircraft stores, gas cylinders, drums of paint, drums of glycerine, drums of oil, lengths of boltstave, reels of electric cable, oily cotton-waste, rust, strange and harassed naval officers who did not yet know each other, men who were leaving the ship tomorrow and men who had joined the ship yesterday.

Formidable had been in Belfast since October 1943 and was due to sail on 9 June, a deadline many considered impractical; there was no great confidence in the Belfast workforce's willingness to meet targets. But the ship's captain made it clear that he

---

* *Anson* was a *King George V*-class battleship displacing 38,000 tons, with an armament of ten 14-inch guns and a speed of 29 knots. Launched in 1940, *Anson* joined the fleet in August 1942.

would sail on time and energized all around him. Even so, some of the shipyard work-
ers remained on board when *Formidable* sailed. Her trials complete, the carrier joined
the Home Fleet and prepared for her first operation of her second commission. This
was Operation MASCOT, a strike on *Tirpitz* in Kaafjord in Norway.

MASCOT was undertaken on 17 July and was not a success: a U-boat had spotted
the British carriers – *Furious* and *Indefatigable* accompanied *Formidable* – and
radioed a warning that allowed *Tirpitz* time to lay a smoke screen in the fjord. A
follow-up operation was cancelled due to bad weather but, on 18 August, another
attack – Operation GOODWOOD – was made on *Tirpitz* in which *Formidable* sailed in
company with *Furious, Indefatigable, Nabob* and *Trumpeter*.

Formidable was then assigned to the British Pacific Fleet and sailed to Gibraltar on
the first leg of its voyage. However, the carrier was once again to spend time in a dock-
yard.

> There was a dreadful scratching sound and this was the main centre gear wheel
> which weighs forty-five tons and stands twelve foot, six inches high and so we
> turned round ignominiously and went back into Gibraltar dockyard and
> waited there for a couple of months. The only spare gear wheel was at Barrow
> in Furness and it had to be shipped out in the face of the full fury of the
> German war effort to us at Gib to be installed.

Formidable finally sailed from Gibraltar to relieve the carrier *Illustrious* in Sydney
on 1 March 1945. The two carriers were soon to meet again. Embarked on
Formidable were Nos. 1841 and 1842 Naval Air Squadrons, both equipped with
Vought Corsair fighters, and No. 848 NAS with Grumman Avenger torpedo-bombers.
From Sydney *Formidable* took part in exercises before refuelling at Manus and sail-
ing for Leyte, which was reached on 4 April.

The British Pacific Fleet operated under the overall command of the United States
Navy's Fifth Fleet, commanded by Admiral Spruance, which included two fast carri-
er task forces: Admiral Marc Mitscher's Task Force 58 and Admiral Rawlings' British
Pacific Fleet as Task Force 57. Mitscher's Task Force 58 comprised four task groups,
each of which was virtually the equal of Rawlings' command. In aircraft, the
American task force disposed 1,218 machines against the 218 of the British Pacific
Fleet.*

> I used to sleep on a camp bed on deck and I remember the first time we joined
> the American fleet in the Pacific off Okinawa, a little back from the operating
> area. We were a big fleet, the biggest fleet the British Navy's ever put out, five
> huge fleet aircraft carriers, battleships, cruisers, destroyers, tremendous thing,
> all spread out over the surface of the Pacific. But we were on the left-hand

---

* Because British aircraft carriers had heavily armoured flight decks there was much less space in the hangars
for aircraft and so British carriers could not accommodate as many aircraft as their American counterparts
with their wooden flight decks.

wing and there were three other groups of Americans exactly the same size ... I've never seen such a collection of aircraft carriers and ships spread out over the surface of the water. There were also groups of smaller aircraft carriers providing aircraft from some hundred miles back.

In October 1944 the US Navy had defeated the Japanese navy at the battle of Leyte Gulf, the largest naval battle ever, involving almost 300 ships and 2,000 aircraft. The destruction of Japanese naval power at Leyte Gulf, where they had lost four carriers, three battleships, nine cruisers and eight destroyers against one American light carrier, two escort carriers and three destroyers, had opened the way to the Japanese home islands, by way of the Phillipines. By March 1945 American naval forces were ready to attack Okinawa in the Ryukyu Islands, the last obstacle before the home islands. The attack on Okinawa was codenamed Operation ICEBERG, and while Task Force 58 covered amphibious operations in the Ryukyus, the British Pacific Fleet was assigned the task of neutralising the Japanese air bases on the Sakashima Gunto, an island group south of Okinawa. This was to ensure that those islands could not be used as a staging post for reinforcement aircraft to reach Okinawa from Formosa.

Task Force 57 began its operations on 26 March and soon made acquaintance with the new Japanese weapon of last resort – the suicide bombers known as *Kamikaze* pilots, who dived their bomb-laden aircraft on to Allied ships in a desperate attempt to prevent Japan being invaded by the Allies.

> We were struck twice by *Kamikaze* aircraft, which is a very odd thing when you think of the young man in there, locked in there, committing suicide on the deck. But the British fleet [carriers] had very powerful steel decks and so when we were struck, although there were casualties and damage, we could be operating again within four hours, whereas the American ships ... had very feeble decks and caught fire and destroyed themselves very easily if they were hit.
>
> I remember the Captain sending to the American Commander-in-Chief after we were hit the first time, saying 'We shall be operating in four hours' time. What do you think of our bloody British flight decks now?' It was a good signal really.

Although the three-inch-thick armour of the British flight deck made it virtually immune to the 'Wind of Heaven' – the translation of *Kamikaze* – it was still a frightening experience to watch a suicide bomber approach:

> I was out on deck and I could see them, these little aircraft, coming round ... What they always did was, they came up over the stern as though they were landing on, like an ordinary aircraft, because that was the best way to come in. And then they would land in the middle of the flight deck as best they could. And one of them didn't come in and he went all the way round and we

were firing at him and didn't knock him down, and then he did come in and killed himself.

One thing that I remember being told and I think it's true is that there was always a mother aircraft watching over these kids who were supposed to immolate themselves, and if you could shoot down the mother aircraft then they tended to turn round and go away. This worked once or twice.

Although the *Kamikaze* tactic was born out of desperation, it fitted in with the culture of the Japanese fighting man. Those who went out to die on the 'Wind of Heaven' were guaranteed their place in Heaven. *Formidable* was struck by such attacks on 4 and 9 May, but neither caused her to be out of action for more than a few hours, although six aircraft on deck were wrecked in the second attack and another ten damaged by fire.

By July the Allied fleet was off the Japanese coast and launching raids on Japan itself. *Formidable* had embarked an additional squadron, No. 1844 with Grumman Hellcats, and Rear-Admiral Sir Phillip Vian was flying his flag from the carrier. Strikes were made on the Tokyo Plain by the carrier's squadrons on 17 July and, on 9 August, No. 1841 attacked Japanese shipping in Onagawa Wan. The squadron was led by Lieutenant Robert Hampton Gray, a Canadian, who

> flew in very low, despite heavy flak from ships and shore batteries, his section of Corsairs following him. His aircraft was hit and set on fire, but he carried on and obtained at least one direct hit before he crashed into the sea.
>
> 'Hammy' Gray was among the top-ranking pilots in the Naval Air Arm, and we had lost one of the most popular officers in the ship.

Gray was posthumously awarded the Victoria Cross. His was the last such decoration of the war. Aircraft continued to strike at Japanese targets for a few days more and then came the news that the war was over: Japan had surrendered unconditionally following the dropping of atomic bombs on Hiroshima and Nagasaki. Harry Barton's war was over, although *Formidable* was to be kept busy for some time yet. The carrier was converted to be a giant troopship and was used to ferry former prisoners and other personnel home to India and to Britain.

The last Irish Victoria Cross of the war was also won in the closing days of the war against Japan. It completed a remarkable trio of naval VCs to Irishmen: the first was won on the surface of the north Atlantic by Captain Edward Fogarty Fegen in HMS *Jervis Bay* in 1940; the second went to Lieutenant-Commander Eugene Esmonde who led 825 Squadron into the maws of death in the air over the straits of Dover in 1942; and the third went to Leading Seaman James Magennis under the waters of the Johore strait, on 31 July 1945. Of the three, only Magennis lived to learn that he had won the Cross and to receive it. He was also the only one of the trio – and of all the Irish VCs of the war – to come from Northern Ireland.

Born in Belfast in 1919, James Joseph Magennis joined the Royal Navy as a teenager in 1935 and was a highly-experienced veteran by July 1945, having seen active service on both surface vessels, large and small, and beneath the waves. He had been sunk off Tripoli in HMS *Kandahar* in Mountbatten's 5th Flotilla in December 1941. Mick Magennis, as he was known in the service, trained as a diver and it was in that role that he won his Victoria Cross. In an effort to devise a weapon to attack the German battleship *Tirpitz* in its Norwegian haven, and inspired by the successes of the Italian navy with its human torpedoes in the Mediterranean, the Royal Navy had developed similar underwater vehicles – known as Chariots – before devising a midget submarine with a four-man crew. These latter were the X-Craft, described as 'undoubtedly one of the most potent and versatile vessels ever constructed for the Royal Navy', capable of being used for striking at targets such as *Tirpitz* that were in heavily defended harbours, or enemy strategic communications, as well as being used for beach reconnaissance before amphibious landings; they could also be deployed as navigational beacons if necessary.

The first operational use of X-Craft was in Operation SOURCE in September 1943 when six of the vessels set off to attack *Tirpitz*, *Scharnhorst* and *Lützow* in Kaafjord.* Magennis was one of the crew of X7, which was towed by HM Submarine *Stubborn* to the release point off Sorøy Sound. X6 and X7 were the only two of the little flotilla to penetrate the defences around *Tirpitz* and X7 was the sole vessel to return. But *Tirpitz* was damaged so severely that she was incapable of sailing operationally. Repairs had to be carried out in Norway as the Luftwaffe could not mount the type of air operation that had covered *Scharnhorst*, *Gneisenau* and *Prinz Eugen* on their dash from Brest in February 1942.

With the subsequent sinking of *Tirpitz* by Bomber Command, and the destruction of *Scharnhorst* at the battle of North Cape, there were few targets for the X-Craft in Europe and a decision was taken to employ them in the war against Japan. Although there was an initial reluctance on the part of the US Navy to have the little vessels in an operational role, a task was eventually assigned to them: the cutting of submarine telegraph cables linking the Japanese forces in Hong Kong, Saigon and Singapore. Then Admiral James Fife, Commander Submarines, US Seventh Fleet, decided that there was an even more aggressive operation that the British midget submarines could undertake. Two Japanese cruisers, *Myoko* and *Takao*, lay in the Johore strait, and Fife's staff believed that the X-Craft of the British 14th Submarine Flotilla could be used to attack the two vessels.

Takao had suffered severe damage from bombing in February, and both ships were moored in the strait as floating anti-aircraft batteries. The United States Navy, believing that both ships were seaworthy and thus represented a danger to Allied shipping, requested that the X-Craft be used to neutralize that danger. In fact, the vessels of 14th Flotilla were XE-Craft, a development of the original vessel designed for use in a tropical zone.

XE1 and XE3 were assigned to attack the two cruisers on the night of 31 July, while two other vessels, XE4 and XE5, were to cut the undersea cables from Saigon

---

* Kaafjord is a branch of Altenfjord. Some sources record *Tirpitz* as being tied up in the latter but all three ships did move from one anchorage to the other from time to time.

to Hong Kong and Hong Kong to Singapore respectively. James Magennis was to sail in XE3, commanded by Lieutenant Ian Fraser and towed by the submarine *Stygian*. As the diver, it was Magennis' job to leave the XE-Craft and attach mines to the hull of *Takao*, the target for XE3. An hour before midnight on 30 July the XE-Craft slipped their tows near the Horsburgh Light at the eastern end of the Singapore strait, leaving the midgets to cover the final forty miles alone.

Fraser had little difficulty in finding *Takao*. XE3 passed through the open gate of the protective boom at about 9 a.m. on 31 July and made its way up channel until the cruiser was spotted. *Takao* was close inshore on the north end of Singapore Island, its stern towards the island. The ship was well camouflaged. Having allowed his three crew members to observe the target through XE3's periscope, Fraser brought the little vessel under the hull of *Takao*. XE3 had two cargo carriers: on her port side was a container with six limpet mines; one large side charge was on the starboard side.

As Magennis tried to leave XE3 to carry out his task of placing the mines on the cruiser, he found that the hatch would open only to a quarter of the normal distance. The tide was falling, and *Takao* was actually coming down on the submarine. The Belfastman managed to get out by deflating his breathing apparatus and squeezing and wriggling his way through the restricted gap. But his problems did not end there. It was no easy matter to fix six limpet mines in a forty-five-foot line along the hull of the Japanese cruiser. Both the curvature of the hull and the fact that it was encrusted with barnacles and other underwater growth meant that Magennis had to scrape clear an area on which to place the mines. To secure them he had to tie them in pairs using a line passing under the hull. This was physically exhausting work but Magennis persevered where:

> A lesser man would have been content to place a few limpets and then to return to the craft. Magennis, however, persisted until he had placed his full outfit [of mines] before returning to the craft in an exhausted condition.

Magennis had been further handicapped by a steady leakage of oxygen from his breathing apparatus that rose to the surface in bubbles and presented the danger of his presence being spotted by an alert sentry. Even when he had returned to XE3's Wet and Dry chamber, his work was not over. Fraser released the starboard charge and then tried to manoeuvre his vessel out from under *Takao*. This was finally achieved after twenty nerve-wracking minutes of applying full ahead and then full astern, as well as blowing and filling tanks. When the vessel did get free, it shot to the surface less than fifty yards from *Takao*, but Fraser took it to the bottom again immediately.

But the craft was very difficult to manoeuvre as the limpet-mine carrier on the port side had not released. Magennis volunteered to don his diving suit again and, although he was physically exhausted from his earlier efforts, he went out with a sledgehammer, crowbar and chisel and succeeded in freeing the recalcitrant container. Fraser then set a course for the Horsburgh Light, which was reached at 3.30 a.m. on 1 August, and the rendezvous with *Stygian*. XE3's crew had been on duty and without sleep for a total of fifty-two hours, sixteen of which had been spent submerged. The midget submarine's coxswain had spent more than thirty hours at the helm without relief.

XE1 had been forced to abandon the attack on *Myoko* but had left another side charge under *Takao* on her way out. At 9.30 p.m. on 31 July the charges exploded, although XE3's main charge, a half-ton of amatol, did not detonate. Some of the limpets did explode and a large hole, over twenty feet by ten feet, was blown in the cruiser's hull. Fire control instruments were damaged and the roller paths for the main gun turrets were also distorted. Although *Takao* did not sink fully, settling on the seabed with its upper deck above water, the ship's useful days for the Japanese navy were over.

Although Fraser and his crew heard an explosion at Singapore, this was later discovered to be an aircraft crashing at Changi and not *Takao* blowing up. At the time of the attack the cruiser had been cleared of ammunition and there was only a small care and maintenance party aboard, which probably explains why Magennis' activities went undetected. The risks taken by the crew of XE3 were very great. They had sailed in harm's way in no uncertain fashion, and their work was recognized by the award of the Victoria Cross to Ian Fraser and to James Magennis. Two DSOs went to the crew of XE1, while the total of awards to the two cable-cutting vessels and the pair that had entered the Johore strait included another DSO, six DSCs, a Conspicuous Gallantry Medal, two DSMs, two OBEs and eleven Mentions in Despatches.

Plans were made to return to the Johore strait to finish off the operation against the Japanese cruisers, but the dropping of atomic bombs on Hiroshima and Nagasaki brought the war to an end. Magennis had played a central role in one of the Royal Navy's final operations of the Second World War. He and his XE-Craft comrades had also earned the admiration of Admiral James Fife, who described their flotilla as 'the little guys with a lotta guts'.

With a little rewording Fife's phrase could also describe the contribution that Irishmen had made to the war at sea between September 1939 and August 1945. They may have been small in number in comparison to the manpower of the Royal Navy, but they made a contribution that was an important part in the final victory at sea and the fact that three VCs went to Irishmen suggests that Ireland, from both sides of the border, punched above its weight in the naval war.

~ I I ~

From Abyssinia to Cassino:
Irish infantrymen at war, part II

TRAMP, TRAMP, TRAMP ...

Field Marshal Montgomery of Alamein, scion of a Donegal family, once wrote of the
infantry soldier that it was he

> who in the end plays the decisive part in the land battle. The infantry is the
> most versatile of all the arms; it can operate in any weather, in any type of
> ground. The infantry soldier remains in the battle day and night, with little rest
> and without adequate sleep. He can use very expressive language about the
> way he has to bear the main burden in battle, but he does it! I salute him.

As an infantry officer in the Great War, Montgomery had real experience of the
subject on which he wrote. As one of the great commanders of the Second World War,
he was better placed than most to assess the value of the infantryman in that conflict.
He admired the 'poor, bloody infantry', as they described themselves, and he knew
how to inspire them to maximum efforts.

Among the 'poor, bloody infantry' of the Second World War were tens of thousands of Irishmen. In chapter Four we have already noted some of their experiences
from the opening clashes of the war, in Norway, to the battles waged in the deserts of
North Africa in late 1941. The campaign in North Africa continued until May 1943;
after the Allied invasion of French north-west Africa – Operation TORCH – in
November 1942, fighting took place in Tunisia as well as in Egypt and Libya.

No Irish infantry battalions were involved in the early part of the North African
campaign although the Irish Brigade arrived in late 1942 to fight in Tunisia. However,
there were many Irishmen in the infantry units that fought the desert war between 1940
and late-1942. William Shorten, from Dublin, served with 2nd West Yorkshire Regiment in 5th Indian Division and was posted to Geneifa in Egypt and, later, to the Sudan:

> We were living in tents and a thing we were never to do was to take off our
> shirts and it was something I done while we were digging dug-outs, air-raid
> shelters, near the tents. I suffered something terrible ... I suffered complete
> sunburn. It wasn't [sun]stroke but I suffered for weeks with the back. And you

couldn't report sick because it was a charge; you weren't supposed to take off your shirt. So I suffered … it was the worst pain I ever suffered. My back was literally bleeding.

Sunburn was regarded as a self-inflicted injury, since the soldier who suffered from it had to have disregarded the very strict rules about acclimatisation. Those rules meant that, in the early days of service in a country such as Egypt, soldiers had to wear shirts; in the initial period they were not even allowed to roll up their sleeves. Stricter rules that involved the wearing of tropical helmets and special clothing to prevent sunburn, including a garment known as a spine pad, were waived in the early days of war. Of course, the link between skin cancers and exposure to bright sunshine was not known at that time.

When Shorten's battalion moved to the Sudan it was posted to the border with Eritrea, which was occupied by the Italians. Fifth Indian Division was to play a major role in the liberation of Eritrea under the command of Dublin-born General Sir Alan Cunningham. But William Shorten was not to see action:

> I didn't go into action there. I fell sick with malaria and was brought back to hospital … I was in hospital for three weeks … and then when I come out of hospital I wasn't sent back to the West Yorks which I was with. I was attached to the First Battalion of the Essex Regiment. I joined them in Haifa in Palestine. I was in Haifa for maybe two or three months and then we were sent across the desert into Iraq.

The move to Iraq came as a result of a pro-Nazi rebellion in that country and 1st Essex deployed to relieve the British embassy in Baghdad. This gave William Shorten his first experience of action, although his battalion's task was principally one of patrolling. From Iraq the battalion moved to Syria and the campaign against the Vichy French forces in that country.

First Essex were sent to take forts that were held by soldiers of the French Foreign Legion. There was no infantry action as artillery pounded the French positions for 'a few days' leading to a French surrender:

> The only shots I fired during those two campaigns was on sentry go outside Palmeira [in Syria]. We were guarding a roadway and these figures appeared. Our orders were [to call] 'Halt, who goes there?', which they didn't. They started moving around and we opened fire. I was on the bren gun with tracer bullets. You could see the bodies going down. We went down and they were unfortunate Arabs we'd shot, and a couple of camels. They didn't understand [the challenge]. It broke our hearts.

So far in the war, William Shorten had learned that the infantryman's life is not all about fighting and that there were enemies other than those armed with rifles and artillery. Sunburn and malaria were afflictions that threatened every European soldier in the region, and the tragedy of the dead Arabs in Syria was a clear example of how war can bring death to those who are not involved.

With the Syrian campaign at an end, 1st Essex moved to Alexandria in Egypt. But the battalion's stay there was brief, and Shorten and his comrades were ordered to board destroyers at Alexandria harbour for a voyage westward along the coast to the Libyan port of Tobruk. As part of 6th Division, the Essex were included in the force that relieved 9th Australian Division of the defence of Tobruk. The handover was complete by 22 October 1941, by which time the division's designation had changed to 70th Division.

Until the launch of Operation CRUSADER in November 1941 (see pp 73-6 above) the soldiers of 1st Essex endured a routine that William Shorten described as 'heavy going'. In addition to the regular enemy bombardment of the port, by artillery and aircraft, the infantry were involved in a daily round of reconnaissance patrols and fighting patrols. The confused fighting during Operation CRUSADER was some of the most complex of the war, having been described as a situation that would never have been contrived for the setting of a training exercise. One of the objectives of the offensive was the relief of Tobruk, part of the garrison of which was to break out through the enemy perimeter to link up with the newly-created Eighth Army; 1st Essex were included in the break-out force. In the muddled battles that followed elements of the battalion came under attack from German armour and were forced to surrender. William Shorten was one of those captured by a German officer who spoke perfect English. Subsequently Shorten and his fellow prisoners were made to bury dead German soldiers. Some of the prisoners were killed by artillery fire from Eighth Army as the battle continued. Then the prisoners were moved to Derna and thence to Benghazi, from where they were transported by Italian vessels to Tripoli. Christmas 1941 was spent outside Tripoli at Tarhuna before another sea voyage took William Shorten to Naples. He remained a prisoner of the Italians until Italy surrendered in September 1943 when, once again, he passed into German custody and was moved to Germany itself where he remained until liberated by the Red Army in 1945.

The desert war was known to many of those who fought in it as the 'Benghazi Stakes', a sardonic reference to the ebb and flow of the fighting as, first, the British pushed forward towards Benghazi and, then, the Axis pushed them back. When, in July 1942, General Sir Claude Auchinleck stopped Rommel's advance at El Alamein in Egypt, the Benghazi Stakes moved into their final phase. At the end of October Eighth Army, now under Lieutenant-General Bernard Montgomery, fought the battle of El Alamein and inflicted a decisive defeat on Panzer Armee Afrika that sent that body retreating to the west for the last time.

When Eighth Army advanced into action at El Alamein on 23 October, one of the leading officers in that advance was William Brownlow from County Down. Brownlow's platoon led 7th Rifle Brigade's advance that October night and continued to be heavily involved. The battle raged until 2 November, when the Germans finally began a withdrawal. Brownlow earned a Mention in Despatches and was badly wounded on the final day of battle. So severe were his injuries that at first he was believed to be dead. (He recovered after a long spell in hospital to rejoin his battalion in Italy as its adjutant.)

One of the best known actions during the fighting at El Alamein took place at the outpost called 'Snipe', where soldiers of 2nd Rifle Brigade carried out a heroic defence of their position against enemy armour. In the course of this action the battalion's commanding officer won the Victoria Cross; among the many other awards was that of the Military Cross to Lieutenant James Benjamin Duncan Irwin, from Moyard, County Galway, who commanded a troop of the battalion's 6-pounder anti-tank guns:

> His troop was ordered to take up position on the northern flank. This flank was attacked by tanks once during the night and four times during the day; on each occasion Lieutenant Irwin's troop repelled the attacks with losses to the enemy. Lieutenant Irwin went from gun to gun encouraging his men and when one gun was knocked out supervized the removal of the wounded and the redistribution of ammunition under heavy fire. In the final attack by 50-60 German tanks at 17.00 hours Lieutenant Irwin's troop had only 20 rounds left. He ordered his guns to hold their fire. When the nearest [tanks] were only 100-200 yards away he gave orders to fire, setting four tanks on fire and helping to turn the attack. Under this officer's cool leadership his troop accounted for 19 enemy tanks burnt and other vehicles hit during the action. His courage was of the highest order.

In the final phase of the Alamein battle Company Sergeant-Major James Ahern (from Cobh, County Cork) of 5th Cameron Highlanders won the Military Medal when he took command of a platoon of D Company:

> ... The only officer in the company who was not a casualty was the Company Commander.
> Company Sergeant-Major Ahern took command of one platoon and Company HQ and led them in a most aggressive manner against seven enemy tanks which he found on the company's objective. He then proceeded to organize these platoons in a defensive position and got them dug in.
> Throughout the action this Warrant Officer's leadership and example were an inspiration to all ranks.

Many Irish soldiers saw action for the first time in North Africa, either in the campaign in Egypt and Libya or the subsequent fighting in Tunisia as the African war drew to a close. In the final phase of the war, which was fought in Tunisia, a number of Irish units were involved: there were three Irish battalions in the Irish Brigade and a battalion of Irish Guards served in 24 Guards Brigade. From Tunisia the Allied armies invaded Sicily in July 1943 as a prelude to the invasion of Italy in September. The Italian campaign had the largest concentration of Irish units in the war: among the infantry were the battalions of the Irish Brigade (6th Royal Inniskilling Fusiliers, 1st Royal Irish Fusiliers and 2nd London Irish Rifles), as well as 1st Irish Guards in 24 Guards Brigade, 2nd Royal Inniskilling Fusiliers in 13 Brigade of 5th Division, and 1st London Irish Rifles in 168 Brigade of 56th (London) Division.*

All of these battalions, save for the Irish Guards, fought in the brief Sicilian campaign in which a number of Irishmen earned gallantry decorations. Among them was the commanding officer of 1st King's Own Yorkshire Light Infantry,† Lieutenant-Colonel Arthur Francis McCausland Riggs, MC, who was awarded the DSO for his leadership and personal courage on 13 July, south of Villasmundo where 15 Brigade's advance was being held up by a strong German force.

> The forcing of this position was of vital importance to subsequent operations. During the reconnaissance for the attack, his Battalion Commander was wounded. He immediately took over the reconnaissance and organisation of his battalion's attack. The objectives necessitated the crossing of a deep nullah under direct enemy observation and fire. The battalion suffered heavily in its efforts to force this obstacle and only isolated parties got across. Lieutenant-Colonel Riggs led a small party on to the second objective; on reaching it he had only one man left and had to withdraw across the nullah.
>
> The battalion, meanwhile, was under heavy fire; Lieutenant-Colonel Riggs started reorganising for a further attack, which, however, was anticipated by the enemy's withdrawing from his positions, and the brigade eventually occupied Villasmundo the same night.

Riggs' personal courage and inspiring leadership had contributed to the eventual success of the attack and the opening of the road to Villasmundo. A native of Dromahair, County Leitrim, Riggs was later killed in action.

In the subsequent fighting around the Primosole bridge Lieutenant-Colonel Robert Peisley Lidwill, commanding a battalion of Durham Light Infantry, also won a DSO. The bridge had been seized in an airborne operation, but many of the paratroopers had landed in the wrong area, and the men who seized the bridge came under severe pressure from German parachutists. Relief came in the form of 8th Durhams who marched twenty miles in stifling heat to reach the bridge. Lidwill's men held the bridgehead until further troops and armour could be sent across the river Simeto‡ to open the way to the Catania plain:

> The position held by his battalion was continually under heavy enemy machine-gun fire and occasional heavy shellfire, and in very close contact

---

* In other arms there were also: 9th (Londonderry) HAA Regiment, 66th and 117th LAA Regiments of the Royal Artillery and the North Irish Horse, an armoured regiment. In addition 16th/5th Lancers maintained some Irish distinctions and attracted Irish personnel.

† The regiment's 2nd Battalion had also been commanded by an Irishman, Lt-Col Keegan from Derry, who won the first DSO of the Burma campaign in 1942.

‡ The Gornalunga river flows into the Simeto just west of the Primosole bridge.

with the enemy, who were eventually only driven out of their positions by our own 'Sherman' tanks. Lieutenant-Colonel Lidwill's conduct during all the operations in Sicily up to date has been of the highest order and an example to all.

John Duane had been commissioned into the Royal Inniskilling Fusiliers from the Irish Guards and had already seen service with 2nd Inniskillings in the Middle East before the battalion embarked at Alexandria for the invasion of Sicily as part of 5th Division.

We, the 13th Brigade, were to land west of the town of Syracuse and proceed inland to laid down objectives. The Inniskillings went ashore from assault landing craft about 8am on 'D' day [10 July]. We were given the task of capturing an important bridge over the Cavadonna river about 8 miles inland. B Company were to lead the assault under Captain Bobby Alexander, a famous rugby player of international fame. I, as a platoon commander in B Company, was in the vanguard to secure the bridge crossing. I had been warned to avoid action against the enemy, get straight to the bridge, capture it and hold on until the full Battalion arrived.

My platoon set off in haste and moved quickly inland. The ground was familiar to me because I had studied air photographs covering the 8 miles up to the bridge. After approximately two hours we approached the bridge and to our delight there were no enemy troops there. However, they were not too far away, just a half mile in a farm house. We hastily took up positions surrounding our target. A main road led away from the bridge towards the town of Syracuse.

We had scarcely settled into our defensive positions when the enemy spotted us. The road was straight towards the bridge with a sharp bend a couple of hundred yards [from] us. We hurriedly erected a road block which was to prove invaluable.

The enemy convoy, a jeep with 5 officers led, followed by 3 lorry loads of infantry, about 150 troops in all. My platoon had only 25 men. We were vastly outnumbered.

The enemy convoy came steaming down the road, came round the bend and came face to face with the road block – head to tail. They presented a favourable target. I had two sections, each of seven men and an NCO in charge ... in a small wood covering the road block. The other section was on the other side of the road behind a fence.

The moment had arrived to engage the enemy. Our three Bren guns opened with automatic fire on the target, supported by the rifle men. The enemy infantry came rapidly out of the trucks presenting an unusual target. There were bullets flying all over the place. The war in Sicily had begun for us.

The enemy succeeded in establishing a machine-gun position about 100 yards from our leading troops. This was a situation which needed immediate attention. Fusilier Bulge, a quiet but very determined man, quickly realized the danger. He charged forward with his machine-gun, routed the enemy and captured their machine-gun.

The battle went on for half an hour and then , to our surprise, a white flag on the end of a pole was hoisted by the enemy. We stopped firing and the white flag came slowly forward to our positions. It was accompanied by an officer and two men. The enemy company were surrendering. We had led them to believe there was a strong force opposing them. We accepted their surrender – all 150 of them with their five officers and supporting guns. It was a great victory for my platoon. Within the hour the Battalion arrived. The prisoners were handed over to battalion HQ. The Company Commander, Captain Alexander, congratulated us. We had some wounded and there were quite a few casualties on the enemy side. They were an Italian contingent, not Germans as we had expected.

As the Inniskillings advanced beyond Syracuse and Augusta they met with German troops who provided much tougher opposition than had the Italians at Cavadonna. One such example of the doughty nature of the German army in defence would be encountered along the Simeto river, a name that would become familiar to most British soldiers in Sicily.

The commanding officers of three Irish battalions also earned the DSO on water crossings. Dublin-born Ian Good, of 1st London Irish, was awarded his decoration for leading his battalion during a silent attack – that is, without artillery support – on the Fosso Bottacetto on the night of 17/18 July. The Fosso, or ditch, is north of the Primosole bridge and 168 Brigade's attack on it was the first operation for 1st London Irish, which

came under extremely heavy enfilade fire from a large number of automatic weapons and from mortars and artillery. Bitter fighting developed and it was extremely difficult to discover the exact situation of the leading companies.

With a complete disregard of danger, Lieutenant-Colonel Good went forward over very open and bullet-swept ground, discovered the exact situation and reported it. Later, during the early hours of July 18th when ordered to withdraw his battalion and take up a defensive position some 400 yards in rear, he extricated his companies with great skill, despite the fact that they were disorganized, due to heavy and confused fighting, and there being only a short period of darkness left.

In spite of its casualties, the battalion was able to dig in to new positions from which to continue the battle. Subsequently, Good gave another example of inspiring leadership at Gravina di Catania where the battalion's advance was held up by heavy mortar- and machine-gun-fire.

It was also on 18 July that Lieutenant-Colonel Joseph Patrick O'Brien-Twohig, commanding 2nd Royal Inniskilling Fusiliers, won the DSO. O'Brien-Twohig's battalion was ordered to capture a new bridgehead over the Simeto that afternoon; this was achieved and three companies had crossed by nightfall. However, the Germans recognized the danger that this presented to their flank and began to reinforce strongly:

> All through the night the enemy mortar and machine-gun fire increased in intensity, and at dawn a determined counter-attack supported by tanks was pushed against the bridge while infantry attempted to cross the river and outflank the Inniskillings.

All but one of the Inniskillings' company commanders were killed or wounded. The battalion's discipline held firm, however, and its commanding officer's personal gallantry and leadership had much to do with this. In spite of the enemy fire, O'Brien-Twohig moved about among his companies to re-organize into new positions as he pulled them back across the river into new positions. These were so strong that the Germans were unable to reach the bridge, and a British counter-attack by tanks and infantry finally forced the Germans to withdraw. Seeing the bridge clear, O'Brien-Twohig went forward alone to reconnoitre and then led his men back across the river to retake their earlier positions. During the battle he had always seemed to be where the threat was greatest, and the 'final success of the operation was very largely due to' his courage and leadership.

A first-hand account of the action from the viewpoint of a platoon commander was provided by John Duane of B Company.

> The Battalion was given the task of forcing a crossing of the Simeto river which blocked our progress to the Catania plain. We were a long way ahead of our artillery support. We had no tanks and our own anti-tank guns were blocked some distance behind with river beds that prevented a crossing. In other words we were exposed to enemy tanks which blocked our advance.
>
> C Company under Major Meade was in the vanguard. A platoon under Lieutenant Harry Christie made the initial crossing of the Simeto followed by the balance of C Company. They immediately came under fire from the Germans holding the river bank. Harry, who was to prove his mettle in no uncertain way, forced the area immediately round the bridgehead on the German side and was counter-attacked by the Germans with tanks and machine-gun fire. He held on to the bridge and during the remaining time before dusk Major Meade's company suffered heavy casualties. B and D Companies were then thrust into battle over the bridge in support of C Company. A bloody battle ensued in which B Company under Captain Alexander was committed. The company commander leading the assault was killed. My platoon was allocated to the left of the bridge. Here we engaged the Germans with machine-gun fire.

Meanwhile Harry Christie with his platoon had knocked out the German tanks. He was later to receive the DSO for this gallant action.*

The battle continued throughout the night. The Battalion held firm to the small bridgehead. Thirteen of our officers had been killed or wounded and [there were] almost two hundred casualties in the Battalion.

As well as the DSO to Harry Christie, C Company's commander, Major Meade, a Dubliner by birth, was awarded the MC for his outstanding courage and leadership.

The Irish Brigade was brought to Sicily with 78th Division, which advanced in the direction of the mountaintop village of Centuripe, captured by the brigade in early August. There followed crossings of the rivers Salso and Simeto, and it was at the latter that the commanding officer of 1st Royal Irish Fusiliers earned the DSO Lieutenant-Colonel Beauchamp Butler, a native of Rathvilly, County Carlow, was given the task of securing the right half of the Simeto bridgehead:

> This officer led his battalion with great gallantry. Throughout a hard day's fighting he was tireless in his efforts to ensure success, personally directing the fire of his anti-tank guns and mortars at centres of resistance; launching attacks and never giving a desperate and determined enemy any loophole. Lieutenant-Colonel Butler was under continuous and accurate short-range machine-gun and rifle fire and mortar fire for many hours, but his complete disregard of danger and his inspiring example to his battalion ensured the success of the operation.
>
> This officer has also rendered distinguished service in the attack on Centuripe and in the crossing of the River Salso.

The capture of Centuripe had brought many plaudits to the Irish Brigade whose achievement was lauded in the house of commons and by General Montgomery. Soldiers of the Inniskillings, led by Major George 'Hobo' Crocker from Cork, had achieved the impossible, ascending a near vertical one-hundred-foot cliff-face to enter the town. Crocker's was the second of two companies to make the climb and after scaling the cliff,

> under heavy cross machine-gun fire, he then organized [A Company] at the summit, still under fire, with complete disregard for his personal safety, and led it into the centre of the town, where it encountered an equal number of a German parachute unit.
>
> In the ensuing hand-to-hand fighting Major Crocker continued to display conspicuous gallantry and leadership and conducted the battle with the greatest skill. Although wounded and suffering from loss of blood he refused to leave his company and remained with it through the night, during which the enemy withdrew.

---

* The award of a DSO to such a junior officer is an indication that he may have been commended for a VC. Christie's DSO is now in the Royal Inniskilling Fusiliers' Museum.

The German retreat from Centuripe was part of a strategic withdrawal to Messina and the evacuation of the island. By 17 August all German resistance on Sicily had ended, with the bulk of the German forces evacuated safely to Italy. The Italian peninsula was the next theatre for the Allied armies in the Mediterranean.

The Italian campaign was a long, brutal slog for the advancing Allied armies as they fought their way up the peninsula against the grain of the country. From the mountainous spine of Italy, rivers run to each coast and every river valley provided a formidable obstacle to the attackers and a partly-made defence system for the Germans. Such is the nature of the terrain that the campaign was largely an infantryman's war. In that respect it differed from the campaign in north-west Europe in 1944-5, or from the North African campaign that had preceded it.

The first landings were made by Eighth Army at Reggio in the toe of Italy on 3 September 1943. British soldiers had, at last, returned to mainland Europe although there was to be almost two more years of fighting before the final victory was achieved. Eighth Army's landings, Operation BAYTOWN, were unopposed and advance elements were soon probing their way through the rugged Calabrian countryside. Six days later, Fifth Army, which included the British X Corps under Major-General Richard McCreery, landed in the bay of Salerno, south of Naples, in Operation AVALANCHE.

AVALANCHE was far from being an unopposed landing. The Germans held back at first, but only until they were certain that the landing was not a feint, and then attacked the beachhead with fury, determined to push the invading Allies back into the sea. Among the many gallantry awards won at Salerno, two Irish soldiers gained the Military Medal.

On 9 September – D-Day – Corkman Patrick McCormack, a stretcher-bearer in a battalion of the Queen's Royal Regiment, won his MM, which was probably the first gallantry award to an Irish soldier in Italy.

> At about 1430 hours on ... September 9th 1943, the company to which Private McCormack was attached as stretcher-bearer suffered several casualties. Quite regardless of heavy machine-gun fire, which was sweeping the field in which these men lay, he immediately moved forward, dressed their wounds, collected them and stayed with them all through the night, and brought them in on the morning of September 10th, 1943. The casualties subsequently survived, which was entirely due to Private McCormack's action. This had a very great moral effect on the men of the company in view of the difficulty in evacuating casualties during this operation.

Among the first soldiers ashore at Salerno had been men of the Army Commandos, then also known as Special Service troops,* one of whom was Sergeant Richard O'Brien, from Newcastle West in County Limerick, who had originally served in the Royal Berkshire Regiment. O'Brien already held the Distinguished Conduct

---

* Commando Brigades were known as Special Service Brigades until 1944. This, of course, meant that the titles of such brigades were abbreviated to SS, which was the main reason for the change in nomenclature.

Medal, and at Salerno he showed complete disregard for personal safety in actions between 10 and 18 September:

> On the morning of September 10th, 1943, he went forward to contact a missing section under heavy fire and led them to safety. Later, in the battle at Piocolette, [15-18 September] after his troop leader had been killed he led a patrol through the enemy lines and brought back valuable information and a prisoner. He then took charge of the troop after all four of his officers had become casualties.

When the battle finally turned in favour of the Allies, and Fifth Army was able to advance from Salerno, it was the beginning of an autumn and winter of hard fighting in which the Allied objective, to reach Rome, was not going to be achieved. As Fifth Army battled at Salerno, Eighth Army was making its way northwards from the toe of Italy. There were no fixed lines of defences, but booby traps, and such simple expedients as felled trees along roads, were used to impede Eighth Army's advance. Fifth Division was one of the leading elements of Eighth Army and Lieutenant John Duane of 2nd Inniskillings had some experience of the traps left for the unwary by the retreating Germans.

> The country was mountainous which meant that the enemy could slow down our progress by demolitions. One incident comes to mind when our Transport Officer, Charlie Ray, lost his life. I had been instructed by the Commanding Officer, Colonel O'Brien-Twohig, to go forward to find a suitable place to harbour our transport for the night. With the aid of a Norton motor bicycle I went rapidly ahead to seek a farm house suitable for this project. I pulled off the main road and quickly discovered that a lot of mines were strewn around the farm house. I was careful to keep the motor bicycle in the centre of the road, not to advance on the area where the wheeled vehicles would move. Later, when Charlie Ray pulled off the main road his vehicle went up on a mine. There were five of these on the 150 yards to the farm house.

Soon after this incident, John Duane was sent ahead of the battalion again, with the full carrier platoon – ten vehicles – to make contact with Fifth Army.

> It was pitch dark and driving into the unknown was daunting experience. As we neared the battle area there was great activity, flares lighting up the darkness, flashes from artillery guns, the rattle of machine-gun fire; all hell was breaking loose. Meeting up with the force – American men as it so happened – was a happy and joyous occasion.

Eighth Army was also advancing on the far side of Italy, pushing up from the heel of the country towards the ankle. Since there were large numbers of assault craft still in the Mediterranean, the opportunity was taken to use some of these to leap frog elements of Eighth Army along the coast. And so the Irish Brigade embarked at Barletta to land at Termoli. The Irishmen were to follow the Special Service and 36 Brigades; and it was intended that when Nelson Russell's battalions landed they would be entering a town and area that had already been secured by the commandos and the infantry of 36 Brigade. At the same time, other elements of 78th Division – the Irish Brigade's parent formation – were pushing towards Termoli by land. However, the flooded Biferno river, and stout opposition, held up the advancing troops. Then a patrol of B Squadron, 56th Reconnaissance Regiment captured a German motorcyclist:

> It was found he was from 16 Panzer Division, thought to be on the West Coast! Termoli was only lightly held by garrison troops, but 7 miles up the road B Squadron bumped into the forward elements of 16 Panzer and found itself in action against German Mark 4 tanks and a considerable force of German infantry. 11 Bde had been advancing on the left of the road and also soon encountered this unexpected opposition.

The Reconnaissance Regiment had acquired the soubriquet Chavasse's Light Horse in honour of its Irish commanding officer, Kendal Chavasse. During the Dunkirk campaign Chavasse had been mentioned in despatches while serving as Brigade Major of 150 Brigade. In 1942 he was appointed to command 56 Recce which he took to Tunisia in Operation TORCH in November of that year and with whom he had won the DSO during the Tunisian campaign. At Termoli he was to earn a Bar to his DSO and become the only officer of the Reconnaissance Corps to be so decorated:*

> B Squadron withdrew to a brickworks on the left of the road and on 11 Brigade's right. I was given command of a mixed force consisting of B Squadron, No. 3 Commando, an SRS troop that had landed with the Commando, and a battery of anti-tank guns with orders to hold the high ground west of Termoli, and defend this position against the advancing Panzer Division.
>
> The Germans launched a heavy attack with tanks and artillery; most of the anti-tank guns were wiped out, and B Squadron lost touch with RHQ as its link wireless vehicle had been destroyed by a shell.
>
> Following confused mortar and machine-gun fire, RHQ moved forward to an olive grove on the east of the road, where B Squadron had parked its vehicles, as it was now defending the brickworks on foot. No. 3 Commando was also there, and the grove dominated the surrounding countryside.
>
> October 5 dawned in a drizzle to find the Argylls (on the left of B Sqn) in the open, holding tanks and infantry with no tank support. So the Brigadier

---

* The only Bar to a Military Medal in the Corps also went to an Irishman, Trooper Paddy Flynn of 45 Recce in Burma.

ordered the Argylls to withdraw and their CO contacted Marcus Mahon
(commanding B Squadron) and advised the withdrawal (as he had no means
of contacting me) which he did, in conjunction with the Argylls.

During the afternoon the enemy advance on Termoli continued, and tanks
and infantry approached the olive grove. I ordered the evacuation of all vehicles except LRCs of RHQ and it soon became clear that RHQ and No. 3
Commando was being encircled. It has been alleged – elsewhere – that when
this became obvious I was reported as having said 'Splendid, we now have an
all round shoot.' I can't remember this myself.

It was now getting dark, and we could hear the voices of enemy infantry,
through the shelling. The order to withdraw came to me from Divisional HQ.
I remember walking through the olive grove with bullets whistling to contact
the CO of the Commando to tell him to withdraw. Then came the problem of
getting our vehicles out. I got on to Division, over the air, and asked for as
much noise as possible, so that the enemy could not hear vehicles starting up.
I remember having to talk in a soft tone, as if I could hear their voices in the
dark they could hear mine! I also remember the gunner saying to me that he
had never been asked for 'noise' before! Anyway they gave it and plenty of it
too and we slipped away unnoticed to behind the firmer line that had been
established behind us.

The subsequent citation for the Bar to Kendal Chavasse's DSO noted that he

Showed exceptional leadership, coolness and devotion to duty. His reports
enabled enemy concentrating for the attack to be dispersed by artillery fire
while his personal example was the mainspring of a gallant and effective
defence which did much to ensure the successful outcome of the operations.

As the Irish Brigade came ashore at Termoli they found themselves embroiled in a
battle that they had not expected. Nonetheless the battalions responded effectively and
an attack was launched that cleared the town of enemy forces. For this operation the
brigade had the support of a Canadian armoured regiment that had crossed the
Biferno. At 11.30 a.m. on 6 October, A Company of 1st Royal Irish Fusiliers, led by
Major Paddy Proctor, advanced on the brickworks where the Argylls had previously
held out. By 1 p.m. the Faughs were secure in the brickworks and ready to move
forward to their next objective, the right side of the San Giacomo ridge; 6th
Inniskillings were to take the other side of the ridge. In those operations Paddy Proctor
won the Military Cross:

His company was moving in rear at the beginning of the attack but when the
forward companies were temporarily held up Major Proctor at once moved
forward on his own initiative up the right flank. Advancing very rapidly in
close co-operation with the tanks he moved his company into a brickworks

which was the first objective. This advance was made in the teeth of fierce opposition from enemy tanks and infantry, but so rapid was it that the enemy were thrown off their guard and the strong-point in the factory was not seriously defended.

After a brief reorganisation the advance was resumed with his company still leading. Opposition from enemy tanks and machine-guns was encountered but rapidly overcome, and by 1530 hours the final objective was gained and the enemy driven off leaving several wounded prisoners in our hands.

Major Proctor's work was consistently of a high order. His leadership and personal example instilled a high morale in his company and sound judgement was responsible for many successful actions in the field.

Paddy Proctor, a native of Rathmullan, County Donegal, was killed in action three weeks later. Also decorated as a result of the battle of Termoli was Sergeant William John Jackson, a Dubliner serving in 1st Royal Irish Fusiliers, who commanded a platoon during the attack on the San Giacomo ridge:

> Throughout the attack Sergeant Jackson commanded his platoon in an outstanding manner. He continually directed the fire of his Brens on to enemy posts and personally led assault groups to clear these positions. His platoon was the first into a large factory which was well known to be an enemy strong-point.
>
> Sergeant Jackson's magnificent leadership, cheery confidence and complete disregard of his own safety were a fine example and inspiration to his men.

Following the Termoli battle the Irish Brigade went on to take the Petacciato ridge and then advanced to another river obstacle, the Trigno. At 78th Divisional Headquarters it was believed that the bridge over the Trigno was still intact, which would ease considerably the task of crossing the river. Patrols were ordered forward to check on the state of the bridge, how steep the river banks might be and the level of water in the river. Two patrols were provided by the London Irish Rifles, the first of which was from H Company and commanded by Captain Desmond Woods, MC, the newly-appointed company commander:

> This was to be the only patrol that I took out in Italy. I was promoted shortly after this to major and majors did not normally command patrols. ... I decided to take a platoon with me and we set off, the idea being to travel by night to try to get to the Trigno unobserved. Now the information about the Germans was very sketchy. We knew that they had outpost positions on our side of the Trigno, mostly based in Italian houses but we didn't know really which houses were occupied, so I took it that most of them would be, from the point of view of trying to take avoiding action.

Desmond Woods' patrol was at platoon strength – about 30 men – and was delayed by terrain difficulties en route to the river. The patrol reached its objective after daylight had broken and occupied an Italian farmhouse from which Captain Woods was able to observe

> down below me ... the most marvellous view of the bridge over the river Trigno. It was intact ... the banks weren't too steep, the level of the water in the river was fairly low and, should the bridge be blown, it would be perfectly possible to make a diversion for tanks on either side of the original bridge and they would be able to get across while a Bailey bridge was being erected.

From the farmhouse the patrol spent the morning observing the ground on either side of the river. Desmond Woods knew that there were Germans about but

> There was a fair amount of cover there and it was absolutely incredible that during that morning I hardly saw any movement by Germans at all. They were very good at lying low by day and not giving their position away. In fact, they were a great deal better than we were.

Shortly after noon, Captain Woods received a wireless message telling him to return as soon as possible to his battalion's headquarters with his report of his reconnaissance. Since this meant moving in daylight he decided to leave most of the platoon in hiding, to be picked up later, and take only a couple of men with him. The return journey was fraught with danger: they had to go through much open country and there was the risk of being spotted by the enemy. However, all the cover that was available was used, but when they came to 'one fairly large open space' it was necessary to resort to other means.

> I saw an Italian with a farmcart spreading manure on this bit of ground and I managed to get in contact with him and the two men and myself decided that the best thing to do was to lie flat in the bottom of this cart and make the Italian drive us across this piece of open ground, which was exactly what we did. It wasn't particularly pleasant but at least we got through it unobserved. And we got across and into cover again and continued on towards Petacciato.

The battalion's second patrol, accompanied by some Royal Engineers, moved right down to the bridge, where they had a brisk firefight with some German troops, and returned to say that the bridge had not been prepared for demolition. Nelson Russell, the Irish Brigade commander, refused to accept that this report was accurate as he did not believe that the patrol had had sufficient time to examine the structure closely. Nonetheless divisional headquarters considered that the river could be crossed by means of the bridge and the Irish Brigade was ordered to 'capture the bridge intact and forthwith'.

Initially the plan of attack went smoothly, but, as the leading troops – C Company of the Irish Fusiliers – reached the bridge, it 'went up like Vesuvius at the top of her form'. In spite of this setback a crossing was made and a bridgehead established on the far side of the river. The Inniskillings then moved up to the village of Montenero, to the left of the bridgehead, as plans were made for the next phase of the advance, against the town of San Salvo, which sat on a ridge some four thousands yards ahead.

The attack on San Salvo, which began on the night of 27 October, proved a traumatic experience for the men of the Irish Fusiliers. Although the Irish Brigade commander had asked for a postponement, due to the very heavy rainfall of the afternoon, this was refused and the Fusiliers and Irish Rifles advanced behind a heavy artillery bombardment. Unfortunately, a number of enemy machine-gun positions were overshot by the guns and these remained in action against the attacking infantry. The muddy ground also slowed the pace of advance and German mortar fire and artillery joined with the machine-guns in taking their toll of the Irishmen.

It was not long before the Irish Fusiliers were pinned down by the intensity of the enemy fire. B Company's commander, Dennis Dunn, was killed by a shell after all his platoon commanders had become casualties. Paddy Proctor, MC, who had been such an outstanding company commander at Termoli, died with all his platoon commanders of A Company when a mortar bomb fell among them as they planned the next phase of their attack, on the final ridge. And the battalion's heroic and inspiring commanding officer, Beauchamp Butler, died from a machine-gun bullet to the head. Butler had been in his usual position, at the front, leading and encouraging his Faughs as they suffered under the intense enemy fire.

The Rifles had also taken a hammering and both battalions were ordered back to the bridgehead where, next morning, Kevin O'Connor, second-in-command of the London Irish, was killed by a German shell. Nelson Russell later wrote that 'We'd had a dusting' and he was especially sad at the loss of Beauchamp Butler, which was:

> A tragedy for the whole Brigade; and the Faughs lost one of the best commanding officers they have ever had – in peace or war … gifted with a quiet charm of manner – and I never heard him say an unkind word about anyone. But his somewhat deceptive exterior held an inflexible will and he was a most determined and skilful leader of troops in action. It was a heavy hearted party which saw him laid to rest in the British cemetery at Termoli to the wail of his pipes.

Butler's battalion was replaced in the bridgehead by the Inniskillings; the Faughs were sent back to San Giacomo to rest, refit and reorganize. But San Salvo remained an obstacle that had to be overcome and its seizure became the first objective of a larger 78th Division plan. The town was taken eventually after much hard fighting and more casualties: the Inniskillings lost Major 'Hobo' Crocker, MC, the Cork man who had led A Company on its 'impossible' assault at Centuripe. Lieutenant Basil

Hewitt, who immediately took over command of the company, was also killed and Company Sergeant Major Stevenson then assumed responsibility for A Company, led it into San Salvo, fighting off an attack by German tanks on the way, and was subsequently awarded the Distinguished Conduct Medal.

But gallantry awards for Irishmen at San Salvo were not restricted to those in the Irish Brigade. Sergeant Michael James Crosby, from Ballinasloe in County Galway, was serving in 6th Royal West Kents in 11 Brigade of 78th Division and won the Military Medal on 4 November. On that morning the West Kents were at the foot of Vineyard Hill, which dominated the battleground. The battalion, supported by tanks of 50th Royal Tank Regiment, was ordered to take the hill. This they did successfully, but:

> as the platoon of which Sergeant Crosby was acting platoon commander reached their objective they came under intense enemy machine-gun fire, which made the positions almost untenable. Sergeant Crosby, acting with extreme promptness and a complete disregard for the devastating fire around him, walked on to the objective, rallied and placed each section in a good fire position, personally directed the fire of his platoon on to the enemy and finally, when this fire became effective, led a bayonet charge which caused the enemy to fall back in disorder, and freed his position.

The citation for Crosby's MM noted that throughout the battle 'his actions ... his disregard for danger, and bravery were an inspiration and splendid example to the men under his command'.

Eighth Army's advance continued through the mud and cold of an Italian winter. At the end of November the army's soldiers were engaged in the battle of the river Sangro, a bloody affair that left the attacking formations, including the Irish Brigade, bruised; but the German hold on the Sangro was broken and Montgomery's army was able to probe forward. At the beginning of December, two companies from 1st Royal Irish Fusiliers, under Major Jimmy Clarke, pushed forward to the small town of San Vito. In doing so they penetrated several miles behind enemy lines. As they moved towards San Vito they found their route barred by a formidable ravine near the road into the town.

> There I was to establish a defensive position from which I could send A Company forward to reconnoitre the approaches to San Vito and under cover of darkness send a patrol further forward to see what was going on there.

When Jimmy Clarke's small force reached the ravine, the forward platoons came under heavy machine-gun and mortar fire from the other side. Clarke ordered one platoon to make its way across the gully and into positions from which the enemy posts could be engaged effectively.

The first section across, of which Fusilier [James] Muldoon was a member, suffered more than 50% casualties and withdrew. Fusilier Muldoon, however, stayed to attend a wounded comrade, whom he carried to a house still on the enemy side of the gulley. There he remained until a party of Germans approached, and he took cover and watched his comrade being carried off.

For the next six hours Fusilier Muldoon lay up and observed the enemy positions, making a sketch of machine-gun posts and other enemy positions. He returned with this after a hazardous journey back across the ravine and reported to his Company Commander, giving invaluable information for any further attack. He arrived with full kit despite having [had] to carry wounded man some considerable distance.

Fusilier Muldoon displayed a devotion to duty of the highest order in remaining on the enemy side of the gulley sketching enemy positions, particularly as our own artillery was engaging targets close to him. His courage was unquestionable, and his action was a great inspiration to his comrades when they saw him return, unhurt and unperturbed.

Muldoon, a native of Mountmellick, County Laois, was not alone in displaying inspiring courage in the advance to San Vito. Just before daybreak, Major Clarke sent a patrol of volunteers, under Lieutenant John Day, into the town while the main body of his small force deployed in defensive positions outside. San Vito's inhabitants welcomed Day's men as liberators and about two dozen Germans were made prisoner, much to their surprise. Clarke and the remainder of his men listened to the sounds of celebration from the Italian townsfolk, including the ringing of the church bell, before the sounds of battle rose again. Ever swift to counter-attack, the Germans had sent two armoured cars into San Vito, and these vehicles had opened fire on the young subaltern's patrol, mortally wounding Day himself. Eight men were captured by the Germans but ten others followed Day's last order and took cover in the town. One of these was Fusilier John Toland, who led two of his comrades to the north end of the town and created havoc with a bren gun:

> With two bursts he killed two German motor cyclists ... He then saw a convoy of horse-drawn ... carts ... and fired three magazines into the leading vehicles. This caused wild confusion and brought heavy fire upon Fusilier Toland's small party, and his number two was hit through the head. Accordingly, with Germans in hot pursuit, he and the remaining Fusilier ... burst into a house and hid in the cellar.

The two Faughs were not content to stay in cover. Emerging to find the German convoy still halted on the main road, they again opened fire, killing several Germans before making their way back to the safety of their hideout. They later rejoined Major Clarke and the other men. For his part in the engagement, Toland was awarded a Russian gallantry medal while Day was recommended, unsuccessfully, for a posthumous Victoria Cross.

Shortly afterwards 78th Division were withdrawn from the line and the Irish
Brigade were given the opportunity to rest and re-organize before their next battles.
On the other side of Italy, Fifth Army was enduring an equally difficult advance with
strong and determined opposition along river lines. One of those had been encoun-
tered by X British Corps in mid-October: elements of X Corps had crossed the river
Volturno with 56th (London) Division, commanded by Major-General Gerald
Templer, an Irishman, in the van.

The Black Cat Division's assault crossing had been carried out by soldiers of 167
and 169 Brigades and, as the leading soldiers crossed the Volturno on the night of 14-
15 October, Captain Patrick Michael Mordaunt, a native of Kildare, won the Military
Cross.* Mordaunt's company was ordered to attack a position almost half a mile
north of the river. This was carried out successfully, with no opposition being encountered, and the Irishman was then ordered to take his company on to the line of a canal
three miles farther on:

> His company carried out this advance and took a position the other side of the
> canal. At dawn they were heavily shelled and counter-attacked by infantry and
> a tank at very close quarters.
>
> [Another] company was then sent to support them and was so heavily
> mortared that it had to withdraw. A further company was unable to get within
> two miles of Captain Mordaunt's position, so that he was left in complete
> isolation and in grave danger of envelopment by the enemy.
>
> In spite of this Captain Mordaunt held on to his position until the CO of
> his battalion was able to re-group at nightfall. During the night Captain
> Mordaunt's company was again heavily counter-attacked, but he did not with-
> draw his company behind the canal until his position had become quite unten-
> able and his Commanding Officer was satisfied that the remainder of the
> battalion positions were secure. When he did eventually withdraw across the
> canal in the face of heavy enemy opposition, Captain Mordaunt personally
> supervized the withdrawal, which was carried on in excellent manner.
> Throughout this action Captain Mordaunt's courage and complete disregard
> for his own safety were a stirring example to his men.

About to move to X Corps at this stage of the campaign was 5th Division, which
included 2nd Royal Inniskilling Fusiliers. On 28 December 1943, Captain John Duane
was ordered to take a patrol out to infiltrate the German lines in the Torricellia area,
ascertain the enemy dispositions, his strength and his supply lines. All this information was to be gathered with a view to mounting a raid subsequently. John Duane was
one of a number of Inniskillings' officers who had already distinguished themselves as
patrol leaders; he now

---

* The citation for Patrick Mordaunt's MC does not indicate his regiment, stating only that he served in the
Infantry. However, the leading troops of his division in the Volturno crossing were from 7th Ox and Bucks
Light Infantry and 9th Royal Fusiliers. As three companies of Fusiliers followed the initial fighting patrols, it
seems most likely that Mordaunt served in the Royal Fusiliers.

Led his patrol with outstanding skill over difficult mountain country to a position 3,000 yards behind the enemy's forward posts, and remained in the area for 24 hours in observation. He brought the patrol back with valuable and detailed information without being detected by the Germans, though at periods they passed within 150 yards of posts.

The intelligence thus gathered was used to plan a raid behind the enemy lines and Captain Duane again took command of the raiding party of thirty men, which set out on 31 December. John Duane led his party to the selected attack area without detection, but that evening there was a most severe blizzard that lasted throughout the night and most of the following day, desisting only towards evening.

This made the projected attack impracticable and Captain Duane with very fine military sense got a contact patrol back, which enabled the supporting [artillery] fire programme to be held up. He brought his raiding party safely back through deep snow drifts under conditions of extreme cold and difficulty, and through enemy posts of a German mountain unit equipped for snow work. The leadership, personal courage and soldierly qualities in the presence of the enemy during both phases of this operation were of a quite outstanding quality, and it is no exaggeration to state that without them this raiding party would almost certainly have suffered severe, if not total, casualties between the enemy and the weather.

John Duane was subsequently awarded the Military Cross for this outstanding example of leadership and courage. Two of his fellow officers in the battalion also distinguished themselves during this period. Captain Bill Vincent, of Muckross House, Killarney, led a fighting patrol that supported another, larger, patrol under Captain Geoff Cocksedge in the capture of a German-held village. The Inniskillings made a bayonet charge – a much rarer event than fiction and Hollywood would have us believe – that evicted most of the Germans; some of the garrison was made prisoner and much 'booty' was also seized. For this and other patrol actions, Cocksedge also received the Military Cross. Then, on 7 January 1944, came the order for the battalion to move with 5th Division to join X Corps on the Fifth Army front.

A new year had begun in Italy and the Allied armies had been brought to a stop by the redoubtable German defence. The aim of reaching Rome before the end of 1943 had proved to be an elusive dream and it was to be another six months before the Allies would liberate the Eternal City. Before that there was to be much hard fighting against the German defences, and especially against the Gustav line which was anchored on an Italian mountain the name of which was to become synonymous with all the suffering that the campaign entailed: Monte Cassino.

As it became clear that the German line was not going to be broken by direct assault, the Allied high command planned a new strategy: an amphibious force would be landed behind the Gustav line and south of Rome with the aim of breaking the enemy defence in conjunction with an attack through the Gustav line by formations of Fifth Army. On 22 January 1944, in Operation SHINGLE, Allied troops of the US VI Corps landed at Anzio. Although the road to Rome was clear, General John Lucas, the corps commander, hesitated to send his troops forward lest they advance into an enemy trap. He preferred to consolidate the bridgehead around Anzio and thus gave the Germans the time they needed to bring up forces to attack the invaders.

The other pincer of the attack, Fifth Army's direct assault on the Gustav line, included 5th Division and 2nd Inniskillings; with the Wiltshires, the Inniskillings were to lead the advance of 13 Brigade. John Duane, commanding the Inniskillings' battle patrol of twenty men, was given the task of leading the battalion's crossing of the Garigliano river,

> A wide river with a powerful flow of water 100 yards across, a huge natural obstacle rather like the Shannon. The Germans were entrenched in the foot hills some half mile from the river bank. They had laid land mines in this area in large numbers to make an advance by the Allied forces difficult.

The Inniskillings' task was to cross the Garigliano in boats, clear the plain on the far side of enemy posts, and then form up before the main German positions to await the opening of an artillery bombardment, following which the battalion would attack. Until that point their advance was to be silent – without artillery support. John Duane's battle patrol was assigned a single boat for the crossing:

> My platoon approached the Garigliano silently. We had the advantage of having been to the river side two nights previously; we knew the way. We were to be followed by A Company under Major Grant and the other two companies C and B. D Company was in reserve but had to make the crossing.
>
> We launched our boat into the river silently and paddled across to reach the far bank a hundred yards downstream because the current carried us along. All was silent in the darkness, a half moon peeped through the clouds. The Battalion followed making what was inevitable, a lot of noise, carrying boats in darkness over difficult terrain. A Very light on the German side of the river came up to light the crossing area and immediately, with A Company in the boats, the withering artillery stonk came down on the bank and river. Over the next half hour part of A Company got across. Many were drowned in the river, the boats were hit one by one until none were left. The crossing, except for part of A Company and the Battle Patrol, had been a failure. A Company went on to attack a German forward position, succeeded, but only just; the casualties were so heavy that the survivors could be counted on the fingers of two hands out of a strength of 100 men.

Instructed to lead his battle patrol forward to the start-line for the attack, John Duane was faced with a dilemma as a result of the disaster that had befallen the crossing. Behind him the CO was also faced with a massive problem and decided to sidestep his battalion to cross in the same area as the Wiltshires. As a result there would be a two-hour delay in the Inniskillings' planned attack:

> All this change of plan was unknown to me. I guessed a tragedy had occurred. I had no choice but to carry on as instructed initially. I reached the assault position soon after midnight and waited for the artillery barrage which was due at 3.30 am. It did not come and I wondered how the situation would unfold. At 5.30 the barrage started to come down. Was I to assault the Gustav line with just 20 brave men? We got up and started to follow the barrage and to our great relief and joy Percy Blake [from Galway] and C Company came up on our left. Right behind the barrage, C Company and the Battle Patrol rushed forward to assault the German position. At this stage John Nixon's B Company arrived on the scene and here the Inniskillings charged forward to assault the Gustav line. Apparently the Germans did not expect us nor indeed the momentum of the assault launched against them. A fierce battle ensued and we did succeed [in capturing] their positions. Our battalion as a whole had suffered heavy casualties but through sheer determination and guts had finally established our bridgehead.

Needless to say the Germans counter-attacked. Over the next twenty-four hours the Inniskillings fought off four or five such attacks and bloodied their attackers' noses. But there were casualties in the battalion, including the redoubtable Captain Harry Christie, DSO, MC, who had so distinguished himself in Sicily. Christie was killed by an enemy shell, which also mortally injured another officer, Lieutenant Bell. At one stage B Company was driven off its objective and withdrew into a small area not more than 100 yards square where it stoutly resisted all enemy efforts to force it to make a further withdrawal. Eventually the line was restored and some of B Company who had been captured by the enemy were liberated. 'Next day the Cameronians came through and enlarged the bridgehead but not to any great extent and the positions gained meant that the Gustav line remained more or less intact.'

The divisional machine-gun battalion was provided by 7th Cheshire Regiment, one of whose platoons gave valuable support to the Inniskillings on the night of 18/19 January. The platoon sergeant was a Dubliner, Thomas Scott, and he earned the Military Medal during the German counter-attacks on the morning of 19 January.

> As the battle developed all of one of Sergeant Scott's gun teams were killed, and the enemy, who by this time were in and around the gun positions, commenced to drag the gun away. Sergeant Scott, without hesitation and with complete disregard of his own safety, directed the fire of his other gun on to the enemy, got back into position and immediately reorganized another team. Throughout the counter-attack Sergeant Scott was continually with both his gun positions maintaining supplies to the guns and inspiring his men by his example of courage.

On the night of 20/21 January the reserve brigade of 5th Division moved through the bridgehead to take objectives to the Inniskillings' left. However, attacks to the right were less successful with 36th (US) Division suffering heavily on the Rapido river, and the overall advance ground to a halt. In fighting in the Minturno area on 22 January, seven Military Medals were won by men of 1st Green Howards, one of whom was Corporal John Murphy from Kilmallack.

> In the area of the Minturno cemetery, the situation of this NCO's platoon became critical, the enemy having infiltrated in some strength and surrounded the platoon locality. Having armed himself with all available grenades and extra ammunition, Corporal Murphy went out with his Platoon Sergeant to attack the enemy.
>
> By superb courage and offensive action of the highest order they overcame great odds, Corporal Murphy himself killing six Germans, wounding others and causing the remainder to break up and run.

Although the Anzio landings took place on the 22nd, the Germans appeared to assess the Garigliano assault to be the more dangerous of the two and thus did not weaken the front, thereby denying Fifth Army an opportunity to make a breakthrough and advance on Rome. It was to be four more months before the Gustav line would finally crumble under the weight of the Allied armies.

In the Anzio beachhead General Lucas' failure to exploit his initial successful landings was probably understandable as his army commander, General Mark Clark, had told him on the quayside at Anzio to be cautious. Having given that initial advice, Clark appeared unwilling to change his subordinate's orders even after it became clear that the other pincer of the assault had met with failure. Thus Lucas felt justified in creating a defensive perimeter around the Anzio beachhead and committing his command to a siege. In due course Lucas was relieved of his command, but the damage had already been done and the men in the beachhead had to endure a purgatory until the Gustav line was finally broken in late May.

Although a US Army formation, VI Corps was not entirely American in composition. The initial landing force included the British 1st Division in which 1st Irish Guards were serving in 24 Guards Brigade. At a later stage, 5th Division, including 2nd Inniskillings, would arrive in the beachhead as would 56th (London) Division with 1st London Irish Rifles. Not surprisingly, a number of Irishmen won decorations during what one regimental historian has described as some of 'the most bitter infantry fighting of the war'.

Typical of the Irish Guards who were decorated at Anzio were Company Sergeant-Major (Drill Sergeant) Michael Moran and Lance-Corporal Maurice Terence O'Brien, both Dubliners, who each received the Military Medal for gallantry on the night of 29/30 January, just a week after their battalion's landing. On that night the Micks were advancing and Moran was in charge of the company transport and acting as second-in-command to the officer commanding the entire battalion transport column.

As the column advanced it came under heavy machine-gun fire from a house some hundred yards away and from other positions on one flank:

> Company Sergeant-Major Moran quickly organized a small party and led an assault on the house and killed the German gunners, thus freeing the column from its most immediate danger. On returning from this task he found that the officer in command had been severely wounded, and that one carrier had been set on fire by mortar bombs which were now falling thickly on the road.

Moran took command of the entire column and ordered flank protection as he organized the turn-round of the column. This was achieved quickly, and he took the column back to a covered position. During this whole period the column was under heavy fire, but Moran was completely cool and showed no concern for his personal safety. Having taken the transport column to safety, Company Sergeant-Major Moran went forward to contact his own company commander and reconnoitre a route to his company position:

> In the subsequent fighting on the flank this Warrant Officer showed outstanding courage and leadership and personally led several attacks on machine-gun posts with complete success. During the whole of the fighting his courage and initiative were remarkable, and he certainly played a large part in securing the number of Germans his company killed. This NCO has fought in Palestine, Norway, Tunisia and now in the Italian campaign, and has on all occasions set the highest example of personal courage and devotion to duty.

During that attack, Corporal Maurice O'Brien was the NCO in command of the 2-inch mortar of one of the forward platoons. His company also came up against strong opposition, including fire from eight machine-gun posts sited between the main Anzio-Albano road and the railway, which was the company axis of advance. Those machine-guns and enemy mortars caused heavy casualties in O'Brien's company and his platoon was in danger of being pinned down by their fire and wiped out,

> when Lance-Corporal O'Brien advanced towards the nearest stream of tracer and brought his mortar into action, totally ignoring his own great danger. He effectively silenced the left-hand machine-gun post, thus enabling the remainder of his platoon to get round the flank. This most courageous and inspiring example and the quick rallying of his platoon through the gap he had made, undoubtedly played a major part in helping his company to reach its objective and saved a good many lives.

O'Brien showed more of his mettle the following day when

> Owing to the presence of enemy tanks in the company's position, the company was ordered to withdraw to another position. Lance-Corporal O'Brien

assumed command of a party of men whom he found had been cut off, and by his initiative, gallantry and example fought his way back with this party. The party was under heavy machine-gun fire from both flanks and all the way this NCO provided, with a Bren-gun, the covering fire for the bounds by which the party made its way back, himself running the gauntlet each time to catch up with them and cover them over the next stretch of open country.

Such bravery continued to be shown by men of the Irish Guards throughout the battalion's time in the beachhead. It was not unique to the Micks and similar examples can be found in the experiences of the other Irish battalions at Anzio and among Irish soldiers in other units, such as Private Thomas Flynn of the Loyal Regiment. Throughout the entire course of his battalion's operations in the beachhead, Flynn, a Sligo man,

> Displayed great courage and devotion to duty.
> During the first two weeks he volunteered for every patrol sent out by the company and displayed great initiative.
> During the hard fighting of February 18th-19th, 1944, he led a section splendidly and by his personal courage and example inspired his men to fierce resistance at a critical period when the Germans had got into the company positions. Private Flynn's actions played a big part in finally driving the enemy out of the area.

There were no major setpiece battles at Anzio. Instead, there was a steady battle of attrition with skirmishes and small-scale actions at battalion, company, platoon and even section level. And all the while, those in the beachhead endured bombarding by Germany artillery and mortars, from which no corner of the Allied-held ground was safe. Even the hospital area was hit by shellfire and those within the beachhead wryly referred to their location as 'Hell's Half Acre'. The soldiers of VI Corps remained at Anzio until Operation BUFFALO at the end of May when the corps broke out from the beachhead to link up with elements of the advancing Allied forces that had finally shattered the Gustav line. That shattering had come about as the result of the final battle of Cassino – Operation DIADEM – when the combined weight of both Fifth and Eighth Armies had been brought to bear on the western side of Italy. Eighth Army had been moved, without detection by the Germans, from the Adriatic side of the country and assaulted the Cassino position to thrust through the Liri valley towards Rome. But it was no easy task, and many lives were lost in its carrying out.

The Irish Brigade played an important part in the battle of Cassino. As part of 78th Division they had the task of expanding the bridgehead across the Rapido that had been formed by 4th British and 8th Indian Divisions. The Irish Brigade were the vanguard of their division, and the brigade's first attack was made by the Inniskillings. That was to be followed by another leap forward by 2nd London Irish Rifles, for whom events did not turn out as planned. As the Rifles' CO, Lieutenant-

Colonel Ion Goff, finalized his plans with John Loveday, the CO of 16th/5th Lancers, the Irish Brigade's armoured support regiment, the area in which the two COs were conferring was targeted by enemy gunners and both Goff and Loveday were fatally injured. As a result the battalion's attack was delayed, and a further delay was imposed to co-ordinate with the Lancashire Fusiliers on the right of the Irish Rifles. When the Rifles went into the attack it was with three companies advancing under cover of an artillery bombardment 'consisting of the entire divisional artillery,* plus the mediums and anything else that they could get hold of'. Major Desmond Woods, MC, was commanding H Company, which had the hamlet of Sinagoga as its objective.

> We were lined up on our start line waiting to go when down came this terrific barrage. I will never forget it; the noise was horrendous and it started to move forward. H Company got up out of their trenches and we started to move forward as well. We'd only been going for a short time when a message came in from one of the forward platoons that they were getting casualties from, they thought, 'shorts' from our artillery barrage.

In fact, the casualties were being caused by German defensive fire, which was extremely accurate as the Germans had 'complete observation of our advance'. H Company's right platoon commander, Michael Clark, was killed by shellfire and the left platoon commander, Geoffrey Searles, was badly injured:

> We kept going forward and I will never forget the noise. You would hear a shell; you had a fraction of a second before it actually burst to dive into cover and one tried to move from one shell-hole to the next and I remember diving into a shell-hole and a chap – one of the riflemen from my company HQ – landing on top of me and I said 'get up, we must go on'. There was no movement, he was dead. He had a bit of shrapnel through his neck ... By now we were about halfway through the attack and the barrage dwelt for ten minutes and we were able to get down to ground. One wondered would anybody be able to live under this barrage as far as the Germans were concerned, but, by God, they could. Then we started moving forward again and I decided to bring up the reserve platoon to try to keep the impetus of the attack going. By then we had some German prisoners and they were moving along at my company HQ and, at times when the shelling was so bad, we were lying flat on the ground as close as we could get to it and there was me beside these German prisoners – we were all made of human flesh, all dignity had gone, it was now a matter of could one stay alive until one got on to one's objective. Things certainly were not getting any better. I was completely deafened by the noise. I was completely dazed as well and I am sure the remainder of the company were.

---

* The divisional artillery consisted of three field regiments, each deploying twenty-four 25-pounders.

The tanks supporting H Company had been held up by a German anti-tank gun, an 88mm weapon, concealed behind a haystack. This was a redoubtable gun and the armour of the Sherman tank, with which the 16th/5th Lancers were equipped, was no match for its shells. Now the presence of this gun threatened the progress of H Company, until one of the section commanders in the left platoon took the initiative:

> Corporal Barnes ... saw what had happened – his platoon commander was very seriously wounded, but that did not deter Corporal Barnes. He realized that he'd have to try to do something about this 88mm which was stopping our tanks getting forward. He advanced with his section and one by one the men were cut down by machine-gun fire on their left flank until Corporal Barnes remained alone. He went on by himself and then he fell dead, cut by a machine-gun, but by then the crew of the 88 had baled out and the tanks were able to get forward once again. Then, suddenly, we were on our objective.

H Company paid a terrible price in achieving its objective: Desmond Woods had lost two of his platoon officers and about two-thirds of his company. With the survivors he consolidated their position in readiness for the inevitable counter-attack, which occurred about half an hour later. The Germans were fought off by H Company and the machine-guns of their supporting tanks after a battle lasting some thirty minutes. Finally, the Rifles had the opportunity to rest and reflect.

For Desmond Woods that reflection led to the decision to write a recommendation for a posthumous Victoria Cross for Corporal Jimmy Barnes:

> This was one of the bravest actions I'd ever seen. Here was this young corporal left on his own, his platoon commander had been knocked out, and it would have been so easy for him to have gone to ground, but not a bit of it. He intended to continue to the end. I am very sorry to say that he was never awarded his Victoria Cross. He was the real hero of that day and I will never forget him as long as I live.

Nor was Jimmy Barnes awarded a posthumous Mention in Despatches – until 1979 the only other gallantry award that could be granted posthumously – and this young man's great courage and self-sacrifice was denied the recognition it deserved. Desmond Woods regarded the Monaghan man as the 'most outstanding' of his nine section commanders:

> He was full of life – always smiling – every time you met him he would greet you. He was great when we were out of the line, a keen footballer and the best type of young corporal you could possibly have.

Desmond Woods' courageous leadership of H Company on that May day was rewarded with a Bar to the Military Cross that he had earned as a young subaltern in Palestine before the war.

On May 16th, 1944, this officer commanding 'H' Company led the attack on the centre of the line. Of all three forward companies in this attack he encountered the fiercest resistance. However, by skilful handling of his company and by his personal example, in spite of severe losses, the enemy strongpoints were overcome. In the attack on the village itself, which was strongly held, he took a part of his company in ahead of the tanks and this alone neutralized to a large extent the enemy anti-tank weapons which then could not be served. During the whole battle Major Woods's company was under very heavy small-arms and shell fire and their capture of the village was very largely responsible for the success of the operation.

One of the other assaulting companies on that day was E Company, commanded by Major Mervyn Davies, which also secured its objective – Sinagoga wood – and began the task of consolidation to meet the expected German counter-attacks:

> I walked through the wood to find G Company on our right had kept up with us. In the wood there was a small farmhouse which I took to be Sinagoga Farm. I went in and in a bedroom on the ground floor there were a very old man and his wife. They were unhurt and I tried to comfort them. I returned to the Company's position in the wood as a dreadful Nebelwerfer Stonk arrived. This killed two of the best men in the Company, Sergeant Mayo, MM and Corporal O'Reilly, MM.

Sergeant Mayo was a Londoner of Irish extraction, while Corporal Edward O'Reilly was a Cavan man, from Arva, who had won the Military Medal in the Sicilian campaign. Both are buried in the Commonwealth Cemetery at Cassino.

As the advancing armies pushed through the Gustav line, the Germans withdrew to a number of prepared positions from which they could delay the Allied advance, and then to the Senger line, originally styled the Hitler line. During this phase of the fighting an Irish sergeant of 5th Buffs (Royal East Kent Regiment), in 36 Brigade of 78th Division, earned the MM at Aquino when his battalion was ordered to attack that location on 19 May:

> Early on in this operation a Platoon Commander in 'D' company of this battalion was wounded. Lance-Sergeant O'Malley immediately took over command of the platoon and led them into the attack with great resolution and courage. Throughout the action he was a great inspiration to all the men under his command, and undoubtedly filled them with great confidence.
>
> His platoon was continually under very heavy machine-gun and mortar fire, and it was very largely due to his great initiative and inspiring leadership that the platoon arrived on the objective.
>
> During the withdrawal of the battalion he once again showed great courage and brought his platoon out complete and in perfect order.

> By his great leadership and devotion to duty Lance-Sergeant O'Malley undoubtedly saved many lives, and gained the complete confidence of the men under his command.

Lance-Sergeant Martin O'Malley was born in County Galway.

On 4 June 1944 the city of Rome was liberated by Fifth Army. The joy of liberation did not obscure the fact that many men had died thus far in the Italian campaign. In directing his formations on Rome, General Mark Clark had thrown away the opportunity to destroy in detail at least one of the two German armies opposing the Allies in Italy. As a result the Italian campaign would drag on for another eleven months, through a further bitter Italian winter, and many more would die before hostilities ended. As ever, Irish infantry would be among those fighting in Italy, and they would rank also among the dead – as they would do in north-west Europe, following the invasion of France two days after the fall of Rome, in Burma, in the Pacific, and in the other lesser-known campaigns that made up the final year of war.

~ 12 ~

Experiences of Irishwomen
at home and abroad

War is an activity that is generally associated with males and that has been the case through much of human history. There have been notable exceptions, and Ireland's legends and history include some of those exceptions: Maeve, the warrior queen of Connaught, Grace O'Malley (Granuaile the pirate queen) and Constance Markievicz are perhaps the best known. But the most common perception of women in war remains the romanticized caring figure, embodied by Florence Nightingale – whose principal lieutenant in the Crimea was an Irishwoman, Agnes Jones from Fahan in County Donegal.

In the twentieth century the role of women in war began to change during the Great War when women not only did factory work to relieve men for military service, but they also took on military tasks that took them much closer to the fighting than before. Thus women drove lorries and ambulances as well as carrying out nursing duties on the western front. By the time the Second World War started there was a much greater acceptance of women in uniform, and Britain's three armed services each had a women's branch: the Royal Navy had the Women's Royal Naval Service, known as the Wrens; the Army had the Auxiliary Territorial Service (the ATS); and the Royal Air Force had the Women's Auxiliary Air Force, the Waafs. We have already seen in chapter One that the recruitment of women for the ATS in Northern Ireland began before the war commenced. There were still, of course, the naval, army and air force nursing services, which continued to be female organizations.

The range of duties performed by women in the Second World War was much greater than had ever been the case before. Women did many jobs that, previously, had been regarded as the prerogative of males, manning the fire-control systems of the anti-aircraft defence of the United Kingdom – and, later, serving on the continent in 21 Army Group – as well as flying aircraft in the Air Transport Auxiliary, deciphering signals in the armed services and at the top-secret Bletchley Park where the German Enigma codes were read regularly throughout the war. Irish women, from both sides of the border, played an important part in the Second World War and were to be found in all three British services.

The senior British service is the Royal Navy, but the women's branch, the Wrens, did not encourage recruitment from south of the border. In this it differed from the other services, which welcomed Irish women. However, there were ways to circumvent this restriction as Elizabeth Chamberlain from Dublin discovered:

> I wanted to join the Wrens because their uniform was the most attractive. But the WRNS wouldn't accept applicants from the south of Ireland, so I had to get to England. Brenda's [Brenda Graham] father made this possible. He was able to arrange jobs for four of us at Chertsey hospital as nursing aides. So I went to England to be able to get into the Wrens.

The four friends travelled to England in two pairs. Brenda Graham, whose doctor father made the trip possible, had been studying languages – English, French and German – at Trinity College, but did not finish her course, preferring the adventure of getting away from Ireland:

> I wanted to get away. There was a sense of adventure and of being able to do something positive, which you couldn't do in Ireland. We all wanted to join the Wrens. Their uniform was so attractive, unlike the other two.
>
> My father was a doctor and he had good contacts and was able to place four of us in the Chertsey hospital.

Dr Thomas Ottiwell Graham, MC, MD, DPH, FRCSI, was one of Dublin's, and Ireland's, best-known doctors. He had served in the Royal Army Medical Corps in France in the Great War, where he had won the Military Cross and met his future wife, who was nursing in France. Known, from his initials, as 'Togo' Graham, he was the president of the Royal College of Surgeons in Ireland in 1942-3. Such a man had little difficulty in arranging nursing-aide jobs for his daughter and her friends in wartime Britain. He also ensured that they had some basic training that would enable them to carry out those jobs. As the driving force of the St John Ambulance Brigade in Dublin, he organized first-aid training courses and all four girls attended one in preparation for England.

The hospital to which the four girls went was the Botley Park War Hospital at Chertsey in Surrey. When the girls arrived in England, in 1941, they found that their accommodation was in wooden huts on the hospital site. Botley Park had been a psychiatric hospital – or lunatic asylum as they were still known at that time – and it continued to house mentally ill patients as well as physically ill patients who had been evacuated from the large London hospitals, such as Guy's, because of the blitz, the German night-bombing offensive during which London was bombed each night for weeks on end. The nursing staff at Botley Park were drawn from St Thomas' Hospital in London. The hospital also had a military wing, but these patients were in the minority. The work of a nursing aide was very hard and involved a range of mundane tasks, such as emptying bedpans, sweeping the floors, serving meals to the patients and the other menial tasks that were part of the daily routine of any hospital.

Both Brenda and Elizabeth stayed at Botley Park for a year before moving on. One of the other girls went to work at the BBC, but the fourth returned to Ireland, as she did not find life in wartime England to her liking. From Botley Park, Brenda Graham went to join the Red Cross in London and found herself based in an office in St James' Palace. Her job was tracing prisoners, which was 'very boring' as it involved sorting through masses of files and other papers. The fact that her office was in the palace's ballroom was no real compensation for the tedium of the task. As a result she volunteered for overseas' service with the Red Cross. She was to be posted overseas in 1943.

Brenda Graham chose not to join one of the three women's services. Although she believed that it was right to contribute towards the defeat of Hitler and the evil that he represented, she regarded herself as being 'very pacifist' and thus felt that her contribution to the downfall of Hitler should be made through an organization such as the Red Cross.

Elizabeth Chamberlain persevered in her desire to join the Wrens. After a year in Chertsey, she applied to join the WRNS, using the local address of a friend of her father, and was delighted to be accepted. From then on the paths of the two friends diverged. But they had shared many experiences: the hard grind of the work in Botley Park, the blackout, which was very severe, and the bombing, although this was nowhere near as bad as it had been in the winter of 1940-41. There were frightening times, but there was also the morale boost that came from seeing the resilience of the civilian population of England, who continued their daily business in spite of all the dangers and difficulties that faced them:

> I was sent for basic training on 23 December 1942 and went to a place called Mill Hill. There we were living in a half-finished factory and we all slept in bunks in cabins, and our living area was called the f'castle. We had to learn all these naval terms.
>
> During the training period we learned about the navy and did drill, as well as a lot of scrubbing, we scrubbed the 'heads', [naval term for latrines] and we marched miles. It was all very hard work but we enjoyed it. We met lots of people and made many friends.
>
> At the end of my training I was told that I was to be a trainee bomb-range marker. That was in the Fleet Air Arm and I had to go to a place called Machrihanish in Scotland.

The role of the bomb-range markers was important in the training programme of the strike aircraft of the Fleet Air Arm. As aircraft dropped their bombloads on the practice ranges, the range markers would take readings of where the bombs had actually landed. These would then be used to ascertain the effectiveness and accuracy of the aircraft crews and show where improvement might be necessary.

Machrihanish in Argyllshire is a remote location, situated near the southern end of the Mull of Kintyre and across the neck of the peninsula from Campbeltown. Its official title was HMS *Landrail*, and it was home to No. 772 FRU* Squadron. Also

---

* Fleet Requirements Unit.

known as RNAS (Royal Naval Air Station) Machrihanish, it accommodated a great variety of aircraft, mostly engaged in training, and these included Blenheims, Chesapeakes, Fulmars, and Masters as well as the ubiquitous Swordfish.

> Machrihanish was very tough. It was very cold when I arrived there and there were these army huts around the place. That was the accommodation. We lived in these awful huts, with washing hanging to dry around the bunks. And you went everywhere at the double. We ran from the huts around the station to wherever we had to go. That was a rule. It was a terrible place, with nothing to do except our jobs. There was nothing there, except the sea. And it was very windy, too. It was so bad, so demoralizing that one girl had a nervous breakdown there.

At Machrihanish Elizabeth Chamberlain learned more about the range-marking instrumentation. At one stage she, with five others, was sent to Skipness, 'up in the wilds of Scotland', where there were about twenty Wrens altogether and they had to do everything for themselves, including cooking. The accommodation at Skipness was a large hut and the location was even less attractive than Machrihanish. A nearby sea inlet was used as a bombing range by the Fleet Air Arm and the Wrens performed their range-marking tasks there as the bombing aircraft flew in from the sea.

Needless to say, Machrihanish was not a station that Elizabeth Chamberlain regretted leaving. She described her feelings as being of 'great joy' when she learned that she was to be posted away from HMS *Landrail*. Her new posting was HMS *Blackcap*, RNAS Stretton, near Warrington in Cheshire. Once again her duties were those of a bombing range-marker. At Stretton the bombing range was a lake and there were huts on either side that housed the instrumentation for range-marking and from which the observations were made. Home was in 'a lovely old house and we used to cycle into work each day'. By now Elizabeth was quite adept at her job:

> An aeroplane would come in over the range and it would drop a stick of three bombs. We would watch and note where each bomb fell. The middle one of the three was supposed to fall on the target. That was the test for accuracy.

The Stretton base was also used as a rest and training centre for Fleet Air Arm crews who had been on operational duties or whose aircraft-carriers were in port. One of the FAA aircrew there was Sub-Lieutenant Michael Beresford-Jones who had been on operational service with HMS *Illustrious* in the Mediterranean.* The pair met at a dance on the young aviator's first night at Stretton and a romance developed. Two months later Mike Beresford-Jones and Elizabeth Chamberlain were married. But the marriage was short-lived:

---

* *Illustrious* was launched in April 1939 and joined the Royal Navy in May 1940. The ship sailed for the Mediterranean in August 1940 and served there and in the Indian Ocean until returning to Birkenhead in early-1943 for a refit.

Mike was sent up to Machrihanish to train on Barracudas, changing over from Swordfish. They were trying to do dive-bombing with the Barracudas but it didn't work properly. Mike just came out of the cloud and went into the sea. He was killed.

Although this was a shattering blow to the young Wren, her husband's death was one among many in wartime and she decided to 'get on with it' and try to live with her loss; the WRNS did send her home for a time on bereavement leave. Later, when her husband's personal effects were returned to her, she realized just how little she had known about him, 'but that was war'. The days at Stretton had been happy ones for Elizabeth Beresford-Jones, but they were soon to come to an end. After her bereavement, the commanding officer of HMS *Blackcap* informed her that he was recommending that she be appointed as a Wren officer. At first she was not keen on this idea as it would mean leaving the many friends that she had made at Stretton. However, she eventually decided to go ahead with the suggestion that she become an officer. The first major hurdle was the selection board:

> I was sent to Liverpool for this board, which had all these admirals on it and I was shaking with nervousness when I went it. But there was a Superintendent, Wrens there, and it turned out that she was Irish. She said to me, 'I see your name is Purefoy. I went to school with a girl called Purefoy.' Purefoy is my second name because that was my mother's name and I told her that 'My mother was Elsie Purefoy.' Then she said, 'I went to Alexandra College with her.' Then I knew I was in.

There followed some months in Liverpool, at Derby House – Headquarters of Western Approaches Command – during which she learned about codes and coding:

> The duties there included de-coding and coding, but new girls spent most of their time running around from office to office with messages. It was very hard work and when it came to learning how to encipher I found it very complicated.
>
> I lived at Sefton Park in a huge Wrennery* there and I worked in the buildings, underground and did watchkeeping duties and then I went into the coding office where we learned about code-breaking. It was very interesting, absolutely fascinating, even though it was very hard work. There were so many different kinds of code. There were code books and each book had a day and you had to match pages with the numbers at the start of a signal. The worst were the ones that you had to work on with machines, and these were very difficult. The machine was like a typewriter with different wheels that you fitted to it. I was never very good at mathematics so it was really quite difficult for me.

** The term *Wrennery* was used throughout the Royal Navy to describe any large building that was used as accommodation for Wrens. Boom Hall, on the northern outskirts of Derry, was taken over for Wren accommodation in the city and was referred to as the *Wrennery* .

However, Elizabeth completed her training at Liverpool and was posted to Greenwich where she was to 'learn how to be an officer'. The college at Greenwich had been bombed and the exigencies of wartime had caused all manner of adaptations in use: the Wren officer cadet accommodation was in the elegant library where some thirty girls slept in three-tier bunks. Much time was spent marching and drilling, for which a petty officer took the cadets, but there were also lectures on naval tradition and on the responsibilities of officers in the service. During her time there the German flying-bombs, the V-1s, began to fall on London and the cadets were evacuated to Stoke Poges in Buckinghamshire where Elizabeth Beresford-Jones completed her officer training. The end of the cadets' course was marked by a concert, attended by a number of senior officers, at which the cadets provided the entertainment.

The newly-appointed Third Officer Beresford-Jones moved to Petersfield for the final phase of her training in cipher skills. She encountered top-secret machines and ciphers on her way to becoming what was known as a 'cipher queen'. Petersfield prepared Elizabeth for her first operational posting as a cipher officer, which was at The Moat in Plymouth.

> Plymouth had been destroyed by German bombing, razed to the ground. We worked in The Moat, which was an underground base that was cut out of a cliff. It was very secret and there were about two hundred people working in it. It had been built for about thirty people. Working there was terrible; the air was so bad in it that we regularly had to climb a ladder to go outside for fresh air.
>
> When I went there, D-Day was looming and we were frightfully busy. There were all these messages that we had to handle, coming in from ships and going out. We knew all that was going on as far as the location of ships was concerned.

The period prior to Operation NEPTUNE – the naval element of the invasion of Europe – and Operation OVERLORD – the invasion itself – was hectic in The Moat and, as the crucial date approached, all ranks were told that all leave had been cancelled for security reasons. Elizabeth Beresford-Jones managed to become a rare exception to that rule. She had applied for an overseas' posting when she had been in Liverpool as she 'was fed up with the job and very sad about Mike's death and wanted to get away'. Her posting came through and with it an entitlement to embarkation leave.

> At that time an old boyfriend, Andy Parsons, whom I'd known when he was studying medicine at Trinity, arrived back, wounded, from Anzio. He was in the Morris Wingfield Hospital in Oxford where they had the very bad casualties. He'd had his sciatic nerve severed but they had decided not to amputate the leg, which had been the usual procedure before.
>
> Andy contacted me and he persuaded the authorities to give me three days' leave to visit him in Oxford on my way home on embarkation leave. He then asked me to marry him and I accepted.

On her return from Dublin, Elizabeth went to Cheyne Walk in London where she was issued with tropical uniform and had lectures from 'funny people, telling us about not getting involved with foreign men, not getting pregnant, and so on'. From Cheyne Walk she travelled in a truck to the station, boarded a train and woke up in Scotland. In the Clyde she joined the SS *Christian Huigens* for the voyage to Naples:

> We wore lifejackets all the time on the ship and although we were in a convoy I was never aware of that. The nearest ship was about a mile away and we couldn't see it. Although the ship was 'dry', the food was excellent, all served by Javanese waiters. Such a contrast to Britain. Because we were officers we had good accommodation but the other ranks were all down in the bowels of the ship, and they really had nowhere to sleep. They had to use hammocks or sleep on the floors. We had cabins and I shared with Barbara Pym and another, terribly la-de-da, girl.
>
> We had no concerns about submarines, or aircraft attacks on the convoy. We used to sit on the deck sewing. I remember making a nightie and a long time later I had a letter from an Irish officer who had been on the ship who sent me a piece of the material that I'd made the nightie from. Sometimes we would sit for hours in lovely hot seawater baths and some people took the chance to have language lessons.
>
> On the lower decks the ORs had very little to do. They used to play housey-housey a lot and we went down to sing for them and put on concerts. Their time was really very boring. There were so many young men on that ship, and the others in the convoy. And so many of them were going to their deaths. My brother, I later discovered, was on another ship in the same convoy. He survived the war. One of the other passengers on the *Christian Huigens* was John Kerans, who was later the captain of HMS *Amethyst* at the time of the Yangstze incident. He was going out to the Med to collect a ship.
>
> We changed into summer uniforms on the voyage and I remember my first sight of Naples. As we approached I went into the loo and looked out through the porthole and there was the bay of Naples, absolutely beautiful. It was marvellous, especially after the blackout.

On arrival in Naples the female officers were taken to a large block of flats at Largo Garofollo where about twenty Wren officers lived. Elizabeth Beresford-Jones' job was as a cipher officer in a large building along the waterfront where she worked with Americans. But, as if to compensate for the dry voyage, she and the other Wren officers with whom she had travelled 'were hardly sober during our first four days there'.

As well as the cipher duties the Wren officers were also expected to share watch-keeping duties and to entertain male officers. This latter task was, according to the head of the Wrens in Naples, a 'duty', but it did have its pleasant side, including many dinners with very senior officers. These latter included a number of dinners with Admiral Sir Andrew Cunningham – ABC as he was known in the service – who was probably the Royal Navy's greatest commander of the Second World War and who was a Dubliner by birth. Cunningham was just one of many senior officers whose acquaintance Elizabeth made during a year in Naples. The dinners were held in the Villa Emma, the one-time home of Nelson's mistress, Lady Hamilton.

For a time Elizabeth Beresford-Jones was a patient in the huge 92nd General Hospital in Naples. She suffered from a neck problem and was admitted to the hospital for treatment. There was a separate ward for female patients, but it was impossible not to be aware of the fact that the hospital was crowded with the casualties of war. Men were even lying on the floors, such was the pressure on accommodation. From the hospital many of the patients would be shipped home to the UK, as Andy Parsons had been many months before. Following her spell in hospital, Elizabeth was sent to convalesce in a hotel in Sorrento where she met several officers of the Buffs. They were all friends of Andy Parsons and they struck up an immediate rapport with their former MO's fiancée. 'They whisked me off to Amalfi, which was their leave centre'.

As the work began to dry up at Naples, Elizabeth applied for a posting to the UK so that she could be married. Her posting arrived at very short notice: 'I was due to go to Rome in a jeep for a weekend. Then, at very short notice, about two days, I was told that I could join a ship that was sailing for Britain. So I had a choice: Rome or home. I chose home.'

And so Elizabeth Beresford-Jones' war came to an end. She recalls it as an exciting time and one that

> I hate to say it, but I enjoyed the war. You forget all the horrible parts. My time in Liverpool and Skipness was pure hell. Then there was the poverty of Naples, seeing people eating out of dustbins. I never regretted joining the Wrens and there was no adverse reaction to my doing so at home. In fact, I remember my first day on the Via Roma in Naples. I met three people from Dublin. All through the war you were meeting Irish people in uniform, in train corridors, streets, everywhere you went, there were Irish people there.

Brenda Graham's application to go overseas with the Red Cross also resulted in a posting to Italy, although she thought at first that she was going to North Africa. However, the war in North Africa had ended and the Allies were advancing in Italy and so she was sent to Naples, but not in quite the same fashion as her friend had travelled. Together with other Red Cross volunteers, or VADs, Brenda travelled in a regular liner in very cramped bunks to Algiers. There she transferred to another ship for the trip across the Mediterranean to Naples but the ship developed mechanical problems and put into another North African port for repairs. Brenda eventually completed her voyage to Naples in a naval hospital ship which was much pleasanter than the liners had been. Conditions were much less cramped with proper bunks and the food was markedly better.

At first Brenda worked in a convalescent home in Sorrento before moving to a hospital further north in Italy:

The casualties ranged from slight to horrific but we didn't see too much of the critical cases. There were very acute wards in Italy but the VADs did not help there as they used only trained nurses, the QAs.*

We were kept busy most of the time. There were a lot of people in hospital with jaundice and we worked with them as well as the slightly-wounded.

Throughout her service in Italy, Brenda Graham was clearly identified as an Iirsh member of the Red Cross, wearing a harp badge to signify her nationality. At home the St John Ambulance Brigade had amalgamated with the Red Cross during the war and the resulting body became the Irish Red Cross. When the war ended in Italy, Brenda was moved into Austria where there were 'halcyon times'. There was much opportunity for leisure and rest time could be spent at Vilden on the Wörtersee where most of the houses belonged to rich Italians or were summer residences. Many were used as leave centres for the occupation forces in Austria.

Included in the occupation forces was the Irish Brigade and Brenda met a young English-born captain of the Royal Irish Fusiliers who, in common with her father, had earned the Military Cross. Brian Clark was the son of a County Down man, and an Irish Fusilier, and he and Brenda were married in January 1946, with snow on the ground. As had been the case with her parents, war had brought her together with the man who was to become her husband.

Although she was a member of a civilian organization Brenda qualified for war medals and received the 1939-45 Star, the Defence Medal and the War Medal.

There were many tasks within the UK that were carried out by women, chief among which were the roles performed by ATS girls in the anti-aircraft defences. Equally important, although not with such a high profile, were the Wrens who worked at the Royal Navy's most important escort base in the battle of the Atlantic: Londonderry on the river Foyle.

Maeve Boyle (see chapter Two) joined the Wrens in 1942, following in her sister's footsteps. A Derry girl, she was posted to HMS *Ferret*, her home town, to become one of some 300 Wrens based in the city, most of whom were Irish girls. She did not regard her wartime role as glamorous or exciting:

We did a job, that was it, but we did it in uniform, and a lovely uniform it was. We were trained in office administration and learned skills that we wouldn't have had the opportunity to learn otherwise.

At first I worked in Smyth's stores right beside the water. We stored blankets there, as well as uniforms and navy-blue pullovers. Those were very heavy pullovers for use in the north Atlantic. As well as the Royal Navy, we also supplied the Royal Canadian Navy and the Newfoundlanders. Newfoundland wasn't part of Canada at that time.

You would see sailors come ashore from the ships after an Atlantic crossing and they would be absolutely weary. One whiskey would have sent them crazy.

---

* Members of Queen Alexandra's Imperial Military Nursing Service were known as QAs.

> There was a great Catholic chaplain in Derry, Father Willie Devine. He was
> a very imposing figure, always very military in his bearing, and his shoes highly
> polished. He did marvellous work there.

In spite of the rigours and shortages of wartime there was still the opportunity to
enjoy a social life. Some of the naval officers who were based in the city or in the
Londonderry Escort Force were members of families that were household names:

> I remember dancing with Fergus Sandemann, of the port wine family, and
> there was also James Robertson, from the jam family, and Bertie Porter. And
> there were officers who became famous, household names, like Hughes-
> Hallett, whom I met in Derry.*
>
> There were dances in places like the [Apprentice Boys'] Memorial Hall, the
> Mem, or the Masonic Hall at Culmore, and we had a great time.
>
> I enjoyed myself during the war. You could go to the pictures and some-
> times I'd make two dates in one day. It was difficult not to use the wrong name
> at times. But the whole experience broadened your outlook. The city was very
> insular in those days.
>
> All the local girls lived out [at home] and the other Wrens lived in Boom
> Hall, the Wrennery. There were about thirty there. If you were living out and
> you were late into work too often you were sent to the Wrennery to clean
> windows or some such chore as a punishment.

Not all the Wrens in the city were accommodated in the Wrennery. Some were
billetted in Ebrington Barracks, which was handed over to the Admiralty in 1943. Just
outside the barracks, in Browning Drive, was a naval hospital where Margaret Little,
from Portadown, was a Wren Chief Petty Officer, paid fourteen shillings a week (70p)
with one half-day off each week and a long weekend every six weeks:

> Wrens had facilities for laundry but drying and ironing at times was a prob-
> lem, as was thieving. Every item had to be named.
>
> The food was bulk cooked and at times left a lot to be desired. Usually
> [there were] four to six Wrens to a room (double metal bunks) and at times it
> was difficult to enjoy a bit of peace and quiet. This was when the Sailors Rest
> came into play. It was a Godsend. I often slipped in there for a quiet read and
> a cup of tea at three old pence per cup.
>
> The two cathedrals provided the odd soothing hour and at times helped
> restore one's equilibrium. Several churches provided canteens and a 'sing song'
> on a Sunday evening, followed by a delightful free supper.

Walking the city's historic walls and strolls across the border into Donegal also
helped Margaret Little keep a sense of proportion. She was able to go home to Porta-

---

* Hughes-Hallett was the captain of HMS *Jamaica* at the battle of North Cape when *Scharnhorst* was sunk
(see chapter Ten).

down whenever she had a long weekend and usually returned with a supply of 'goodies': 'homemade bread, jam, bacon and Billy Mays sausages with a few eggs thrown in for good measure' meant an enjoyable Sunday evening supper when 'the smell coming from the hospital galley ... would have knocked one for six'. In the hospital recreation hall there was a weekly dance, or 'shuffle' for those who were not so good on their feet and these were always lively occasions.

Some patients brought special problems with them:

> A young sailor (Polish I think) ... came in as a patient off a ship in great mental agony, could not be consoled, cried all the time and refused all medication and food and repeatedly tried to break free. A concerned sick-berth man asked if any of us had any suggestions as to helping this lad.
>
> It was suggested that a Wren should accompany a sick-berth man with an attractive dainty dish and some homemade titbits. This was tried and it took quite a few visits before any result: a spoonful to the Wren and then one to the lad. He thought they were going to poison him. No language needed. This went on for days. After a few months' medical treatment, together with the catering staff help, it was a great joy to all staff to see him wave 'Good bye' to his new found Irish friends.
>
> Oh, Lord, what miracles you do.

Dubliner Romie Lambkin joined the Auxiliary Territorial Service and spent much of her war in Northern Ireland, some of it in company with other ATS girls from south of the border. She trained as a driver and avoided the opportunity of officer selection. Her duties took her over much of Northern Ireland, driving senior and not-so-senior officers and she was able to spend leaves in England. Eventually she obtained a posting to 21 Army Group in north-west Europe.

Romie Lambkin's personal memoir of her wartime experiences paints a fascinating picture of those days and conveys a real sense of wartime Britain and Ireland. When she went to Europe in the closing months of war, she was stationed in Belgium and was in Brussels when the war ended. She recorded the scenes of ecstatic celebration in the city which had endured more than four years of German occupation:

> It's been magnetic ... we surged out into the night streets flowing in rivers of berserk humanity past the little Mannekin Pis statue (wearing US Naval uniform) to the Grande Place, where the Belgique multitude went into such demented frenzies of shouting, screaming and singing about La Paix that, joyful or not, it was unnerving. The heaving mobs pinned my arms rigid, my battledress tearing apart at the seams, until a group of Tommies forced themselves into a circle round us, manoeuvring and shoving us like a rugby scrum to a side street bistro haven, where we stayed put until the crowds diluted and let us crawl back to the billets dog tired.

There was a very different emotional reaction when her unit, 721 Company, RASC, went to the cinema in Brussels a few days later. The main feature was American, but it was not a Hollywood production with the stars of the day. Instead it was the US official footage of the horrors of some of the Nazi concentration camps:

> The horrors made many of us retch … countless bodies you can hardly recognize as human thrown in gross heaps like rubbish and, inside hundreds of huts, half-alive people lie together in twos on wooden tiers, often enough an already dead one beside a still living person. Who would believe such a terrifying degradation of humanity could be deliberately brought about by other so-called humans? I could barely watch the film but I couldn't look away either. The eyes in those awful skeletonic faces won't leave my mind. As a consequence of seeing it, not one of us would be too troubled if every German was wiped from the face of the earth overnight. I am glad I didn't see the film before yesterday's trip [to Main HQ 21 Army Group in Germany]. How dare those Germans smile at us? The occupants of a village adjacent to one concentration camp have been forced to walk through it to view the horrors for themselves, so it is said, after which the local Herr and Frau Mayor committed suicide. So well they might.

Not far from the edge of the Atlantic the end of the war was marked by the formal surrender of German U-boats at Lisahally on the river Foyle, signifying the importance of the role of that river and its great naval base in the battle of the Atlantic. Both Maeve Boyle and Margaret Little were present on the jetty at Lisahally when Admiral Sir Max Horton took the surrender:

> I was in Ebrington Barracks at the time and we were invited to see a couple of submarines coming in at Lisahally by Lieutenant Linstead. A bus was laid on and we stood on the battered jetty and watched the U-boats coming in. Sailors were lined up on the submarines and I can remember the senior German officer coming ashore. He was terrible looking, very tired and with sunken cheeks. Then Sir Max Horton strutted out to take the surrender. At the time I just didn't appreciate the immensity of the occasion, didn't realize that I was watching history being made.

The war was over but the memories would remain:

> I wished to tell you the most important experience. That of extreme sadness, to know that never again would I see the young men who left Derry by air, by warship, who were shot down and drowned in the North Atlantic.
> No more loving letters and bunches of flowers, just memories.
> All of this so long ago but clear in my mind but balancing the fun memories with the sad memories the scales just swing even.

For most of the Irishwomen who gave the years of their youth to the defeat of Hitler, the scales do, just about, swing even.

Epilogue

This book was originally planned as a single-volume history of the contribution made by Irish people to the Second World War. As the research and writing progressed it became clear to me that it would not be possible to do justice to the subject within the confines of one book. The range of material that was made available to me, through my own contacts, through the Volunteers' Project at University College Cork and through Myles Dungan, defied any efforts on my part to reduce it to a manageable size.

It thus became apparent that there were two basic choices: the first was that much editing would be required to condense the material; the second was that a second volume should be embarked upon to allow all the available material to be used. The final decision was made by Four Courts Press who decided that this book should have a companion volume.

The reader who has persevered thus far will be acutely aware of many aspects of Irish involvement in the war that swept the globe between 1939 and 1945 that have not been covered in this first book. Sailors, soldiers and airmen and the women of Ireland are included, but no mention is made of the contribution that was made by Irish men and women in the civilian services in Britain – the nursing, fire and police services all included Irish members who were decorated for their devotion to duty during the war. Nor is the record of those in the services complete: there are no soldiers from the armoured units, nor the artillery, nor the engineers and yet many Irish served in those bodies. In the air this volume confines its attention to bomber and fighter crews and does not cover those who served in Coastal or Transport Commands. And there is much more to be told of the story of Irishmen in the Royal Navy, both above and below the waves as well as the part played by Irish merchant sailors in the long war at sea.

The part played by Irish men and women in forces other than those of the United Kingdom is but briefly alluded to in this book. However, there were many Irish men, and some women, who served in the Australian, Canadian, New Zealand, South African and United States forces. The next volume will examine their experiences.

During the Second World War many countries were overrun by the Axis nations and underground movements were organized in those countries to oppose the conquerors. Irish men and women played their part in the resistance movements of occupied Europe and in the Allied special forces that assisted those movements. Those individuals included one of the greatest literary figures of the twentieth century, the writer and playwright Samuel Beckett, as well as men and women whose names have been forgotten by all but their families. Their story will also be told in the next volume.

The Second World War saw a proliferation of special forces, intended to strike behind enemy lines. Needless to say, there were Irishmen involved in special forces and they saw service in the North African campaign, in Italy and in north-west Europe as well as the Far East. Irishmen in the commandos, the Special Air Service and the Chindits will feature in volume two.

This book includes two chapters on Irish infantry soldiers during the war and it only begins to tell their story. Much remains to be told of the service of Irishmen in several campaigns, including the longest land campaign of the war – in Burma, the final year of the Italian campaign, the last year of the war in north-west Europe including the invasion of France – Operation OVERLORD – on 6 June 1944 and some forgotten campaigns, such as that in the Dodecanese islands in late-1943.

Much of the story of Ireland's involvement in the Second World War has died with those who were that involvement. As each year passes, their ranks grow even thinner and even the youngest veteran is now in his or her early seventies. While there are still veterans living, it is appropriate that Ireland should remember what they did as they fought, in the words of Pope Pius XII, for peace with justice between 1939 and 1945. The Royal Dublin Fusiliers had as their motto the Latin words *Spectamur Agendo*. They thus asked people to judge them by their deeds. This book, and the volume to follow, make that same exhortation: that Ireland's contribution to the Second World War be judged by the deeds of those who served.

Notes

PAGE 9 **people to the Union** Barton, *Northern Ireland in the Second World War*, p. 4; Fisk, *In Time of War*, p. 396. **to the British forces** Fisk, op. cit., pp 522-7. **Britain's eventual victory'** Ibid., p. 526. **in the British Army** Doherty, *Clear the Way!*, p. 7. **join the British forces** Fisk, op. cit., pp 521-2.

PAGE 10 **loyalty to the Empire'** P.R.O.N.I./CAB 4/597/7; Fisk op. cit., p. 526. **standards of the time** Notes from Royal Army Pay Corps (now Adjutant General's Corps). **fought in the Great War'** In Cooper, *The Tenth (Irish) Division in Gallipoli*, p. 7. **farms and hospitals** *Neutral Ireland and the Third Reich*, pp 258-9. **Berehaven and Lough Swilly** McIvor, *A History of the Irish Naval Service*, p. 61.

PAGE 11 **British government may require'** Ibid. **Egyptian Treaty of 1936** Raugh, *Wavell in the Middle East*, p. 48. **only lightly manned** McIvor, op. cit., p. 61. **thereafter used that facility** Smith, Action Stations 7, p. 29. **enormous sum at the time** P.R.O., Kew, CO267/678 Ctte Imp Def, Dec 1936. **for each of them'** Gibbs, *Grand Strategy*, vol. I, p. 820. **occupation of all of Ireland** PRO, Kew, CO267/678 Ctte Imp Def, Dec 1936.

PAGE 12 **defending the Irish coast** Ibid. **with the Labour party** Lyons, *Ireland since the Famine*, p. 504. **to the British crown** Ibid., pp 511-4. **the link with Britain** Ibid., pp 519-22. **described as 'external'**, Duggan, op. cit., p. oo **by 31 December 1938** Foster, *Modern Ireland 1660-1972*, p. 553; Lyons, p. 522. **this monumental blunder**, McIvor, op. cit., p. 64.

PAGE 13 **underpinning of Irish neutrality** Churchill, *The Second World War*, vol. I, p. 249. **shadows and for ease** Ibid., p. 248. **been settled to his satisfaction** Ibid. **saw service in Buncrana** P.R.O.N.I. Blake papers, CAB 3/A/22. **independence from all belligerents** Lee, *Ireland 1912-1985*, p. oo. **men and food to Britain** Ibid., p. 244.

PAGE 14 **for much of the war** Ibid. **towards non-alignment** Dungan, *Distant Drums*, p. 91. **decisions much easier** Gallagher papers, N.L.I. MS18, 375 (6), p. 52. **government could have adopted** *The Times*, 9 September 1939. **the local fishing fleet)** Doherty, *Key to Victory*, p. 86.

PAGE 15 **from Britain to Japan** Keegan, *The Second World War*, pp 590-1. **it ... a good war'** Taylor, *The Second World War*, p. 234. **and Royal Dublin Fusiliers** Ascoli, *A Companion to the British Army*, p. 110.

273

PAGE 16   its Great War identity Ibid., pp 123, 132 & 140. existed only on paper
Frederick, *Lineage Book of British Land Forces, 1660-1978*, vol. I, p. 32. vanished
with partition.) Ibid., p. 33. the linkage was broken.) Cunliffe, Marcus, *The Royal
Irish Fusiliers 1793-1968*, pp 371-6. of the Royal Ulster Rifles Frederick, vol. I, op.
cit., pp 148-9. continued in existence Harris, *The Irish Regiments*, p. 273. extended
to Ireland Gailey, Gillespie and Hassett, *An Account of the Territorials in Northern
Ireland*, p. 13.

PAGE 17   Imperial defence only Ibid. was therefore rejected Bartlett and Jeffrey, *A
Military History of Ireland*, p. 434. Northern Ireland government P.R.O., Kew,
HO45/18349. territorial infantry organization Bartlett and Jeffrey, op. cit., p. 434.
previously had an affiliation *The London Irish at War*, p. 17.

PAGE 18   the same fortifications Gailey et al., op. cit., p. 32. by the Air Ministry Ibid.,
pp 70-1. Royal Artillery was made Doherty, '3rd (Ulster) Anti-Aircraft Brigade, RA
(SR)', IS, vol xviii, no. 71, p. 120. on paper since 1920 Gailey et al., op. cit., p. 23.
Special Reserve squadron, Halley, *The Squadrons of the Royal Air Force*, p. 304.
auxiliary squadron in 1937 Gailey et al., op. cit., p. 77. maintaining the aircraft
Halley, op. cit., p. 10. after the Great War Gailey et al., op. cit., p. 23.

PAGE 19   Horse were unique Doherty, 'Supplementary Reserve Regiments', IS, vol.
xviii, no. 72, pp 237-8. telegraphs employees respectively National Army Museum,
letter and contemporary leaflet *National Service* (HMSO, 1939) to author. searchlight
defence of the UK Ibid. in the Army List Frederick, op. cit., vol. II, pp 766 & 890. AA
(LAA) battery Doherty, IS vol. xviii, no. 71, p. 121. anti-aircraft branch The author
was told, in a letter from the Royal Artillery Institution, that such an order of battle
did not exist. being in August 1939.) Frederick, op. cit., vol. II, p. 780. Ordnance
Corps (RAOC) Doherty, IS vol. xviii, no. 72, p. 121.

PAGE 20   Londonderry and Antrim Ibid. Lurgan in County Armagh Ibid. less than
three months Gailey et al., op. cit., p. 27. 000 men to their ranks Ibid.; Doherty, IS vol.
xviii, no. 72, p. 121. (Ulster) Searchlight Regiment Frederick, op. cit., vol. II, pp 766
& 890. two light AA batteries Ibid. order to become soldiers See *Irish Independent*,
13 June 1945. by the recruiting staff P.R.O.N.I. McFarland Papers, partial nominal
roll of 25 Bty.

PAGE 21   of Wight and Malta Fox, Sir Frank, *The Royal Inniskilling Fusiliers in the
Second World War*, pp 8-9; Graves, *The Royal Ulster Rifles*, vol. III, pp 35-7; Cunliffe,
op. cit., p. 381. and 1st Irish Fusiliers Ibid. reactivated in July 1939 Verney, *The
Micks*, p. 89. 16th/5th Lancers in India Bredin, A *History of the Irish Soldier*, p. 489;
Lunt, *The Scarlet Lancers*, p. 125. and absorbing volunteers Gailey et al., op. cit., p.
23. Guards, there were 138 Gibbs, Grand Strategy, vol. I, p. 450. This figure includes
only regular battalions. nominal strength of 786 Ellis and Chamberlain, *Handbook
on the British Army*, p. 24. 53,951 men in India Gibbs, vol. I, op. cit., p. 00.

PAGE 22   of the *Manchester Guardian Manchester Guardian*, 13 March 1944. in a
Daily Telegraph Daily Telegraph, 18 October 1944. the figure at 250,000 P.R.O.,
Kew, DO35/1230 WX132/1/140, Sedgwick to Costar, 3 November 1945. an opti-
mistic estimate P.R.O., N.I., Spender Diaries, D715/18 21 January 1942; quoted in

Fisk, op. cit., p.522. **forces during the war**, P.R.O., Kew, DO35/1230 WX132/1/124 Machtig to Maxwell, 12 March 1946. **and 11,050 in the RAF** P.R.O., Kew, DO35/1230 WX132/1/124. **provided for that reduction** Fisk, op. cit., p. 523. **service-men and women** Carroll, *Ireland in the War Years*, p. 182. However, there is no letter from Gough in the London *Times* in August 1944 quoting the number of next-of-kin addresses in Éire. Carroll may have mistakenly identified the *Times*.

PAGE 23   **18,600 Éire recruits** Barton, op. cit., p. 54. **not include nationality** Commonwealth War Graves Commission, letter to author, April 1996. **individual joined the Army** P.R.O., Kew, WO304. **Bomber Command personnel.**) Ellis, *The World War II Databook*, p. 254. **were in the majority** P.R.O., Kew, WO304. **representing 5% of the total** Ibid.

PAGE 24   **regiments quoted earlier** Ibid. **whom (45) were from Éire** Ibid. **no Irish dead at all** Ibid. **in the armoured regiments** Ibid. **regiments were born in Ireland** Ibid.

PAGE 25   **on to specialist training** Myatt, *The British Infantry 1660-1945*, p. 211. **Second World War was 1 in 22** Ellis, op. cit., p. 254. **served in both services** Ibid.

PAGE 28   **living in neutral Ireland** Devlin, *Reminiscences of a Rifleman in Normandy, France – 1944*, pp 6-7. **twenty did not need either** Ibid., pp 9-10. **obvious that I wasn't 20** Ibid. **routine of basic training** Ibid., pp 10-11.

PAGE 29   **in the Irish Fusiliers** Gannon, interview with Myles Dungan. **selected as a sniper** Ibid. **following the invasion in 1944** Clarke, interview with Myles Dungan. **Corps in November 1940** Frederick, vol. I, op. cit., p.20. **in the British Army** Jameson, interview with Myles Dungan.

PAGE 30   **in the course of the war** Baker, interview with Tina Neylon for the Volunteers' Project, University College, Cork. **linen trade in Ulster** Obituary, *Daily Telegraph*, 23 July 1997. **wounded, at El Alamein** Obituary, *Daily Telegraph*, 1 June 1998; interview with author, October 1995. **wipe out whole populations** Gorman, interview with author, March 1995.

PAGE 31   **So I gave that up** Ibid. **Guards Armoured Division** Ibid. **slavery if he'd succeeded** d'Alton, interview with author, August 1998. **into the Royal Navy** Ibid.

PAGE 32   **would do the same thing** Previty, interview with Myles Dungan. **the wireless just now!** Ross, *All Valiant Dust*, p. 13. **trivial and irrelevant** Ibid., p.14. **Battalion at that time** Col A.D. Woods, MC, letter to author.

PAGE 33   **of 2nd Parachute Battalion** Col A.D. Woods, MC, interview with author, September 1995. **painted on his aircraft** Obituary, *Daily Telegraph*. **the dotted line and went** Mooney, interview with Myles Dungan. **of the Royal Engineers** Ibid. **volunteer in September 1939** Whyte, interview with author, February 1989. **whenever war broke out** Parsons, *Exit from Anzio*, p. oo.

PAGE 34   **would like to meet them** Revd S. Eaton, interview with author, May 1998. **force chaplain in 1941** Revd S. Eaton, letter to author. **had enlisted in 1937** Revd D. Henderson, letter to author. **when war broke out** Obituary, *Faugh A Ballagh Gazette*. **Division in North Africa** RACh.D. Museum, letter to author. **to serve as chaplains** Johnstone and Hagerty, *The Cross on the Sword*, p. 195. **to the Australian forces** Johnstone, letter to author. **becoming military padres** Church of Ireland records.

Eighth Army in Italy RACh.D. Museum, letter to author. who became chaplains Revd H. Sloan, letter to author. the South African forcesDr E. Ritchie, letter to author; K. Rea, *The Best has yet to Come*, passim. if it wants me to'Coyle, interview with author, April 1986.

PAGE 35   given him employment Tracey, interview with author, January 1989. I'm earning my keep Fitzgerald, *The Irish Guards in the Second World War*, p. 324. on medical grounds Hugh Doherty, interview with author, June 1985. prior to overseas service Information from Mrs Bridie Williams, sister of Hugh Doherty, Jun 1985. for training to Devonport Mannion, interview with Myles Dungan. to get rid of them Fenning, interview with Myles Dungan.

PAGE 36   I had at that time Cassidy, interview with Myles Dungan. the Germans was demanded' Duane, letter to author, February 1998. remain for over a year Duane, letter to author, December 1997. think that's the reason McCaughey, interview with Myles Dungan. a conventional sailor Ibid.

PAGE 37   step such as I took Dunlop, interview with Myles Dungan. was the end of it' Ibid. about the same time Ibid. the jungles of Burma Dungan, *Distant Drums*, pp 104-5.

PAGE 38   in the summer of 1938 Stokes, *Paddy Finucane Fighter Ace*, p. 25. his English-born wife Ibid., p. 17. de Valera in the IRA Ibid., p. 21. into the Royal Artillery Ibid., p. 14. most of it as a prisoner Power, *Long Way from Tipperary*, pp 13-19. Rifle Brigade battalion Clark, interview with author, October 1989. Indian Army Service Corps Ibid. numbers of officers Frederick, vol. I, op. cit., p.307.

PAGE 39   that for the world' Ormsby, journal tape no.1; interview with author, Feb 1995. immediately to lance-sergeant Matt Mulhern, interview with author, September 1986. into an active-service job Richard Mulhern, interview with author, February 1987. birth of the young Stott *Soldiers Died in the Great War*, part 32, p. 40. regiment as he had wanted Robinson, interview with author, June 1998. Military Pioneer Corps Army Order 200, 1939 (renamed Pioneer Corps in 1940).

PAGE 40   from personal conviction McCready, interview with author, October 1986. taking the king's shilling Logue, interview with author, November 1988. obvious, is not stated' quoted in Barton, op. cit., p.19. would not support him Ibid. I'd a family. I had to go Byrne, interview with Myles Dungan. smashed them all over Ibid. were quite proud of it Brehony, interview with Myles Dungan. wanted him to do Murnane, interview with Myles Dungan.

PAGE 41   to a Swordfish squadron Gibney, letter to author. before the war Killanin, interview with Myles Dungan. to the South Staffords Shorten, interview with Myles Dungan. leave], so I skipped Berrill, interview with Myles Dungan. units after eight weeks Ibid. were subsequently apprehended' Duggan, *History of the Irish Army*, p. 198. as high as 7,000 Fisk, p. 523.

PAGE 42   join the British forces' *Irish Independent*, 13 June 1945. Nuremberg and Leipzig Ibid. paid by the Irish forces Ibid. honour and deserved reward Ibid. from the Defence Forces *Irish Independent*, 16 June 1945. he had great respect M. Mulhern, interview with author, September 1986.

PAGE 43 for two shillings a day Dungan, op. cit., p.146. the Royal Ulster Rifles' Ibid. to the recruiting officer Lapsley, interview with author, June 1998. some two years later Doherty, *Wall of Steel*, p. 79; *The Sons of Ulster*, p. 56. and domicile as Éire P.R.O., Kew, W.O. 304 Army Roll of Honour 1939-45. Bridge Street in the city Doherty, *Wall of Steel*, p. 215. soldier and a good friend Jim Dinsmore, interview with author, June 1988. 2nd New Zealand Division Doherty, op. cit., pp 213-5. brothers were to die flying R.G. Lovell Webster Browne, letter to author. wouldn't have come back Jarvis, interview with author, February 1989.

PAGE 44 and the Big World War Lambkin, *My Time in the War*, p. 5. behind the Four Courts Ibid. when war broke out Mrs Brenda Clark, interview with author, August 1998.

PAGE 45 Hospital in Chertsey, Surrey Ibid. was to join the Wrens Mrs Elizabeth Dobbs, interview with author, August 1998. became a radar mechanic Mrs F. Galloway, letter to author. accepted for pilot training Ibid. battle of the Atlantic Doherty, *Key to Victory*, passim. were based in the city P.R.O., Kew, ADM. example of her older sister Maeve Kelly (née Boyle) interview with author, September 1998. about a sizeable response Ibid.

PAGE 46 and most were Catholic Ibid. north of the city Ibid. marrying a soldier Barbara Coyle, interview with author, March 1994.

PAGE 48 days we got used to it Jarvis, interview with author, February 1989. That finished me altogether Ibid. to hear that Derry voice Ibid.

PAGE 49 then onto the shoulder Devlin, op. cit., p. 13. better form of punishment Ibid., pp 17-18. shalt not be found out" Ibid., p. 18. from our platoon' Ibid.

PAGE 50 give us the ports Murnane, interview with Myles Dungan. from the Shankill Road Ibid. well from Dublin Ibid.

PAGE 51 and become 'Irish' McAughtry, interview with Myles Dungan. education was concerned Dunlop, interview with Myles Dungan. was severe about it' Ibid.

PAGE 52 offenders on this occasion Cuthbert, interview with author, January 1988. You see, he's Irish! Ross, *All Valiant Dust*, p. 93.

PAGE 53 graves for the dead Ibid., p. 94. his strength and faith Ibid., p. 95. I can tell you Lambkin, op. cit., p. 42. whitewash 'the Last Post' Power, op. cit., p. 22. to fight the British Ibid., pp 113-129.

PAGE 54 was no antagonism McCaughey, interview with Myles Dungan. out to soothe it away Hansard, 28 Oct 1948, cols 247-250.

PAGE 55 South Wales Borderers Fitzgerald, *History of the Irish Guards in the Second World War*, p. 6. via the port of Adams, *The Doomed Expedition*, p. 16. German forces invaded Narvik Ibid., pp 1-2. training per year Ibid., p. 6; Fitzgerald, op. cit., p. 4. day of the invasion.) Adams, op. cit., p. 6; Fitzgerald, op. cit., p. 4. before the invasion Fitzgerald, op. cit., p. 4; Adams, op. cit., p. 6.

PAGE 56 down from the sky' Fitzgerald, op. cit., p. 4. Commander on 20 April Fraser, *And We Shall Shock Them* p. 37; Greenwood, *Field Marshal Auchinleck*, p. 77. after the German landing' Fitzgerald, op. cit., p. 13. volunteers and unemployed' Ibid., p. 18. two weeks of May Ibid., pp 12-28.

PAGE 57   **low-flying admiral'** A.E.C. Bredin, *History of the Irish Soldier*, p. 480.
advanced on Narvik Fitzgerald, op. cit., p. 40; Adams, op. cit., p. 67. **hot knife
through butter** Fitzgerald, op. cit., p. 42. **was the sole attacker** Quoted in Adams, op.
cit., p. 68. **brought all four to safety** Fitzgerald, op. cit., pp 44-46. **create a strong
defence** Ibid., pp 51-52. **directing the withdrawal** Ibid., pp 59-60; Adams, op. cit., p.
81.

PAGE 58   **strafing the German troops** Bredin, op. cit., p. 480. **had been left behind**
Fitzgerald, op. cit., p. 62. **concentration area at Fauske** Ibid., p. 66. **was to be abandoned** Adams, op. cit., p. 82. **to sail for England** Fitzgerald, op. cit., p. 70. **to speed
their return** Ibid., p. 75. **belt under his shirt** Ibid., p. 76. **road to The Hague** Ibid., p.
79. **sharply by the quay'** Ibid.

PAGE 59   **sail for England** Ibid. **government had arrived** P.R.O., Kew, WO167/695,
War diary, 2nd Irish Guards, 1940. **on the battalion area;** Ibid. **twice and destroyed**
Fitzgerald, op. cit., pp 80-1. **relief to stricken refugees** Ibid., p. 82. **after leaving that
port** WO167/695, op. cit. **BEF from France** Ibid.; Fitzgerald, op. cit., p. 85. **might be
obtained locally** Fitzgerald, op. cit., p. 81. **of going to see him** Bredin, op. cit., p. 481.

PAGE 60   **L/Corporal Mawhinney** Fitzgerald, op. cit., p. 93 and p. 583; WO167/695.
Royal Navy's efforts Fitzgerald, op. cit., pp 94-98. **giving a damn for anything** Ibid.
one and a half miles Ibid., p. 92. **other – as close as that** Dick Connell, Royal Ulster
Rifles, interview with author, December 1988.

PAGE 61   **and W.D. Tighe-Wood** Graves, *The History of the Royal Ulster Rifles*, vol.
III, pp 44-5. **course of repetition** Ibid. **probing the Rifles' defences** Ibid., pp 45-6. **day
Gibbens was killed** Ibid., pp 46-7. **the same manoeuvre** Ibid., p. 47.

PAGE 62   **got shot completely off** H.E.N. Bredin, notes on the Campaign in 1940. **forc-
ing the German withdrawal** Graves, op. cit., p. 47. **and took two prisoners** Fox, *The
Royal Inniskilling Fusiliers in the Second World War*, p. 28. **I Corps from the Dyle**
Ibid., p. 27. **the timetable laid down** Ibid., p. 28. **things weren't quite right** Billy
Megaw, interview with author, December 1988. **everybody, including us'** Ibid.

PAGE 63   **happening all round us** Ibid. **It was a pathetic business** Ibid. **were not called
forward** Fox, op. cit., p. 29; P.R.O., Kew, WO167/758, War diary, 2nd Inniskillings
1940; WO167/244, War diary, 5th Division. **never saw them again** Megaw, interview
with author, op. cit. **put on half rations** Fox, op. cit., p. 30; Megaw, op. cit;
WO167/758, War diary, op. cit.

PAGE 64   **didn't even have shovels** Megaw, interview with author, op. cit. **to the
Channel coast** WO167/758, op. cit; WO167/244, op. cit; Fox, op. cit., pp 31-32. **the
line from Ypres** Fox, op. cit., p. 32; Megaw, interview with author, op. cit. **back in a
little village** Megaw, interview with author, op. cit. **party were captured** Fox, op. cit.,
pp 32-3. **Germans were supposed to be** Ibid., p. 33. **to the advancing Germans** Ibid.,
pp 33-4.

PAGE 65   **700 officers and men** Ibid., p. 34. **good meal out of that** Connell, interview
with author, op. cit. **as the Ulster Rifles** John Donovan, interview with author,
December 1988. **they had fought him** Connell, interview with author, op. cit. **nobody
really in charge** Ibid.

PAGE 66   our waists in water Ibid. likelihood of being evacuated Ibid. and he was dead Ibid. with their bren guns Ibid. outside the harbour H.E.N. Bredin, notes, op. cit; Graves, op. cit., p. 59.

PAGE 67   Fusiliers deployed at Meerbeke Cunliffe, *The Royal Irish Fusiliers 1793-1968*, pp 382-3. caused sixty casualties Ibid., pp 384-5. Colonel Guy Gough, DSO, MC Horsfall, *Say Not the Struggle*, pp 46-50. have been much worse Ibid. that you could name David Laird, interview with author, December 1988. best part of three days Cunliffe, op. cit., pp 386-9. urgent passage for ourselves Gough, *Thirty Days to Dunkirk*, p. 48. Company and an open flank Horsfall, op. cit., p. 77; pp 83-4.

PAGE 68   and alive by a miracle Ibid., p. 76. action with German armour Ibid., p. 91. something to do with this Ibid., p. 73n. fresh supply of ammunition Ibid., p. 99. with courage and determination Gough, op. cit., pp 89-90; Horsfall, op. cit., pp 67-8, 91-2. Totenkopf SS Divisions Horsfall, op. cit., pp 105-6; Cunliffe, op. cit., pp 387-9. front dissolved about us Horsfall, op. cit., p. 107.

PAGE 69   back to England immediately Gough, op. cit., p. 123. bothered to think about it Ibid., p. 114. sight of Murphy's pistol Ibid., pp 142-3. and burning Dunkirk' Ibid., p. 143. the Faughs re-assembled Cunliffe, op. cit., p. 392. he got to the pier Megaw, interview with author, op. cit. bought it the next trip Ibid.

PAGE 70   the Dunkirk perimeter Lummis File E 20. divisions of the BEF Smyth, *The Story of the Victoria Cross*, pp 342-3. reduced to forty men Lummis File E 20. told the *Daily Telegraph* Doherty, *The Sons of Ulster*, p. 48.

PAGE 71   water for over a mile *London Gazette*, 30 July 1940. miles short of Dunkirk The 'Halt' Order, put into effect on 24 May 1940. attribute of a victory' Hamilton, *Montgomery, the Making of a General 1887-1942*, p. 393. headline BLOODY MARVELLOUS Whiting, *The Poor Bloody Infantry 1939-1945*, p. 54. home was in great danger Montgomery, *Memoirs*, p. 68. battle-honours' system Ibid. memory of that episode' Connell, *Auchinleck*, p. 68. couldn't understand that …' Donovan, interview with author, op. cit.

PAGE 72   was a tremendous defeat Megaw, interview with author, op. cit. Joseph Bernard Jackman Lummis File J 2. to Stonyhurst College *Irish Independent*, 26 June 1945. had an Irish origin Frederick, vol. I, op. cit., p. 276. served with a friend' Obituary, *St George's Gazette* (regimental journal of the Royal Northumberland Fusiliers), 28 February 1942, p. 12.

PAGE 73   four 2-pounder weapons Myatt, *The British Infantry 1660-1945*, p. 206. way out and link up Fraser, op. cit., pp 164-5. that was expected of it Obituary, *St George's Gazette*, op. cit. tanks of 7th Armoured Humble, *Crusader*, p. 111. Watch suffered 75% casualties Ibid.

PAGE 74   escarpment south of Tobruk Barclay, *The History of the Royal Northumberland Fusiliers in the Second World War*, p. 61. brought to a standstill Ibid., pp 61-2. driven away to safety Ibid., p. 62. Distinguished Conduct Medal Ibid. eight hours in arrears Ibid. anything but [the] objective' Royal Northumberland Fusiliers' Museum; Notes by Fusilier R.J. Dishman.

PAGE 75   **Hughes with his flag** Barclay, op. cit., pp 62-3. **was in friendly hands** Humble, op. cit., p. 145. **and Corporal Gare instantly** Dishman, Notes, op. cit. **and capable commander** Ibid. **awards for one action** Laffin, *British VCs of World War 2*, p. 81.

PAGE 76   **which they had gained** Barclay, op. cit., p. 63. **officer of the Fighting Fifth'** Ibid. **Britain's greatest gallantry award** Kenneally, *Kenneally, VC*, passim.

PAGE 77   **five long years of war'** Harvey, *The Allied Bomber War*, p. 85. **suffered its first casualties** Middlebrook and Everitt, *The Bomber Command War Diaries*, pp 22-3. **the declaration of war** H. Barton, interview with author, January 1998.

PAGE 78   **massive stupidity had begun** Ibid. **on 26 August 1939** Doherty, *Key to Victory*, p. 3. **declaration of war on Germany** Barnett, *Engage the Enemy More Closely*, p. 66. **crew of 1,000 men** Ibid., p. 69. **at the second attempt** Ibid., p. 71. **death toll was 833 men** Ibid. **was in need of refurbishment** Ibid., p. 80.

PAGE 79   **to attack Allied shipping** Ibid., p. 79. **in North Atlantic waters** Ibid., p. 78. **engage his British pursuers** Ibid., p. 89. **vessel from destruction** Ibid., pp 84-5. **Conspicuous Gallantry Medal** *Volunteers from Éire*, p. 4. **battleship was recommissioned** Barnett, op. cit., p. 117. **had destroyed 54 ships** Ibid., p. 196. **skin of a true warship** Ibid., p. 197; Turner, *VCs of the Royal Navy*, pp 56-7. **command of Jervis Bay** Turner, op. cit., p. 56. ***Pinguin, Thor* and *Widder*** Barnett, op. cit., p. 196.

PAGE 80   **officer in the Royal Navy** *Irish Independent*, 23 June 1945; Lummis File F 7 (Military Historical Society). **Moy and Paladin** Lummis File F 7. **at Jervis Bay** Lummis File F 7. **by the Admiralty** Ibid.; Obituary, *The Times*, 14 November 1940. **more for his men's** Turner, op. cit., pp 55-6. **the commodore's ship** Ibid., p. 56; Barnett, pp 196-7. **age of fourteen** Forde, *The Long Watch*, pp 35-6.

PAGE 81   **Kapitan Theodor Krancke** Turner, op. cit., p. 56; McAughtry, *The Sinking of the Kenbane Head*, p. 112. **Ar196 floatplane** McAughtry, op. cit., p. 112. **targets of opportunity** Turner, op. cit., p. 56. **waiting for them** McAughtry, op. cit., pp 113-14. **and make smoke** Turner, op. cit., pp 56-7. **of Coastal Command** Barnett, op. cit., pp 196-7. **there were no hits** Turner, op. cit., p. 57. **thick armour plate** Ibid.; Barnett, op. cit., p. 197.

PAGE 82   **useless by his side** Turner, op. cit., pp 57-8; Lummis File F 7. **began to list** Turner, op. cit., p. 58; Lummis File F 7. **straight for *Scheer*** Turner, op. cit., p. 58. **been shot away** *The Times*, 14 Nov 1940. **list grew greater** Turner, p. 58. **men on the liferafts** Ibid., p. 59.

PAGE 83   **from Fegen's crew** Ibid., pp 59-60. **to see the prey** *Wexford People*, 19 May 1945. **that the note was genuine** P.R.O., Kew, ADM1/17330. **Clyde by a destroyer** Turner, op. cit., p. 61. **except five ships** Roskill, *War at Sea*, Vol. I, pp 288-9. **would have wished'** Turner, op. cit., p. 61.

PAGE 84   **until 17 November** Ibid. **Dreyer had spotted** Barton, interview with author, Jan 1998. **sister ship *Gneisenau*** Barnett, op. cit., p. 279. **RHEINÜBUNG (Rhine Exercise)** Ibid., p. 300, p. 278. **crew of 1,419 survived** Ibid., p. 294. **that *Hood* had gone** Barton, interview with author, Jan 1998. **the enemy capital ship** Ibid.; Barnett, op. cit., p. 300.

PAGE 85   **now parted company** Barnett, op. cit., 294-302. **aircraft-carrier respectively** Ibid., pp 300-1. **biplane torpedo-bombers** Ibid., p. 301; Bowyer, *Eugene Esmonde*,

VC, *DSO*, p. 80. family home at Drominagh Bowyer, op. cit., pp 15-18. in the 1798 rebellion Ibid., pp 17; Lummis File E 21. was not for him Lummis File E 21.

PAGE 86 considerable operational experience Bowyer, *For Valour*, pp 271-2. carrier in the dark Bowyer, *Eugene Esmonde*, p. 85. aircraft was blown away Ibid., pp 86-7. as 'suicidal courage' Wragg, *Carrier Combat*, p. 52. as the light faded Ibid.; Barnett, op. cit., pp 301-2.

PAGE 87 aircraft carrier Ark Royal Bowyer, *Eugene Esmonde*, p. 90. Distinguished Service Order *London Gazette*, 16 September 1941. the whole squadron P.R.O., Kew, ADM1/11260. 825 Squadron, failed Barnett, op. cit., pp 302-3. Erne in County Fermanagh Smith, *Action Stations 7. Military Airfields of Scotland, the North-East and Northern Ireland*, p. 59. one hit on its rudder Bowyer, *Eugene Esmonde*, p. 92. brother of Eugene Ibid., p. 90. down with *Bismarck* Barnett, op. cit., pp 310-15. officer of HMS *Zulu London Gazette*, 14 October 1941. night of 26/27 May P.R.O., Kew, ADM1/11260. was appointed OBE Ibid. was a mining engineer Bowyer, *Eugene Esmonde*, pp 90-2.

PAGE 88 for Britain on 19 June Ibid., pp 93-4. of a downed Swordfish Ibid., pp 100-2. turned for Gibraltar Ibid., p. 104. destroyer HMS *Laforey* Ibid., pp 105-6. Gibraltar to attend them' Ibid., p. 108. attacks on the enemy' *London Gazette*, 20 January 1942.

PAGE 89 command 825 Squadron Bowyer, op. cit., pp 108-9. them would not return Ibid., pp 109-12. March 1941 for refitting Ibid., p. 112. dock undergoing repair Barnett, op. cit., p. 117. became Operation FULLER Bowyer, op. cit., pp 112-15.

PAGE 90 naval and air effort Ibid., pp 115-16. invasion of that country' Ibid., p. 117. following his Christmas leave Ibid., pp 117-18. without being intercepted Ibid., p. 119. Le Havre to Boulogne Ibid., pp 120-1.

PAGE 91 in a surface engagement Ibid., p. 121. blizzard to get there Ibid., pp 121-2. the effect of their fire Ibid., pp 122-3. beginning to unfold Stokes, *Wings Aflame*, pp 147-58; Stokes, *Paddy Finucane*, pp 121-7; P.R.O., Kew, AIR27/2076, Operations Records Book, no. 602 Squadron. returning to Manston Bowyer, op. cit., p. 124. very few senior officers Ibid.

PAGE 92 through the English Channel Ibid., pp 124-126; Barnett, op. cit., p. 447. make their run undetected Barnett, op. cit., p. 447. German luck was holding Bowyer, p. 129. luck was still holding Ibid., p. 130. Commander Finlay Boyd Ibid., pp 130-1; Stokes, *Wings Aflame*, p. 147. the Germans picked it up Bowyer, op. cit., p. 135.

PAGE 93 by one of the pilots Stokes, op. cit., pp 147-8. to be a daylight attack Bowyer, op. cit., p. 141. rendezvous with the Spitfires Ibid., pp 141-4. Admiral Ciliax's force Ibid., p. 145. became instantly plain Ibid.

PAGE 94 coming across 825 Squadron Ibid., p. 148. men were planning to do Ibid., p. 149. Esmonde's tiny force Ibid., pp 149-50. the crews of the *Swordfish* Ibid., p. 150. heading for *Prinz Eugen* Ibid., pp 151-2. Kingsmill lost sight of it Ibid.

PAGE 95 towards the huge warship Ibid., p. 152. torpedo fired by Esmonde Ibid., pp 152-3. least three RAF pilots Ibid., pp 153-62. Squadron would not return Ibid., p. 142. award of the Victoria Cross Ibid., p. 167. fine and stirring memory' *London Gazette*, 3 March 1942.

PAGE 96   by either side that day' Bowyer, *For Valour*, op. cit., p. 278. **war has yet witnessed**' Bowyer, *Eugene Esmonde*, p. 168. **as 'courage personified**' Bowyer, *For Valour*, p. 278. **receive her son's award** Bowyer, *Eugene Esmonde*, p. 170. **are fighting this war**' Bowyer, *For Valour*, p. 271. **the Second World War**Lummis Files E 21, F 7 and M 2.

PAGE 97   **on an adversary** Nesbitt, *Illustrated History of the RAF*, pp 72-4. **retaliation from the Luftwaffe** Ibid., p. 102; Sheppard, *France 1940*, p. 17. **came under Luftwaffe control** Nesbitt, p. 102. **and Bristol Blenheims** Ibid.

PAGE 98   **was the first to perish** Bowyer, *For Valour*, p. 215. **Fairey Battle light bomber** Ibid.; Halley, *The Squadrons of the Royal Air Force*, p. 36. **German border zone** Bowyer, op. cit., p. 216; Franks, *Valiant Wings*, p. 18.

PAGE 99   **one crew being decorated** Franks, op. cit., pp 40-3. **Battles were stopped** Ibid., p. 43. **cold winter conditions** Bowyer, op. cit., p. 216. **routine of flying began** Ibid. **followed** NICKEL **leaflet raids** Franks, op. cit., p. 66. **little effect, on Amifontaine** Bowyer, op. cit., p. 216. **carry out the attack** Franks, op. cit., pp 81-2. **fire from the ground** Ibid., p. 82. **George Irvine, was killed 16** Ibid. **gunner and the aircraft**' *Volunteers from Éire*, p. 52.

PAGE 100   **Veldwezelt and Vroenhoven** Bowyer, op. cit., p. 216; Franks, op. cit., p. 117. **to be the strike force** Franks, op. cit., p. 117. **approach to his target** Bowyer, op. cit., p. 217. **seek out their target** Ibid. **prove woefully inadequate** Franks, op. cit., pp 118-19. **rearward-firing machine-gun** Bowyer, op. cit., p. 217. **to the concrete bridge** Ibid.; Franks, op. cit., pp 120-1. **around the bridge area** Bowyer, op. cit., p. 217.

PAGE 101   **desperately for survival** Franks, op. cit., p. 119. **made prisoner of war** Bowyer, op. cit., p. 217. **diving into the ground** Ibid., pp 217-18. **Garland's cool attack**' Ibid., p. 218. **die during the war** Ibid.

PAGE 102   **four boys to die** Ibid., p. 215. **waters in September 1942** Ibid. **causes in March 1943** Ibid. **seventy enemy aircraft**' *Volunteers from Éire*, p. 22.

PAGE 103   **Odell received the DFM** Franks, op. cit., p. 94; *Volunteers from Éire*, p. 62. **in his native Dublin** *Volunteers from Éire*, p. 62. **lovely aircraft to fly** Doug Cooper, interview with author, January 98. **that port and Brunsbüttel** Fearnley, *Blenheim Odyssey*, p. 17; Middlebrook and Everitt, *Bomber Command War Diaries*, p. 22. **against the Blenheims** Franks, op. cit., p. 26. **machines in the raid** Middlebrook and Everitt, op. cit., p. 22.

PAGE 104   **bombs hitting the ship** Ibid. **Wyton on 2 November** Fearnley, op. cit., p. 17. **killing two civilians** Middlebrook and Everitt, op. cit., p. 22. **casualties of the war** Barton, op. cit., p. 87. **prior to landing** Cooper, interview with author, January 98. **failed to return** Moyes, *Bomber Squadrons of the RAF*, p. 156. **running fight ensued** Cooper, interview with author, January 98. **on 4 September 1939** Fearnley, op. cit., p. 17.

PAGE 105   **Dornier Do18 flying-boat** P.R.O., Kew, AIR 27/857, Operations Record Book (O.R.B.), no. 110 Squadron; Middlebrook and Everitt, p. 36. **courage and initiative** *Volunteers from Éire*, p. 52. **service in March 1941** Ibid. **town' over that bridge** Franks, op. cit., p. 105. **that is what he did** Cooper, interview with author, January 98.

PAGE 106   part in the Maastricht raid Ibid. two non-operational flights) From Doug
Cooper's logbook. could have jumped through Cooper, interview with author, January
98. piece of cake really' Ibid. others suffered damage Franks, op. cit., p. 278. safely
with two aircraft *Volunteers from Éire*, p. 60.

PAGE 107   appeared to be on fire Ibid. on 20 February 1941 Cooper, interview with
author, Jan 98. frightening than in daylight Ibid. sky to land safely Ibid. unfavourable
weather conditions' P.R.O., Kew, AIR27/263, O.R.B., no. 21 Sqn.

PAGE 108   the rest of the war Cooper, interview with author, Jan 98. from Bomber
Command Ellis, *The World War II Databook*, p. 254; Overy, *Bomber Command
1939-1945*, p. 204.

PAGE 109   destroyed the enemy Air Ministry Bulletin no. 1101, Air Historical Branch
(A.H.B.) to author. Distinguished Flying Meda Ibid. Wellingtons and Hampdens
A.H.B. letter to author. also affected vision Middlebrook and Everitt, op. cit., p. 85.
all five crew members A.H.B. letter to author. Schloss Charlottenburg Middlebrook
and Everitt, op. cit., p. 85.

PAGE 110   were all Australians Sean Drumm, interview with Myles Dungan. be one
of the survivors Ibid.

PAGE 111   anti-submarine patrols Halley, *The Squadrons of the Royal Air Force*, p.
107. in the Middle East *Volunteers from Éire*, p. 62. the end of the war Halley, op.
cit., p. 107.

PAGE 112   superiority over Burma Eric Dunlop, interview with Myles Dungan. on its
return to base Ibid. provided for the bombers Ibid. but nothing else Ibid.

PAGE 113   was always very short Ibid. hills in bad weather Ibid. faced with enemy
opposition *Volunteers from Éire*, p. 55.

PAGE 114   seven enemy fighters Ibid. earned him the DFC Ibid., p. 52. commissioned in 1942 Ibid., p. 56. and devotion to duty Ibid., p. 58. of all the risks Ibid.,
p. 59.

PAGE 115   or anti-aircraft gunfire Ibid., p. 61. otherwise have been abandoned' Ibid.,
pp 61-2. between 70 and 80 degrees Pitt, The *Military History of World War II*, p.
220. raid on Peenemunde Middlebrook and Everitt, op. cit., p. 424. encounters with
nightfighters Denis Murnane, interview with Myles Dungan.

PAGE 116   off the engagement Ibid. came off completely Ibid. nightfighter the whole
way Ibid.

PAGE 117   That was pretty shattering Ibid. Halifax crashed in Belgium Middlebrook
and Everitt, op. cit., p. 673. we all had to jump Murnane, interview with Myles
Dungan. in the height of battle Ibid. not once but twice Ibid.

PAGE 118   allow the others to escape Ibid. RAF Kirkby in Lincolnshire Sean Drumm,
letter to author. Lancaster Is and IIIs Halley, op. cit., p. 341. atmosphere afterwards:
'*tense*' Drumm, notes to author. straighten up afterwards Drumm, interview with
author, Oct 98. from the turret's glazing Drumm, notes to author.

PAGE 119   Kinloss in Scotland Drumm, notes to author. Europe, was destroyed
Middlebrook and Everitt, op. cit., p. 609. mission of their tour Drumm, notes to
author.

PAGE 120   force of the explosions Ibid. this stage of the war Middlebrook and Everitt, op. cit., pp 613-614. Trondheim in November Drumm, interview with author, Oct 98. home on railway warrants' Ibid. and thirty-five minutes Ibid.

PAGE 121   flashes from falling bombs Drumm, notes to author. crew members survived Drumm, letter to author. to die in service Ibid.

PAGE 122   perished there in 1944 David Truesdale, notes to author.

PAGE 123   Missing at Runnymede Middlebrook and Everitt, pp 577-578. joined up in 1942 Mrs F. Galloway, letter and notes to author. P.O. Tottenham, DFC Ibid.

PAGE 125   abuse their power 1 Luke, Ch. 3; v. 14. 'Soldiers likewise asked him, "What about us?" He told them, "Don't bully anyone. Denounce no one falsely. Be content with your pay."' saint of chaplains Johnstone and Hagerty, *The Cross on the Sword*, p. v. wounded on the battlefield Ibid., preface, passim. carried out their duties Ibid., p. 198. been the Crimean War Ibid., pp 5-6. last rites to dying men Ibid., p. 88. Langemarck in August 1917 Denman, *Ireland's Unknown Soldiers*, p. 123. nature of the sacraments Johnstone and Hagerty, op. cit., p. 198.

PAGE 126   at the battalion's RAP Ibid., p. 197. clearing stations (CCSs) Ibid. services as a chaplain Volunteers from Éire, p. 22. Army Chaplains' Department Ibid. to 151 Infantry Brigade Johnstone and Hagerty, op. cit., p. 199. beginning of February 1940 Joslen, *Orders of Battle Second World War*, p. 335. as being 'outstanding' *Volunteers from Éire*, p. 22. MC to Father Duggan Ibid.

PAGE 127   arrived in Northern Ireland Johnstone and Hagerty, op. cit., p. 199. the British Empire (OBE) Ibid., p. 170. 1961 at the age of seventy-one Ibid. the Military Cross *Volunteers from Éire*, p. 22. Calais on 23 May Fraser, op. cit., p. 67. 1st Armoured Division Ibid. England on 22 April Ibid. Queen Victoria's Rifles Ibid., p. 68. in an uneven struggle Ibid.

PAGE 128   very gallant chaplain *Volunteers from Éire*, p. 22. Queen Victoria's Rifles P.R.O., Kew, WO167 Index. and asked for wounded' P.R.O., Kew, WO167/813, narrative of 1 R.B. in Calais, p. 9. repatriated in his place Johnstone and Hagerty, op. cit., p. 200. Headquarters, BEF near Arras Ibid., pp 196-7. comfort where they could Ibid., pp 198-9. them were trained nurses Ibid.

PAGE 129   night of 29/30 May Ibid., p. 199. with 1st Division's artillery Ibid. the battle for France *Volunteers from Éire*, p. 7. awarded the Military Cross P.R.O., Kew, WO373/15; Johnstone and Hagerty, op. cit., p. 199. at the War Office Johnstone and Hagerty, ibid, p. 202. Shanghai, Egypt and Britain Ibid.

PAGE 130   HMS *Ferret*, at Londonderry Doherty, Key to Victory, op. cit., p. 8. Melbourne in Australia Daly and Devlin, *The Clergy of the Diocese of Derry*, p. 54. element of the Anzacs Johnstone and Hagerty, op. cit., p. 275. the Croix de Guerre John Connor, Australian Defence Force Academy, letter to author and summary of Father Devine's service from the Australian War Memorial. finally to Derry in 1932 Daly and Devlin, op. cit., p. 54. 48th Battalion, AIF Connor, letter to author. Londonderry naval base Bishop Edward Daly, interview with author, November 1997. as First Sea Lord Johnstone and Hagerty, op. cit., p. 273. and effective chaplain Ibid., p. 276; Bishop Edward Daly, interview with author, November 1997. the military

chaplain Maeve Kelly, interview with author , September 1998. **had made confessions** Johnstone and Hagerty, op. cit., p. 276; Bishop Edward Daly, interview with author, November 1997.

PAGE 131 **elderly very charming Irishman'** Taylor, *Sea Chaplains*, p. 444. **on 26 March 1941** Information from Royal Army Chaplains' Department Museum. **a time in Palestine** Ibid. **78th (Battleaxe) Division** Ibid. **problem quickly disappeared** Clark, interview with author, October 1989. **overall sense of occasion** Ibid. **for him elsewhere** Colonel J. Trousdell, letter to author.

PAGE 132 **they were fighting for** Horsfall, *The Wild Geese are Flighting*, p. 19. **when it was necessary** Broadbent, letter to author. **the going was tough** Trousdell, letter to author.

PAGE 133 **– who can say?** Gunner, Front of the Line, p. 82. **unfailing devotion to duty** *Faugh A Ballagh Gazette*, vol. xxxvi, no. 159, p. 227. **and the pope concurred** Scott, *Narrative of the Service of the Irish Brigade*. **being entirely Catholic** Ibid. **blessed by a pope** Ibid.; Jim Hamilton, MM, interview with author, June 1990. **the most popular tune** Scott, op. cit.

PAGE 134 **in post-war Austria** Mgr J. Shortall, letter to author. **Doyle of our war'** Gunner, letter to author. **of the confessional helps** Gunner, op. cit., p. 105. **Webb of the Faughs** Webb, letter to author; interview with author, November 1990.

PAGE 135 **Irish Fusiliers in Austria** Ibid. **Gunner described him** Gunner, op. cit., p. 146. **capital on 15 June** Obituary, *Faugh A Ballagh Gazette*, vol. xli, no. 189, p. 267. **his beloved Kerry** Mgr J. Shortall, letter to author. **as a Columban missionary** *Faugh A Ballagh Gazette*, vol. xliii, no. 196, Autumn 1959, p. 64. **Japanese invasion in 1942** Johnstone and Hagerty, op. cit., pp 253-4. **join 1st Burma Division** Ibid., p. 254; Fox, *The Royal Inniskilling Fusiliers in the Second World War*, p. 39. **serve them as a chaplain** Johnstone and Hagerty, op. cit., p. 254. **him to a chaplaincy** Ibid. **accepted with no hesitation** Ibid.

PAGE 136 **Army for that alone** Royal Inniskilling Fusiliers' Museum, transcript of tape in possession of the Columban Fathers. **had orders to destroy** Fox, op. cit., pp 39-40. **aircraft on 10 April** P.R.O., Kew, WO304/11 Army Roll of Honour. **by a sniper's bullet** Fox, op. cit., pp 40-1. **by machine-gun bullets** Fischer, *Mission in Burma*, p. 58. **blazing oil wells** Ibid. **and occupy the ridge** Fox, op. cit., p. 40. **The attack was halted** Slim, *Defeat into Victory*, pp 67-8. **battalion reached India** Fox, op. cit., p. 42.

PAGE 137 **the armoured skin** Obituary, *Columban Intercom*, November 1993, p. 217. **terrible campaign began'** Revd L. Carroll, quoted in Fischer, op. cit., pp 58-9. **with Jim Cloonan'** Obituary, *Columban Intercom*, op. cit. **until liberated in 1945** Johnstone and Hagerty, op. cit., p. 255. **very well in captivity** Obituary, *Columban Intercom*, op. cit. **part of the perimeter** *Volunteers from Éire*, supplement, p. 12. **Durham Light Infantry** RACh.D. to author.

PAGE 138 **and an example to all** *Volunteers from Éire*, supplement, p. 12. **Willie Doyle of Burma** Johnstone and Hagerty, op. cit., p. 257. **overseas service in 1943** *Interfuse*, no. 41, p. 82. **energy and indomitable courage** Ibid. **forward to celebrate Mass** Ibid., p. 84.

PAGE 139   January 1945, he died Ibid., p. 83. May he rest in peace Johnstone and Hagerty, op. cit., p. 257. Father Hayes' Provincial Interfuse, no. 41, p. 84. battle for the Mareth line *Volunteers from Éire*, p. 31. three of their objectives Blaxland, *The Plain Cook and the Great Showman*, p. 194. with the utmost bravery *Volunteers from Éire*, p. 31. actually hitting the RAP' P.R.O., Kew, WO169/10165, War diary, 6th Grenadier Guards, 1943.

PAGE 140   unpleasant and dangerous task *Volunteers from Éire*, p. 31. the victims had fallen P.R.O., Kew, WO169/10165, op. cit. diocese of Derry and Raphoe Doherty, *Wall of Steel*, p. 102. complaint was ever made George Lapsley, interview with author, June 1998. his Protestant friends Ibid. also became a bishop Information from RAChD and *Church of Ireland Gazette*.

PAGE 141   Hymn of the Irish Church' Cloake, Templer, p. 104. course of the war Ibid. of the desert war Doherty, *Wall of Steel*, pp 78-79. a much-needed rest Dr D. Henderson, notes and tape to author; Verney, *The Desert Rats*, p. 60. Deputy Chaplain General Dr D. Henderson, notes and tape to author.

PAGE 142   ground below them Johnstone and Hagerty, p. 215. to be killing here' Ibid. which it was isolated *Volunteers from Éire, supplement*, p. 10.

PAGE 143   off and was blinded.' Rea, op. cit., p. 41. leaflets in return Ibid., pp 42-4. who had been wounded Ibid., pp 46-9. for personal safety Ibid., p. 57. bomber over the Ruhr Hamilton-Pollock, *Wings on the Cross*, p. 75.

PAGE 144   won't find him coming.' Ibid., p. 76. O'Reilly's bomber, C-Charlie Johnstone and Hagerty, op. cit., p. 231. of those you've had it Hamilton-Pollock, op. cit., p. 79.

PAGE 145   fighters on the way back Ibid. who had died that night Ibid., p. 80. and God bless you' Revd Samuel Eaton, notes to and interview with author, June 1998.

PAGE 146   wrote back to thank me Ibid.

PAGE 147   the Medical Staff Corps Hallows, *Regiments and Corps of the British Army*, p. 242. of a more regular system Ascoli, op. cit., p. 153. in the Great War Hallows, op. cit. the Second World War Ibid. of Army Medical Services RAMC to author.

PAGE 148   with the outbreak of war Mrs Elizabeth Dobbs, interview with author, August 1998. to join the BEF Parsons, *Exit at Anzio*, p. ii. 13 Brigade of 5th Division Ibid., p. iii; Joslen, op. cit., p. 47. General Harold Franklyn Joslen, op. cit., p. 47. and one English battalion Ibid., p. 251. retreat to Dunkirk Parsons, op. cit., p. 29. well in local restaurants Ibid., pp 4-5. of the two companies Ellis and Chamberlain, op. cit., p. 89. troops on the roads Billy Megaw, interview with author, December 1988; Parsons, op. cit., pp 7-10. strapped to the roofs of cars Parsons, op. cit., p. 7. also to his officers Fox, op. cit., pp 27-8.

PAGE 149   advice or help from me Parsons, op. cit., p. 13. aircraft flown by Germans Ibid., pp 13-14. flesh and powder Ibid., p. 30.

PAGE 150   as quickly as possible Ibid., p. 31. than 700 all ranks Fox, op. cit., p. 34. there in the darkness Parsons, p. 36. wounded man's kit Ibid., p. 37. chaplain had expired Ibid. Egypt, via South Africa Ibid., pp 39-42. on an orthopaedic ward Ibid., pp 44-9.

PAGE 151   shattered by mines Ibid., p. 49. regimental medical officer Ibid., p. 50. in 10th Armoured Division Joslen, op. cit., p. 160. as a motor battalion P.R.O., Kew. WO169/4994, War diary, 1st Buffs. name to the Buffs Chicester and Burges-Short, *Records and Badges of the British Army, 1900*, p. 326. Royal East Kent Regiment) Ascoli, op. cit., p. 116. had been a senior officer P.R.O., Kew, WO169/4994, op. cit. accompany the other two groups Parsons, op. cit., p. 58.

PAGE 152   and considerable confusion Delaforce, *Monty's Marauders*, p. 114. have lost their lives *Volunteers from Éire*, p. 27. corridors in the minefields Delaforce, op. cit., pp 111-4; P.R.O., Kew, WO169/4230, War diary, 8th Armoured Brigade. tended the wounded Parsons, op. cit., p. 64.

PAGE 153   the body was lying Ibid. possible booby trap Ibid., p. 74. on the white sand' Ibid., p. 75. crawling with flies Ibid., p. 76. he was relieving himself Ibid. withdrawn after El Alamein Delaforce, op. cit., p. 119.

PAGE 154   the town that afternoon P.R.O., Kew, WO169/4994, op. cit. heavy enemy shellfire Delaforce, op. cit., p. 123; *Volunteers from Éire*, p. 27. immediately he was hit' Parsons, op. cit., p. 96. saved a valuable life' *Volunteers from Éire*, p. 27. believed to be alive Ibid. again saved several lives Ibid. continuous periods of action Ibid.

PAGE 155   now in 18 Brigade Joslen, op. cit., p. 244. Anzio in late-February Parsons, op. cit., pp 172-3. and moved in daylight Ibid., p. 198-9. by a 105 mm shell Ibid., p. 216.

PAGE 156   to the United Kingdom Ibid., p. 221. rest of his days Mrs E. Dobbs, interview with author, August 1998. General Orde Wingate Bidwell, *The Chindit War*, pp 45-6. he had been wounded Desmond Whyte, interview with author, January 1997. Palestine and then to India Ibid. attack on Pearl Harbor Ibid., December 1988.

PAGE 157   learned a lot of lessons Ibid., January 1997. included Desmond Whyte Ibid. He was sincere Ibid. transport and facilities Rooney, *Burma Victory*, p. 108.

PAGE 158   take on the Japanese Rooney, *Wingate and the Chindits*, p. 103. allotted to Wingate's scheme Ibid. India from Quebec Bidwell, op. cit., p. 69; Rooney, *Wingate and the Chindits*, p. 104. next operation in Burma Rooney, op. cit., p. 104. of rotary-winged aircraft Bidwell, op. cit., p. 64. carrying heavy packs Whyte, interview with author, January 1997; Doherty, *Only the Enemy in Front*, p. 104. the Gangan reservoir Doherty, op. cit., p. 104. to his fellow officers Bidwell, op. cit., p. 47.

PAGE 159   they were very tough' Whyte, interview with author, December 1988. operation were agreed Rooney, op. cit., p. 108. with 1,100 animals Slim, *Defeat into Victory*, p. 265. 7,000-foot high mountains Rooney, op. cit., p. 116. the movement by air Masters, *The Road past Mandalay*, p. 165. course of their work.) Ibid., p. 172. Cameronians on 24 March Rooney, op. cit., p. 132. other two battalions Ibid.

PAGE 160   were completely exhausted Ibid. it would go off Whyte, interview with author, December 1988. from the fighting zone Masters, op. cit., pp 185-6. one or two casualties Whyte, interview with author, December 1988. derelict was blown up Rooney, op. cit., p. 132. was suffering from strain Ibid., p. 133; Masters, op. cit., pp 199-200.

PAGE 161   no badges of rank Whyte, interview with author, January 1997. command of Special Force Masters, op. cit., p. 203; Bidwell, pp 155-6. step into the breach

Rooney, op. cit., p. 126, 133-4; Bidwell, p. 160. **major's rank, however** Rooney, op. cit., pp 133-4; Masters, op. cit., pp 206-7. **order to engage elsewhere'** Masters, op. cit., pp 204-5. **and railway to Mogaung** Ibid., p. 222.

PAGE 162   **doctors with the brigade** Whyte, interview with author, December 1988. **don't need to elaborate** Ibid. **their attention to it** Masters, op. cit., p. 226. **over-ruled by Lentaigne** Rooney, op. cit., p. 135. **That was repulsed** Whyte, interview with author, December 1988. **rotted on Blackpool's perimeter** Ibid.

PAGE 163   **unpleasant and very wearing** Ibid. **opposite could happen** Masters, op. cit., pp 226-30. **were also flown in** Ibid., pp 234-9. **strengthen the defences**Ibid., p. 248. **That was very sad** Whyte, interview with author, December 1988. **back to his command** Masters, op. cit., pp 248-9. **Chindits a signal victory** Ibid., p. 251. **the rain was incessant** Ibid., pp 251-3. **many of those casualties** Ibid., p. 254.

PAGE 164   **Henley days are over'** Whyte, interview with author, December 1988. **pieces under his hands** Masters, op. cit., p. 278. **had lost his face** Ibid., p. 258. **without light in them.'** Ibid., p. 259. **to see any Japanese'** Ibid. **shut out the sound.'** Ibid.; Whyte, interview with author, January 1997. **600 men in total** Masters, p. 265.

PAGE 165   **a matter of days** Ibid., p. 268. **which was awarded immediately** Ibid., pp 275-6. **Brigade Medical Officers** Copy of citation in author's possession via Mrs Patricia Whyte. **as 'not good enough'** Masters, op. cit., p. 278.

PAGE 166   **Indian Airborne Division** Whyte, interview with author, January 1997. **service 'would be fun'** Dungan, *Distant Drums*, p. 96.

PAGE 167   **recommendation was made** Ibid. **heavy machine-gun fire** *Volunteers from Éire*, p. 27. **that short campaign** Ibid., p. 23. **being machine-gunned** *Irish Independent*, 25 May 1945. **January of that year** P.R.O., Kew, WO222/246 Canal no. 18 Area, Middle East Forces, notes by Brig G.F. Allison.

PAGE 168   **carried out so smoothly** *Volunteers from Éire*, p. 7. **from time to time** P.R.O., Kew, WO222/246 op. cit. **sitting or walking** Ellis and Chamberlain, op. cit., p. 86. **an example to all** *Volunteers from Éire*, p. 8.

PAGE 169   **was beyond praise'** Ibid., p. 16. **'most unusually low'** Ibid., p. 17. **in September 1940** P.R.O., Kew, WO222/246, op. cit. **treatment of septic wounds** *Volunteers from Éire* , p. 19. **many difficult times'** Ibid., p. 21. **less than two months** Ibid., pp 19-20.

PAGE 170   **brought to safety** Ibid., p. 30. **or in slit trenches** Ibid., p. 26. **of limb amputation** Ibid., p. 25. **up to relieve him** Ibid., p. 29. **casualties were suffered.'** Parsons, *Outline History of 17 Fd Regt*, p. 6. **on those around him** *Volunteers from Éire*, p. 26.

PAGE 171   **and example to all** Ibid., *Supplement*, p. 14. **to be called up** Pantridge, *An Unquiet Life*, p. 13. **at Selerang barracks** Ibid., pp 13-16. **be useless in action** Ibid., p. 19.

PAGE 172   **provide air cover** Ibid., pp 20-1. **for the next encounter** Ibid., p. 21. **came] flying past me'** Ibid., pp 21-2. **for quick movement** Ibid., p. 22. **suffer at Japanese hands'** Ibid., pp 22-3.

PAGE 173   **Distinguished Conduct Medal** Ibid. **reason for their survival** Desmond Whyte, interview with author, December 1991. **officers and men alike** *Volunteers from*

Éire, supplement, p. 14. Cross for his courage Obituary, *Daily Telegraph*, December 1997.

PAGE 174 formidable army in Europe' P.R.O., Kew, ADM116/4572. awarded the DSO Ibid.; *Volunteers from Éire*, p. 4. Lieutenant in 1942 *Volunteers from Éire*, p. 48. down in his turret Ibid.

PAGE 175 the award of the MBE Ibid. most appalling circumstances Ibid., p. 59.

PAGE 176 first became apparent Stokes, *Paddy Finucane Fighter Ace*, pp 22-3.

PAGE 177 British in April 1916 Ibid., p. 17. air force blue Ibid. was on other things Ibid., p. 24. at the end of August Ibid., p. 25. at Hornchurch in Essex Ibid., pp 28-35. and a dead engine Ibid., p. 37.

PAGE 178 down into the Channel Ibid., p. 38. the second as damaged Ibid., p. 39. chances of hitting it Ibid., p. 31. days' operational flying Ibid., pp 38-9. and is learning quickly Quoted in ibid, p. 41.

PAGE 179 on his fourth attack Ibid., p. 44. increasing all the while Ibid., pp 44-5.

PAGE 180 with an 'exceptional' rating Ibid., p. 46. pilots of the squadron *London Gazette*, 13 May 1941.

PAGE 181 its first circus operation Ibid., pp 49-55. favourable to our fighters P.R.O., Kew, AIR 16, Headquarters Fighter Command. height and sun Ibid.

PAGE 182 way back to England Stokes, op. cit., pp 60-61.

PAGE 183 spirit of the unit *Volunteers from Éire*, p. 49; *London Gazette* 9 and 26 September 1941. stood at fifteen *Volunteers from Éire*, p. 49. leadership and example *London Gazette*, 21 October 1941. be a great figure Churchill, op. cit., vol. VI, p. 329.

PAGE 184 by King George VI Stokes, op. cit., pp 105-11. shamrock of Ireland Ibid., pp 118-19. from the day of his arrival Ibid., p. 120.

PAGE 185 fire on the fighters Ibid., pp 121-3. the overall advantage Ibid., pp 125-7. gave up the chase Ibid., p. 127.

PAGE 186 FW190 at those heights Ibid., pp 128-32. inflicted on the enemy Quoted in ibid, p. 134. them at 350 m.p.h. Stokes, op. cit., pp 136-7.

PAGE 187 achieved by Finucane Ibid., pp 146-7. or had been downgraded Ibid., pp 148-9. Finucane's finest achievements Ibid., pp 152-4. Kenley on 21 June P.R.O., Kew, AIR 27/2076, Operations Records Book, no. 602 Sqn.

PAGE 188 fighter Roadstead to Ostend Stokes, op. cit., pp 176-183. must remain unanswered Ibid., pp 183-5. of the 'fighter boy' Quoted in ibid, p. 186.

PAGE 189 sitting at a desk again Ibid., p. 13. and Eugenyi Gorbatyuk RAF Museum, notes to author. the French Beaumais Stokes, *Wings Aflame*, pp 16-17. who lived in London Ibid., p. 18. Central Flying School Ibid., pp 21-26.

PAGE 190 establishing the flight Ibid., pp 43-59. charm, and very friendly' Ronald Harker, quoted in ibid, p. 65. would not do himself Ibid. remaining bombs and fled Ibid., pp 68-75. own and a Dornier Do215 Ibid., Appendix B, p. 179.

PAGE 191 with great energy and dash *London Gazette*, 23 July 1940. daylight bomber offensive Stokes, op. cit., pp 92-102. lifted off the ground Ibid., p. 107. coolness and courage' *London Gazette*, 8 November 1940.

PAGE 192   descended to 4,000 feet Stokes, op. cit., p. 109-10. claimed only as a probable Ibid., pp 117-18. on 25 January 1942 Ibid., pp 122-46. example' he had set *London Gazette*, 25 September 1941. on to 11 Group HQ Stokes, op. cit., pp 147-8. report what he saw Bowyer, *Eugene Esmonde*, p. 133. was not picked up Ibid.

PAGE 193   he had seen Stokes, op. cit., p. 155. be his last claims Ibid., pp 165-171. at about 12,000 feet Ibid., pp 171-3. him a magnificent leader' *Volunteers from Éire*, p. 53. Lieutenant in July 1940 Ibid. later rose to fourteen Stokes, *Paddy Finucane*, Appendix F, p. 206.

PAGE 194   ranks of the 'aces' *Volunteers from Éire*, p. 50. and weather reconnaissance Halley, op. cit., p. 129. damaged three enemy aircraft *Volunteers from Éire*, p. 54. leadership, skill and courage Ibid., p. 56. as a priest or a monk R.G. Lovell Webster Browne, letter and notes to author. officer in October 1938 Ibid.

PAGE 195   in January 1939 Halley, op. cit., p. 75. when war was declared' R.G. Lovell Webster Browne. was out of ammunition Ibid. wounded in the legs Ibid. at North Fambridge Ibid. to earth in a tree Ibid.

PAGE 196   East in February 1942 Halley, op. cit., p. 173. operational squadron R.G. Lovell Webster Browne. his outstanding leadership Ibid. Distinguished Flying Cross Ibid. shot down an opponent Ibid., and telephone conversation with author. seldom, if ever, equalled' R.G. Lovell Webster Browne.

PAGE 197   some 21 enemy aircraft Ibid. Tony's best teenage friend Ibid. to No. 263 Squadron Ibid. cannon in the nose Nesbit, op. cit. p. 153. Flight on 29 October R.G. Lovell Webster Browne.

PAGE 198   body in the wreckage Ibid. where he lies to this day Ibid. R.G. Lovell Webster Browne laid a wreath on Stuart Lovell's grave in January 1994. was very, very sad Bill Polley, interview with author, January 1989.

PAGE 199   use its own radar Pitt, op. cit., pp 34-5. damaged two enemy aircraft *Volunteers from Éire*, p. 50. of five enemy aircraft Ibid., p. 54.

PAGE 200   lieutenant in November 1940 Ibid., p. 55. who serve under him Ibid., p. 57.

PAGE 201   a Mention in Despatches Doherty, *Only the Enemy in Front*, p. 41 & p. 80. battleship *Benbow* in 1925 Obituary, *Daily Telegraph*, 10 Oct 1994. incapacitated by the gale P.R.O., Kew, ADM1/ 11675, Report by CO, Princess Victoria on minelaying operations commendations for bravery.

PAGE 202   Distinguished Service Cross Ibid. preyed upon our shipping Evelyn Chavasse, *Business in Great Waters*, p. 3. troopship arrived in Liverpool Ibid. I was given command' Ibid., p. 4. in the western Atlantic Barnett, op. cit., p. 183. angle of 45 degrees Ibid., p. 256 & pp 587-589.

PAGE 203   knew what hit them Chavasse, op. cit., p. 8. of *Broadway*'s steering gear' Ibid., p. 12. across the North Atlantic Ibid., p. 15. bring the Allies defeat' Ibid.

PAGE 204   outcome of this debate Ibid., pp 16-17. away from the enemy Ibid., p. 36.

PAGE 205   the convoy was reunited Ibid., pp 31-2. slog across the Atlantic Ibid., pp 27-8.

PAGE 206   death, and said No Ibid., pp 42-3. perhaps if I was right Ibid. of the convoy escorts Barnett, op. cit., pp 584-5. ever for shipping losses Ibid., p. 597. Atlantic to the Allies Ibid., p. 612.

PAGE 207 protection of the convoy Chavasse, op. cit., pp 92-3. zone around HX237 Ibid., p. 94. speed of 20 knots Ibid., p. 97.

PAGE 208 her fair and square Ibid., pp 97-8. they rest in peace Ibid., p. 99. without further interruption Ibid., p. 100.

PAGE 209 high state of efficiency P.R.O., Kew, ADM1/14453. damage to the enemy' Ibid. looking after her father-in-law Chavasse, op. cit., p. 103. concentrating its attentions Ibid., p. 104. in the Arctic convoys McCaughey, interview with Myles Dungan. left Iceland for Russia Barnett, op. cit., p. 710. had it, I'm afraid McCaughey, interview with Dungan, op. cit.

PAGE 210 descended on PQ 17 Barnett, op. cit., pp 713-17. to scatter on 4 July Ibid. Germans had a field day McCaughey, interview with Dungan, op. cit. went down was grim Barnett, op. cit., pp 719-21. pleasant afternoon's fun McCaughey, interview with Dungan, op. cit. until September 1942 Pitt, op. cit., p. 161. of one merchant ship Chavasse, op. cit., p. 127.

PAGE 211 Garwood in June 1944 Ibid., p. 144. deserved and most unusual! Ibid., pp 159. career to a premature end Ibid., p. 161. to some life buoys Paul Chavasse, *A Sailor's War Memoirs*, p. 3.

PAGE 212 fifty were hospitalized Ibid. assessed was confidential Ibid., p. 4. proudly, the White ensign Ibid., pp 4-5. coast of the island Ibid., p. 8.

PAGE 213 troops from the island Ibid., p. 9. of 31 May–1 June Barnett, op. cit., p. 362. *Jackal* and *Kimberly* Ibid. we could have carried' Chavasse, op. cit., p. 9. would have been hit Ibid. been rescued from Crete Hill, *Oxford Illustrated History of the Royal Navy*, p. 361. returning to Alexandria Barnett, op. cit., p. 363.

PAGE 214 our own air cover Chavasse, op. cit., p. 10. first run to Tobruk Ibid. bade farewell to her Ibid., pp 12-13. resupply of Tobruk *London Gazette*, 13 Oct 1942. shore, and all this Jarvis, interview with author, Feb 1989.

PAGE 215 put it like that Ibid.

PAGE 216 stop to pick him up Ibid. go through it again Ibid. Malta's national holiday Barnett, op. cit., p. 524. the invasion of Sicily McCaughey, interview with Dungan, op. cit.

PAGE 217 Germany's summer offensive Barnett, op. cit., p. 517. standard of proficiency Ibid. evening, her task completed Ibid., p. 518. no damage was done Ibid., p. 519.

PAGE 218 continue with the convoy Ibid. continue on its way Ibid., pp 522-3. *Santa Elisa* and *Wairangi* Ibid., p. 523. steamed on for Malta Ibid. convoy had reached Malta Ibid., pp 523-4.

PAGE 219 for about two months Ibid., p. 524. others' mission to an end Ibid. the invasion of France McCaughey, interview with Dungan, op. cit. 24 hours later! Chavasse, op. cit., p. 15. it the next day Ibid.

PAGE 220 luxury in wartime Britain Ibid., pp 16-17. and Torpedo Officer Ibid., p. 19. our man. And yours?'! Ibid. naval pressure on Japan Barnett, op. cit., p. 739.

PAGE 221 number of smaller vessels Ibid., pp 740-741. as were the destroyers Ibid., p. 741. about three miles ahead Chavasse, op. cit., p. 20. were most spectacular Ibid., pp 20-21. **fire and shell burst** Paul Chavasse, letter to Mrs Elizabeth Chavasse, 30 Dec 1943.

PAGE 222   **my proudest possessions** Paul Chavasse, *Memoirs*, p. 21. **engage with torpedoes:** Letter to Mrs Elizabeth Chavasse, op. cit. **She sank shortly afterwards** Ibid. **some four years earlier** *London Gazette*, 7 Mar 1944. **with coolness and speed** P.R.O., Kew ADM1/16676 Recommendations and awards for personnel who participated in the sinking of the German battlecruiser *Scharnhorst*. **only thirty-six were rescued** Barnett, op. cit., p. 744. **of flag staff aboard** Paul Chavasse, op. cit., p. 21. **either aircraft or submarines'** Col K.G.F. Chavasse, letter to author.

PAGE 223   **life ebbed away** Ibid. **occasion at Scapa Flow** P. Chavasse, op. cit., p. 21. **or Royal Air Force** Ibid., pp 21-2. **and Wolff of Belfast** Barton, interview with author, May 1995. **joined the ship yesterday** *A Formidable Commission*, p. 18.

PAGE 224   **Kaafjord in Norway** Ibid., p.18-19. *Nabob* and *Trumpeter* Ibid., pp 23-8; Barnett, op. cit., pp 745-6. **Gib to be installed** Barton, interview with author, op. cit. **reached on 4 April** Ibid.; Hobbs, *Aircraft Carriers of the Royal and Commonwealth Navies*, p. 91. **British Pacific Fleet** Barnett, op. cit., p. 885.

PAGE 225   **some hundred miles back** Barton, interview with author, op. cit. **way of the Phillipines** Barnett, op. cit., p. 884. **Okinawa from Formosa** Ibid., pp 885 & 891. **good signal really** Barton, interview with author, op. cit.

PAGE 226   **worked once or twice** Ibid. **ten damaged by fire** Hobbs, op. cit., p. 91. **shipping in Onagawa Wan** Ibid., p. 92. **officers in the ship** *A Formidable Commission*, p. 114. **awarded the Victoria Cross** Ibid. **India and to Britain** Barton, interview with author, op. cit.

PAGE 227   **in December 1941** Lummis Files, M 2. **with a four-man crew** Kemp, *Underwater Warriors*, p. 115. **beacons if necessary** Ibid., p. 128. **Brest in February 1942** Ibid., pp 146-55. **attack the two vessels** Ibid., pp 176-8. **neutralize that danger** Ibid., p. 178. **in a tropical zone** Ibid., p. 132.

PAGE 228   **forty miles alone** Ibid., pp 178-9. **on the starboard side** Ibid., p. 179. **the Japanese cruiser** Padfield, *War beneath the Sea*, p. 473. **passing under the hull** Kemp, op. cit., p. 179. **an exhausted condition** *London Gazette*, 13 Nov 1945.

PAGE 229   **the helm without relief** Kemp, op. cit., pp 179-80. **Japanese navy were over** Ibid., p. 180. **not** *Takao* **blowing up** Ibid. **activities went undetected** Ibid., p. 182. **Mentions in Despatches** Ibid., pp 181-2. **the war to an end** Ibid., p. 182. **with a lotta guts'** Quoted in ibid, p. 182; Lummis Files, M 2.

PAGE 230   **does it! I salute him** Montgomery of Alamein, *A Concise History of Warfare*, p. 331.

PAGE 231   **was literally bleeding** William Shorten, interview with Myles Dungan. **the desert into Iraq** Ibid. **forces in that country** Ibid. **It broke our hearts** Ibid.

PAGE 232   **the defence of Tobruk** Harrison, *Tobruk*, p. 9. **changed to 70th Division** Joslen, op. cit., p. 49. **of a training exercise** Playfair, *The Mediterranean and the Middle East*, vol. III, p. 46. **the Red Army in 1945** Shorten, interview with Dungan, op. cit. **into their final phase** Bates, *Dance of War*, p. 2. **west for the last time** Lucas, *War in the Desert*, p. 7. **to be heavily involved** Brownlow, interview with author, Oct 1995.

PAGE 233 **believed to be dead** Obituary, *Daily Telegraph*, 1 June 1998. **against enemy armour** Perrett, *Last Stand!*, pp 117-26. **won the Victoria Cross** Ibid., p. 125. **of the highest order** *Volunteers from Eire, Supplement* (to Nov 1944), p. 12. **inspiration to all ranks** Ibid., p. 14.

PAGE 234 **strong German force** *Volunteers from Éire*, p. 11. **Villasmundo the same night** Ibid., pp 11-12. **was later killed in action** Ibid., p. 12. **also won a DSO** Ibid., p. 10. **to the Catania plain** Ibid.

PAGE 235 **and an example to all** Ibid.

PAGE 236 **as we had expected** Duane, notes to author. **DSO night of 17/18 July** *Volunteers from Éire*, p. 9. **period of darkness left** Ibid. **and machine-gun-fire** Ibid.

PAGE 237 **Fusiliers, won the DSO** Ibid., p. 10. **outflank the Inniskillings** Ibid. **courage and leadership** Ibid.; Fox, op. cit., pp 74-5.

PAGE 238 **casualties in the Battalion** Duane, notes to author. **courage and leadership** *Volunteers from Éire*, p. 28. **the Simeto bridgehead** Ibid., p. 11. **of the River Salso** Ibid. **and by General Montgomery** Doherty, *Clear the Way!*, pp 80-1. **the enemy withdrew** *Volunteers from Éire*, p. 25.

PAGE 239 **evacuated safely to Italy** Doherty, op. cit., p. 79. **on 3 September 1943** Ibid., p. 82. **rugged Calabrian countryside** Ibid., p. 83. **in Operation** AVALANCHE Ibid. **back into the sea** Hickey and Smith, *Operation Avalanche*, p. 126. **during this operation** *Volunteers from Éire*, p. 46. **Royal Berkshire Regiment** Ibid., p. 45.

PAGE 240 **had become casualties** Ibid., pp 45-6. **yards to the farm house** Duane, notes to author. **contact with Fifth Army** Ibid. **happy and joyous occasion** Ibid.

PAGE 241 **infantry of 36 Brigade** Russell, *Account of the Irish Brigade*. **a German motorcyclist** K.G.F. Chavasse, *Some Memories of My Life*, p. 74. **this unexpected opposition** Ibid. **Brigade Major of 150 Brigade** P.R.O., Kew, ZJI/943. **the Tunisian campaign** *Volunteers from Éire*, p. 14.

PAGE 242 **established behind us** K.G.F. Chavasse, op. cit., pp 74-5. **outcome of the operations** *Volunteers from Éire*, p. 14. **side of the ridge** Doherty, op. cit., p. 87.

PAGE 243 **actions in the field** *Volunteers from Éire*, p. 28. **three weeks later** Doherty, op. cit., p. 94. **inspiration to his men** *Volunteers from Éire*, p. 46. **crossing the river** Doherty, op. cit., p. 92. **take avoiding action** A.D. Woods, MC, H Company, 2nd London Irish Rifles in Italy.

PAGE 244 **bridge was being erected** Ibid. **better than we were** Ibid. **of men with him** Ibid. **continued on towards Petacciato** Ibid. **bridge intact and forthwith'** Russell, op. cit.

PAGE 245 **the top of her form'** Ibid. **thousands yards ahead** Doherty, op. cit., p. 93. **toll of the Irishmen** Ibid., p. 94. **bullet to the head** Ibid. **by a German shell** Ibid., p. 95. **wail of his pipes** Russell, op. cit.

PAGE 246 **Distinguished Conduct Medal** Fox, op. cit., p. 97. **Medal on 4 November** *Volunteers from Éire*, p. 44. **and freed his position** Ibid. **under his command'** Ibid. **behind enemy lines** Doherty, op. cit., pp 100-1. **was going on there** James Clarke, notes to author.

PAGE 247 **unhurt and unperturbed** *Volunteers from Éire, Supplement* (to Nov 44) pp 22-3. **of battle rose again** Doherty, op. cit., p. 101. **cover in the town** Ibid. **and hid in** the cellar *Faugh A Ballagh Gazette*, vol. xxxvi, no. 158, p. 192. posthumous Victoria Cross Doherty, op. cit., p. 103.

PAGE 248   Irishman, in the van Williams, *The Black Cats at War*, pp 59-60. the Military Cross *Volunteers from Éire*, p. 27. three miles farther on *Volunteers from Éire*, p. 27. example to his men Ibid. a raid subsequently *Volunteers from Éire, Supplement* (to Nov '44), p. 11. themselves as patrol leaders Fox, op. cit., p. 102. served in the Royal Fusiliers Williams, op. cit., pp 60-1.

PAGE 249   150 yards of posts *Volunteers from Éire, Supplement* (to Nov '44), p. 11. desisting only towards evening Ibid. enemy and the weather Ibid. the Military Cross Fox, op. cit., p. 103. the Fifth Army front Ibid.

PAGE 250   landed at Anzio Bidwell and Graham, *Tug of War*, p. 141. attack the invaders Pitt, *The Military History of World War II*, p. 279. advance of 13 Brigade Fox, op. cit., p. 105. Allied forces difficult Duane, notes to author. boat for the crossing Ibid. strength of 100 men Ibid.

PAGE 251   Inniskillings' planned attack Fox, op. cit., p. 107. established our bridgehead Duane, op. cit. enemy were liberated Ibid.; Fox, op. cit., pp 112-13. more or less intact Duane, op. cit. 7th Cheshire Regiment Joslen, op. cit., p. 47. example of courage *Volunteers from Éire, Supplement* (to Nov '44) p. 24.

PAGE 252   ground to a halt Bidwell and Graham, op. cit., pp 147-9. of 1st Green Howards Powell, *The History of the Green Howards*, p. 205. break up and run *Volunteers from Éire, Supplement* (to Nov '44), p. 23. Anzio to be cautious Bidwell and Graham, op. cit., p. 141. fighting of the war' Verney, *The Micks*, p. 141. their battalion's landing *Volunteers from Éire, Supplement* (to Nov '44), pp 22-3.

PAGE 253   positions on one flank Ibid., p. 22. thickly on the road Ibid. and devotion to duty Ibid. the forward platoons Ibid., p. 23. saved a good many lives Ibid.

PAGE 254   stretch of open country Ibid. out of the area Ibid., p. 20. Liri valley towards Rome Doherty, op. cit., p. 128. and 8th Indian Divisions Ibid., p. 131. made by the Inniskillings Ibid., pp 132-3.

PAGE 255   of the Irish Rifles Ibid., pp 136-7. could get hold of' Woods, op. cit. from our artillery barrage Ibid. Searles, was badly injured Ibid. of the company were Ibid.

PAGE 256   were on our objective Ibid. thirds of his company Ibid. lasting some thirty minutes Ibid. him as long as I live Ibid. could possibly have Ibid.

PAGE 257   success of the operation *Volunteers from Éire, Supplement* (to Nov '44), p. 9. Corporal O'Reilly, MM Davies, notes to author. Cavan man, from Arva Eamon Crowe, notes to author (Volunteers gives Edward O'Reilly's residence as Mullaghbawn). Medal in the Sicilian campaign *Volunteers from Éire*, p. 40. location on 19 May Ibid., *Supplement* (to Nov '44), p. 24.

PAGE 258   under his command Ibid. born in County Galway Ibid. the Allies in Italy Bidwell and Graham, p. 340.

PAGE 260   get into the Wrens Mrs Elizabeth Dobbs, (née Chamberlain) interview with author, August 1998. in the Chertsey hospital Mrs Brenda Clark, (née Graham) interview with author, August 1998. preparation for England Ibid. routine of any hospital Ibid.

PAGE 261   posted overseas in 1943 Ibid. as the Red Cros Ibid. difficulties that faced them Dobbs interview, op. cit. Machrihanish in Scotland Ibid.

PAGE 262   as the ubiquitous Swordfish Smith, op. cit., pp 146-7. nervous breakdown there Dobbs interview, op. cit. flew in from the sea Ibid. the test for accuracy Ibid. early-1943 for a refit Hobbs, op. cit., pp 110-11.

PAGE 263   the sea. He was killed Dobbs interview, op. cit. Then I knew I was in Ibid. quite difficult for me Ibid.

PAGE 264   provided the entertainment Ibid. ships was concerned Ibid. to embarkation leave Ibid. him and I accepted Ibid.

PAGE 265   after the blackout Ibid. first four days there' Ibid.

PAGE 266   mistress, Lady Hamilton Ibid. was their leave centre' Ibid. home. I chose home Ibid. were Irish people there Ibid. food was markedly better Clark interview, op. cit.

PAGE 267   as the slightly-wounded Ibid. forces in Austria Ibid. become her husband Ibid.

PAGE 268   marvellous work there Mrs Maeve Kelly (née Boyle) interview with author, September 1998. chore as a punishment Ibid. delightful free supper Mrs Margaret Little, letter to author.

PAGE 269   always lively occasions Ibid. what miracles you do Ibid. in north-west Europe Lambkin, op. cit., p. 131. to the billets dog tired Ibid., p. 134.

PAGE 270   So well they might Ibid., pp 138-139. took the surrender Kelly interview, op. cit. history being made Ibid. scales just swing even Mrs M. Kelly, letter to author.

Sources

Adams, Jack, *The Doomed Expedition. The campaign in Norway 1940* (London, 1989)

Allen, Trevor, *The Storm Passed By* (Dublin, 1996)

Barclay, Brigadier C.N., *The History of the Royal Northumberland Fusiliers in the Second World War* (London, 1952)

Bardon, Jonathan, *A History of Ulster* (Belfast, 1992)

Barnett, Correlli, *Engage the Enemy More Closely. The Royal Navy in the Second World War* (London, 1991)

Bartlett, Thomas & Jeffery, Keith (ed.), A *Military History of Ireland* (Cambridge, 1996)

Barton, Brian, *Northern Ireland in the Second World War* (Belfast, 1995)

Blaxland, Gregory, *The Plain Cook and the Great Showman. The First and Eighth Armies in North Africa* (London, 1977)

Blumenson, Martin, *Mark Clark* (London, 1985)

Bowyer, Chaz, *Eugene Esmonde, VC, DSO* (London, 1983)

—, *For Valour. The Air VCs* (London, 1992)

Bredin, Brigadier A.E.C., DSO, MC, DL, *A History of the Irish Soldier* (Belfast, 1987)

Buckland, Patrick, *A History of Northern Ireland* (Dublin, 1981)

Buzzell, Nora, *The Register of the Victoria Cross* (Cheltenham, 1988)

Carroll, Joseph T., *Ireland in the War Years 1939-1945* (Newton Abbott, 1975)

Churchill, Sir Winston, *The Second World War* (London, 1950)

Cloake, John, *Templer. Tiger of Malaya* (London, 1985)

Daly, Edward and Devlin, Kieran, *The Clergy of the Diocese of Derry. An Index* (Dublin, 1997)

Delaforce, Patrick, *Monty's Marauders – Black Rat and Red Fox* (Brighton, 1997)

Denman, Terence, *Ireland's Unknown Soldiers. The 16th (Irish) Division in the Great War* (Dublin, 1992)

Doherty, Richard, *Clear the Way! A History of the 38th (Irish) Brigade, 1941-1947* (Dublin, 1993)

—, *The Sons of Ulster: Ulstermen at War from the Somme to Korea* (Belfast, 1992)

—, *Only the Enemy in Front: The Recce Corps at War 1941-1946* (London, 1994)

—, *Key to Victory: The Maiden City in the Second World War* (Antrim, 1995)

—, *A Noble Crusade. The History of Eighth Army 1941-1945* (Staplehurst, 1999)

Duggan, John P., *Neutral Ireland and the Third Reich* (Dublin, 1985)

—, *A History of the Irish Army* (Dublin, 1991)

Dungan, Myles, *Distant Drums – Irish Soldiers in Foreign Armies* (Belfast, 1993)

Ellis, C. and Chamberlain, P. (ed.), *Handbook on the British Army 1943* (United States Army, 1943; reprinted London, 1975)

Ellis, John, *The World War II Databook* (London, 1993)

Fearnley, Len, *Blenheim Odyssey. Epic Saga of an Aircraft and Its Crews* (Farnham, 1990)

Fevyer, W.H., (ed.) *The George Medal* (London, 1980)

Fischer, Edward, *Mission in Burma. The Columban Fathers, Forty-three Years in Kachin Country* (New York, 1980)
Fisk, Robert, *In Time of War – Ireland, Ulster and the Price of Neutrality 1939-45* (London, 1983)
Fitzsimons, Bernard (ed.), *Tanks and Weapons of World War II* (London, 1973)
Forde, Frank, *The Long Watch* (Dublin, 1981)
Forester, C.S., *Hunting the Bismarck* (London, 1970)
Foster, R.F., *Modern Ireland 1600-1972* (London, 1988)
Franks, Norman, *Valiant Wings. The Battle and Blenheim Squadrons over France 1940* (London, 1988)
Frederick, J.B.M., *Lineage Book of British Land Forces, 1660-1978*, 2 vols (Wakefield, 1984)
Gilbert, Adrian (ed.), *The Imperial War Museum Book of the Desert War* (London, 1992)
Glover, Michael, *An Improvised War – The Abyssinian Campaign of 1940-1941* (London, 1987)
Gough, Brigadier Guy F., DSO, MC, *Thirty Days to Dunkirk – The Royal Irish Fusiliers May 1940* (Wrexham, 1990)
Gray, Tony, *The Lost Years – The Emergency in Ireland 1939-45* (London, 1997)
Gunner, Colin, *Front of the Line – Adventures with the Irish Brigade* (Antrim, 1991)
Halley, James J., *The Squadrons of the Royal Air Force* (Tonbridge, 1980)
Hallows, Ian S., *Regiments and Corps of the British Army* (London, 1991)
Hamilton-Pollock, P., *Wings on the Cross – A Padre with the RAF* (Dublin, 1954)
Harris, R.G., *The Irish Regiments. A Pictorial History 1683-1987* (Tunbridge Wells, 1989)
Harvey, Maurice, *The Allied Bomber War 1939-45* (Tunbridge Wells, 1992)
Hennessy, Thomas, *A History of Northern Ireland 1920-1996* (Dublin, 1997)
Hobbs, Cdr David, MBE, *Aircraft Carriers of the Royal and Commonwealth Navies* (London, 1996)
Horsfall, John, DSO, MC, *The Wild Geese Are Flighting* (Kineton, 1976)
—, *Say Not The Struggle* (Kineton, 1977)
—, *Fling Our Banner to the Wind* (Kineton, 1978)
Humble, Richard, *Crusader. The Eighth Army's Forgotten Victory November 1941–January 1942* (London, 1987)
Johnstone, Tom & Hagerty, James, *The Cross on the Sword – Catholic Chaplains in the Forces* (London, 1996)
Kemp, Paul, *Underwater Warriors* (London, 1996)
Kenneally, John Patrick, VC, *Kenneally VC* (Huddersfield, 1991)
Laffin, John, *British VCs of World War 2 – A Study in Heroism* (Stroud, 1997)
Lambkin, Romie, *My Time in the War – An Irishwoman's Diary* (Dublin, 1992)
Lee, Joseph, *Ireland, 1912-1985* (Cambridge, 1989)
Lewis, Bruce, *Air Crew. The Story of the Men Who Flew the Bombers* (London, 1991)
Lucas, James, *Storming Eagles. German Airborne Forces in World War Two* (London, 1988)
Lyons, F.S.L., *Ireland since the Famine* (London, 1971)
Marrinan, Patrick, *Churchill and the Irish Marshals* (Belfast, 1986)
Masters, John, *The Road past Mandalay* (London, 1961)
Middlebrook, Martin and Everitt, Chris, *The Bomber Command War Diaries* (London, 1985)
McAughtry, Sam, *The Sinking of the Kenbane Head* (Belfast, 1977)
Moorehead, Alan, *The Desert War. The North African Campaign 1940-1943* (London, 1965)
Moyes, Philip, *Bomber Squadrons of the RAF and Their Aircraft* (London, 1964)
Myatt, Frederick, *The British Infantry 1660-1945. The Evolution of a Fighting Force* (Poole, 1983)
Nesbit, Roy Conyers, *An Illustrated History of the RAF* (Godalming, 1990)
Ó Drisceoil, Donal, *Censorship in Ireland 1939-1945* (Cork, 1996)
Overy, Richard, *Bomber Command 1939-1945* (London, 1997)
Pantridge, Frank, *An Unquiet Life* (Antrim, 1989)
Pitt, Barrie (ed.), *The Military History of World War II* (London, 1986)
Quigley, A.A., *Green Is My Sky* (Dublin, 1983)
Quinn, John (et al), *Wings over the Foyle. A History of Limavady Airfield in WWII* (Belfast, 1995)
Raugh, Harold E. Jr, *Wavell in the Middle East 1939-1941. A Study in Generalship* (London, 1993)

Rea, Kathleen, *The Best Is Yet to Be* (Harare, 1992)

Rooney, David, *Burma Victory* (London, 1992)

—, *Wingate and the Chindits – Redressing the Balance* (London, 1994)

Roskill, S.W., *The War at Sea*, 3 vols (London, 1954-61)

Ross, Peter, *All Valiant Dust – An Irishman Abroad* (Dublin, 1992)

Share, Bernard, *The Emergency, Neutral Ireland 1939-45* (Dublin, 1978)

Shepperd, Alan, *France 1940 – Blitzkrieg in the West* (London, 1990)

Slim, Field-Marshal Sir William, *Defeat into Victory* (London, 1956)

Smith, David J., *Action Stations 7. Military airfields of Scotland, the North-East and Northern Ireland* (Cambridge, 1983)

Smyth, Sir John, *The Story of the Victoria Cross* (London, 1963)

Stokes, D., *Wings Aflame – The biography of Group Captain Victor Beamish, DSO and Bar, DFC, AFC* (London, 1985)

—, *Paddy Finucane: Fighter* Ace (London, 1983; Kansas, 1998)

Taylor, G., *Sea Chaplains* (London, 1978)

Turner, John Frayn, *VCs of the Royal Navy* (London, 1956)

Verney, Maj-Gen. G.L., DSO, MC, *The Desert Rats – The 7th Armoured Division in World War II* (London, 1954)

Volunteers from Éire who have won distinctions serving with the British forces – Revised edition Sept. 1939-Feb. 1943

—, Revised list Sept. 1939-Feb. 1944

—, Supplementary list to Nov. 1944

Whiting, Charles, *The Poor Bloody Infantry 1939-1945* (London, 1987)

Wragg, David, *Carrier Combat* (Stroud, 1997)

REGIMENTAL, UNIT & SHIP HISTORIES

Boardman, Captain C.J., *Tracks in Europe – The 5th Royal Inniskilling Dragoon Guards 1939-1946* (Salford, 1990)

Cunliffe, Marcus, *The Royal Irish Fusiliers 1793-1968* (Oxford, 1970)

Evans, R., *The 5th Royal Inniskilling Dragoon Guards* (Aldershot, 1951)

Fitzgerald, Major D.J.L., MC, *The Irish Guards* (Aldershot, 1949)

Fox, Sir Frank, *The Royal Inniskilling Fusiliers in the Second World War, 1939-1945* (Aldershot, 1951)

Graves, Charles, *The History of the Royal Ulster Rifles*, Vol. III (Belfast, 1950)

On behalf of the London Irish Rifles' Old Comrades' Association, *The London Irish at War* (London, n.d.)

Lunt, James, *The Scarlet Lancers: The Story of 16th/5th The Queen's Royal Lancers 1689-1992* (London, 1993)

Strawson, J.M. et al., *Irish Hussar. A short history of the Queen's Royal Irish Hussars* (London, 1986)

The Wardroom Officers of HMS *Formidable*, *A Formidable Commission* (London, n.d.)

UNPUBLISHED, PRIVATE PAPERS

Chavasse, Commander Evelyn H., 'Business in Great Waters – War Memories of a Semi-sailor'

Chavasse, Colonel K.G.F., DSO and Bar, 'Some Memories of My Life'

Chavasse, Captain P.M.B., DSC and Bar, RN, 'A Sailor's War Memoirs'

Devlin, Patrick R., 'Reminiscences of a Rifleman in Normandy, France – 1944'

Ormsby, John J., 'Personal Journal/Diary 1939-1945'

Parsons, Andy, 'Exit at Anzio'

ARTICLE

Whyte, Desmond, 'A Trying Chindit (in Medicine and War)', *British Medical Journal* no. 285, pp 18-25, December 1982

Acknowledgements

A book such as this could not have been written without the advice and help of many individuals and organisations. I wish, therefore, to place on record my gratitude to all those who helped me while I was researching and writing this work. A number of institutions were invaluable.

These were, in the United Kingdom: Public Record Office, Ruskin Avenue, Kew, Surrey; National Army Museum, Royal Hospital Road, London, especially the staff of the Reading Room; Imperial War Museum, Lambeth Road, London, especially the staff of the Departments of Printed Books, Documents and Photographs; British Library Newspaper Library, Colindale, London; The Lummis Files of The Military Historical Society, held at the National Army Museum, London; The Fusiliers' Museum of Northumberland, Alnwick Castle, Alnwick, especially Captain (Retd) P.H.D. Marr; Royal Army Chaplains' Department Depot, RAChD Association, Netheravon House, Netheravon, Wilts, especially Major (Retd) Margaret A. Easy; Royal Air Force Museum, Hendon, London; Ministry of Defence, Naval Staff Duties (Historical Section), Great Scotland Yard, London; Ministry of Defence, Air Historical Branch, Theobalds Road, London; Commonwealth War Graves Commission, Maidenhead, Berkshire; The Royal Inniskilling Fusiliers' Museum, Castle Barracks, Enniskillen, Co. Fermanagh, especially Major G.E.M. Stephens MBE; The Royal Irish Fusiliers' Museum, Sovereign's House, The Mall, Armagh, especially Mrs Amanda Moreno, Major Noel McConnell and Major Cormac Finnegan MBE; The Royal Ulster Rifles' Museum, War Memorial Building, Waring Street, Belfast, especially Major Mike Murphy; Public Records Office of Northern Ireland, Balmoral Avenue, Belfast; The Linenhall Library, Belfast; The Church of Ireland Gazette, Lisburn; The Methodist Church in Ireland (Revd Edmund T. Mawhinney), Fountainville Avenue, Belfast; The Presbyterian Church in Ireland, Church House, Belfast; Central Library, Foyle Street, Londonderry.

In Ireland I would like to acknowledge the following institutions: National Library, Kildare Street, Dublin; History Department, University College Cork (The Volunteers' Project); Missionary Society of St Columban, Navan, especially Teresa Caldwell, Librarian.

The following Australian institutions must also be acknowledged: Australian Defence Academy: The University of New South Wales, Canberra, A.C.T.; Australian War Memorial, Canberra, A.C.T.

Many individuals gave generously of their time to talk to me about their experiences or to write about them for me. Their names appear throughout this book and there is no need to repeat them here. I owe them all a special debt.

My research was eased considerably by the assistance I was given by Myles Dungan who allowed me to borrow tapes of interviews he conducted with many Irish veterans of the Second World War. Likewise, Dr Geoff Roberts and his team at University College Cork's History Department's Volunteers' Project provided an invaluable resource for me and I would especially like to commend the work of Tina Neylon in carrying out a wide range of interviews with Irish veterans. The Volunteers' Project is a timely and much needed addition to Ireland's historical archives.

Several sources, and documents, of which I might otherwise have been unaware, were drawn to my attention during the course of my research for which I thank Colonel Kendal Chavasse, DSO and Bar, Co. Waterford, Colonel Robin Charley, OBE, Co. Down, Most Reverend Dr Edward Daly, DD, retired bishop of Derry (Diocesan Archivist for the diocese of Derry), the late Colonel Desmond Whyte, DSO, Londonderry, Mr Eamon Crowe, Tralee, Co. Kerry, Mrs Elizabeth Dobbs, Monkstown, Co. Dublin, Mr David Truesdale, Newtownards, Mr John Conor, Australian Defence Force Academy, Canberra, A.C.T., Australia and Mr Tom Johnstone, Mt Eliza, Victoria, Australia.

Throughout the book I have used quotations from a number of books and I wish to express my thanks for permission to do so to Mr Chaz Bowyer (*Eugene Esmonde, V.C., D.S.O.* and *For Valour. The Air VCs*); Mr James Gibbons on behalf of the family of the late Brigadier Guy F. Gough, DSO, MC (*Thirty Days to Dunkirk*); Colonel John Horsfall, DSO, MC (*Say Not the Struggle* and *Fling Our Baanner to the Wind*); Appletree Press, Belfast (*Distant Drums* by Myles Dungan); Mr Fergal Tobin, Gill and Macmillan (*Neutral Ireland and the Third Reich* by John P. Duggan); Mr Bryan McCabe, The Greystone Press, Antrim (*Front of the Line* by Colin Gunner and *An Un-quiet Life* by Frank Pantridge); The Lilliput Press, Dublin (*All Valiant Dust* by Peter Ross); Wolf-hound Press, Dublin (*My Time in the War* by Romie Lambkin); Cambridge University Press (*Ireland 1912-1985* by Professor Joseph Lee and *A Military History of Ireland* edited by Thomas Bartlett and Keith Jeffery); Frank Cass and Co. Ltd (John Bowman's introduction to *The Tenth Irish Division in Gallipoli* by Bryan Cooper and *The Irish Naval Service* by Aidan McIvor); Cassell Ltd (*The Second World War* by Winston Churchill); Geoffrey Chapman Ltd, an imprint of Cassell & Co. (*The Cross on the Sword* by Tom Johnstone and James Hagerty); Crécy Publishing Ltd (*Paddy Finucane. Fighter Ace* by Doug Stokes); André Deutsch Ltd (*In Time of War. Ireland, Ulster and the price of neutrality, 1939-45* by Robert Fisk); Grub Street Ltd (*For Valour, the Air VCs* by Chaz Bowyer); HarperCollins Ltd (*Memoirs* and *A Concise History of Warfare* by Viscount Montgomery of Alamein); Public Record Office, Kew, Surrey for permission to quote from official documents held in the British National Archives (the document references will be found in the chapter notes); The Fusiliers' Museum of Northumberland, for permission to quote from documents held in the Museum relating to Captain J.J.B. Jackman, VC, and from the *History of the Royal Northumberland Fusiliers in the Second World War* by C.N. Barclay; The Royal Inniskilling Fusiliers' Museum for permission to quote from *The Royal Inniskilling Fusiliers in the Second World War* by Sir Frank Fox; TAVRA (NI) for permission to quote from *An Account of the Territorials in Northern Ireland* edited by I.B. Gailey, W.F. Gillespie and J. Hassett.

United Kingdom Crown Copyright material is reproduced with the permission of the Controller of Her Majesty's Stationery Office and includes extracts from *Grand Strategy, Vol I* (History of the Second World War, UK Military Series) by N.H. Gibbs, and *War at Sea, Vol I* by S.W. Roskill as well as various extracts from *The London Gazette*.

Revd Alan McGuckian, SJ, Editor, *Interfuse*, a private Irish Jesuit publication, published by the Jesuit Communication Centre, Dublin, gave permission to quote from 'Our Single Casualty: the death in Burma of Fr John Hayes' (*Interfuse*, No. 41).

In spite of best endeavours it has not proved possible to trace current copyright owners in a number of instances but the author and publisher are prepared to make the necessary arrange-ments to rectify this at the earliest opportunity.

Photographs are reproduced by permission of the copyright holders as indicated in the list of illustrations.

My thanks are also due to Michael Adams and his team at Four Courts Press for their enthusiastic support for this project at all stages and for their tremendous professionalism in the production of the book.

To my wife, Carol, and children, Joanne, James and Catríona, I record, once again, my appreciation of their patient support and understanding without which this book would never have been possible.

Richard Doherty
July 1999

Index

Under the headings 'Battalions', 'Regiments' and 'Units (Misc)' the listings are given in order of precedence in the appropriate army, generally British. An * after a medal awarded indicates that the individual was awarded the medal twice, ** indicates three times.